The Middle Ages

An Encyclopedia for Students

William Chester Jordan, *Editor in Chief*
for the
American Council of Learned Societies

Volume 2

CHARLES SCRIBNER'S SONS
Macmillan Library Reference USA
Simon & Schuster Macmillan
New York

SIMON & SCHUSTER AND PRENTICE HALL INTERNATIONAL
London Mexico City New Delhi Singapore Sydney Toronto

Developed for the American Council of Learned Societies by Charles Scribner's Sons and Visual Education Corporation.

PRINTING
    4 5 6 7 8 9 10

Library of Congress Cataloging-in-Publication Data

The Middle Ages / William Chester Jordan, editor in chief for the American Council of Learned Societies.
        p.   cm.
    Includes bibliographical references and index.
    ISBN 0-684-19773-1   (hard/libr. bind. : alk. paper)
    1. Middle Ages—Encyclopedias, Juvenile.   I. Jordan, William C., 1948– .   II. American Council of Learned Societies.
D114.M54 1996
909.07´03—dc20   95-49597
                                                                          CIP

ISBN 0-684-80483-2 (vol. 1)
ISBN 0-684-80484-0 (vol. 2)
ISBN 0-684-80485-9 (vol. 3)
ISBN 0-684-80486-7 (vol. 4)

Coronation

Coronations were religious ceremonies in which popes and monarchs were dressed in rich garments, placed on their thrones, and crowned. Early papal coronations were modest events, but the ceremonies became much grander as the papacy's political power grew. Coronation ceremonies of monarchs varied from country to country but included many of the same symbolic stages, such as acclamation*, consecration* or anointing with oil, and crowning.

In the 300s, the pope was elected by the Roman clergy and laity* on a Sunday. That same day, bishops from neighboring areas gathered to consecrate the new pope by laying their hands on his head. This ceremony developed during the Middle Ages. By the 700s, newly elected popes were invested* on their election day at a ceremony in the papal palace, with people showing respect by kissing the new pope's feet and pledging their allegiance. Consecration took place in St. Peter's church on a later day, after which the pope came out on the church steps to receive his crown and the cheers of the crowd. By the later Middle Ages, the central feature of the papal coronation was the crowning of the pope with a tiara* in front of St. Peter's and a procession through the city afterward.

Royal coronations also included investing and crowning. The first ceremony of this type in western Europe took place in Rome, where Pope Leo III crowned CHARLEMAGNE as Holy Roman Emperor on Christmas Day in 800. Customs from this coronation were later adapted for the crowning of kings of the developing European nations.

Different church officials presided at different royal coronations: the archbishop of Cologne in Germany, the archbishop of Canterbury in England, and the archbishop of Rheims in France. In Germany, the new king had to answer a series of questions before his anointing. In France, a special oil that had supposedly anointed King Clovis in 481 was used. In England, newly crowned kings swore to preserve the laws and customs of the kingdom. However, all the ceremonies featured an acclamation in which subjects called out a phrase such as "God save the king."

Coronations were religious ceremonies in which popes and monarchs were crowned. Church officials presided at all royal coronations. On Christmas Day in 800, Charlemagne received his crown from Pope Leo III.

Cortes

* **cleric** church official qualified to perform church ceremonies

The cortes were parliamentary institutions that began in the Christian kingdoms of Spain—CASTILE, PORTUGAL, ARAGON, and CATALONIA—in the 1200s. The word *cortes* comes from the Spanish word for court. *Cortes* can be singular or plural. The cortes developed when town representatives joined the courts of nobles and clerics* who traditionally gave advice to the kings. They became the main political assembly in a Spanish kingdom.

Each cortes could be summoned only by the king, whose presence was essential to its legality. It was usually called every two to four years. Sessions lasted for a few weeks or a month and took place in centrally located palaces, cathedrals, or monasteries. Once the cortes gathered, the king explained the reasons for the assembly and often asked for a tax subsidy. Important issues were then debated. For example, in 1407, the cortes of Castile requested that money from a particular tax be used solely in the war against the Muslims. After the cortes made decisions and approved tax subsidies, the session ended.

The cortes discussed matters related to royal succession, legislation, taxation, and other policy issues. No important statute could be enacted and no tax could be levied without their consent. Statutes that the cortes drew up and the king approved had the full force of law. Up until the late Middle Ages, the cortes were forums in which groups could express their views on public issues. Their influence declined in the 1400s and 1500s as a result of civil wars, the unification of Spain, and the rise of absolute monarchy.

Cosmetics and Beauty Aids

* **Byzantine** referring to the Eastern Christian Empire that was based in Constantinople

Cosmetics and beauty aids were used in ancient Egypt, Greece, and the Roman Empire. Many makeup formulas were written down, though it is not clear which were actually used. In the Middle Ages, the traditions and formulas were passed on to the Christians in CONSTANTINOPLE and to the Muslim world. Makeup practices among the barbarians of western Europe are not so well known. It was once thought that few cosmetics were used after the barbarian invasions until the crusaders brought perfumes back to western Europe. Evidence from Anglo-Saxon graves suggests otherwise. In the 800s, CHARLEMAGNE's court at Aachen was familiar with perfumes from Baghdad. After the CRUSADES, however, makeup fashions changed, and a greater variety of beauty products were available in western Europe.

Cosmetic Preparations. Wealthy people in Rome wore thick makeup, and this custom continued under the Byzantine* Empire and perhaps in western Europe. White was commonly the preferred color for base makeup because a pale complexion was admired. Green, gray, or brown tones might be used for eyeshadow. Rouge was sometimes applied to the lips and cheeks; in Anglo-Saxon times this might be orange- or rose-colored. In Italy in the 1200s, however, a "natural" look, consisting of a flesh-colored base and bright pink rouge, became popular.

In medieval times, people purchased makeup from wandering merchants or cosmetics makers in the towns. It was usually stored as powder, then moistened (often with saliva), and applied by finger or with a fine

Medieval mirrors were generally pieces of polished metal. Glass mirrors were first made in the 1200s. This ivory mirror case was made in France in the 1300s. Its back is decorated with scenes of courtly love.

* **fixative** chemical used to stabilize a scent, preventing it from evaporating too fast

stick. Some preparations included toxic elements. White lead, often used for the base coloring, could cause pimples and spots that needed special healing creams. Recipes for these medieval face creams were sometimes written down with the formulas for makeup.

In Constantinople, as earlier in Rome, perfumes played an important part in personal adornment. They were also used in public festivals and religious ceremonies. The Arabs of the Middle Ages greatly treasured perfumes. The prophet MUHAMMAD placed them third on his list of joys, after children and women. IBN SINA, the Muslim physician and philosopher, found a way to distill the scent of rose petals.

Perfumes were less available in the West because the ingredients were hard to obtain there. However, after the crusades, growing trade with the East brought spices and perfumes to Europe in larger quantities. In 1190, King Philip Augustus chartered a perfumers' guild in France. Two technical developments—the use of animal extracts as fixatives* and the invention of alcohol-base perfumes in the 1300s—further promoted perfume's effectiveness and popularity.

Breath deodorizers made of natural products were often used. Based on aniseed, wild mint, and similar materials, they were often dissolved in wine. Arab physicians also developed preparations for cleaning teeth that, like today's toothpastes, used calcium compounds. However, the calcium was often mixed with honey and sugar, whose role in promoting tooth decay was not yet known. The resulting paste was applied with a cloth or the flattened end of a twig.

Many people in the Middle Ages paid much attention to care of the skin and hair. Facial masks were made of many unusual ingredients, from asses' milk to beef marrow. Their effectiveness varied greatly because their makers rarely took care to prevent contamination. Artificial hair coloring was widely practiced. Anglo-Saxon hair dyes included blue and, if the paintings in manuscripts are to be believed, green and orange. A bleaching formula recorded in France in the 1200s included yellow arsenic. In one shampoo, a key ingredient was mercury, now known to be a dangerous poison. Not surprisingly, there were also recipes for preventing dandruff and hair loss and for giving hair more body. Finally, there were treatments for killing hair lice. With regard to hair health, not much had changed since the Roman poet Ovid noted that hair dyes often caused hair loss.

Beauty Devices.   Bronze and jeweled fillets for the hair, tweezers, and combs made of bone have been discovered in medieval graves. At first, such objects may not have been used very often: around the 800s, an Anglo-Saxon complained that Danish men, because they combed their hair and bathed every Saturday, were too attractive to women.

The medieval mirror, or speculum, was usually a small circular piece of polished metal, often fitted into a richly decorated case of gold or silver or carved ivory. Glass mirrors were first made in the 1200s. In the later Middle Ages, mirrors became very fashionable with men, who had them fixed into the hilts* of their swords or concealed in silken cases.

Scissors, tweezers, and razors were widely used. English nuns in the 600s were criticized for cutting their nails in a fashionable talonlike shape. Some men shaped their beards; others shaved them. The church generally

* **hilt** handle of a sword, particularly the protective hand guard

preferred shaving and strongly disapproved of any long hair on men. In the later Middle Ages, women often plucked their eyebrows and shaved their hairline to produce the illusion of a high forehead.

Other popular hair-care devices were curling irons, hairpins, and braid ornaments. Beginning in the 1100s, braid cases decorated with ribbons were used to hold braids in place, and men might use beard bags to protect their carefully waxed beards during the night. More medieval beauty devices were made for the hair than for anything else. (*See also* **Clothing.**)

Count, County

Originally, the word *count* meant companion, specifically a prince's companion. Throughout most of the Middle Ages, however, it referred to a noble who represented the ruler locally. From the time of CHARLEMAGNE, counts supervised fairly large areas called counties, upholding law and order, exercising military authority, and maintaining justice. In all of the CAROLINGIAN Empire, there were approximately 300 counties.

Counts were generally members of great aristocratic families. At first, the emperor might transfer them to other parts of the empire or send them on special missions. By the later Middle Ages, however, the counts had managed to make their positions hereditary, and many had increased the size of their holdings by taking over additional counties. As a result, some became powerful and independent dukes and lords.

The French and English kings protected their authority by curbing the power of the dukes and counts (called earls in England). However, the German counts (known as *Grafs*) retained their independence. The inability of the German kings to bring the counts under their authority delayed the unification of Germany until the 1800s.

Almost everywhere in western Europe, the county remained the basic unit of local government no matter who controlled it. Most counts relied on lower local officials as well as their own staffs to run the county. In general, counts ranked below dukes, who had lower status than princes and other royalty. But there were few firm rules about rank in the Middle Ages.

Courtesy Books

* **aristocrats** people of the highest social class, often nobility

Courtesy books were the how-to manuals of the Middle Ages. They instructed men, women, and children about good manners, how to behave in public and private, and how to treat other people. Some courtesy books were written for the middle classes, but most were addressed to members of the nobility. The courts of nobles and bishops served as the training grounds for young aristocrats*, and courtesy books were their textbooks. Learning these codes of behavior was useful for anyone who wished to be a part of the world of lords and ladies, knights and squires.

Courtesy books probably first appeared in the 1100s, in the courts of Provence, the region of southern France where the codes of CHIVALRY and COURTLY LOVE developed. From there, they spread to the rest of Europe. By

> **Remember:** Consult the index at the end of Volume 4 to find more information on many topics.

the 1400s, courtesy books could be found in northern France, Italy, Spain, Germany, and England.

There were many kinds of courtesy books. The most common kind dealt with the behavior of pages, squires, and knights—the young men of the medieval aristocracy. These books provided guidelines on how to succeed in public life. Pages, the boys who served at court, received the most basic instructions. Proper behavior for a page consisted of walking with dignity, greeting people courteously, performing the proper rituals in church, following the orders of a lord or master, and treating women graciously. Boys were warned against boisterous conduct, such as wrestling with dogs or throwing stones and sticks. Table manners were also important, and pages had to learn the proper way to hold an eating utensil and to carry on polite conversation. They were instructed not to pick their teeth with a knife or use a tablecloth as a handkerchief. Instead of providing a list of dos and don'ts, one book illustrated bad behavior through the example of a character called "reckless Ruskin."

Squires, the knight's helpers, also received instruction in proper behavior. Courtesy books advised a young squire to be generous, truthful, bold but not immodest, and well-spoken. He should dress neatly, be discreet as a lover, and be ready to obey his lady's will. Most important, he should serve a worthy lord and be loyal both as soldier and as counselor.

One type of courtesy book, the book of chivalry, was written specially for knights. Books about knightly behavior first appeared in the early 1200s and discussed the knight's clothing and equipment as well as his behavior. Modesty, respect for women, and truthfulness were important qualities. One of the most widely read books of chivalry was Ramon Lull's *Book of the Order of Chivalry,* written in Spain about 1276. Besides providing rules for being a knight, Lull discusses the origins, religious duties, and symbolism of chivalry. Such knowledge was as important as practical rules for behavior.

Women, too, received instruction about behavior from courtesy books. While men were told how to behave in order to succeed in their public lives, women were advised on leading proper private lives. No matter what a woman's social rank, she was regarded as primarily a wife and mother.

Courtesy books written for women—such as the one Geoffroy de La Tour-Landry, a French knight of the 1370s, composed for his own daughters—placed great emphasis on dutiful behavior and piety. Women were expected to attend church, pray, fast, give money to the poor, obey their husbands, and be good mothers. They were advised to read only the Bible and other religious works. Bold language or speaking one's opinion was unacceptable.

In marriage, a woman's role was to get along with her husband, make his life as comfortable as possible, and manage his household well. In addition to her tasks as wife and mother, she was expected to walk, sing, dance, and speak gracefully. On the whole, women were encouraged to be modest, meek, and humble.

The most interesting and detailed courtesy book for women was written by a woman, CHRISTINE DE PIZAN, in 1405. A French poet of Italian descent, Christine addressed her book *The Book of Three Virtues* to several types of readers: princesses, noble ladies, and women of the middle and working classes. In it, she advises a princess not to become spoiled by her position of privilege and to help keep peace between her husband and his BARONS. She tells a noblewoman how to run an estate while her husband is away or, as in the case of Christine herself, in the event of her husband's death. She gives middle-class women advice on helping their husbands with their work. Filled with practical advice, the book gives the most complete picture we have of the busy lives of medieval women.

A more personal kind of courtesy book contained advice from parents to their own children. These books taught children about moral behavior and the right way to treat people. Another of Christine de Pizan's works, for example, advises her son to respect his wife and let her run his household rather than treat her as a servant. (*See also* **Knighthood; Women, Role of.**)

Courtly Love

The idea of courtly love was popularized in the late 1000s by poet-entertainers called TROUBADOURS, who went from castle to castle in PROVENCE in southern France. They wrote lyrics addressed to the lady of a castle, singing her praises and pledging to serve her faithfully. They expressed the feelings of love as a polite game, a clever flirtation. This idea of "true love" spread to courts in northern France, Italy, Germany, England, and Spain and became part of Europe's literary tradition.

In the poetry of courtly love, the poet puts his beloved on a pedestal to worship her. He declares himself her vassal*, offering to perform noble deeds for her. Love is often described as an illness that makes him pale and sickly. Yet, striving to be worthy of his lady helps him to be noble.

* **vassal** person given land by a lord or monarch in return for loyalty and services

Courtly love was one of the major literary themes of the Middle Ages. This scene from the *Divine Comedy* shows Dante's encounter with his beloved Beatrice, who leads him through Paradise. Dante's idealization of Beatrice, a woman he barely knew, exemplifies the tradition of courtly love.

Courtly love poetry borrowed elements from the Latin love poems of the Roman poet Ovid and the Arabic poetry of Muslim Spain. The troubadours adapted these traditions to the social setting of the Provençal courts. Later poets incorporated themes of courtly love in the romance, a type of poem telling the story of a hero and his beloved.

Courtly love appears in the work of most of the major authors of the Middle Ages, including CHAUCER, DANTE, MALORY, and CHRÉTIEN DE TROYES. Some parts of the tradition—love at first sight, secret love, the suffering of the lover—influenced later Western ideas of love and can be found in today's songs, poems, plays, and novels. (*See also* **Arabic Language and Literature; Classical Tradition in the Middle Ages; French Language and Literature; Roman de la Rose.**)

Croatia

See map in Ottomans and Ottoman Empire (vol. 3).

* **Frankish** referring to the Germanic tribe called the Franks, who dominated western Europe in the early Middle Ages

* **protectorate** city or state that is under the military protection of a larger, more powerful state

Croatia is one of the nations of the Balkan peninsula, the region of southeastern Europe located between the Adriatic and Black Seas. Each country of the Balkans has its own complex medieval history of dramatic events and vivid personalities.

Croatia was once part of the Roman Balkan provinces of Dalmatia and Pannonia. At the start of the Middle Ages, these provinces were within the BYZANTINE EMPIRE. Slavs invaded the Balkan provinces in the middle 500s, forming the basis of a common ethnic stock in the region. These Slavs were soon dominated by Croatians, however, a people who entered the Balkans from the north but may have originated in Iran in Asia. Byzantines kept several important Dalmatian coastal cities, such as Dubrovnik (Ragusa). But the Croatians established control over central and northern Dalmatia and in Pannonia. As they ruled, they adopted the culture and language of the Slavs. Their version of the Slavic language came to be called Croatian.

In 788, CHARLEMAGNE conquered Lombardy in northern Italy and continued eastward. He subdued northern Dalmatia and Pannonia as far east as the Hungarian border. This opened the way for missionaries to bring Frankish* Christianity into the region. Disciples of CYRIL AND METHODIOS later tried to organize Slavic Orthodox churches in Croatian lands, which used Slavic instead of Latin in their church services. Their efforts were opposed by the Croatian clergy. Slavic was forbidden several times, though it continued to be used locally in some northern churches throughout the Middle Ages.

In the early 900s, Tomislav, the greatest medieval Croatian ruler and the first one to be called king, came to the throne of Dalmatia. He challenged the Magyars, a nomadic people from Asia who had invaded Hungary in the 890s and were now threatening the Croatians in Pannonia. Tomislav went to the aid of his fellow Croatians, defeating the Magyars in several battles. This brought much of Pannonia into his kingdom, creating a united Croatia for the first time.

Croatia flourished in the 900s and 1000s. In its mountainous interior, towns were few and small and served primarily as royal residences, forts, or local markets. Its main cities, Split and the Byzantine protectorate* of Dubrovnik, were on the coast. Trade across the Adriatic was profitable for both cities. Dubrovnik, a fortress city, was a merchant republic that rivaled nearby VENICE. It continued to be independent of Croatia in the handling of its affairs, but it became a center of Croatia's Slavic culture. It had a mint, a customs house, palaces, and monasteries and experienced considerable development of art and learning.

In later centuries, the kingdom of Croatia grew weaker and smaller. There were struggles with SERBIA over the mountain region that became BOSNIA. There were clashes with Venice, with the Byzantine Empire, and with the Normans of SICILY. There was also a long war with Hungary, which did not end until Hungary's King Koloman claimed both Pannonia and Dalmatia in 1107. From that time on, the Hungarian king was also officially the king of Croatia, though this meant that most Croatian nobles were able to act as independent lords on their lands. This remained the situation until the OTTOMAN Turks conquered much of Hungary and Croatia in the 1500s.

Crusades

Crusades were wars Christians undertook in the second half of the Middle Ages to recapture the Holy Land from the Muslims and to defend the Christian world against its enemies. These wars were called for and often financed by the Roman Church. The crusades were largely unsuccessful in the long run. Yet they were important for many reasons. They helped establish a western European presence in the eastern Mediterranean area. They encouraged a trade that benefited both western Europeans and Muslims. They exposed western Europe to the ideas and impressive civilization of the Islamic world.

In the three centuries after the Muslims captured the Holy Land from the BYZANTINE EMPIRE in 638, Christians were usually given the freedom to visit the holy sites of Jerusalem. By the 1000s, however, the world of Islam was undergoing some major changes. The old Abbasid caliphate* was still in place in Baghdad, but the main Islamic powers near the Mediterranean were the new FATIMID caliphs of Egypt and the SELJUK Turks. The Seljuks controlled most of Islam's northern lands, including Syria and areas of ANATOLIA (present-day Turkey). Hostility between these two powers caused a basic weakness in the Muslim world and also made life hard for Christians in the Holy Land. Then in 1071, at the Battle of Manzikert in Anatolia, the Seljuks defeated Byzantine emperor Alexios I KOMNENOS who appealed to the Latin* West for help.

Western Europe was in a period of growth and expansion. Religious and secular leaders were seeking to extend their influence, and new nations were beginning to emerge. In addition, the restless growth of FEUDALISM at this time led to a military spirit that sought outlet in war.

The First Crusade (1095–1099). Emperor Alexios's appeal for help was heard by Pope URBAN II. In 1095, Urban gave a powerful speech to Western leaders, calling Christians to a military pilgrimage to recover the Holy Sepulcher in Jerusalem. The pope promised church protection of the homes and other properties of those who would join the expedition and said they would be earning God's forgiveness for their sins. Crosses, the symbol of Christianity, were passed out at the meeting. (The word *crusade* comes from the Latin for cross; joining a crusade was called "taking the cross.")

* **caliphate** office and government of the caliph, religious and political head of the Islamic state

* **Latin** referring to western Europe and the Roman Church, which used the Latin language for its services

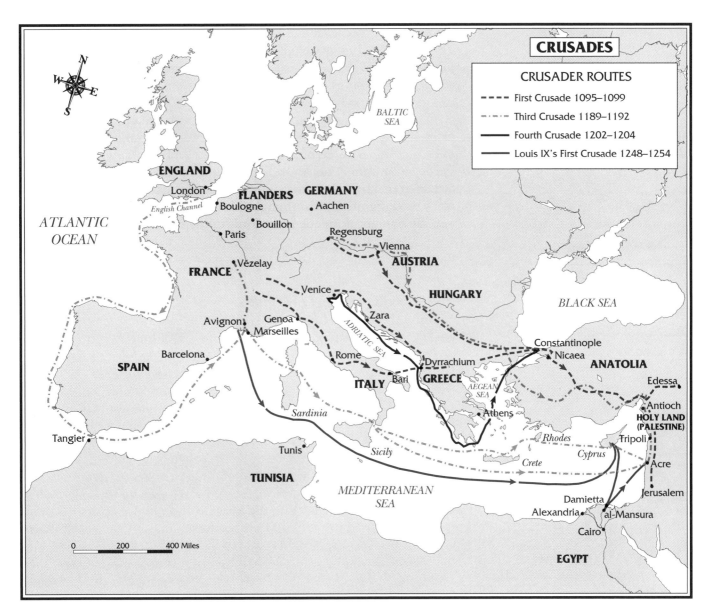

The First Crusade (1095–1099) was the most successful and established Christian states in the Holy Land. Some later crusades from Europe were largely military expeditions to prevent the Muslims from regaining these lands. With the fall of Constantinople in 1464, the crusading movement ended.

* **crusader states** states established in the East by Western Christians during the crusades. They included Jerusalem and Antioch.

Inspired by the pope's call to arms, many Western leaders took the cross and began raising armies for the crusade. Among these leaders were Godfrey of Bouillon, Baldwin of Boulogne, and BOHEMOND of Sicily. However, the planning was poor, as was the case in many subsequent crusades. While the nobles were preparing for the expedition, a number of traveling preachers, including PETER THE HERMIT, urged peasants to form their own crusade. The Peasant's Crusade arrived in CONSTANTINOPLE in 1096 and ended in disaster. Many peasants were killed, and others were taken captive.

The nobles and knights began to arrive later and had their first success in June 1097, when they forced the city of Nicaea in Anatolia to surrender. During the next few months, the crusaders split into several groups and moved deeper into Turkish territory, recapturing several other cities for Alexios. Then a group led by Baldwin of Boulogne conquered the town of Edessa and set up the first Latin crusader state* in the Near East. Another group took the powerful fortress of Antioch after a long siege and founded a second state under the rule of Bohemond of Sicily. The crusaders then marched on to Jerusalem, which they conquered in July 1099, and they cruelly slaughtered its Muslim inhabitants. The city and its surroundings became the Latin Kingdom of Jerusalem, with Godfrey of Bouillon as its ruler.

The First Crusade was the only truly successful crusade. It achieved its main goal of freeing the Holy Land*. In addition, three crusader states were established in the region, bringing power and wealth to the western European settlers. A fourth state, Tripoli, was later created, and crusading orders of CHIVALRY, such as the Knights Hospitalers and the Knights Templars, were founded to protect the Holy Land. They built many castles, and their knights fought long and hard against the Muslims. For the next 200 years, these knights and the rulers of the crusader states did much of the fighting in the Holy Land. Later crusades were military expeditions to help these Christians against further Muslim threats.

The Second Crusade (1147–1149). In 1144, the crusader state Edessa was captured by the Muslims, and Antioch and its surrounding territories were threatened as well. Pope Eugenius III called for a new crusade, and the French cleric BERNARD OF CLAIRVAUX persuaded King Louis VII of France and Emperor Conrad III of Germany to lead the forces. Louis's queen, ELEANOR OF AQUITAINE, joined the expedition.

The Second Crusade was a failure. While marching through Anatolia, the crusaders suffered heavy losses. Troops that were left to defend cities along the way were massacred or sold into slavery. Jerusalem's Christian rulers also persuaded the crusaders to ignore the plight of Edessa and Antioch and to attack the Syrian capital of DAMASCUS instead. As a result, the crusaders suffered a costly defeat, due partly to treachery by the Jerusalem Christians, who negotiated with the Muslims and withdrew from the siege.

The failure of the Second Crusade lessened the West's enthusiasm for crusades. Western knights had been unable to gain new lands, and they felt betrayed by the rulers of the crusader states. However, they could still be attracted by the promises of the church and their own religious feelings.

The Third Crusade (1189–1192). The capture of Edessa was only the beginning of reversals for the crusader states. Under the great leader SALADIN, the Muslim regions of Egypt and Syria were reunited. In 1187, Saladin defeated King Guy of the crusader states at the Battle of HITTIN and moved on to conquer Jerusalem. Though Saladin is reported to have dealt humanely with the Christians, the West's forces were once again called on for help.

The Third Crusade, like the Second Crusade, was a crusade of kings. King RICHARD I THE LIONHEARTED of England and King PHILIP II AUGUSTUS of France sailed to the Holy Land. FREDERICK I BARBAROSSA of Germany marched overland. Frederick died in Anatolia, but in 1191 the remaining crusaders reached the city of Acre and joined a siege begun earlier by knights from the crusader states. Eventually, the siege was successful, and Acre was recaptured from the Muslims.

After this victory, Philip learned that his young son and only heir was sick, and he returned to France. This left Richard the task of fighting Saladin. After a number of encounters, the two leaders reached a stalemate.

* **Holy Land** Palestine, the site of religious shrines for Christians, Jews, and Muslims

See color plate 10, vol. 3.

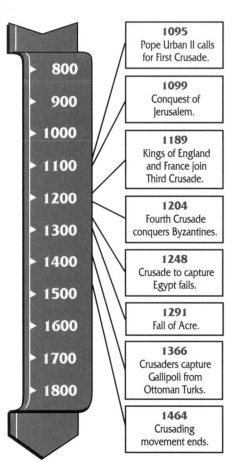

1095
Pope Urban II calls for First Crusade.

1099
Conquest of Jerusalem.

1189
Kings of England and France join Third Crusade.

1204
Fourth Crusade conquers Byzantines.

1248
Crusade to capture Egypt fails.

1291
Fall of Acre.

1366
Crusaders capture Gallipoli from Ottoman Turks.

1464
Crusading movement ends.

800
900
1000
1100
1200
1300
1400
1500
1600
1700
1800

In September 1192, they signed a three-year truce. Under this agreement, Jerusalem remained in Muslim hands, but its holy shrines were to be accessible to Christian pilgrims, and the crusaders regained control of much of the coastal region of Palestine. In October 1192, Richard set sail for England, and the Third Crusade came to an end.

The Third Crusade was a partial success. It gained important safeguards for Christian pilgrims and delayed Muslim conquest of the crusader states for several decades.

The Fourth Crusade (1202–1204).

A new pope, INNOCENT III, called for a crusade in 1198. He hoped that this crusade would not only drive the Muslims from the Holy Land but also resolve conflicts between the Western rulers by uniting them in a religious cause. Initially, few people responded to the pope's appeal. It took until 1202 to attract sufficient crusaders for the expedition.

The crusade was a largely French venture, though led by the Italian count Boniface of Montferrat and Baldwin IX of Flanders. Ships for the journey were hired from VENICE, and its planned target was Egypt. The belief was that Jerusalem would be easier to recapture if the Egyptian Muslims were defeated. Instead of pursuing this goal, however, the crusaders ended up attacking and conquering two Christian cities, one of which was Constantinople.

The Fourth Crusade was diverted from its original goal because of intrigues within the Byzantine Empire. Prince Alexios, the pretender* to the Byzantine throne, met with the crusade leaders and persuaded them to help depose his uncle, the current emperor. In return, he would provide much needed financial and military aid for the crusade and also unite the Greek and Roman churches. The crusaders agreed.

* **pretender** noble who claimed to be the rightful ruler when another held the power

The crusaders also came to an agreement with the city of Venice, which was demanding payment for the 500 ships provided. Because the crusaders could not supply the funds, they agreed to recapture from the Byzantines the Adriatic port of Zara, which Venice needed for its seafaring power.

The crusaders captured Zara in October 1202. Nine months later, they made a show of force outside Constantinople and arranged for Prince Alexios to become Emperor Alexios IV. The crusaders did not enter the city until 1204, however, when the citizens of the city rebelled against the new emperor. Alexios was deposed and murdered, and the crusaders fought their way into the city. Baldwin IX of Flanders was declared the new emperor of Constantinople. Instead of moving on to the Holy Land, the crusaders became involved in securing and extending their Byzantine conquests.

The Fifth Crusade (1217–1221).

Pope Innocent III again called for a new crusade in April 1213. Few knights from France joined this crusade, but many from England and Germany did. Major leaders included King Andrew II of Hungary, Duke Leopold VI of Austria, and John of Brienne, who held the title, king of Jerusalem. The goal of the Fifth Crusade was once again to capture Egypt. Once again, the goal was not attained.

The leaders of the crusade decided that the most effective way to break Muslim power was to attack the city of Damietta in the Nile delta. From there, they would move to Cairo, Egypt's capital. The crusaders arrived in Damietta in May 1218 and took more than a year to capture the

See color plate 9, vol. 3.

city. Then they waited for reinforcements from Germany. When the Christians finally moved in 1221, the Muslims had had plenty of time to create a stronghold at al-Mansura. There they cut the crusaders off from their supplies and from the best route of retreat. Rather than fight and lose many men, the Christians decided to surrender and agreed to give up Damietta. By the end of August 1221, the Fifth Crusade was over. All of Egypt was still under Muslim control.

The Crusades of Frederick II, Thibaut of Champagne, and Richard of Cornwall (1228–1240). After the failure of the Fifth Crusade, the Holy Roman Emperor FREDERICK II took up the burden of a new crusade. After nearly seven years of preparation, his army departed for the Holy Land in June 1228. Frederick regained Jerusalem, but he did it through diplomacy.

Frederick's main goal was apparently to gain control of the crusader states rather than to fight a holy war. He held secret talks with the Muslims, promising to aid them in some local conflicts and to permit freedom of worship for Muslims in the crusader states. In return, the Muslims agreed to a ten-year truce and ceded Jerusalem and other holy places to the Christians. However, the agreement was criticized by both sides. Many Muslims thought it was a disgrace to surrender Jerusalem to gain the favor of Christians. Many crusaders felt that Frederick's actions were a betrayal and renounced his leadership.

To continue the arrangement beyond ten years, Pope Gregory IX began calling for a new crusade in 1234. Among those who answered his call were Thibaut, who was count of CHAMPAGNE and king of Navarre, and Richard of Cornwall, the brother of King HENRY III of England.

Thibaut's expedition left for the Holy Land in 1239. On arrival in Jerusalem, he saw that the city's fortifications and supplies were very inadequate. To remedy the situation, Thibaut found Muslim leaders ready to help him in return for aid against their Muslim rivals. By playing Muslim leaders against each other, he secured promises that the Christians would retain Jerusalem as well as additional territories. With these assurances, Thibaut and his crusaders returned home. Meanwhile, Richard of Cornwall and his crusaders arrived in Jerusalem. They did little but confirm the agreements between Thibaut and the Muslims. Christian Jerusalem was still not adequately refortified and was thus left exposed to future dangers.

The Crusades of Louis IX (1248–1254, 1270–1272). In August 1244, the Muslims recaptured Jerusalem and nearly destroyed a Christian army near Gaza. Total loss of the Holy Land seemed possible. In response to this threat, King LOUIS IX OF FRANCE initiated a new crusade. This crusade was better prepared than any in the past, with large numbers of troops and supplies.

Louis's crusade followed a pattern similar to that of the Fifth Crusade. Its first target was Damietta, which was quickly captured. Once again, however, the expedition ran into problems at al-Mansura, where King Louis was captured in early 1250. After he was ransomed and released, he left Egypt for Palestine. There he worked to improve the fortifications of Christian outposts and to end bitter rivalries among the various crusader kingdoms. However, when Louis returned to France in 1254, he had not accomplished his goal of defeating Egypt.

See color plate 6, vol. 3.

> **Remember:** *Words in small capital letters have separate entries, and the index at the end of Volume 4 will guide you to more information on many topics.*

The crusades were a series of largely un-successful wars and confrontations be-tween Muslims and Christians that lasted for nearly two centuries. King Louis VII of France and Emperor Conrad III of Ger-many led the forces of the Second Cru-sade, which began in 1147. This manu-script page shows the two rulers entering Constantinople.

This crusade not only resulted in a defeat for King Louis. The Muslim army, made up mostly of freed slaves, took advantage of its victory to revolt against Egypt's Ayyubid dynasty. Under BAYBARS AL-BUNDUQDARI, the for-mer slaves established themselves as a new and powerful force in the world of Islam—the so-called MAMLUK, or slave, dynasty.

In 1267, Louis decided to launch another crusade. The target of this one was Tunisia. The king's troops began a siege of the city of Tunis in July 1270, but less than a month later Louis died. His brother Charles of An-jou, who had become king of Sicily, agreed to a truce with the Muslims that gave trading rights in Tunisia to the Sicilians. This may have been a major goal of the expedition.

Crusades of the Later Middle Ages.   During the last centuries of the Middle Ages, western Europe underwent several economic and social crises, including the BLACK DEATH and the HUNDRED YEARS WAR between France and England. The Byzantines recaptured Constantinople in 1261, and the Mamluks of Egypt conquered the last remaining Christian strong-holds in the Holy Land in 1291. This effectively ended nearly two centuries of Latin presence in the East. The western Europeans never managed to re-cover what they lost. Nevertheless, the crusading movement did not die.

Between 1291 and 1336, almost every French king made plans for a crusade to the Holy Land. These plans never materialized, however, be-cause of long-term disputes with England and the very high cost of such expeditions. Instead, supporters of crusades began to aim for more lim-ited objectives. Western powers with interests in Greece, especially Italian cities such as Venice, gained the pope's support for some important naval victories there in the 1330s and 1340s. King Peter de Lusignan of Cyprus used the appeal of crusading to attract troops and money for a successful raid on the Egyptian port of Alexandria in 1365. However, though this was the greatest crusading victory in the 1300s, Peter probably arranged it to

See map in Black Death (vol. 1).

lessen competition for his own rival trading ports. He abandoned Alexandria at the first approach of the Mamluk army, whose enormous strength was a huge obstacle to any lasting successes.

In 1366, crusaders also recaptured Gallipoli near Constantinople from the OTTOMAN Turks. The Ottomans were fast rivaling the Mamluks as the chief military threat of the Muslim world. This initiated a long struggle in which crusaders occasionally joined the Byzantines and other Balkan powers in an attempt to resist an Ottoman advance into eastern Europe. Though the Christians won some significant victories, they also suffered heavy defeats.

The fall of Constantinople to the Turks in May 1453 shocked the Christian world and led to the last major crusade. This crusade was organized in 1464 by Pope Pius II, who took up the cross himself. Most Western powers showed little interest, and those that did backed out as the departure date drew near. Pius left Rome in July 1464, but he died en route to Constantinople. His death marked the end of the crusading movement.

Other Crusades of the Middle Ages.   Crusades to the Holy Land were religious wars against the religion of Islam, though for many knights, greed for land and the other spoils of war was also an important motive. Another area of fighting against Islam was SPAIN, where the wars were also known as crusades. Combined Christian forces also waged fierce campaigns against surviving pagans in the BALTIC COUNTRIES of northern Europe. In all cases, victorious knights won much wealth as well as glory. Finally, several joint campaigns were fought against Christian heretics*, whom the popes saw as a major threat to the Roman Church's beliefs. Directed against such groups as the CATHARS and the Hussites, these expeditions were also religious crusades supported by the church.

The Roman Church called for other wars that seem to have had less religious motivation. These wars were against Christian rulers who were disobedient or hostile to the popes and arose from CHURCH-STATE RELATIONS that had troubled the Holy Roman Empire through much of the Middle Ages.

There had been a long-standing conflict between the popes and the emperors about who had greater control over the empire. By the 1120s, the popes had established their religious independence. The emperors still had overall political power throughout Germany and Italy, including the Papal States, a small area of central Italy directly ruled by the pope.

As long as the emperors focused their attention on Germany, the popes could wield influence in Italy and stand up to the emperors politically. By 1200, however, Emperor Frederick II had inherited direct control in Sicily and southern Italy. This weakened the pope's independence in the Papal States and even more in the nearby independent cities of northern Italy. When Frederick died in 1250, his son Manfred, though never an emperor, fought to remain king of Sicily and posed a similar threat to the popes. Later still, in 1282, Manfred's son-in-law Peter III of ARAGON was invited to rule Sicily, once again renewing the troubles of the papacy.

The popes called for several crusades against these rulers. In 1248, Frederick II lost Aachen, the royal seat in Germany, although he managed to hold on to his Italian possessions. In a 1266 crusade led by the French count Charles of Anjou, Manfred was killed in Sicily. (Charles, brother of

* **heretic**   person who disagrees with established church doctrine

Castles in the East

The crusaders from the West who stayed in the Holy Land after the First Crusade wanted to rule there forever. They built many huge castles on commanding sites and rebuilt forts taken from the Muslims. These castles were often called *kraks,* from a Syrian word meaning fortification.

King Baldwin of Jerusalem built the Krak de Montreal in his kingdom, sited to command tribute from those using nearby trade roads. The Knights of St. John built the Krak des Chevaliers to strengthen a site captured in 1110.

When these castles fell to the Muslims, many were fortified still further. They remain there today, huge fortresses baking in the sun.

the crusader King Louis IX, himself became king of Sicily for a time.) Yet another French crusade attacked Peter III's kingdom of Aragon.

The political crusades helped make the Papal States and northern Italian cities safer from outside interference, but they had other results as well. The rulers of western Europe had seen church money used for political wars and realized that it could also be available for their own campaigns. Moreover, the German emperors of the Holy Roman Empire had lost considerable power. This caused instability in both Germany and Italy, so much instability that the popes themselves had to take refuge at AVIGNON for much of the 1300s.

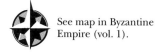

Cyprus, Kingdom of

See map in Byzantine Empire (vol. 1).

* **crusader states** states established in the East by Western Christians during the crusades. They included Jerusalem and Antioch.

* **dynasty** succession of rulers from the same family or group

* **fief** under feudalism, property of value (usually land) that a person held under obligations of loyalty to an overlord

* **vassal** person given land by a lord or monarch in return for loyalty and services

Located at the eastern end of the Mediterranean Sea, the island of Cyprus was a crossroads for many peoples and cultures. Byzantines, Muslims, French crusaders, and Italian merchant princes all ruled the island during the Middle Ages. Cyprus prospered most during the 250-year rule of its French kings. Settlers were attracted to the island, and its economy grew. It became an outpost of Christian culture in a region dominated by Muslims. The kings established a Western-style monarchy, expanded Cypriot power in Asia Minor, fought Turkish pirates, and traded across the Mediterranean.

In 500, Cyprus was part of the BYZANTINE EMPIRE. However, it came under continual pressure from Arab expansion after 632, and its capital was ruled by Muslims in the 700s and 800s. Cyprus was reunited under the Byzantines in the mid-900s and achieved independence in 1184.

Seven years later, RICHARD I of England conquered the island on his way to the Third CRUSADE, claiming that pilgrims were being mistreated there. Richard's rule over the island was brief: in 1192, Cyprus was purchased by Guy of Lusignan, former ruler of the kingdom of JERUSALEM, a crusader state* in the Holy Land. King Guy founded a feudal dynasty* on Cyprus that ruled until 1384. Guy seized the greater estates, including church lands, and gave fiefs* to knights from the Holy Land and the West. (He kept the richest lands for himself and his family.) The knights became his vassals* and promised to defend the new kingdom.

Cyprus became a rich domain of towns, villages, and castles. The royal court was at Famagusta, the most important town on the island and a major trading center. A government patterned after that of the Byzantine Empire handled the royal holdings and finances. High courts of the king's councilors heard cases involving fiefs and vassals of the king. Most fiefs remained with the old crusader families. Their impressive wealth, however, was soon matched by that of Greek and Syrian merchants, who managed Cyprus's exports of wheat, barley, wine, and textiles of spun gold. Other groups on Cyprus included craftsmen, mainly Syrian, and peasants, for the most part Greek. The peasants paid taxes, which were collected for the benefit of the lords.

Cyprus reached its peak of power under Peter I, who ruled in the mid-1300s. Peter had imperial ambitions, making raids into Asia Minor and even declaring himself king of ARMENIA. He fought the MAMLUK sultan* of Egypt and conquered Egypt's port of Alexandria in 1365. He also made alliances with other Christian lords against Turkish pirates who

* **sultan** political and military ruler of a Muslim dynasty or state

were disrupting Mediterranean trade. At home, Peter granted charters of freedom to Greek towns, giving them privileges similar to those of French and Syrian communities.

Many Christian communities in Cyprus coexisted in a spirit of tolerance. DOMINICANS and FRANCISCANS flourished alongside Greek monks from the Byzantine Church. In addition, some people still followed the Syrian and Armenian churches and other old foundations from the East.

The island entered a period of decline after Peter I was assassinated in 1369. Genoese forces seized Famagusta and also captured the young king, Peter II. In 1384, Peter's uncle, James I, finally turned Cyprus over to the Genoese, who held it until 1464. Twenty-five years later, another Italian city-state, Venice, annexed the island.

Cyril and Methodios, Sts.

Cyril
ca. 826–869
Byzantine missionary

Methodios
ca. 825–885
Byzantine missionary

* **liturgy**   form of a religious service, particularly the words spoken or sung

* **Orthodox**   referring to the Eastern Byzantine Church

* **patriarch**   head of one of the five major centers of early Christianity: Alexandria, Antioch, Constantinople, Jerusalem, and Rome.

* **heresy**   belief that is contrary to church doctrine

Cyril and Methodios were Byzantine Christian missionaries to the SLAVS of central and eastern Europe. Their impact on Christianity in the East was great. They introduced a Slavic alphabet, preached in the Slavic vernacular (the everyday language of the people), and helped found national churches based on local cultures. From their time until the present, vernacular languages have been used in the Christian liturgy* of the Orthodox* churches of eastern Europe, including the Russian Orthodox Church.

Cyril and Methodios were brothers, born in Thessaloniki, Greece. The nearby Slavs did not have their own writing, and Cyril invented an alphabet that contained modified Greek characters for a written Slavic language. (The Cyrillic alphabet used in Russia and in parts of eastern Europe today is named after Cyril though it is not his original version.) With this alphabet, Cyril and Methodios translated religious texts to use for spreading Christianity.

In 863, the Byzantine emperor and the patriarch* of CONSTANTINOPLE sent the brothers on a mission to Moravia, a region inhabited by Slavs but conquered by Louis the German, a ruler of the CAROLINGIAN Empire. Cyril and Methodios were determined to introduce worship in the everyday language of the people. However, German rulers and clergy favored Latin, the language of the Western Church based in Rome. The brothers' use of the vernacular brought them into conflict with the powerful German bishops, who forced them to leave. By opposing Cyril and Methodios, the bishops also sought to limit the spread of other Byzantine Christian beliefs in the region.

In 867, the brothers traveled to Italy, where they debated with Latin clerics over the use of the vernacular. Many people in the Roman Church believed that Christian worship should be conducted only in Hebrew, Greek, and Latin, a belief that the brothers called "the heresy* of three languages." In Italy, the brothers received an audience with Pope Adrian II, who gave his support to the use of Slavic in the liturgy.

Cyril was unable to continue the mission, dying in Rome on February 14, 869. However, Methodios was made archbishop over several Slavic regions, including Moravia. His mission to the Slavs was now sponsored by both the pope in Rome and the Eastern patriarch, the two heads of the Christian church.

When Methodios returned to Moravia as archbishop, the opposition he and Cyril had experienced earlier continued. Despite the pope's approval of the Slavic liturgy and his sponsorship of Methodios, a new Moravian prince joined the Carolingians in supporting Latin-speaking bishops. In 870, Methodios was arrested and tried by a council of German bishops. He was imprisoned until 873, when a new pope, John VIII, arranged for his release. For the next 12 years, Methodios fought the Latin liturgy and was able to strengthen and expand the Byzantine Church in the region.

Methodios died in Moravia on April 6, 885. After his death, his followers were persecuted and imprisoned. Upon their release, they traveled to BULGARIA and SERBIA, where they successfully organized Orthodox churches. Although the Slavic liturgy in Moravia was replaced by Latin, eastern and southern Slavs continued to employ the Slavic liturgy, and it remains in use in eastern Europe today. (*See also* **Bohemia-Moravia; Christianity.**)

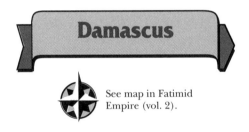

Damascus

See map in Fatimid Empire (vol. 2).

* **provincial** referring to a province or an area controlled by an empire

* **oasis** fertile area in a desert

* **Byzantine** referring to the Eastern Christian Empire that was based in Constantinople

* **caliph** religious and political head of an Islamic state

D amascus was an important Muslim political and religious center during the Middle Ages. It was the capital of the Islamic Empire for a century. After BAGHDAD was built in the late 700s, Damascus became a relatively minor provincial* capital for a few hundred years. Later, during the 1200s and 1300s, the city reemerged as an important center of Muslim learning.

Beginnings. Located in Syria about 60 miles from the Mediterranean coast, Damascus was in a large, fertile oasis* known as the Ghuta. Its climate—long, dry summers and short, cold winters with moderate rainfall—was good for growing crops. Damascus was well situated as the hub of many overland trade and pilgrim routes. It was an important Roman and Byzantine* city, located on the fertile land bridge connecting Egypt and Palestine to the south with Anatolia and Mesopotamia to the north and west. It later became a key storage and distribution center for the Mediterranean ports of Acre, Tyre, and Beirut.

In addition to being in the Ghuta, Damascus was near two other agricultural areas—the Bika Valley of central Lebanon to the west and the fertile Hauran plateau to the south. It was the main trade and government center of central Syria, and its economic importance and strategic location made it an especially attractive prize for rulers in Cairo and Baghdad.

Damascus Under the Arab Caliphates. The Arabs captured Damascus from the Byzantines in 635, and when the Syrian governor MU'AWIYA became the first UMAYYAD caliph* in 661, Damascus became capital of the entire Muslim Empire. The city's legacy from Roman times was visible everywhere in the remains of Roman construction. Mu'awiya built his palace inside the Roman walls of the city next to the old temple complex, which at the time was shared by a mosque and a church. The Umayyad mosque built in the northwest corner of the walled city was revered by many later generations of Syrians. Under the Umayyads, Damascus became a major center of Islamic scholarship, though it retained a large non-Arab population. Arab historian Ibn Shihab al-Zuhri spent the last 20 years of his life in the city, and another great scholar, al-Awza, was born there.

* **dynasty** succession of rulers from the same family or group

When the ABBASIDS overthrew the Umayyad dynasty* in 750, they moved the capital of the empire to Baghdad. Damascus spent its next 300 years as a provincial backwater under the Abbasids, and then under the FATIMID rule of Egypt. During this period, the city grew with the arrival of poor peasants from the countryside. It became divided into four quarters. Wealthy Muslims and government officials lived in the northwest quarter. Poor Muslims—day laborers and rural migrants—lived in the southwest quarter. The city's original inhabitants, Christians and Jews, occupied the other two quarters.

During these years, Damascus gained a reputation as a city of violent, ungovernable people. By the 900s, armed urban militias* posed a serious challenge to the city's foreign governors. The militias had their own infantry and cavalry units and remained a major political force in the city well into the 1100s. The city revolted several times against Abbasid rule. The Abbasid governors dismantled the Roman walls to allow free movement throughout the city. Later the walls were rebuilt in mud brick and then solid stone.

* **militia** army of citizens who may be called into action in a time of emergency

Damascus Under Later Rulers. In 1079, the city was occupied by the Turkish prince Tutush, beginning an era of rule by the SELJUKS. Tutush built a new fortified citadel*, with a royal palace and a government compound,

* **citadel** stronghold or fortified place commanding a city

During the Umayyad era, Damascus became a major center for Islamic religion and scholarship. In this courtyard is the Bayt al-Mal (treasury), which was built by al-Walid I in the early 700s. Also seen is one of three towers that were the first minarets in Islam.

* **crusader states** states established in the East
by Western Christians during the crusades.
They included Jerusalem and Antioch.

in the northwest corner of the city. Under the Seljuks, Damascus became a local power center, virtually independent of both Cairo and Baghdad. It vied with other local powers, including the new crusader states*, as well as Muslim centers such as Aleppo and Mosul.

In 1154, the prince of Aleppo, Nur al-Din Mahmud, seized control of Damascus. Under Nur al-Din, the city became the capital of a united Muslim Syria and command headquarters for military campaigns against the crusader states. His popularity allowed him to control the Damascus militias and lessen their influence, and again the city became an important center of Islamic learning. Many new religious schools were built, and distinguished Muslim scholars came from Iran and Mesopotamia. One of Damascus's most effective rulers, Nur al-Din campaigned as far away as Egypt, which his general SALADIN occupied in 1168.

Saladin became ruler of Egypt and succeeded Nur al-Din as the main Muslim leader against the crusades. Under Saladin and his AYYUBID dynasty, Damascus was the foremost center of religious learning in the Muslim world. The city and the surrounding area had many sites of interest to pilgrims and scholars, including the tomb of the caliph Mu'awiya and shrines to ALI IBN ABI TALIB and earlier figures in Islamic and Jewish history.

Ayyubid rule was ended by a Mongol attack in 1260, after which Damascus was occupied by the Egyptian MAMLUK dynasty. The city became a key staging area for Mamluk military campaigns against the Mongols, against later Christian crusades, and against rival Muslim groups. It continued to thrive as a religious center, and a new marketplace was built that was famed for its silk and brocade and its enameled glass, inlaid metalwork, and leather. The Mamluks ruled Damascus until the OTTOMAN Turks conquered the city in 1516. (*See also* **Crusades; Islam, Conquests of.**)

Dance

Dance played an important part in social and religious life throughout the Middle Ages. Dances took place at court, at festivals, and at other public gatherings. They were also part of weddings and other church celebrations, though not always approved of by the church.

Dances are shown in paintings and mentioned in literature, but few pieces of music or descriptions of dance steps survive from before 1400. The evidence shows that some dances had instrumental backing and others were accompanied by songs. More often than not, dances were done by pairs or groups of dancers rather than by single performers. Instruments included the harp, lute, organ, bagpipe, rebec*, and percussion such as tambourines and drums to give the beat. Two paintings from the 1300s show a singer playing a tambourine for a group of dancers. No pictures, however, show people playing from written music, and there are also very few music manuscripts, so it is assumed that the music was usually learned by heart or improvised.

BALLADS may have begun as a form of dance song (the Latin verb *ballare* means to dance). Rounds were sung to dances that were done in a circle. There was a dance called the estampie, which had irregular rhythms and needed great concentration from the dancers. Some dances were quite energetic, involving leaping steps.

Dancing was an important part of medieval social life. It was popular at court and at festivals and other public events. Dancing was usually done by pairs or groups rather than by single performers.

See color plate 9, vol. 1.

Popular Dancing

Many popular dances had their origin in rites performed in Europe before Christianity became the established religion. The church, therefore, issued frequent warnings against dance. It is clear, however, that dances took place during church celebrations, and that these did not differ greatly from the dances at festivals and in nobles' courts.

In 1325 in Paris, the church forbade its clergy from dancing at any time of the year other than Christmas and the feasts of St. Catherine and St. Nicholas. Anyone who disobeyed faced expulsion from the church.

* **shawm** double-reed woodwind instrument similar to a bassoon

At first, the different classes in society appear to have all performed the same kinds of dances. But after 1400, a new, more stately dance called the basse danse became very popular with the upper classes. More information is available about this dance than about earlier ones. Music and dance manuals from France, Italy, Germany, England, and Spain give detailed descriptions.

The basse danse started in the courts of Burgundy and Lombardy and spread rapidly through Europe. Its name refers to the fact that the feet were kept low, instead of performing the jumping and leaping steps of other dances. In one northern Europe version, couples moved forward, hand in hand. After beginning the dance with a formal bow, they performed a complicated series of steps: two slow steps forward, left foot, then right; three steps forward, ending with the feet together; turns of the body left, right, left, right, with the feet together; and then a move called a reprise that involved putting one foot behind the other, rising on the toes, and putting the feet together again.

The details and sequence of these steps varied for each different basse danse. In Italy, it was called the *bassadanza,* and it combined the dignified steps of the north with more active ones, including leaps. Another related Italian dance, called the *ballo,* combined quick and slow steps and was sometimes designed to show a theme such as ungraciousness or jealousy. Dancers had to practice in order to learn the different variations, and some nobles spent several hours a day in dance class.

The musical instruments most often used for the basse danse and its Italian variations were the shawm*, trombone, trumpet, flute, and drum. From the 1400s, hundreds of music manuscripts of these dances survive—close to 100 each of the basse danse and *bassadanza* and 70 of the *ballo.* These dances were popular well into the 1500s, when new fashions of dance became popular. (*See also* **Music; Musical Instruments.**)

Danegeld

I n the 800s and 900s, VIKINGS from SCANDINAVIA, whom the English called Danes, attacked and plundered many coastal communities in western Europe and defeated some of the ANGLO-SAXON kingdoms in ENGLAND. To prevent the Danes from looting and destroying, other Anglo-Saxon rulers chose to buy off the Danes with tribute, or money payments, called danegeld. Frankish kings made similar payments on the European mainland. Even after the Danish threat passed, the term continued to be used in England for taxes levied to defend against attacks from the sea.

The custom of paying tribute to Viking invaders began with King ALFRED THE GREAT, who made a large payment to the Danes in the early 870s before he defeated them in battle and drove them north out of his kingdom. In 991, however, after the Danes had invaded once again and defeated the English forces, King Ethelred began to pay tribute to the Danes on a regular basis. To help pay for the tribute, he had to collect danegeld from his subjects. The Vikings took back large amounts of danegeld from England. There are massive numbers of silver coins from King Ethelred's reign found in Scandinavia, and memorial inscriptions also mention the payments.

Long after the end of the Danish threat, danegeld was a land tax that English kings imposed on their subjects, originally to pay for ships and crews to defend the English coast. This annual danegeld tax continued well into the 1100s. The last danegeld tax was collected in 1162 during the reign of King HENRY II.

Dante Alighieri

1265–1321
Poet

D ante was the most accomplished poet of the Middle Ages. He grew up in the Italian city of FLORENCE, where he was active in city politics. After political opponents exiled him from the city in 1302, Dante spent the last 20 years of his life in exile. During his exile, he wrote an epic poem—*Commedia,* or *Comedy* (later called the *Divine Comedy*)—a triumph of world literature that has placed Dante in the company of Homer and Shakespeare as among the greatest writers who ever lived. The *Divine Comedy* was full of Dante's political beliefs. He took revenge on his enemies in Florence by placing them in Hell. He placed his allies and heroes in Heaven.

***The* Divine Comedy.** Dante's work is filled with a dazzling display of medieval ideas, symbols, and people. Written in beautiful Italian musical verse, the poem pictures a changeless universe ordered by God according to gradations of sin and righteousness. Critics agree that the *Divine Comedy* is a unique masterpiece and one of the great poems of all time.

Consisting of 100 cantos, or sections (more than 14,000 lines), the poem tells of Dante's imaginary journey during Easter Week of 1300 through the three realms Christians believed people's souls could go to after death—Hell (Inferno), Purgatory, and Heaven (Paradise). Virgil, the Latin poet of ancient Rome, guides Dante through the Inferno and Purgatory. Beatrice, a young woman in Florence whose early death made a deep impression on Dante, guides him across the heavens to Paradise. There the role of guide is taken over by BERNARD OF CLAIRVAUX, famed Cistercian orator of the early 1100s.

In the *Inferno,* Dante goes deep inside the earth through the nine circles of Hell. He sees people who are spending eternity being punished for sins they committed in their lifetimes. The sins range from gluttony, waste, and sullenness to violence, fraud, and treachery. Dante recognizes many of his enemies there, including Popes BONIFACE VIII and Clement V.

In the second part of the poem, *Purgatorio,* Virgil and Dante return to the surface of the earth shortly before dawn on Easter Sunday and climb the mountain of Purgatory. In Purgatory, sinners also suffer for their sins, but there is a difference. People in Purgatory confessed their sins, asking forgiveness, so they will be cleansed and will one day be with God. Because Virgil is not a Christian, he cannot enter Paradise with Dante. At the top of the mountain, Virgil passes Dante on to Beatrice.

In the third and final part of the poem, *Paradiso,* Beatrice is Dante's guide through the nine heavenly spheres of space. These spheres of Paradise are populated by saints; heroes; biblical figures such as Joshua, David, and Solomon; theologians* such as Thomas AQUINAS; and Christian emperors such as CONSTANTINE I, JUSTINIAN I, and CHARLEMAGNE. In the final canto of the poem, Dante's journey ends when he sees God's truth "in a great flash of light."

> * **theologian** person who studies religious faith and practice

The *Divine Comedy* has probably received more attention than any other poem ever written. Thousands of books and articles have been written about it, and hundreds of thousands of people have read it, either in the original Italian or in translation. Each year new readers discover the poem's scope, brilliance, and freshness. Their enthusiasm is the best evidence of the poem's greatness and of the enduring fame of the man who wrote it.

Dante's Youth and Early Works. The writer of the *Divine Comedy* was born in Florence at a time when TUSCANY was torn by continuous civil war. Five years before his birth, forces from Florence loyal to the papacy (called GUELPHS) had been defeated by forces from SIENA loyal to the HOLY ROMAN EMPIRE (called Ghibellines). The Florentine Guelph party, to which Dante's family belonged, had suffered 20,000 casualties.

By the time Dante was born in 1265, the Guelphs had staged a comeback. They had avenged their earlier defeat by expelling all of Florence's Ghibelline citizens and then decisively defeating the Sienese Ghibellines at the Battle of Colle Val d'Elsa. By the time Dante was five years old, Florence was a completely Guelph city, and so it remained for the rest of his life.

Dante's mother died when he was 5, and his father died when he was 16 or 17. As was the practice at the time, his family chose the girl who was to be his future wife, Gemma Donati. Dante married her when he was 20. As a young man, Dante fought in two battles for his city as a citizen-soldier. Except for a few lyric poems he wrote at that time, he seemed more directed toward a life of action than of literature.

The death of a young woman, Beatrice Portinari, in 1290 had a profound impact on Dante. She was married and a year younger than Dante, and it is not clear how well Dante knew her, or even if he knew her at all. However, Beatrice became his literary inspiration in the tradition of COURTLY LOVE. In *Vita nuova,* consisting of 31 love poems and 42 prose chapters written in the vernacular* (Italian rather than Latin), Dante described Beatrice as the perfect representative of Christian love on earth.

> * **vernacular** language or dialect native to a region; everyday, informal speech

Dante is one of the greatest poets of world literature. His masterpiece, the *Divine Comedy,* has received more attention and analysis than perhaps any other poem ever written. This painting from Florence Cathedral in Italy shows Dante posed before the three settings of his poem: Hell, Purgatory, and Paradise.

At the end of the work, Dante made a promise "to say of her what has never been said of another woman." He kept that promise years later when he assigned Beatrice a central place in the *Comedy.*

Between 1295 and 1301, Dante was an active politician in Florence. He served on several city councils and represented the city in delegations to other cities. However, trouble developed when the Guelph families who ran the city split into two factions called the Whites and the Blacks. In 1300, the Whites, the faction to which Dante belonged, banished the leader of the Blacks. Dante was then elected to the main six-member city council, and his political career reached its highest point.

In 1301, forces supporting Pope Boniface VIII enlisted the banished Blacks to help them gain control of Florence. Dante went to Rome as part of an embassy sent by the Whites to plead their case to the pope. During his absence, forces loyal to the pope entered Florence and allowed the banished Blacks to return. For five days, the Blacks robbed, destroyed, and murdered, driving the Whites who were still alive into exile. The Blacks fined Dante, who was still away from the city, and condemned him to exile for two years. When Dante refused to pay the fine, they took his belongings and property and condemned him to be burned at the stake if he returned to Florence. Dante, who blamed the pope, never saw his native city again.

Exile.   While the exiled Whites tried unsuccessfully to regain the city, Dante lived in exile, first in Verona and then in Arezzo. At this point in his life, he wrote two major works that he never finished.

The first was *De vulgari eloquentia,* a work in Latin defending the use of the vernacular in literature. At the time, Latin was widely regarded as the best language for scholarship, but Dante argued forcefully, as he had earlier in *Vita nuova,* that the vernacular Italian was more noble, natural, universal, and eloquent than Latin.

Dante's second great unfinished work of this period was *Convivio,* which was intended to be a massive 500-page treatment of the literary, philosophical, and moral issues that interested Dante most. Even unfinished, the work was the longest piece ever written in Italian. Dante championed the wisdom and greatness of Lady Philosophy and explored in detail the nature of true nobility. For the first time, he showed a keen interest in poets of the CLASSICAL TRADITION, especially Virgil, who was to have a central place in the *Comedy.*

When Henry VII, who was chosen king of Germany in 1308, announced that he planned to go to Italy to be crowned emperor of the Holy Roman Empire, Dante supported his decision. Though Dante had grown up in a pro-papal Guelph family, he now saw the emperor and the idea of empire as the best way to unify Italy and to check the power of the papacy. Dante hoped Henry would rule in the tradition of Charlemagne, the Christian king of the FRANKS who had been crowned the first medieval emperor of Rome on Christmas Day in 800.

Henry had enemies in Germany who tried to delay his departure, but in 1310 he crossed the Alps into Italy with 5,000 troops. He was crowned first in Milan and then in Rome, despite the growing opposition of Clement V and his Guelph supporters. Henry also laid siege to Florence, and Dante's hope of returning to the city was raised. However, he was disappointed; Henry was unable to take the city and died the following year.

During Henry's years in Italy, Dante was writing the *Comedy,* which champions the idea of empire throughout. In the first part of the poem, Dante assigns punishments to those who oppose the emperor and the principle of empire. At the very center of the Inferno, placed in the jaw of Satan, are Brutus and Cassius, who murdered Julius Caesar to prevent him from becoming the first Roman emperor. In the third part of the poem, Christian emperors such as Charlemagne have honored places in Paradise.

While Henry was in Italy, Dante also wrote a treatise* in Latin called *Monarchia,* about the relationship between the papacy and the empire. He argued against the growing power of the papacy and the papal claim that the church was the source of the state's power. He declared that the emperors were independent of the popes and equal to them in status and authority.

After Henry's death, Dante spent several years in Verona at the court of its ruler, Can Grande della Scala. Della Scala had welcomed Henry and had been one of his strongest supporters. Dante continued work on the *Comedy,* probably finishing the *Inferno* and *Purgatorio* in Verona. Dante's *Letter to Can Grande,* which he wrote to his host in 1316, explains the poem's style, technique, and meaning. The letter is now regarded as the briefest and clearest explanation of the poem ever written.

Dante spent his final years in RAVENNA at the court of Guido Novello da Polenta, where he finished the *Divine Comedy.* He was joined by several of his children, was honored by the court, and undertook several important diplomatic missions for his host. While in Venice on an embassy for Guido Novella, Dante caught a fever. He died in Ravenna at the age of 56. (*See also* **Church-State Relations; Italian Language and Literature; Italy; Paradise, Idea of; Purgatory, Idea of.**)

Remember: *Words in small capital letters have separate entries, and the index at the end of Volume 4 will guide you to more information on many topics.*

See color plate 8, vol. 3.

* **treatise**   long, detailed essay

Death and Burial in Europe

Religious beliefs about death and burial played an important part in the Middle Ages. Christians and Muslims both believed that an afterlife of peace in paradise would reward the faithful. Religious ideas about death affected burial rites. Details of such beliefs and rites changed during the Middle Ages, however, as described here for western Europe.

Beliefs About Death.   By the start of the medieval period, the pagan* ideas about death held by the German tribes and in ancient Rome had been largely replaced by Christian beliefs. Some pagan practices continued, however, such as the preparation of the body, the wake*, and the funeral procession.

Early Christians were unusual in that they believed death was not to be feared. Instead, it was a joyful, victorious experience connected with Christ's rising from the dead. Some saw death as a sleep in preparation for the afterlife. Others saw it as the soul's passage to paradise guided by Christ and the angels. To emphasize the joyous aspect of death, early Christians were encouraged to dress in colorful clothes rather than the mournful black worn by pagans. Death was even referred to as a day of birth because it was the time when the deceased attained peace and light. As the Middle Ages progressed, however, there was more of an emphasis on the power of God as judge, the sinfulness of humans, and fear of hell and damnation for those who were not pardoned by God. Later still, the church began to play down the fear of death and to emphasize God's mercy.

The church taught that death separated the soul from the body; thus, prayer and final forgiveness were more important than care of the corpse. However, even at the start of the Middle Ages, the bodies of Christians, especially saints, were believed to have holy powers. By the end of the period, there was an almost macabre fascination with the physical remains of the dead.

Rites of Death and Burial.   Western death and burial ceremonies varied greatly, but they had basic features in common. They began with last rites for the dying person. After death, the body was prepared, taken to the church, and then taken to the grave. The deceased was also often remembered later in prayers.

In the early Middle Ages, last rites included readings from the Bible about the last sufferings of Christ and a final Mass* for the person who was dying. Later, additional ceremonies and prayers were added. For example, the dying person would be anointed with oil, and the whole community might be summoned by church bells to his or her final Mass. By the end of the Middle Ages, anointing had became less important, and more emphasis was placed on confession and forgiveness. It was believed that confessing one's sins and receiving absolution* shortly before dying were the best preparations for Judgment Day.

During the last rites and throughout the remaining preparations and services, prayers were read and psalms* and antiphons* were sung. The body was made ready for burial. It was washed and clothed in garments and shoes appropriate to the person's status, so that the person would be properly clothed for God's Judgment. If the body was that of somebody of high standing, it might be embalmed to preserve it, or, after about 1100,

* **pagan** word used by Christians to mean non-Christian and believing in several gods

* **wake** funeral watch in which family and friends sit with the dead body before burial

* **Mass** Christian ritual commemorating Christ's Last Supper on earth, also called Communion or Eucharist

* **absolution** forgiveness granted by a priest after a Christian has confessed to his or her sins

* **psalms** sacred songs from the Old Testament of the Bible

* **antiphons** psalms, anthems, or verses sung alternately between two groups of singers

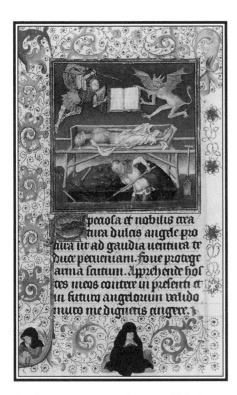

Death is an important theme in Christian art. Some illuminated manuscripts show different stages of death and burial. This manuscript page, from the *Book of Hours of Catherine of Cleves,* shows a guardian angel and a demon battling for possession of a soul.

* **relic** object cherished for its association with a martyr or saint

* **bier** ceremonial stand for a coffin or a corpse

* **psalms** sacred songs from the Old Testament of the Bible

* **chalice** cup used at the Mass to represent Christ's cup at the Last Supper

* **sarcophagi** ornamental coffins, usually made of stone

* **votive** referring to fulfillment of a vow, devotion, or gratitude

* **Office of the Dead** service commemorating the dead, often added to the regular daily prayers

* **fresco** method of painting in which color is applied to moist plaster and becomes chemically bonded to the plaster as it dries; also refers to a painting done in this style

The Cluniac Way of Dying

When a monk at the monastery of Cluny was dying, he confessed his sins in front of the entire community. The monks went in a procession to his room to sing psalms as he was given his last Mass. Then the dying monk was left with a cross and lighted candles at the head of his bed, and he was prepared for death by being sprinkled with ashes. At the moment of death, the monks were summoned again by a loud knocking, affirmed their belief in God by saying the creed, and prayed for the monk's soul. Then they gathered in the chapel to say the Office of the Dead, and the bells sometimes were tolled.

parts of it might even be removed. This unusual practice was sometimes performed so that several churches or religious orders could have relics* if the person became a saint. Or the dying person might wish to have certain parts of the body, such as the head or the heart, buried at different sites, or to have prayers for the soul said in more than one place. Church leaders, including Pope Boniface VIII in 1299, condemned dismemberment, but the practice continued.

Once the body was prepared, it was placed on a bier* to lie at home for the wake ceremony, or be carried in procession directly to the church. The funeral service might include recitation of psalms*, spreading of incense, and another Mass. It would end with prayers for the deceased to share Christ's Resurrection and to receive peace, light, and a place with the saints.

After these prayers, another procession was formed, and the body was carried to the graveside, preceded by lamps or candles and incense. The grave was sprinkled with incense and holy water. Laurel leaves were placed in it to signify the victory of those dying in Christ. The body of a poor man might be buried in the ground without even a sheet, but the bodies of wealthier people were placed in large earthen jars or elaborate coffins. Members of religious orders and the clergy were often buried with symbols of their rank; for example, priests might have a small wooden chalice*. Persons of very high rank were put in elaborate sarcophagi* that stood above ground. All bodies were supposed to face east, ready for God's appearance on Judgment Day.

After a burial, Christians were encouraged to remember the dead. Masses were said for the deceased 30 days after their departure as well as on the day of death. The dead could also be remembered by having their names inserted into the regular Mass. From the 800s on, there was a marked increase of votive* Masses in honor of the dead. The dead were remembered in the Divine Office by having the Office of the Dead* recited regularly. Churches and orders kept lists of the dead according to the day of their death so that prayers could be said on the anniversaries of their deaths.

Artistic Portrayals of Death.   Understanding of medieval attitudes toward death comes not only from religious writings, wills, and other historical documents but also from many works of art: illuminations in manuscripts, paintings on walls, and sculptures on tombs.

From ancient times, death was an important theme in Christian art. The ancient catacombs, or tombs, were decorated with images and symbols representing triumph over death. In Romanesque church decoration, the Last Judgment was often carved in stone over the main doorway. Sarcophagi were often carved with elaborate scenes of death as well as images of the deceased. Ornate crosses marked locations where funeral processions had stopped and chapels where Masses could be said.

The subject of death was often depicted in illuminated manuscripts, especially in Books of Hours, which often show the various stages of death and burial. Fresco* paintings also frequently represented themes of death. A particularly somber theme in later medieval wall painting was the dance of death, or danse macabre. This showed skeletons dancing with the dead and leading or dragging them away, regardless of what their class in life had been.

See *Scandinavia.*

D
evils and demons were part of the religious beliefs and traditional folklore of medieval society. The devil, or Satan as he was often called, was part of the common religious heritage of JUDAISM, ISLAM, and CHRISTIANITY that had its origins in the Jewish BIBLE. In the book of Job, for example, Satan is described as the adversary of God. Ideas about his evil influence on people's behavior affected popular forms of medieval Judaism, but he was not believed to possess independent power.

In Islamic tradition, the devil was called Iblis but was also known as al-Shaytan (Satan). He is described as an enemy of Allah, or God, from the beginning. Iblis refused to join the angels in bowing down before the newly created Adam, and he successfully tempted Adam and Eve to disobey God. According to the Islamic mystical* tradition of Sufism*, the devil's greatest sin was that he tried to put himself on the same level as God.

Muslims believed Iblis was always trying to disrupt prayers, interfere with natural functions such as eating and drinking, and find ways to tempt men and women into sins of ambition, greed, and lust, especially during the night. Many medieval Islamic texts provide special prayers and ritual formulas so the faithful can ward off the devil.

In early medieval Christianity, Satan was a similar figure, who knew the best way to get people to commit sins and engage in superstitious practices. He was also a great deceiver. According to St. Paul, Satan had the ability to transform himself into "an angel of light" to fool people and get them to believe what was untrue.

European Christians also believed in evil spirits called demons. Although they did not think demons could transform things, they believed demons could fly, appear and disappear suddenly, and speak different languages. Since they could do many things humans could not do, people believed they were the force behind the performance of magic.

Belief in devils and demons increased during the Middle Ages. Christianity began to stress the conflict between God and Satan for human souls. Satan became a more powerful figure, capable not only of deceiving people but of actively recruiting them for his evil plans. The belief that the

* **mystical** referring to the belief that divine truths or direct knowledge of God can be experienced through meditation and contemplation as much as through logical thought

* **Sufism** belief that suggests ways to attain loving intimacy with Allah

One of Christianity's greatest concerns was the struggle between God and the devil for human souls. Such conflict is illustrated here in *The Temptation and Prayer of St. Anthony* by Agnolo Gaddi.

devil was enlisting supporters paved the way for charges of WITCHCRAFT and the trials that became common in Europe. It was believed that witches chose to worship the devil because of his great powers and the earthly rewards he promised his followers. Christian belief in the devil reached its peak at the end of the Middle Ages. (*See also* **Angels; Magic and Folklore; Mysticism.**)

Dinis, King of Portugal

1261–1325
King and poet

Dinis, sixth king of PORTUGAL, was one of the most effective royal patrons of poetry during the Middle Ages. He encouraged and supported the poetic tradition of COURTLY LOVE established by the TROUBADOURS of Provence in southern France in the 1100s. He also wrote many fine poems of his own.

Dinis was the son of Alfonso III of Portugal. While growing up, he was sent on many embassies to his grandfather, ALFONSO X EL SABIO of Castile and León, whose court was famed for its poets, scientists, and scholars. There and at other Spanish courts, he met the most talented poets of his time.

Dinis became king of Portugal at age 18. An excellent ruler, he also made his court into an international poetry center for the almost half century he ruled. Portuguese became the language of poetry for all of central and western Spain. He supported many poets, and he himself wrote and collected poems, as did his two sons, Alfonso Sanches and Pedro. Dinis also founded the University of Coimbra.

The work of Dinis that has survived shows the range and diversity of his talent. Most of his poems are *cantigas d'amor,* or love poems, about the pain and sorrow of love. He also wrote more lighthearted love poems, as well as some satirical ones that poke fun at hypocrisy and cowardice.

Dinis was the last important royal supporter of troubadour poetry. When he died, Castilian began to establish itself as the literary language of Spain. French pilgrims to SANTIAGO DE COMPOSTELA also brought a new popular literature with them, the tales of King Arthur from Wales and Brittany.

Diplomacy

* **emissaries** official agents of a ruler or government sent on a special mission or errand

Diplomacy is the basic means of communication between states or rulers for settling disputes peacefully. It can also be a government's approach to getting its way in international affairs. Attitudes toward other states differed in the Middle Ages, and so did diplomatic practices, but every state had to send, and receive, emissaries*. This article examines the ways in which diplomacy was practiced in the Byzantine Empire, the Islamic Empire, and the states of western Europe.

Byzantine Diplomacy

Diplomacy was a major factor in the survival of the Byzantine Empire during the Middle Ages. The empire was involved in many wars, but Byzantines preferred diplomacy to costly military action. The main purposes of their diplomacy were to defend the empire and to expand its influence. They also sought to divide their enemies by playing one against the other.

Medieval rulers were judged by the way they treated visiting foreign nobles and diplomats. This manuscript illumination from the 1300s shows King Edward III of England paying homage to Philip of Valois, king of France.

The Byzantines used many methods, including spying and propaganda, to achieve these goals.

The Byzantines viewed their emperor as the leader of all world rulers, and they considered that he was issuing orders to his inferiors rather than trying to negotiate terms. This arrogant view was, however, carefully balanced by very practical diplomacy. Despite their claim to world leadership, the Byzantines often made concessions and compromises. They paid large amounts of tribute* to different states during their history, though they always maintained that the payments were "gifts" to foreigners.

* **tribute** payment made to a dominant foreign power to stop it from invading

In choosing emissaries to foreign nations, the Byzantines drew on people of various backgrounds and experiences, from the military, the church, and the bureaucracy*. Ambassadors were selected for acceptability to a particular foreign ruler, language skill, and willingness to sacrifice themselves for the good of the empire. They were also expected to return with as much data as they could about the nation they visited. In fact, Byzantine travelers were all expected to gather information both inside and outside the empire.

* **bureaucracy** large departmental organization such as a government

Though the empire had no permanent foreign emissaries, it kept a regular diplomatic staff that operated within its borders. This staff, supervised by an official called the logothete, not only handled diplomatic communications within the empire but acted as escorts to all envoys from abroad who came to negotiate with the emperor. Next to the emperor, the logothete was the most important host at receptions of foreign ambassadors.

Because the Byzantines preferred diplomacy to war and violence, "peace and a treaty" was their goal. They favored ingenious and subtle maneuverings that required skill and careful planning. They saw nothing wrong in using money and favors to gain peace or military allies. At the very start of the Middle Ages, their emperor wrote: "There is a law that orders the emperor to lie and to violate his oath if it is necessary for the well-being of the empire." To protect the empire, they would use whatever means were available.

Islamic Diplomacy

In contrast to Byzantine diplomacy, the basic principle underlying Islam's relations with other nations was the idea of JIHAD, or holy war. A founding belief of Islam was that it had a continual state of war with non-Muslim states. For early Islam, therefore, diplomacy usually served either to deliver the message of Islam before fighting began or to negotiate an exchange of prisoners after the fighting stopped.

Beginning with the ABBASID period in 750, diplomatic relations took on a broader scope. The Abbasids saw the need to communicate with non-Muslim nations without military action. Diplomacy helped Muslim leaders achieve this goal. Truces were negotiated, peace agreements were achieved, and ransoms were paid. Even so, Islamic diplomacy remained primarily a way to reach immediate objectives, not to maintain long-term relationships. As a result, Muslim states did not establish permanent embassies in other countries. Islamic emissaries were viewed as temporary representatives who returned home after they had delivered their message.

Such emissaries (called *rasuls* or *safirs*) were usually respected and trusted by Islamic rulers. *Rasuls* were known for their knowledge, skill, reliability, good appearance, courage, and charm. Muslim rulers often sent several emissaries to foreign courts because they could not find one person with all the necessary qualifications.

Islamic diplomacy was considered an important way of maintaining economic and cultural contacts with other peoples and, ultimately, of extending Islamic influence and control.

Diplomacy in Western Europe

Compared with the Byzantine and Islamic diplomacy, the diplomacy of western Europe was more straightforward and, at first, more primitive. In the early Middle Ages, kings or other leaders would themselves meet at a neutral site—for example, on a bridge over a river dividing their lands—to settle differences. As their lands became larger, however, personal contacts between rulers became more difficult. It became necessary for them to send emissaries in their place.

Diplomatic Personnel and Missions.   The method of choosing emissaries differed from state to state and from one period to another. In a monarchy, the king or queen usually selected the ambassadors. In the Italian republics, they were often elected. Social status was perhaps the most important quality for a leading diplomat, and wealth was also necessary. Nationality was usually less of an issue.

High social standing helped ensure that an ambassador was personally acceptable to the ruler being visited. Using an ambassador of low status would be considered a sign of great disrespect. This was done on purpose during the HUNDRED YEARS WAR: Charles V of France sent a defiant message to England's Edward III in the hands of a kitchen servant. But leading diplomats were nearly always chosen from the nobility or from the clergy.

Wealth was also important. Emissaries sometimes received payment for their services and expenses, but in the early Middle Ages especially, they were often expected to cover many of their costs themselves. Not surprisingly, people tried to avoid diplomatic appointments. They also complained of the time and dangers involved in their missions. There was a

Remember: *Words in small capital letters have separate entries, and the index at the end of Volume 4 will guide you to more information on many topics.*

The Carolingian Connection

One of the most fabulous errands of medieval diplomacy was in the late 700s, between the early Carolingian kings of the Franks and the Abbasid caliphs al-Mansur and Harun al-Rashid.

This was at a time when travel across Europe was still very difficult and there was little knowledge about far-off cultures. Yet four missions took place—one sent by Pepin III the Short, one sent by al-Mansur, and two sent by Charlemagne.

The goal of the missions is not clear, but among the gifts exchanged was an elephant, sent from Baghdad back across Europe, from Harun al-Rashid to Charlemagne.

* **plenipotentiary** a person with full authority, such as a procurator

risk of being robbed or captured while on the road. Being imprisoned by the foreign power was always another danger.

It was therefore not uncommon for friendly foreigners to be hired as diplomats. A respected noble from another nation might be an excellent choice. It was sometimes convenient, and less costly, to use a person who was already present at a foreign court. Such appointments made sense in the Middle Ages because the idea of national identity was not strong; matters were being negotiated between the leaders more than between the nations.

Types of Diplomats.   Terms used to describe diplomatic officials in western Europe included legate, *nuncius*, ambassador, and procurator. These words were not used precisely, but they do correspond to different types of messengers. Some emissaries merely carried messages to a fellow ruler, acting as a kind of "living letter" who repeated the words his lord, or sender, had given him. Such a messenger was usually called a legate or *nuncius*. He could be sent to offer treaties, truces, marriage alliances, and other pacts. He had no flexibility to suggest or agree to any other terms unless specifically instructed. It was as if the king or ruler was speaking through him.

The name *ambassador* was also sometimes used for messengers of this kind. In the later Middle Ages, however, *ambassador* came to mean something a little different. Ambassadors were often charged with other tasks that might lead to good relations with the ruler they were visiting. They participated in, and arranged, ceremonies of entertainment that were becoming increasingly important in diplomacy. They attended marriages or funerals as official representatives to friendly states and rulers. As diplomatic activity in Europe increased, it became practical to have an ambassador remain in another city or royal court for an extended period rather than travel back and forth continually. Resident ambassadors were especially useful for gathering information (about the condition of routes or the size of an army) and for keeping their rulers informed on what was going on elsewhere. In other words, they made good spies.

Some legates and ambassadors, especially those to distant places (such as Muscovy), were given full powers to negotiate and conclude treaties, truces, and the like. If they had these plenipotentiary* powers, they were more properly called procurators. A procurator was an emissary who could act on his own initiative without waiting for specific instructions from his ruler. Whatever the procurator agreed on had the same force of law as if the king agreed to it.

Sometimes procurators were given blank documents already marked with their royal seal. Whatever they wrote would become the agreement. Henry III of England sent a bishop to Rome as an emissary to appoint a new diplomat. The emissary carried a document that was complete except for the new diplomat's name, which the bishop was to fill in once an acceptable person was chosen.

Diplomatic Immunity in the Middle Ages

Diplomatic missions were important to states throughout the medieval world. Whatever their basic attitude toward using emissaries, therefore, all nations tried to ensure the safety of ambassadors—their own and those of other states. One type of protection offered was diplomatic immunity. According to this principle, governments considered the ambassador, his goods, and those accompanying him to be untouchable.

Under the laws of immunity in western Europe, ambassadors could not be tried for criminal or civil offenses. Those who seriously abused this right, however, might have immunity withdrawn from them. Diplomatic immunity generally worked in the Middle Ages although violations sometimes occurred. The most famous example in medieval times took place in 1241 when Holy Roman Emperor FREDERICK II imprisoned more than 100 clergy, *nuncii,* and procurators who had come to him from rebel towns in Lombardy. Public outrage and a royal rebuke forced Frederick to release them.

Immunity did not extend so far in Islamic countries. Visitors and diplomats were all expected to respect the laws of Islam. But an important element of Islamic diplomacy was the granting of safe conduct. For most foreigners, this was done by granting an *aman,* which was like a passport. It entitled non-Muslims to enter Islamic lands under the protection of Muslim authorities. Emissaries were, however, given the same protections without an *aman.* Even in times of war, this protection was usually honored.

The Byzantine Empire did more than granting safe conduct to emissaries from other nations. It also assigned agents to welcome them at the border and to guard their safety at all times. There were, of course, other motives for this human escort: the agents were expected to collect all the information they could from the foreigners.

Diplomatic Ceremony in the Middle Ages

Diplomacy involves a great deal of courtesy and etiquette. The late Middle Ages especially have been called a period of a thousand formalities. But formalities were always important for easing relations between rulers and maintaining civilized behavior. A ruler was judged on the basis of his treatment of visiting foreign diplomats. Ambassadors were thus welcomed, feasted, and made to feel honored and respected.

In Islamic lands, the arrival of an ambassador and his companions was usually met with great ceremony. They were given luxurious quarters, were lavishly entertained, and were given gifts. However, if the mission was a failure, they could be coldly dismissed. If war broke out between the states, the visiting diplomats were occasionally imprisoned or even killed.

Pomp and ceremony also greeted emissaries in Europe. An ambassador to France in the 1400s described how he was brought into a great hall where not only the king but all his barons were seated. The envoy was motioned to sit on a bench at the far end of the hall to explain his visit. Great skill at speaking and a loud voice were necessary for such envoys.

There was no more impressive audience than the one given at the Byzantine emperor's court. Foreigners were led into the imperial audience hall past the imperial guard and throngs of dignitaries. At the end of the procession, a curtain was drawn aside to reveal the emperor, dressed in glittering robes and seated on his throne. When the diplomats prostrated themselves on the ground, as they were required to do, the throne was hoisted above the assembly to symbolize the unapproachability of the emperor. Later on, the emperor might dine with the visiting diplomats in a less formal setting.

Though diplomats were honored on visits to other nations, however, they were hardly trusted. In Constantinople, the logothete and his numerous agents watched foreign ambassadors closely to make sure they did not see more than they should or journey where they should not. Emissaries to

> **Remember:** Consult the index at the end of Volume 4 to find more information on many topics.

Muslim countries, though allowed to enter without an *aman* or passport, were courteously accompanied by a guide who ensured that they did not spy or gather material that would be useful in a war. Western nations were also suspicious of ambassadors, often trying to isolate them and limit their access to information. In England during the 1200s, English messengers were assigned to accompany foreign envoys. Then in the late 1400s, Venetian nobles were forbidden to discuss matters of state with all foreigners, and especially foreign ambassadors. (*See also* **Byzantine Empire; Chronicles; Consuls, Consulates; Crusades.**)

Divine Office

* **antiphons** psalms, anthems, or verses sung alternately between two groups of singers

* **canticle** song from the Bible traditionally used in religious services

The Divine Office was a set of eight Christian religious services performed throughout the day and night by monks, nuns, and clergy. Its purpose was to offer continuous prayer and worship to God. The services consisted of prayers, psalms, readings, hymns, antiphons*, and canticles*.

The individual services of the Divine Office were called "hours." The eight hours were matins, lauds, prime, terce, sext, none, vespers, and compline. During the Middle Ages, the length of each service, the text used, and the time of day it was performed varied from place to place.

Matins was the longest of the hours. It usually lasted more than an hour and was performed at about two o'clock in the morning. The hours that followed were said at roughly three-hour intervals. The last two—vespers and compline—were said close together at the end of the day, with compline ending at bedtime. This allowed the worshipers to get several hours' sleep before the Divine Office began again the next morning.

Reciting the Divine Office as a group called for a religious community that could keep up with its demanding schedule. As more clergy lived on their own, and as monks began to work outside the monasteries, they found it difficult to find time for the Office. By the end of the Middle Ages, the practice was declining. For monks and clergy, the Divine Office often became a private devotion, rarely performed together as a group. Many communities of nuns, however, continued to practice the complete service until the end of the Middle Ages and beyond. (*See also* **Benedictines; Book of Hours; Breviary.**)

Dmitrii Ivanovich Donskoi

1350–1389
Prince of Moscow and
military hero

* **tribute** payment made to a dominant foreign power to stop it from invading

Dmitrii Ivanovich Donskoi was the first Russian prince to defeat the GOLDEN HORDE. The Golden Horde was part of the MONGOL EMPIRE, and it dominated most of Russia during the last quarter of the Middle Ages. Under the Golden Horde, Russia's princes kept their lands but had to pay tribute* to the khans, the Mongol leaders. The khans also made decisions about who should rule over the local Russian states. They set up Dmitrii's ancestors as grand princes of Vladimir, a part of northeast Russia that included the regions of Suzdal and Tver as well as MUSCOVY, the area around Moscow.

Despite its power over Russia's princes, the Golden Horde was not unified. In 1359, rival Mongol groups backed the princes of Suzdal and

Tver in their claims to Vladimir. An army from Moscow put down the Suzdal prince by invading Suzdal in 1363. Seven years later, young Dmitrii himself led his army into Tver. LITHUANIA threatened to help Tver, however, and it was not until 1375 that Dmitrii confirmed Moscow's dominance in Vladimir by assembling an army large enough to deal with the Lithuanian threat.

With control of the rival princes confirmed, Dmitrii began fighting the Mongols themselves. In 1380, his army routed the Mongols in a bitter battle at Kulikovo, on the Don River near Moscow. Kulikovo was the only major Russian victory over the Golden Horde, and it won Dmitrii the name Donskoi (meaning "of the Don").

Moscow's independence was short-lived. In 1382, the Golden Horde sacked Moscow. However, the Mongol khan endorsed Dmitrii to remain grand prince, knowing that a satisfied Dmitrii Donskoi would remain a loyal ally.

Domesday Book

The Domesday Book consists of two huge handwritten volumes containing a thorough description of England at the end of the reign of WILLIAM I THE CONQUEROR. The census that produced the work is considered the greatest administrative achievement by any royal government in the Middle Ages.

Just 20 years after he invaded England, William I arranged to have the Domesday Book prepared. In one year's time—during the year 1086—most of William's kingdom was investigated. Royal officials collected data on the wealth and people of each county. The accuracy of the information about each locality was confirmed under sworn oath by groups of local villagers called together at an inquest*.

* **inquest** official examination of evidence by a jury

William I's survey of England was not called Domesday Book until the mid-1100s. Domesday, or doomsday, was a reference to the biblical day of final judgment, the day of doom. The authority of the book and its entries, like the decisions to be made by God on Judgment Day, were considered final and not to be appealed.

* **scribe** person who hand-copies manuscripts to preserve them

Though each county's information was methodically collected village by village, it was carefully rearranged in so-called feudal order, according to landowners and their holdings. These materials were then sent to a treasury scribe*, who shortened most of the county descriptions and combined them into a single volume called Great Domesday. The second volume, called Little Domesday, includes the full information for three eastern counties. This information was never shortened for inclusion in the main volume, perhaps because the project was interrupted by the king's death in 1087.

* **manor** farming estate, usually with a house for the lord and a village for the local farmworkers

* **fief** under feudalism, property of value (usually land) that a person held under obligations of loyalty to an overlord

For each county, the king's manors* and estates are described first. These descriptions are followed by similar entries on the properties of the king's major tenants in fief*. Each entry indicates the tenant at the time of the survey and also at the time of the Norman conquest. Also included are the property's size; the numbers and classes of people who work on it; its mills, ponds, meadows, woods, and other resources; and its value. Value is quoted three ways: before the conquest, when the present tenant received the manor, and at the time of the survey.

Domesday helped the Normans collect tax revenues and was also useful in settling land disputes. Because it was accepted as authoritative, the work became a main support of Norman power in England and the feudal rights of the king. It survives as the essential source of information about England in the 1000s. (*See also* **England; Normans.**)

Dominic, St.

ca. 1171–1221
Founder of the Order of
Friars Preachers

* **friar** member of a religious brotherhood of the later Middle Ages who worked in the community and relied on the charity of others for his livelihood

* **heretic** person who disagrees with established church doctrine

* **crusades** holy wars declared by the pope against non-Christians. Most were against Muslims, but crusades were also declared against heretics and pagans.

See color plate 9, vol. 3.

* **canonize** to officially declare (a dead person) a saint

Dominic was a Spanish priest from the city of Osma, Castile. He won permission from the pope in 1216 to establish the Order of Friars Preachers to teach and preach against heresy. These friars*, called DOMINICANS, were among the most illustrious and influential teachers of the Middle Ages. They founded some of the leading schools and universities in Europe.

In 1206, Dominic joined the bishop of Osma on a mission to preach to the CATHAR heretics* in southern France. The Cathars fiercely argued that the Roman Church lacked purity. Dominic tried to convert them by persuasion even after Pope INNOCENT III ordered a crusade* against them. The mission convinced Dominic that no headway could be made against dedicated heretics until missionaries of the church could match the zeal of their opponents.

By 1215, Dominic collected enough gifts and volunteers to found a religious order devoted to teaching and preaching against heresy. Pope Honorius III approved Dominic's new order and granted it a universal preaching mission. Dominic sent new members of the order to the university to give them the strongest religious education possible. His own preaching to students in Paris, Rome, and Bologna won the Dominicans many new recruits. Dominic held the first meeting of the order at Bologna in 1220.

Dominic attached great importance to the help of women in the order's work, and he founded several convents for nuns, once again with an educational mission. He died and was buried in Bologna in 1221. Thirteen years later, he was canonized*.

Dominicans

* **friar** member of a religious brotherhood of the later Middle Ages who worked in the community and relied on the charity of others for his livelihood

* **laypersons** nobles or common people who were not official clergy in the church and had not taken vows as monks or nuns. Some monasteries accepted lay brothers and sisters to help them with their work.

* **heresy** belief that is contrary to church doctrine

* **asceticism** way of life in which a person rejects worldly pleasure and follows a life of prayer and poverty

The Dominican order is a religious order founded by St. Dominic in the early 1200s. Its official name is the Order of Friars Preachers. The friars*, nuns, and laypersons* of the order combine a life of prayer with a mission to defend and spread Christianity, primarily through preaching. In the 1200s and 1300s, the order grew throughout Europe and beyond. The Dominicans stressed education and learning and, with the FRANCISCANS, became one of the church's most effective and influential religious orders.

Origins and Organization. In 1206, DOMINIC, a Spanish priest, joined the church's mission in southern France to counter the CATHAR heresy*. One aspect of this heresy was a belief in purity and rigid asceticism*, a reaction to dissatisfaction with wealthy and worldly priests. Dominic's and his companions' life of strict poverty won the approval of many heretics and the notice of the church.

On December 22, 1216, Pope Honorius III confirmed Dominic's order of preachers as a religious organization. The following month the pope gave it the right to preach anywhere in the world. This was unusual; up to this time, only bishops had been allowed to preach.

Dominic established the order in Rome, Bologna, and other Italian cities. In 1220, he held the first meeting of the order. The general chapter, the governing body of the order, grew out of this first meeting. It adopted strict rules against owning property and earning income, making the friars dependent on the charity of others. In 1221, groups of friars were sent to establish Dominican centers in such places as Germany, England, Denmark, Poland, and Hungary. Houses for nuns were also founded in Madrid, Rome, and Bologna in recognition of the important work women did for the order.

The general chapter had sole power to change the order's rules. Dominican provinces, which included religious houses called priories, were governed by a provincial and a provincial chapter or council. Leaders were

The Dominican order became one of the church's most important religious orders. The Dominicans had strict rules regarding property and earning income, and they depended on charity to meet their needs. This painting by Fra Angelico shows Jesus visiting a Dominican hospice.

usually selected by vote; a provincial would be chosen by the provincial chapter, and members of priories could elect their prior. Sometimes, however, provincials might appoint priors in their districts. The superior of the entire order, called the master general, could also appoint provincials.

Preaching and Scholarship. Dominican priories were centers of the order's preaching ministry. Each priory was responsible for its own area. Within that area, preaching friars were assigned to districts, where they delivered sermons. The Dominicans built churches with large interior spaces to allow more people to hear their sermons. They also preached outdoors.

Nuns were important members of the Dominican Order. Dominic himself founded several convents for nuns, and many more were established after his death. Dominican nuns lived totally enclosed in their convents and supported the work of the friars with their prayers. To win popular support, the Dominicans organized a Third Order of Penance of St. Dominic. Lay* men and women could join this order for spiritual direction and a rule of life that followed Dominican principles. St. CATHERINE OF SIENA, a leading church scholar, was a member of the Dominican Third Order.

Dominicans often performed special missions for the papacy and served many kings and princes as royal confessors. They also went to distant places—Sweden, Lithuania, the Baltic region, and Russia—to spread their message. Later Dominicans made contact with Jews and Muslims in Spain, North Africa, and the Middle East.

Scholarship and education were a central part of Dominican life. Friars studied the Bible and established priories in university cities such as Paris, Oxford, and Bologna. Dominican scholars taught theology* and became prominent in many fields of knowledge as wide-ranging as biblical studies, history, languages, translation, and medicine. The greatest medieval theologian, Thomas AQUINAS, was a Dominican.

* **lay** not linked to the church by clerical office or monks' and nuns' vows

* **theology** study of the nature of God and of religious truth

Dondi, Giovanni de'

1318–1389
Italian physician and inventor

* **patron** person of wealth and influence who supports an artist, writer, or scholar

Giovanni de' Dondi designed and constructed a clockwork model of the universe as it was known in his time. The machine, which he described as a "planetarium" or an "astrarium," showed the movements of the sun, the moon, and the planets around a stationary earth as explained by the Greek astronomer Ptolemy. It also had a 24-hour time dial, as well as dials for the fixed and movable feasts of the church.

The son of a physician, de' Dondi was appointed professor of medicine at the University of Padua in 1350 or 1352, and he later joined its faculty of astrology, philosophy, and logic. He worked on his "astrarium" while at Padua. The machine, one of the earliest mechanical CLOCK devices known, took 16 years to complete, from 1348 to 1364. De' Dondi also prepared several illustrated manuscripts that describe the machine and its construction.

For a time, the prince of Padua was an important patron* of de' Dondi. In 1371, the prince sent him as his ambassador to Venice. De' Dondi served on a committee to establish boundaries between the prince's domain and the Venetian republic, then voted with the Paduans to wage war on Venice.

After the war, de' Dondi lost the prince's favor and was befriended by the duke of Pavia. De' Dondi's, "astrarium" was moved to the duke's library in 1381, and a year later de' Dondi was appointed to the faculty of the University of Pavia. The "astrarium" was seen by a number of famous individuals, including PETRARCH and Leonardo da Vinci, but by 1529, it had fallen into serious disrepair. All trace of it is now lost. (*See also* **Astrology and Astronomy.**)

See *Vlad Tepes.*

D ramatized plays, important in the literature and culture of ancient Greece and Rome, were banned by the church during the early Middle Ages. For more than 300 years, they seem to have become a forgotten art. By 1500, however, there was a thriving tradition of popular drama in most European countries.

Many of the late medieval plays had religious themes, being based on stories from the Bible and other accounts of religious history. There were also original morality plays*, and farces* mocking the follies of the times. Some were in Latin, others in the vernacular* languages of Europe.

Unlike ancient plays, medieval plays on the most serious themes often had comic elements. There was no attempt to divide drama into comedy and tragedy. Plays in the later Middle Ages also rarely took place in a theater. There was little distinction between the acting area and the audience, between the make-believe world of the play and the actual world of the town where it was performed.

Sponsored by the town government, guilds*, the church, or a rich individual, plays were usually free. They might begin with a costume procession through the town. This often included wagons on which people performed mime or dumb shows, like the floats in parades today. Stages, or scaffolds, might be set up for the actual play, perhaps in a town square.

Plays were used to teach religion, to instruct children, to entertain, and sometimes to make political statements. Together with public speeches or sermons, drama was one of the few ways that ideas could be conveyed to a large number of people. Groups who sponsored plays gained broad prestige.

Origins of Medieval Drama.   In the early 400s, soon after Christianity became the recognized religion of the Roman Empire, performance of plays of all kinds was officially forbidden. They were viewed as deceptive, sinful, and non-Christian. Other entertainments such as minstrel and mime shows survived and may have influenced later medieval dramas. However, there is little evidence of plays in Europe until the early 800s. Before then, ancient drama was known only to scholars. To help them learn Latin, early medieval monks read the works of famous Roman authors, including the comedies of Terence.

During CHARLEMAGNE's revival of culture, plays were again allowed for a time. One of his bishops, Amalarius of Metz, even encouraged dramatized episodes about truths from the Bible, perhaps after seeing similar plays in Byzantine churches. Some of these dramatizations became a part

* **morality play** type of drama similar to allegory, with characters representing different aspects of human nature and human existence

* **farce** light, humorous play characterized by broad comedy and an improbable situation

* **vernacular** language or dialect native to a region; everyday, informal speech

* **guild** association of craft and trade workers that set standards and represented the interests of its members

* **liturgy**   form of a religious service,
  particularly the words spoken or sung

of the Latin liturgy* and were used for the rest of the Middle Ages. One such episode is a musical dialogue between three followers of Jesus and an angel on Easter Morning, called the *Quem quaeritis? (Whom Do You Seek?).* It is considered a vital link in the survival of drama into the later Middle Ages and beyond.

Though drama was now part of the Latin church service, nonreligious plays were soon banned again. No popular performances are recorded after 900 for at least two centuries, though in the 960s a Benedictine nun named HROTSWITHA VON GANDERSHEIM from Lower Saxony wrote six Latin dramas. These plays were in old Roman comedy style, except that they were about virtuous rather than sinful women. There may have been performances, but many think that Hrotswitha's plays were merely an exercise in writing Latin.

Gradually, however, the brief musical dialogues in the liturgy seem to have given rise to longer religious dramas for Easter, Epiphany, and other feasts. These dramas have large casts and involve several scenes. Many are in Latin. Some mix Latin with the local vernacular language: for example, French choruses in a Latin play, or a Latin play with a closing hymn in German. Comic episodes are often included; a popular scene in many Easter plays shows Christ's followers buying ointments from a spice merchant. Then, around 1200, drama began to be written totally in the vernacular.

By this time, many plays were performed outside churches in the town streets. Drama was growing independent from worship. Plays in 1500 had become part of both the sacred and secular lives of most European peoples.

French Drama.   The earliest-known French-language drama produced outside the church is from the thriving city of Arras, famous for its textiles. Around 1200, Jean Bodel wrote a *Play of St. Nicholas,* which includes crusaders and a religious miracle but also has comic tavern scenes in an urban setting. This and a few other plays from urban areas survive from the 1200s. During the following century, a set of 40 plays called the Miracles of Notre Dame was written in Paris. Each play is about someone who was saved by a miracle of the Virgin Mary. One was produced each year by the guild of goldsmiths.

In addition to miracle plays, the main types of drama popular in France were Passion plays (about the final suffering and death of Christ), morality plays, and farces. In the 1300s, Passion plays were fairly short. By the end of the Middle Ages, however, some were enormous productions, with 200 or more players and lasting several days. These plays had expanded to portray all of Christ's life and, like miracle plays, were regarded as important presentations of living history.

Unlike religious plays, morality plays and farces were both purely make-believe. Morality plays, however, have a serious, religious purpose—to instruct the audience in how to behave well. In farces, however, bad behavior is expected and jeered at. Disorder reigns instead of reason. The most celebrated farce of the late medieval period is *Maître Pierre Pathelin* (about 1465), the story of a down-and-out lawyer who cheats a draper out of some cloth and is cheated in turn by a simple shepherd.

There were no professional acting troupes in France before the 1500s, but longer plays cost large sums to produce and were at first organized and financed by city governments. Later, wealthy aristocrats invested in these

Medieval drama included religious plays, morality plays, and farces. Performances were generally sponsored by the town government, guilds, churches, or even wealthy individuals. Plays rarely took place in a theater. They were usually performed on moving wagons, stages, or scaffolds that were set up in a town square. This picture shows the performance of a farce in a French village in the late Middle Ages.

Costumes

In the Middle Ages, actors dressed in costumes of their day instead of in historical ones. Roman soldiers, for example, would be dressed as medieval knights. Herod and Pilate might appear as medieval princes or Muslim sultans. Nudity in the Garden of Eden was simulated by means of body stockings.

Women very rarely took parts. Even when they were allowed to take minor roles—for example, during a Passion play in Austria—the leading parts, the Virgin Mary and Mary Magdalene, were still acted by men in women's costumes.

* **allegorical** pertaining to allegory, a literary device in which characters represent an idea, moral, or religious principle

* **Lent** Christian period of fasting that precedes Easter

* **disembowel** to cut open a victim's abdomen before death

plays and charged admission fees. Short plays, including farces, were most often small, informal affairs, frequently staged in people's homes. Members of the society of law clerks were especially clever at writing such plays, often making fun of the nobility as well as of townspeople and peasants.

English Drama.   Though dramas in English appear later than those in French—toward the end of the 1300s—England was the first nation to use paid actors. In many towns, a tradition developed of parades and processions on Corpus Christi day, which falls near midsummer. Many included performances of so-called mystery plays associated with these processions. Different mystery plays were staged by the different guilds in the town. Together the plays would often portray the whole spiritual history of humankind, with titles ranging from the *Creation of the World* to the *Last Judgment.*

Each town had its own cycle of plays and staged them differently. Some of the productions used their "pageant" wagons as stages. These were moved from one location to another in the streets. For each audience, the actors would act from the wagons and would also leap down onto the street.

Perhaps the most famous English medieval play is the morality play called *Everyman.* Like other morality plays, it uses allegorical* characters. God sends Death to summon Everyman. Everyman tries to bribe Death and also to get help from his friends. Most of them, including two characters called Fellowship and Kindred, fail him. Only Good Deeds and Knowledge stay with him, to prepare him for the end.

German Drama.   The first plays written in German, from the 1200s, were Passion plays. As in France, some of these covered much more than Christ's death. A few even had a scope as broad as England's Corpus Christi cycles, though they were performed at Easter and had no procession. There were also plays about the other parts of Christ's life—in fact, well over half of all German plays are religious and "historical" in nature.

Only a few morality plays were written in Germany—this was not a popular form of drama there. Several types of nonreligious plays were apparently presented, however: not only comedies and farces, but also political and instructional plays. These tended to be put on at the end of winter, in the carnival season that preceded Lent* and Easter.

Scenery in German plays was quite simple until late in the Middle Ages. An ordinary barrel, for instance, could represent a mountaintop and also the roof of a temple. However, spectacular effects began to be produced during the late 1400s. In one play, Judas Iscariot, the follower who betrayed Christ before Easter, was seen to hang himself on a tree. Then he was attacked and disemboweled* by Satan; after which his body flew along a rope on a pulley, straight from the tree into the mouth of Hell.

In another production, after Christ had died on the cross, several choirs sang mournful music. A golden "sun," hung as scenery outside a city tavern near where the play was being performed, was reversed to show a somber, dark-red side. A dove, representing the soul, was released from a box on top of the cross. Rifle shots and boulders shaken in barrels produced sounds of thunder and earthquake. Finally, actors representing the dead climbed out of a "grave" and stood around the town square with the audience. (*See also* **Allegory; Feasts and Festivals.**)

Dublin

* **Danelaw** area of England that was ruled by the Danish Vikings during the 800s and 900s

* **Gaelic** word used to describe the Celts of Ireland and Scotland, and especially their language

* **pagan** word used by Christians to mean non-Christian and believing in several gods

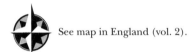

See map in England (vol. 2).

* **consecrate** to declare someone or something sacred in a church ceremony

Today Dublin is the capital of the Republic of Ireland. During most of the Middle Ages, however, Dublin was a VIKING and then an English stronghold. It was founded by Viking raiders. At the same time that they invaded northern ENGLAND and created the Danelaw* settlements, they attacked the Irish coast. In 841, they created a harbor for their ships near a black pool—Dubh Linn in Gaelic*—formed by the Poddle River. This became a trading settlement and later grew into the present city.

Under the Vikings, Dublin was distinct from the rest of Ireland because of its ethnic makeup and religion. Other Irish kingdoms were Gaelic and Christian, but Dublin was mainly Scandinavian and pagan*. During the 900s, its port grew as a result of trade, and Dublin became an important European commercial center. It was also linked to the Danish settlements in England. At the same time, prosperity made Dublin the envy of its Gaelic Irish neighbors. It became involved in power struggles between rival Irish kingdoms and was often attacked by the warring factions.

The Vikings were driven from Dublin in the early 1000s, and many Dubliners accepted Christianity. Their conversion helped remove one barrier between Dublin and Gaelic Ireland, and control of the town shifted back and forth between the Gaelic kingdoms for the next 100 years. However, instead of looking to the Irish church for guidance and inspiration, Dublin's Christians looked to England instead. Throughout the 1000s and 1100s, Dublin's bishops were consecrated* by England's archbishop of CANTERBURY. The townspeople kept a separate identity and were referred to as Ostmen (men from the east).

In 1169, the English invaded Ireland, drawn in part by interest in Dublin's fleet of ships, which they wanted to use in their own wars. The English conquest of Dublin a year later opened a new phase in the town's history. Large numbers of English immigrants flooded into Dublin and forced the Ostmen from the town. Dublin now became the center of English power in Ireland, a position it held for the next 750 years. Dublin Castle was the headquarters of a growing English colony. The townspeople were loyal to the English crown and considered the Gaelic Irish to be their enemies.

The greatest threat to English power in Dublin came in 1317, when the town faced attack by a Scottish army. The Scots, who were also Gaelic, had defeated their English overlord EDWARD II in 1314 and were now attempting to overthrow the English in Ireland. Faced with this challenge, Dubliners tore down homes to fortify the town walls, destroyed a strategic bridge, and set fire to outlying areas. Much damage was done, but this show of resistance put off the Scots, who marched away from the town.

In the later Middle Ages, England's power in Ireland declined until it controlled only a small area known as the Pale—Dublin and its immediate surroundings. Dublin itself tried to maintain its English character. Attempts were made to curb Irish migration into the town, and citizenship and GUILD membership were restricted to people of English descent. Gradually, however, Gaelic influence within the town grew, and by the modern period Dublin had become primarily Irish in character. (*See also* **Ireland; Patrick, St.**)

Duke, Duchy

Dukes were important medieval nobles. Their lands were called duchies. The power of dukes varied, depending on the region, state, or kingdom of which they were a part. The duchies in GERMANY became particularly powerful and were known for a time as the stem duchies.

Dukes evolved from Roman generals and Germanic leaders. In the late Roman Empire, *duces* were military or civilian commanders of frontier areas. The name was also used among the Germanic tribes, for nonroyal military leaders who gained authority as a result of their victories in battle. In the MEROVINGIAN Frankish Empire, dukes were appointed to rule in the more remote parts of the Frankish kingdom, over such tribal groups as the Saxons, Bavarians, and Gascons. By the late 600s, as Merovingian power lessened, dukes in these border areas took more power to themselves and built their own small domains.

When the CAROLINGIAN rulers took power, they suppressed these dukes and used the title *duke* for leaders to whom they gave temporary command over large armies or regions. However, independent duchies began to emerge again in the 900s. Such regions as BAVARIA, Saxony, and Swabia became the seats of powerful families, who loosely combined their lands to form the German kingdom, core of the Holy Roman Empire. In France, the term *duchy* was used in only a few areas, such as Normandy and BURGUNDY. England's royal power was more centralized. Dukes did not exist there until the late 1300s and had little territorial significance. (*See also* **Nobility and Nobles; Normans.**)

Duma

* **clergy** church officials qualified to lead church services

* **boyar** Slavic term for powerful lord, similar to medieval baron

Princely councils in medieval Russia were called dumas. Through dumas, a ruling prince obtained the advice and support of the other influential people in his realm. Dumas included royal relatives, high clergy*, key landowners, and military chiefs. Because the army's loyalty was vitally necessary, the boyars* became the leading duma members.

Dumas were probably called as the need arose. In return for the prince's favor, boyars pledged loyalty, collected taxes, governed provinces, and enforced royal laws. Dumas were especially important when a ruler was incapable of ruling. For example, a duma helped rule Muscovy until DMITRII IVANOVICH DONSKOI was old enough to govern.

By the early 1300s, the duma in Moscow became particularly influential. Its boyars led the armies of Muscovy, the most powerful Russian principality. The duma was consulted by the Muscovite prince in matters of state, and it also supervised day-to-day government. To keep the duma loyal, the prince insisted that the senior boyar be related to him by marriage.

* **autocratic** ruling with absolute power and authority

Duma members served long apprenticeships at court, at least 25 to 30 years. In that time, they could acquire great influence. However, the duma's authority went only as far as the prince allowed. Members who displeased him were disgraced, deposed, stripped of their wealth, or even executed. Russian princes could thus be very autocratic*. Over the years, the word *duma* has come to mean a representative body. Today it is the name of the lower house of Russia's Parliament. (*See also* **Ivan III of Muscovy.**)

Easter

See *Feasts and Festivals.*

Eastern Orthodox Church

See *Christianity.*

Échevin

The legal officers known as *échevins* are descended from medieval town officials who served in FLANDERS and northern France. Their counterparts in Italy, southern France, and Germany were called *consules.* In other parts of Europe, they were known as *jurés,* and in England they were termed aldermen or councillors.

The original *échevins* in Flanders served on the public courts of feudal administrative districts. The lord of the local castle presided over each court. Towns grew around some of the castles, and territorial princes allowed the new urban communities to have their own *échevins* to handle justice for the townspeople. After towns gained political independence and self-rule as part of the COMMUNE movement, the *échevins* were elected by townspeople to serve on town councils. They took on the added responsibility of collecting taxes, constructing public works, and organizing militias*, schools, hospitals, and similar institutions.

* **militia** army of citizens who may be called into action in a time of emergency

The medieval office of *échevin* was never democratic. Though guilds played an important part in the elections, working people rarely became *échevins.* By the 1200s, the office of *échevin* in Flanders had become dominated by rich and powerful families. Their apparent disregard for the rights of citizens outside their social class provoked tensions and led to worker revolts in the late 1200s and 1300s. When the powerful dukes of BURGUNDY became rulers of Flanders in the late 1300s, the dukes broke the power of the *échevins* and placed them under tight control. (*See also* **Bruges; Cities and Towns; Ghent.**)

Eckhart, Meister

ca. 1260–ca. 1328
Teacher, preacher, and mystic

* **friar** member of a religious brotherhood of the later Middle Ages who worked in the community and relied on the charity of others for his livelihood

* **Beguines** pious laywomen in northwestern Europe, who lived in communities and cared for the poor and the sick

* **mystical** referring to the belief that divine truths or direct knowledge of God can be experienced through meditation and contemplation as much as through logical thought

* **heresy** belief that is contrary to church doctrine

* **Reformation** emergence of a new, Protestant Christianity after 1500

Meister Eckhart was one of the most original religious thinkers of the Middle Ages. He was an influential preacher in Germany, but near the end of his life his ideas caused him trouble with the church.

Eckhart von Hochheim was born in Thuringia in central Germany. He became a Dominican friar* and studied in Paris and Cologne. While still in his 30s, Eckhart held important administrative positions among the German Dominicans and was regarded as a leading intellect. In the early 1300s, as a visiting professor at the University of Paris, he won the title "master of sacred theology," translated into German as *Meister.*

Eckhart's writings and sermons, some of which were addressed to the Beguines* of Cologne, urged individuals to seek a mystical* union with God. In Eckhart's philosophy, this union can occur when people empty their souls of desires through prayer and meditation. A state of empty "nothingness" ignites the soul like a "spark" and links it to God. Although Eckhart's training was rooted in SCHOLASTICISM, he was influenced by St. AUGUSTINE, by mystical ideas from the Byzantine world, and by the writings of the Jewish philosopher MAIMONIDES on the existence and nature of God.

Eckhart was the first Dominican ever accused of heresy*, for claiming that the distance between God and humans could be bridged. Though he is said to have renounced his ideas before he died, his writings inspired many people, including Martin Luther, the German theologian who sparked the Protestant Reformation*. (*See also* **Beguines and Beghards; Mysticism; Scholasticism.**)

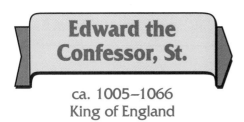

Edward the Confessor, St.

ca. 1005–1066
King of England

* **canonize** to officially declare (a dead
person) a saint

See map in Vikings (vol. 4).

See
color plate 4,
vol. 2.

Edward the Confessor is best known for his religious piety, for which he received the name "the Confessor." Popularly regarded as a saint in his own lifetime, he was canonized* in 1161. While Edward managed to keep England relatively peaceful while he was king, his reign was also marked by constant struggles over who would succeed him.

As son of King Ethelred II the Unready and Emma of Normandy, Edward was a descendant of the famed Anglo-Saxon king ALFRED THE GREAT. During his early years, Edward was educated at a monastery in eastern England. However, when the Danish VIKINGS invaded, Emma fled with her children to her brother's court in Normandy. Later, after Ethelred's death in 1016, Emma returned to England and married the new king, CNUT THE GREAT, who was a Dane. Their son Hardecnut, Edward's half brother, succeeded his father as king, but Hardecnut was childless and soon fell ill and died. Edward, finally proclaimed his successor, returned from Normandy to England and was crowned in CANTERBURY on Easter Sunday 1043.

Though Edward was king, the real power in England rested in the hands of the earls of Wessex, Mercia, and Northumberland. In 1043, they advised Edward to take action against his mother, whose loyalties as Cnut's widow seemed to make her more sympathetic to the Danes than to the English. Under pressure from the earls, Edward seized his mother's treasure and banished many Danes who were in her service.

The most powerful of the English earls was Godwin of Wessex. His influence grew with the marriage of his daughter Edith to Edward in 1045. Their failure to have children increased tensions over the issue of the succession. By 1050, Edward was turning increasingly to Norman advisers to help counteract Godwin's influence. Godwin died in 1054, but his son Harold became the leading candidate to succeed Edward as king.

When Edward died on January 5, 1066, he was buried at WESTMINSTER ABBEY, which had just been built. A struggle to take the English throne

Edward the Confessor's reign was relatively peaceful for his subjects, but it was marked by constant struggles over who would succeed him. His death in 1066 began a fight for the English throne that ended with William the Conqueror's invasion of England. Edward is shown here in a panel from the Bayeux Tapestry.

arose between Harold and Duke William of Normandy (later called WILLIAM THE CONQUEROR), and the NORMANS invaded England later in the year. The Norman conquest ended ANGLO-SAXON rule and ushered in a new era in English history. (*See also* **England; Hastings, Battle of.**)

Edward I of England

1239–1307
King of England

* **coronation** ceremony during which a leader, king, or queen is crowned

* **homage** formal public declaration of loyalty to the king or overlord

Edward I, the son of King HENRY III OF ENGLAND and Eleanor of PROVENCE, was a warrior king who also influenced the development of England's PARLIAMENT.

On his way back from a CRUSADE in North Africa and Syria, Edward received word of his father's death. Before returning to England, he put down a series of revolts in AQUITAINE, one of the regions of France then under English rule. On arriving back home in 1274, Edward was crowned king.

His greatest military achievement was his conquest of WALES. At Edward's coronation*, the leading Welsh prince, Llewelyn ap Gruffudd, refused to pay the homage* that Wales had paid to Edward's father. War was inevitable.

As a result of intensive fighting between 1277 and 1284, Edward conquered Wales and placed most of it under English rule, building many large castles to dominate the countryside. He then made his son the first English prince of Wales. This established the custom of calling the heir to the English throne Prince of Wales. During the last part of his reign, Edward was involved in less successful battles in Scotland and France.

Today Edward is best remembered for his governmental reforms. His Statute of Gloucester, issued in 1278, established the principle that all English justice derived from the authority of the king. Edward also enlarged his council, or Parliament, to include representatives of towns and rural areas throughout England, especially for gaining authority to levy taxes and for deciding how the laws should apply in novel situations. (*See also* **England.**)

Edward II of England

1284–1327
King of England

* **abdication** giving up the throne voluntarily or under pressure

Edward II of England was the son of King EDWARD I and Eleanor of Castile. His father had conquered Wales, so he was the first heir to the English throne to be called Prince of Wales. Edward became king of England on his father's death in 1307. His reign was marked by military disasters and misrule that led eventually to his abdication* and murder.

Edward inherited a number of problems from his father. The country had a foreign policy dominated by warfare, which had emptied the treasury and left enormous debts. Unfortunately, Edward had a talent for making bad situations worse. In 1314, he suffered a crushing defeat in Scotland. Ten years later, he lost English territory in AQUITAINE, France.

Edward relied on favorite advisers instead of consulting Parliament about government policy. Angered by such actions, Parliament restricted the king's power in 1311 and had his chief adviser executed. The king fought back and by 1322 regained full power.

Edward's final downfall, however, began in 1325 when trouble threatened to erupt again between England and France. He sent his wife, Isabella of France, to Paris to negotiate with her brother, the French king. Isabella was angry at her husband because he was unfaithful, and while in France she became the lover of Roger Mortimer, an English nobleman living in exile. The two gathered a force and invaded England in 1326. Edward fled westward; few barons would support him. He was captured, and in 1327 he was forced to abdicate in favor of his young son, EDWARD III. Later that year, Edward II was brutally murdered.

Edward III of England

1312–1377
King of England

* **chivalry** rules and customs of medieval knighthood

* **succession** the transmission of authority on the death of one ruler to the next

* **Commons** part of Parliament consisting of knights and nonnoble representatives from towns and the countryside

Edward III became king of England at the age of 14. During his long reign, he fought wars in Scotland and France, including the early conflicts of the HUNDRED YEARS WAR.

In 1327, Edward's father, King EDWARD II, was forced to abdicate by Edward's mother, Isabella, and her lover, Roger Mortimer. They continued to hold power for the first few years of Edward's reign, but in 1330 he seized control, had Mortimer executed, and made his mother enter a convent.

Edward was more interested in fighting than in governing. His devotion to chivalry* and knighthood led to the creation of the famous Order of the Garter. He began his own military career in the 1330s with several victories in Scotland, at one point capturing its king. However, Scotland later regained its independence.

In 1337, territorial and succession* disputes between England and France led to the Hundred Years War. The English won major victories at the Battles of Crécy (1346) and of Poitiers (1356), where Edward's son, EDWARD THE BLACK PRINCE, led the forces. But by the end of Edward's reign, England had lost much of its territory in France to the French king, Charles V.

Edward relied on the barons in PARLIAMENT to help run his government. To finance his wars, he frequently requested money from them, but he allowed Parliament to make policy decisions in many other areas. As a result, Parliament, especially the Commons*, gained power as a growing force in English government.

Edward the Black Prince

1330–1376
Prince of Aquitaine and heir to the English throne

* **duchy** territory ruled by a duke or a duchess
* **principality** region that is ruled by a prince

Edward, the oldest son of King EDWARD III of England and Philippa of Hainault, was famed for his courage and chivalry. He never became a king because his father outlived him. However, he was made prince of AQUITAINE in southern France during the HUNDRED YEARS WAR, when England won back all of the duchy* of Aquitaine from the French and made it an independent principality*.

From an early age, Edward assumed major responsibilities. At 8 years of age, he was given the title "Guardian of England" while his father fought in France. Several years later, at age 16, he fought in the Hundred Years War himself, showing great courage while leading the English at the Battle of Crécy (1346). He became known as the Black Prince, perhaps

Edward the Black Prince was the eldest son of King Edward III of England and the father of King Richard II. He was one of England's ablest commanders during the Hundred Years War. This image of the Black Prince is from his tomb in Canterbury Cathedral.

because he wore black armor at Crécy. His greatest triumph was at the Battle of Poitiers (1356), when his soldiers, heavily outnumbered, captured the French king, John II. According to legend, Edward chivalrously helped the defeated King John remove his armor and then waited on him at supper.

Edward was not a skillful ruler in Aquitaine and was unable to assert his authority. To finance a military expedition to help CASTILE in Spain, he tried to tax the Aquitaine nobles, but they rebelled against him.

Sickness contracted in Spain forced Edward to return to England in 1371. He probably suspected that he would not live to become king. Meanwhile, his brother, JOHN OF GAUNT, challenged Edward's authority with the support of a group of followers. Edward spent his final years opposing his brother and securing the succession for his own son, who became RICHARD II.

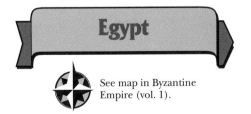

Egypt

See map in Byzantine Empire (vol. 1).

E gypt was a great power during the Middle Ages. Formerly it had been a vital center of Greco-Roman culture and of Byzantine Christianity. In 639, Arab armies conquered Egypt, and it continued to influence the eastern Mediterranean with its new and enduring Islamic civilization.

Early History. The Egyptian city of Alexandria was a hub of ancient Greek culture. It was taken over by the Roman Empire in 30 B.C., and later it became part of the BYZANTINE EMPIRE. Alexandria's strong scholarly tradition continued as Egypt shifted from one empire to another. This created a heritage of Greek, Latin, and Christian learning in early medieval Egypt.

See color plate 14, vol. 2.

The Arab conquest shifted Egypt's political and economic ties from the northern Mediterranean to the Islamic Empire. Egypt was now ruled by governors appointed by Arab rulers, called caliphs, seated first in DAMASCUS and later in BAGHDAD. The Islamic religion and the Arabic language came to Egypt, and many Arabs settled there in the 700s and 800s. The settlers were easily accepted into Egyptian society, and many Egyptian Christians converted to Islam. Egypt became the base for new Islamic conquests across North Africa.

Islamic Dynasties. A new phase of Egypt's history began in 969, when the FATIMIDS conquered Egypt and founded their own caliphate in CAIRO. The Fatimids were an Islamic dynasty* from Tunisia in North Africa who belonged to the Shi'ite* branch of Islam. They rejected the rule of the ABBASID caliph in Baghdad and became lords of a vast empire that included North Africa, Sicily, Syria, Palestine, and Yemen. However, the Fatimids failed to overthrow the Abbasid caliphs, and the Fatimids' power declined in the late 1000s.

The Fatimid dynasty ended in 1171 when the Muslim warrior SALADIN took over. He founded the Ayyubid dynasty, which restored Sunnite* Islam in Egypt and governed it on behalf of the Abbasids. Egypt was the main base for the wars that finally forced the crusaders from the Holy Land.

Key to Egypt's strength was an elite corps of Turkish mamluks, or freed slaves. In 1250, a MAMLUK DYNASTY seized control of Egypt from the Ayyubids and established a government of sultans*. When a sultan died, the strongest warrior nearly always seized power next. Each sultan was leader of a highly trained group of slaves, who were freed by him and formed a privileged ruling class within the government. In 1260, an important

* **dynasty** succession of rulers from the same family or group

* **Shi'ites** Muslims who believed that Muhammad chose Ali and his descendants as the rulers and spiritual leaders of the Islamic community

* **Sunnite** Muslim majority who believed that the caliphs should rule the Islamic community

* **sultan** political and military ruler of a Muslim dynasty or state

Before the Arab conquest in 639, Egypt was a Byzantine province. The Egyptian Christian church, known as the Coptic church, was an important branch of early Christianity that continued under Arab rule. Coptic Christianity had its own artistic traditions. Shown here is a detail of Jonah, from a tapestry entitled *Triumph of the Cross,* made in Egypt in the 500s or 600s.

Mamluk victory over Mongol invaders from Asia saved Egypt from great destruction. The Mamluk dynasty controlled Egypt until 1517.

Although Egypt was very prosperous under the Fatimids, Ayyubids, and early Mamluks, it began to decline in the 1300s. One cause was the BLACK DEATH, which decimated the population and damaged the economy. Another cause was competition from Italian cities, which hurt Egyptian industries. Discovery of a sea route to India also reduced Egypt's importance for trade between the Mediterranean and the Indian Ocean.

The invasions of the Mongol warrior TAMERLANE further weakened the Mamluks. The Mongols were driven back by the OTTOMANS, who built a powerful empire in the 1400s. Finally, in 1516–1517, the Ottomans destroyed the Mamluk sultanate and brought all of its territories under their rule.

Egyptian Culture. Egypt made important contributions to Islamic culture. Cairo was a major center of Islamic law in the Middle Ages, producing distinguished judges and theologians*. It also attracted many other scholars. The great North African historian IBN KHALDUN settled in Egypt, as did the Spanish Jewish philosopher MAIMONIDES. Islamic mysticism* also flourished when Sufi religious orders were founded under the Mamluks.

Egyptian scientists played an important part in reviving Greek science and medicine, making advances in many areas. The well-known collection of tales called the THOUSAND AND ONE NIGHTS was compiled in Egypt in the 1300s. In art and architecture, native techniques were combined with Eastern ones to produce a distinctive style. The surviving artwork and monuments are evidence of the cosmopolitan* nature of medieval Egyptian society.

* **theologian** person who studies religious faith and practice

* **mysticism** belief that divine truths or direct knowledge of God can be experienced through faith, spiritual insight, and intuition

* **cosmopolitan** having an international outlook, a broad worldview

Einhard

ca. 770–840
Scholar, poet, teacher,
and historian

See
color plate 8,
vol. 3.

Without the work of Einhard, we would know far less about one of the great figures of the Middle Ages, the Frankish emperor CHARLEMAGNE. Einhard wrote a biography of Charlemagne, one of the most important works of his time.

Educated at a monastery in central Germany, Einhard went to the court of Charlemagne at AACHEN when he was in his early 20s. He eventually succeeded ALCUIN OF YORK as the director of the palace school. Einhard was in charge of Charlemagne's literary and mathematical studies and undertook several major missions as ambassador for the court. After Charlemagne's death, Einhard became personal secretary to the next emperor, Louis I the Pious, and taught Louis's oldest son, Lothar. In 830, he retired with his wife to a monastery built on an estate given to him by Louis.

Einhard wrote several religious works and many letters, but his greatest literary achievement was the life of Charlemagne, which he wrote during his retirement. In addition to being the only contemporary account of Charlemagne and his time, it is an important contribution to the history of German literature, language, and culture.

Eleanor of Aquitaine

ca. 1122–1204
Queen of France and England

* **annul** to cancel.

* **vernacular** language or dialect native to a region; everyday, informal speech

* **courtier** person in attendance at a royal court

Upon the death of William X, count of Poitou and duke of Aquitaine, his daughter Eleanor inherited his vast lands and became the greatest heiress in Europe. She was the queen of Louis VII of France and of Henry II of England. A skilled politician and a patron of the arts, she is one of the most famous women of the Middle Ages. Eleanor's tomb, shown here, is in the abbey of Fontevrault in France.

When she was about 15 years old, Eleanor of Aquitaine inherited the county of Poitou and the duchy of Aquitaine in France, a territory larger than that belonging to the French king. This made her the greatest heiress in Europe. She was a ruler who worked hard to make her family powerful, and she married two kings. She was also an active patron of the arts whose court was one of the most brilliant of the time.

The strong-willed and energetic Eleanor was the granddaughter of WILLIAM IX, duke of Aquitaine and count of Poitou. When she received her vast inheritance in 1137, she married Louis, the 16-year-old son of the king of France. Her father-in-law died a year later, and she became Louis VII's queen. In 1147, Eleanor accompanied Louis on a crusade to the Holy Land, creating legends about her as a warrior and causing rumors that she was unfaithful. After the birth of their second daughter, tensions arose between Eleanor and Louis, and their marriage was annulled* in 1152.

Only two months after the annulment, Eleanor married Henry Plantagenet, duke of Normandy and count of Anjou. Two years later, Henry became King HENRY II OF ENGLAND, and Eleanor was once again a queen. Between the two of them, Henry and Eleanor controlled the territories of Poitou, Aquitaine, Normandy, and Anjou—the whole western part of France as well as England.

Eleanor and Henry had eight children, including two future kings—RICHARD I and JOHN of England—and two queens—Eleanor of Castile and Joanna of Sicily. In the 1170s, internal disputes began to tear this family apart. Henry gave his sons empty titles (without any power), and they rebelled against him, unsuccessfully. Because Eleanor sided with her sons, Henry imprisoned her. She was released for short periods but did not get complete freedom again until after Henry's death in 1189.

Eleanor's son Richard I (the Lionhearted) then became king, and she was drawn back into politics. When Richard was captured and held captive by the duke of Austria in 1192, Eleanor governed the kingdom until she could raise the enormous sum demanded for his ransom.

After Richard died in 1199, Eleanor supported her youngest son, John, in his claims for the throne against the claims of her grandson Arthur of Brittany. Her last great political accomplishment was arranging the marriage of her granddaughter Blanche of Castile to the heir to the French throne.

Eleanor is also noted for her enthusiastic support of the arts. Under her patronage, the vernacular* literature of northern and southern France flourished. The brilliant circle of poets, TROUBADOURS, and courtiers* that she gathered at her court in Poitiers cultivated refined manners and the concept of courtly love. She especially encouraged the writers of romances, such as Wace, Benoît de Sainte-Maure, and the renowned CHRÉTIEN DE TROYES.

Encyclopedias and Dictionaries

Reference works like encyclopedias and dictionaries existed before the Middle Ages. A book called *On the Meaning of Words* was written by a Latin author named Flaccus in 5 B.C., and two important works—Varro's *Disciplines* (50 B.C.) and Pliny's *Natural History* (A.D. 77)—were important ancestors to the encyclopedia tradition, particularly in western Europe. But medieval reference works go well beyond those from classical times. Such works were important in all three geographical areas discussed in this article.

Old Notes

Patriarch Photios of Constantinople read widely. The books he read dated from the fifth century B.C. up to his own time in the 800s. He liked to make notes about the books he read.

His notes became a book called the *Bibliotheke*. Some of the notes are very brief, some provide detailed summaries of the books he read, and others are passages from the books he copied down. The *Bibliotheke* was often used as a reference work by readers in Constantinople.

Without this work, we would never have known about many of the books he read. Almost half of them no longer survive.

* **secular** nonreligious; connected with everyday life

* **etymology** explanation of the origin and the history of words; study dealing with linguistic changes

Byzantine Works.   Many volumes of reference materials were produced under the Byzantine Empire, suggesting that easy access to information was prized. Some of these works were built on materials borrowed from earlier works, while others were original.

Handbooks of military and naval tactics date from the 600s to the 1000s and beyond, and lists of government officials and procedures also span the Middle Ages. But the greatest century for dictionaries and encyclopedias was the 900s, when the Byzantine Empire was powerful and culture and learning flourished.

A wide-ranging volume called the *Suda,* produced in the 900s, was an alphabetically arranged regular dictionary. However, it also included literary excerpts and commentaries, lists of proverbs, and historical biographies. The biographies are known to have been compiled by a writer called Hesychios at the very start of the Middle Ages.

Many of the century's encyclopedias were compiled under the patronage of Emperor Constantine VII. Some of these encyclopedias were quite lengthy. For example, the *Constantinian Excerpts,* with extracts from Greek historians from the fifth century B.C. to the 800s, had 53 volumes. There is an agricultural encyclopedia called the *Geoponica* that includes material on popular magic and superstitions. Two other works are a medical encyclopedia called the *Iatrika* and an illustrated veterinary handbook, the *Hippiatrika.*

Muslim Works.   The earliest Arabic dictionaries were compiled right after the death of the prophet Muhammad to explain words from the QUR'AN. Secular* Arabic dictionaries to explain words in poetry began about the same time. Early dictionaries were often arranged by theme (for example, clothes, food, and people). However, the most complete and authoritative medieval Arabic dictionary, containing 80,000 entries, is ordered alphabetically, by sound.

The first Arabic encyclopedic work, *Adab al-Katib (The Knowledge of the Scribe),* was written for traditional public officials by Ibn Qutayba (828–889). It included sections on law, language, literature, history, ethics, mathematics, and astronomy. Some later works were more revolutionary. In the 900s, al-FARABI produced a work based on the thoughts of the ancient Greek philosopher ARISTOTLE. A group called the Brethren of Purity produced a 52-part encyclopedia that attacked traditional Islamic law and incorporated ideas from Persian, Hindu, and Christian sources. More traditional works continued to be produced, however, containing medical and scientific material as well as material on religious topics.

In Islamic society, dictionaries and encyclopedias were guides for the faithful, serving as memory aids for people who were committed to living according to Muslim religious principles. These works were also used by doctors of religion and public officials.

European Works.   The first Western medieval dictionary was *Rudiments of Learning,* written by Papias of Lombardy in about 1053. Arranged in alphabetical order according to the first three letters of each word, the dictionary included the origins and definitions of words and more general knowledge of the kind found in encyclopedias. Later works such as Osbern of Gloucester's *Book of Derivations* (ca. 1150) were devoted more to the etymology* of words than to general information. This led to dictionaries that were ordered not alphabetically but by related groups of words. By the

* **vernacular** language or dialect native to a region; everyday, informal speech

* **liberal arts** seven traditional areas of knowledge—grammar, rhetoric, logic, geometry, arithmetic, astronomy, and music

* **concordance** alphabetical index of the principal words in a book or in the works of an author

end of the 1400s, however, Western dictionaries were again using strict alphabetical order. By then, they focused on word meanings, and they covered vernacular* languages as well as Latin.

For the encyclopedia writers of western Europe, Roman writer Pliny's *Natural History* was the main inspiration. Not only did writers use information he had collected, but they also used his format, starting with the heavens and moving down to earth, humans, other animals, plants, and minerals.

Two early works survive. In Italy, CASSIODORUS wrote his *Institutiones* in about 560 to summarize divine and human learning for the monks in his monastery. In its second volume, on human learning, it presents the seven liberal arts*. Isidore of Seville's *Etymologiae,* written in 620 well before the Muslims invaded Spain, covers practical human learning also—such topics as food, tools, furniture, public games, ships, and cities. It was the most extensive and influential encyclopedia in the early Middle Ages.

After the 600s, Western encyclopedias tended to repeat the ideas of these two early works in different forms. But the situation changed in the 1200s. As a result of the crusades and improved trade, there was more information to collect and organize. New knowledge based on the ancient texts of Aristotle and the learning of Islamic scholars was making its way into Europe. The philosophy of SCHOLASTICISM encouraged examination of the parts as the best way to understand a whole topic. Also, advances in the format of books—paragraphs, chapter titles, and tables of contents—made collecting information easier.

There was a sudden explosion of new reference works in Europe. Besides encyclopedias, other works appeared—Bible concordances*, library catalogues, and alphabetically arranged indexes. Many of these new works were written to help traveling FRIARS of the new preaching orders to prepare their sermons. In the mid-1200s, the FRANCISCAN Bartholomaeus Anglicus wrote a 19-volume encyclopedia *On the Properties of Things*. It was translated into six languages and became the most widely read and quoted reference work in the late Middle Ages. At about the same time, a Dominican, VINCENT OF BEAUVAIS, wrote a massive work called *Speculum maius (The Larger Mirror),* which collected and organized statements from authorities in all the known fields of knowledge. *Speculum maius*—more than three million words long—was the most ambitious effort ever undertaken to gather all knowledge together in one work. (*See also* **Arabic Language and Literature; Byzantine Empire; Byzantine Literature.**)

England

The kingdom of England developed during the Middle Ages. Off the coast of mainland Europe on the island of Britain, England at the start of the period was inhabited largely by pagan* Germanic tribes. By 1500, it was a single kingdom with unique institutions that drew from many different traditions.

* **pagan** word used by Christians to mean non-Christian and believing in several gods

The Anglo-Saxon Period

Like other parts of the Western Roman Empire after the fall of Rome, the old Roman province of Britain was invaded by Germanic tribes in the 400s and 500s. These tribes were ANGLO-SAXONS who came from the German

* **Celts** ancient inhabitants of Europe and the British Isles

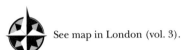

See map in London (vol. 3).

* **Picts** northern British Celts who are said to have used a bluish dye for war paint

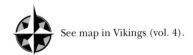

See map in Vikings (vol. 4).

coast of northern Europe. As they settled in the new land, they forced many of the native, Christianized Celts* to move west into Cornwall and Wales and north into Scotland.

Early Kingdoms. The Anglo-Saxons were several distinct peoples whose beliefs and practices differed considerably. They set up eight separate kingdoms, each one ruled by a small aristocracy of warriors headed by a king.

Many of the Anglo-Saxons landed at the mouth of the Thames River. A group that came to be called the East Saxons founded a kingdom named Essex, to the northeast of the old Roman city of LONDON. The West Saxons founded Wessex, to the west of London. Other Saxons traveled south and founded Sussex. Two groups called the Jutes and the Frisians set up the kingdom of Kent in the southeast. Closest to the European mainland, Kent was at first the most prosperous and dominant kingdom.

Other Germanic groups invaded along rivers farther north, creating the kingdoms of East Anglia (land of the east Angles), Deira, and Bernicia, which later joined to become Northumbria, and, in the interior, Mercia.

The Bretwaldas and the Supremacy of Wessex. During the early Anglo-Saxon period, warfare raged between the different kingdoms. The head of the kingdom that was dominant was often called the Bretwalda (Britain's ruler). King Ethelbert of Kent was the first Bretwalda. During his rule in the 590s, missionaries from Rome came to CANTERBURY and began to preach Christianity to the pagan tribes.

In the 600s, the most powerful kingdom was Northumbria. It dominated politically, and there was a remarkable flowering of religion and culture at its capital in York. Northumbria was defeated by Picts* in 685 and became a political backwater, but York remained an important cultural center throughout the 700s.

The kings of Mercia were the Bretwaldas of the 700s. One of these kings, called Offa, built a defensive wall 200 miles long at the border between England and Wales. This can still be seen and is known as Offa's Dyke. Offa was well-known on the European mainland. He negotiated with the pope, corresponded with CHARLEMAGNE, and encouraged international trade.

In the 800s, a West Saxon prince named Egbert made Wessex the most powerful Anglo-Saxon kingdom. After defeating Mercia in 825, he was acknowledged as the Bretwalda by Kent, Sussex, Essex, and East Anglia. He also subdued the Celts in Cornwall. All southern England was under the control of one king. For the rest of the Anglo-Saxon period, Wessex dominated the politics of England.

For more than 200 years after the death of Egbert in 839, the British Isles were threatened by VIKINGS from Norway and Denmark. The Danes conquered Northumbria and East Anglia, an area that became known as the Danelaw. Mercia, too, was partly invaded, and Wessex, inland and further south, was seriously threatened. But in 871, ALFRED THE GREAT became king of Wessex. An outstanding general and king, Alfred became a hero to the Anglo-Saxons because of his successful wars against the Danes.

Alfred preserved the independence of all of Wessex and part of Mercia. All Anglo-Saxons not living in the Danelaw viewed him as their king. Under Alfred's successors, Wessex came to dominate the whole of England. His son and grandson reconquered many of the Danish territories.

* **dynasty** succession of rulers from the same family or group

His great-grandson Edgar completed the process. Edgar was known for the peace he kept with the Danes and for his newly minted Anglo-Saxon currency. He was also famed for his laws, which applied to Anglo-Saxons and to the many Danes who remained living in England.

Troubles with the Vikings were not over, however. Ethelred, Edgar's younger son, was defeated in 991 by a new wave of Danish attacks. To secure peace, he paid a tribute called the DANEGELD. Then, in 1013, there was an invasion by the Danish king Sweyn Forkbeard and his son CNUT THE GREAT. This time the Danish victory was complete. Cnut served as king of all England for 19 years, and his two sons succeeded him. They died without heirs, however, and the Anglo-Saxon dynasty* of Wessex was restored under Ethelred's son, EDWARD THE CONFESSOR. Edward's death in 1066 paved the way for the NORMAN conquest.

Anglo-Saxon Achievements. Perhaps the Anglo-Saxons' greatest achievement was creating a well-organized kingdom. A regular structure of government developed. The countryside was divided into areas known as hundreds and boroughs, ruled according to local customs by appointed officials called reeves. These areas were grouped into larger territories called shires, which were administered by SHERIFFS (shire-reeves). The Normans inherited this pattern of local government in 1066.

The regional economy also developed steadily. Slavery was common, but many Anglo-Saxons were free farmers, though they rarely owned their own property. Large landowners would provide land for them to build homes and raise food, demanding in return that the peasants work in the owners' fields for a proportion of their time. Rural England developed patterns of settlement in villages and hamlets that remained a familiar feature of England into modern times. The last years of Anglo-Saxon rule also saw the start of urban growth. Industries such as wool production led to the growth of larger cities and new towns, each with its own local customs, laws, and organization.

During the Anglo-Saxon period, too, the pagan Germanic peoples were converted to Christianity. After the mission to Kent in the late 500s, Christianity slowly spread to all the Anglo-Saxon kings and royal courts. Archbishoprics were set up in Canterbury and in York. In the 600s, Celtic missionaries from Ireland and Wales joined the Romans in spreading Christianity, especially in the north of England. Religious customs of the Roman and Celtic churches differed, but these were settled at the Synod of Whitby in 663. The church became united under the authority of Canterbury. By the early 700s, the Anglo-Saxon kingdoms were all Christian.

Supported by several Bretwaldas, including Offa and Edgar, there was a monastic revival in the 800s and 900s. Monasteries gave stability to the English church and state. They produced a steady stream of well-educated, powerful men to serve the church and to act as advisers to the rulers. A strong organized Christian church was vital to the unification of England.

Christianity, as an international religion, brought England into more frequent contact with the Frankish Empire and the Mediterranean culture. The church encouraged a sense of law and of the responsibility of public office. It provided English kings with educated officials to write down laws and government records. It also led to a flowering of scholarship, especially

* **vernacular** language or dialect native to a region; everyday, informal speech

in York, Northumbria, which produced outstanding vernacular* literature and superb illuminated manuscripts.

The Norman/Early Angevin Period

The year 1066 was a turning point in English history. It marked the rise of a new political regime that brought fundamental changes to the country. In that year, the Normans—descendants of a Viking people who had earlier settled in northwestern France (Normandy)—conquered England. The Normans ruled from 1066 to 1154, and their direct descendants, the Angevins, from 1154 to 1399. These two dynasties developed political institutions that set England apart from the rest of Europe, and that still function with some modification today. At the same time, the Normans brought England into still greater contact with the European mainland. This contact changed England's culture and also affected the history of France and Europe.

The Norman Rulers. When Edward the Confessor died without an heir, the English nobles offered the crown to Harold, the powerful earl of Wessex. But his succession was challenged by Duke William of Normandy. William's claim, based on an earlier promise by Edward, was approved by the pope. He invaded England and defeated Harold at the Battle of Hastings on October 14, 1066. William I (the Conqueror) thus became the first Norman king of England. He quickly consolidated his power. A year before his death, he assembled a council of his barons, and everyone, from greatest to least, swore an oath of loyalty to him.

William died in 1087. His eldest son, Robert, took Normandy, and his second son, William Rufus, took England. But Robert later went on the First CRUSADE, leaving Normandy in William's hands. In the year 1100, William Rufus was shot while hunting, and his younger brother Henry I took the throne.

Robert returned from the crusade and tried to regain his inheritance, but in a long war Henry succeeded in conquering Normandy. However, he was unable to pass on his expanded kingdom peacefully. His only legitimate male heir died in 1120. So in 1127, Henry persuaded the English barons to accept his daughter Matilda as his lawful successor. Matilda was married to the count of Anjou, lord of the land to the south of Normandy.

When Henry I died in 1135, many English barons were reluctant to be ruled by a woman. Instead they supported Stephen, a grandson of William the Conqueror through his daughter. Stephen rallied the barons and took the throne of England. Matilda and her husband controlled Normandy and Anjou, however, and a civil war erupted. For almost 20 years, Stephen and Matilda fought each other for control of England. Royal government weakened, and the English barons gained much independence.

In 1153, Matilda's son, Henry, invaded England from Normandy and arranged a truce. The Treaty of Winchester stated that Stephen would rule England until his death, at which time Henry would succeed him. Stephen died in 1154, and Henry took firm control of the realm as HENRY II.

The Early Angevin Rulers. Henry II was the first Angevin king of England. The word *Angevin* comes from his title as count of Anjou in France. Both Henry and his son and heir RICHARD I THE LIONHEARTED spent more time on the mainland than they did in their new island kingdom. Richard

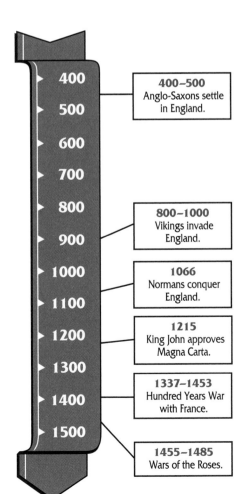

400

500

400–500
Anglo-Saxons settle
in England.

600

700

800

900

800–1000
Vikings invade
England.

1000

1066
Normans conquer
England.

1100

1215
King John approves
Magna Carta.

1200

1300

1337–1453
Hundred Years War
with France.

1400

1500

1455–1485
Wars of the Roses.

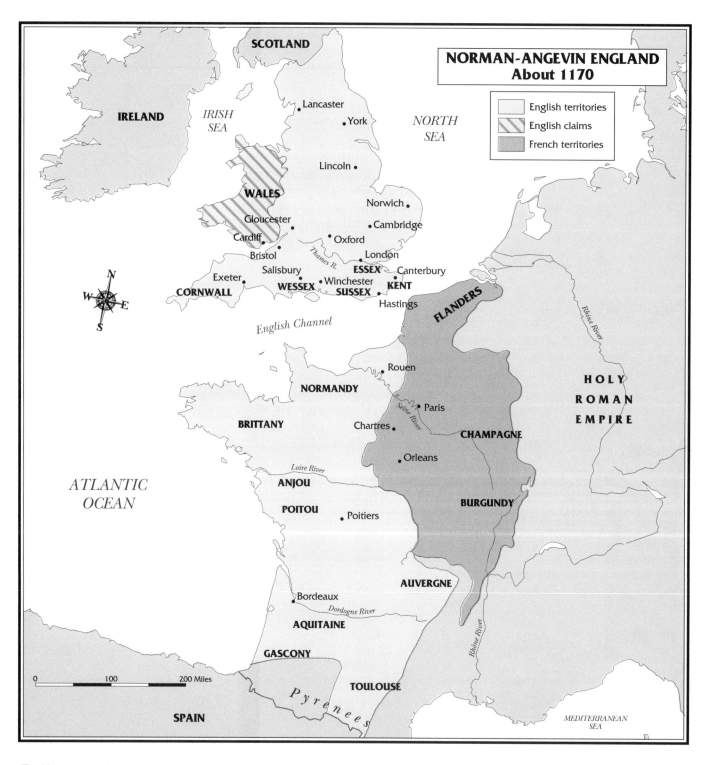

NORMAN-ANGEVIN ENGLAND
About 1170

English territories
English claims
French territories

SCOTLAND

IRELAND

IRISH SEA

NORTH SEA

Lancaster

York

Lincoln

WALES

Norwich

Gloucester

Cambridge

Cardiff

Oxford

Bristol

London

Salisbury

ESSEX

Canterbury

Exeter

Winchester

KENT

CORNWALL

WESSEX

SUSSEX

Hastings

FLANDERS

English Channel

Thames R.

Rhine River

Rouen

NORMANDY

HOLY ROMAN EMPIRE

Paris

BRITTANY

Chartres

Seine River

CHAMPAGNE

Orleans

Loire River

ANJOU

ATLANTIC OCEAN

POITOU

BURGUNDY

Poitiers

AUVERGNE

Bordeaux

Dordogne River

Rhine River

AQUITAINE

GASCONY

TOULOUSE

0   100   200 Miles

Pyrenees

SPAIN

MEDITERRANEAN SEA

The Normans and Angevins had a profound influence on England. Not only did they bring their feudal customs, law, and culture, but they also added huge territories to the English realm. Henry of Anjou became the first Angevin king of England in 1154 A.D., and the marriages of Henry and his children extended Angevin territory from northern England to the Pyrenees Mountains.

was also heavily involved in the Third Crusade. But under their rule, the combined lands became stable, powerful, and influential. The marriages of Henry and his children made the Angevins heirs not only to England, Normandy, and Anjou but also to Aquitaine, Saxony and Bavaria, Sicily, and Castile.

Richard's brother JOHN succeeded him as king. John's greed, cruelty, and military failures brought about the collapse of the Angevin Empire. By the end of his reign, King PHILIP II AUGUSTUS of France had driven the

English out of Normandy and Anjou. In addition, John's power as king of England had been severely challenged. Not only had he become unpopular because of unfair taxes. A dispute with the church had led to an interdict, or suspension of church services in all of England, from 1208 to 1212. With the help of the archbishop of Canterbury, the nobles rebelled and forced John to approve a document called MAGNA CARTA, which set bounds on the king's powers.

The king was to be able to raise special funds only with the "common consent of the realm." The Magna Carta also demanded that a council of barons share power with the king. This document, which played an important part in later English history, was soon disregarded, however. The barons rebelled again, inviting the threat of an invasion from France. Then John died in 1216, leaving England to his son Henry III. Normandy and Anjou were no longer a part of the English king's lands.

Achievements of the Normans and Early Angevins. As rulers of England and a large part of France, the Normans and early Angevins were the leading kings in western Europe. They governed with great authority as lords of the realm. They called the barons together on occasion but did not need baronial approval for their actions. Instead, the barons owed everything to them: rank, power, and property.

Before 1066, Anglo-Saxon lords on whose property the farmers worked usually owned that land. But William of Normandy brought with him the feudal* customs of Normandy. He claimed all the land for himself and his family, granting parts of it as fiefs* to his leading warriors and churchmen—who in turn granted some as fiefs to their followers. Anglo-Saxon landholders were replaced by Norman vassals*.

Administrative control over England was established very quickly and efficiently. William organized a unique feudal survey of England in which all lands and landholding vassals were identified and recorded. The results of two years of inquiry were written up in a book called the DOMESDAY BOOK, which could be used to settle disputes about land. The book helped give the royal government great authority.

Non-feudal ideas from Anglo-Saxon government were used when it was to the royal advantage, however. Instead of granting whole shires or counties to his vassals and allowing the vassals to govern these, as was usual on the European mainland, William kept the system of Anglo-Saxon sheriffs and reeves. This gave the king closer control. Only in dangerous areas such as the Welsh border were barons given full governing authority.

The Normans made other important administrative changes in England. There were new officials—including a chancellor, chamberlains, and a constable—to handle the routine business of the kingdom. A new permanent financial office was set up to store royal income, pay royal bills, and keep track of all financial transactions. Later, under the Angevins, a new court was added to judge financial disputes: the court of Exchequer. As the population grew larger, other courts were created for cases between private citizens and between the king and his subjects. Judges regularly traveled around the country to make justice more obtainable.

The Normans accepted many aspects of local Anglo-Saxon law, but they added their own features too. For example, the inquest system, in which people gave evidence under oath, was expanded and improved in Norman times. It became a central means of getting information for settling cases.

* **feudal** referring to the social, economic, and political system that flourished in western Europe during the Middle Ages

* **fief** under feudalism, property of value (usually land) that a person held under obligations of loyalty to an overlord

* **vassal** person given land by a lord or monarch in return for loyalty and services

* **regent** person appointed to govern a kingdom when the rightful ruler is too young, absent, or disabled

* **depose** to remove from high office

* **Capetians** princely and royal family that controlled the west Frankish kingdom for several centuries

Another important change was the separation of public and church courts, which had been joined together under the Anglo-Saxons.

Other new legal procedures included trial by jury in property disputes and the use of grand juries to formally accuse those suspected of major crimes. But the basis of the law was still traditional Anglo-Saxon customs.

England's economy prospered under the Normans and early Angevins as a result of their contacts with Normandy and France. More towns and markets arose, merchants gained power, and GUILDS were formed. Rural change also occurred. The prosperity of towns led some peasants to flee the countryside to find other employment. This forced local lords to improve the treatment of peasants, and many lords then accepted rent payments instead of demanding labor in their fields.

Culture and learning reached a high point under the early Angevins. The royal court encouraged scholarship and learning, becoming the patron of historians, philosophers, theologians, and poets. ELEANOR OF AQUITAINE, the wife of Henry II, was celebrated for her patronage of TROUBADOURS and their poetry. A number of celebrated scholars wrote important prose works. One of these works was the popular *History of British Kings* by Geoffrey of Monmouth. In architecture, the ROMANESQUE style of the Normans was gradually replaced by the English GOTHIC, of which Lincoln Cathedral is a fine example.

The Beginnings of Parliament

After the loss of much of its mainland territory during the reign of King John, England continued to create institutions and laws that distinguished it from the rest of Europe. The Norman and early Angevin kings had great freedom and power. However, there had been two lapses in royal control over England: first during the struggles of Stephen and Matilda and then during the reign of John.

When John's young son HENRY III came to the throne, his regent* reissued and confirmed the Magna Carta. Toward the end of Henry's reign, Parliament emerged as a regular institution for consulting nobles and churchmen as well as representatives of the shires and towns. The decisions reached in Parliament were said to represent the judgment of "the community of the kingdom of England."

During the next three centuries, Parliament became the recognized place for addressing problems of law, making adjustments in England's legal system, and authorizing taxation. During this time, three English kings were deposed*. In each case, Parliament approved the deposition and also approved the new king's right to rule. Strong kings were still able to enforce their own decisions. But when the kings needed community support, groups and factions represented in Parliament were sometimes able to gain rights from the kings.

EDWARD III launched the HUNDRED YEARS WAR to establish his claim to the French throne after the last Capetian* king died without a direct heir. For this, he needed to raise taxes, and he invited wealthy commoners from the cities to join the barons and bishops in Parliament. The power of these commoners became more secure as the war dragged on. Fighting continued during the reigns of four other kings, during which England conquered Normandy, lost it, won it again, and lost it again. The high point for the English was in 1422, when HENRY V's infant son was recognized by treaty as king of France as well as England. But many French nobles refused to accept this settlement, and after almost 30 years of fighting, that son, as HENRY VI, had lost all the English territories for the last time.

The loss of France caused new waves of popular and baronial discontent. Many commoners from the south of England stormed London during the shortlived CADE'S REBELLION. Then the duke of York led a campaign that started the so-called WARS OF THE ROSES, resulting in Henry VI's being deposed. The duke's son Edward IV was confirmed as king by Parliament, but the rivalry between Henry's and Edward's families continued after both of them were dead.

The Wars of the Roses were settled on a hot August day in 1485 at the Battle of Bosworth Field. RICHARD III, the duke of York's second son, was defeated by a distant relative who became England's Henry VII. One of Richard's supporters made it clear how much the authority of Parliament had grown since the time of the Angevins. Defending his actions to the new king, he said: "(Richard) was my crowned king, and if the parliament authority of England set the crown upon a stock, I will fight for that stock. And as I fought for him, I will fight for you, when you are established by the same authority."

Later kings of England, including Henry VII, still retained great power. The authority of Parliament was not fully established until the late 1600s. However, between the Battle of Hastings and the Battle of Bosworth Field, Parliament had established itself as an important institution in the government of the English kingdom. (*See also* **Feudalism; Kingship, Theories of.**)

English Language and Literature

During most of the Middle Ages, the preferred language for writing, in England as well as in other western European countries, was Latin. Latin was the language of the Roman Church. Especially before 1100, educated people—rulers and officials as well as churchmen—used Latin for most of their official work. However, they learned their Latin in school or from tutors, as a second language. The language people learned when growing up, which differed according to where they lived, was known as the vernacular. In England, the vernacular went through several stages of development before it became Modern English.

The oldest form of the English vernacular is the language brought to Britain in the 400s by its Germanic invaders—the Angles, Saxons, and Jutes. Their language—Old English—is also called ANGLO-SAXON, and it remained the language of most of England until the NORMAN conquest in 1066. The word *English* comes from *Engle,* the Anglo-Saxon word for Angle. There are many surviving manuscripts written in Anglo-Saxon from this period—more than in any other vernacular of the early Middle Ages.

After the Norman conquest, England had two vernaculars—the Norman French spoken by the new overlords and the English spoken by the common people. Latin remained the language of the church, but for more than 300 years French became the language of England's royal court, its law, and its government. The English written during this period began to be influenced by Norman French, and it is known as Middle English.

In 1204, the English kings lost Normandy to France and became less influenced by French ways. Gradually the two vernaculars began to mix. It

A Gift from God

Caedmon was an uneducated cowherd who worked in an abbey. One night, as he was sleeping in the cowshed, he had a vision in which he was commanded to sing of the Creation. The following morning, he sang these lines to the abbess and the brethren:

"Now it is our duty to praise the Guardian of the heavenly kingdom, the Maker's might and purpose, the acts of the Glory-Father, just as He, the eternal Lord, established the origin of everything wondrous. He, the holy Creator, first created heaven as a roof for the children of men; then the Guardian of mankind, the eternal Lord, the almighty God, later fashioned the land, middle earth, for men."

The abbess and the learned brethren agreed that Caedmon's hymn was a gift from God.

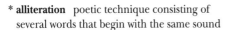

* **alliteration**   poetic technique consisting of several words that begin with the same sound

* **rood**   early word for cross

was a slow process. The first king to speak English rather than French as his first language was Henry IV, who came to the throne in 1399. But by 1500, English had changed enough for us to call it Modern English—the language of William Shakespeare and Ernest Hemingway.

Old English (Anglo-Saxon)

There are 400 manuscripts surviving from the Middle Ages that preserve Anglo-Saxon literature. Most of this was written for very practical purposes. The leaders of the Christian church wanted its teachings to be understood by the less educated—especially by beginning students in school—but knew that these people could not read Latin. Much of the writing in Old English is quite accomplished. It also records some of the old oral poetry of the Anglo-Saxon peoples and some original writing in Anglo-Saxon poetic style.

Poetry.   Anglo-Saxon poetry is largely anonymous. It is preserved in very few documents, and the names of the poets are rarely indicated. In fact, we know the names of only three Anglo-Saxon poets—Caedmon, Aldhelm, and Cynewulf. Caedmon, the best known of the three, is the only one credited with one of the Anglo-Saxon poems that survive, a nine-line *Hymn* in praise of God. He lived at an abbey at Whitby in northern England in the 600s, and he has been called "the father of English poetry." According to the medieval English historian BEDE, Caedmon "sang about the creation of the world, the origin of the human race, and many stories taken from the sacred Scriptures."

The most famous Old English poems are those that deal with the heroic past of the Anglo-Saxons. *Beowulf,* a poem of more than 3,000 lines, is considered the first major poem in the English language. Set in Scandinavia in the distant past, it gives a vivid picture of old Germanic life, as it tells the story of Beowulf's successful fights with three monsters. Many scholars have compared it to Homer's *Iliad.*

Beowulf and other Old English poems do not use rhyme as a regular feature. Instead they are characterized by their strong rhythms and by their use of alliteration*. For example, there is a poem called *The Battle of Maldon,* about an Anglo-Saxon hero who died fighting the Vikings in 991. Near the end, one of his oldest supporters says: "Though I am feeble I will not flee, But by my beloved lord I will lie forever."

Many Anglo-Saxon poems have religious subjects. There are four long narrative poems about saints' lives. One of them—*Juliana*—tells about the life and death of the virgin martyr of Nicomedia who sacrificed her life to defend her Christian beliefs. The poem focuses on a series of debates between Juliana and the devil, who visits her in prison.

Other debate poems have also survived. The longest is *Christ and Satan,* presenting the conflict when Satan tempts Christ during 40 days in the wilderness. Another debate poem, *Solomon and Saturn,* is a dialogue between the wise Jewish king from Bible times (Solomon) and the pagan god Saturn, who is presented as a magician.

One of the most beautiful of the Old English poems is the *Dream of the Rood*,* a meditation about the cross of Christ. In the poem, a jeweled cross speaks to a dreamer about what the cross means and how it helps sinners, and the dreamer decides to place his trust in the cross. The poem ends with a vision of the Kingdom of Heaven, where the dreamer hopes he will one day join his friends who have died. A similar, shorter poem presenting a speech by the cross is carved in RUNES on an outdoor stone cross that is still standing today in Northumbria in northern England.

Prose.   Much more Old English prose has survived than poetry. Some of the writing shows great skill. The best-known writer of Old English prose is ALFRED THE GREAT, king of the West Saxons from 871 to 899. Most of his writing involved translating and adapting books from Latin into Old English. Among the translations and adaptations credited to him are Pope GREGORY THE GREAT's *The Book of Pastoral Care,* a manual for parish priests; St. AUGUSTINE's *Soliloquies;* and the *Ecclesiastical History of the English People* by Bede.

Among the most accomplished types of original prose writing to survive are informal SERMONS known as homilies. The best of these use rhythmical alliteration that is almost like Anglo-Saxon poetry. Two of the greatest homily writers were Aelfric, abbot of Eynsham, and Wulfstan, archbishop of York. Aelfric's homilies were so popular that scribes* continued to copy them into the 1200s.

Other Old English prose includes lives of saints, BIBLE translations, handbooks, treatises, tracts, medical texts, laws, monastery rules, legal documents, charters, and wills. One of the most notable prose works is the Anglo-Saxon Chronicle, a record of important public events first kept in King Alfred's reign and continued almost to 1100.

* **scribe**   person who hand-copies manuscripts to preserve them

Middle English

After the Norman conquest, French became the language of the court, the upper classes, the law courts, and the schools. French joined Latin as a language of government and law. Increasingly, however, the nobles began to speak English as well as French and Latin—especially if they married English wives. When the Normans spoke English, they naturally used many French words and ways of speaking.

The English spoken by the common people, which had many regional dialects*, began to absorb French words from their rulers. As English slowly became the main language of the nobles, French words and grammatical habits became even more common. There was a great mixing of different vocabularies and dialects. English was used for education and business instead of Latin or French. At first, it was written differently in different regions, depending on the dialect of the speakers. Later, especially after William CAXTON started England's first printing business in 1476, spelling and grammar became more standard. It had essentially become Modern English, and since then, the language has changed far more slowly.

* **dialect**   form of speech characteristic of a region that differs from the standard language in pronunciation, vocabulary, and grammar

Early Middle English.   Between 1066 and 1350, works in Middle English included both popular literature, such as chronicles and songs, and religious educational materials. Such works were aimed mainly at two groups—educated common people and nobles with an English background.

The first Middle English chronicle was Layamon's *Brut* (1189). A poem of more than 16,000 lines, it begins with the founding of Britain and ends with the Anglo-Saxons driving the Britons into WALES. Almost one-third of the poem tells the story of King Arthur. Although the work did not contribute significantly to the development of ARTHURIAN LITERATURE, *Brut* ranks as one of the most important works of English literature before Chaucer.

Many of the songs from the early Middle English period are included in sermon collections. The practice of setting religious words to popular tunes to help spread the Christian message began with the FRANCISCANS in Italy. After they came to England in 1224, they composed popular gospel songs in English. The songs were not alliterative in style but used rhyme.

There were also rhyming Middle English poems with moral messages, including debate poems. *The Owl and the Nightingale* (ca. 1200) is a debate between secular* and monastic life and between art and philosophy. In *The Thrush and the Nightingale* (ca. 1275), the Nightingale argues that women are always true and gracious, while the Thrush contends that women are not to be trusted.

* **secular** nonreligious; connected with everyday life

Notable works from the early 1300s include *Cursor Mundi* (ca. 1300), an encyclopedic collection of Bible stories from the Creation to the Day of Judgment, and *Handlyng Synne* (ca. 1303) by Robert Mannyng of Brunne, a manual of religious stories adapted from the French. Later in his career, Mannyng wrote a chronicle called *Rimed Story of England* (1338), which begins with Noah and ends with the death of King EDWARD I in 1307.

Much devotional writing in Middle English during this period—sermons, homilies, manuals, allegories, treatises, lives of saints, and adaptations of works written in Latin—was intended for members of the English-speaking nobility, many of them women. An outstanding example is *Ancrene Riwle (Rule of the Anchoresses*), written about 1220. It was a manual for the guidance of three noble Englishwomen in the western part of England who had retreated from the world to live as recluses. Its eight chapters cover Devotions, Custody of the Senses, Regulation of Inward Feelings, Temptations, Confession, Penance, Love, and External Rules. The work is written in a lively, witty style and shows great psychological insight and knowledge of the writings of the leading mystics* and theologians*.

* **anchoress** female hermit

* **mystic** person who experiences divine truths through faith, spiritual insight, and intuition

* **theologian** person who studies religious

Another writer, Richard Rolle (died 1349), wrote similar works for three different women who sought to lead a mystical life. He shows a very personal and almost poetic style as he writes about spiritual ecstasy. Later, women writers authored two important Middle English devotional works. In *Revelations of Divine Love,* JULIAN OF NORWICH meditates on the meaning of the 16 mystical visions of Christ's suffering she had during a severe illness in 1373. The other work, from the early 1400s, is the *Book of Margery Kempe,* a candid autobiography by a mother of 14 children about her personal and spiritual struggles.

Golden Age. The late 1300s were the first golden age of English literature. At the urging of John WYCLIF, the Bible was translated into Middle English and, together with his sermons, was popularized throughout England. Though the church did not approve of this action, it gave new dignity to the vernacular language. At the same time, important literary writers in London began to produce significant works in the maturing language.

> **Remember:** *Words in small capital letters have separate entries, and the index at the end of Volume 4 will guide you to more information on many topics.*

An important prose writer, John MANDEVILLE, wrote a very popular book pulling together descriptions of travels throughout the medieval world. It is not clear that he himself traveled at all, but his book captured the imaginations of readers then and later. His work can be considered a part of the history of the English novel. The book was written in Norman French about 1356, then was translated into Middle English many times.

A famous Middle English poet of this period was John GOWER. In fact, he wrote in three languages, with important poems in Norman French and in Latin as well. However, his most popular poem was *The Lover's Confession,* which weaves many stories into a frame built around the Seven Deadly Sins.

Although a number of other authors and their works made the period a rich one, Geoffrey CHAUCER was its leading figure. Chaucer was the son of a London merchant who went on to a varied career as a soldier and diplomat. He authored many works, including one of the great love poems in the English language, *Troilus and Criseyde.* However, Chaucer's masterpiece was his *Canterbury Tales,* which he worked on for 14 years before his death in 1400.

Both Chaucer and Gower wrote rhyming verse. During the late 1300s, there was also a revival of alliterative poetry. The most important poem of this revival was William Langland's *Piers Plowman.* The poem moves from political to spiritual allegory in a series of dream visions of a "field full of folk" that represents society. Its informal alliterative patterns and rhythms give it a personal and meditative flavor.

Another impressive poem of the alliterative revival is *Sir Gawain and the Green Knight.* The poem tells about the chivalric adventures of Gawain and contains rich descriptions of clothing, furniture, architecture, the seasons, hunting, and Gawain and the other characters. Other alliterative poems of the period include *Pearl,* a poem that begins with the death of the infant daughter of the poet-dreamer and moves on to an exploration of such religious topics as baptism, divine grace, and heaven. *Patience* and *Purity* are homilies in verse that use unrhymed alliterative lines and employ Bible stories to teach the virtues of humility and obedience. Although the alliterative revival died out in England after 1425, it continued in Scotland in the work of William Dunbar and other Scottish poets to the end of the 1400s.

The two leading English literary figures of the 1400s were Sir Thomas MALORY and William Caxton. Malory was the author of the *Book of King Arthur and His Knights,* an acknowledged prose masterpiece and the last major work of the Middle Ages to take CHIVALRY seriously. Caxton was the first to print books in English. After learning printing in COLOGNE in Germany, he returned to England and printed about 100 books in English, 24 of which were his own translations of Latin and French works. They also included the works of Chaucer, Gower, and Malory. For some of the books he printed, he wrote prologues and epilogues. Caxton played a leading role in moving English literature from church and court circles out to the wider audience of middle-class English readers. By printing large numbers of books, he encouraged standardization of the spelling and of the language, thereby paving the way for Modern English. (*See also* **Allegory; Ballads; Beowulf; Drama; Kempe, Margery; Mysticism.**)

William Caxton was one of the leading figures of English literature in the 1400s. In addition to writing books, he also printed books—his own works, translations of French and Latin works, and the works of earlier English authors. This illustration shows Caxton presenting a printed book to the queen in the late 1400s.

Ethiopia (Abyssinia)

At the beginning of the Middle Ages, Ethiopia—also called Abyssinia—was a powerful kingdom to the southeast of Egypt in Africa. One of the first Christian states, it was almost as large as western Europe. Its port city of Adulis controlled international trade through the Red Sea, with links to the Mediterranean world and to Asia. Although the spread of Islam isolated Ethiopia from the rest of the Christian world during much of the early Middle Ages, contact was reestablished during the crusades and later.

Early History. Ethiopia began as a small state on the south coast of the Red Sea with its capital at Aksum. By the 300s, it controlled lands on both sides of the Red Sea, and its emperor Ezana made Christianity the official state religion. Christianity spread quickly; when the Egyptian monk Cosmas returned after a visit to Ethiopia in about 525, he reported "everywhere churches of the Christians, bishops, martyrs, monks, and hermits, by whom the gospel is proclaimed."

During the same period, Ethiopian forces mounted a great expedition against a Persian* alliance, aiding Byzantine emperor JUSTINIAN I by helping to save the Christian city of Najran in southern Arabia. Ethiopia's links with the Byzantines also ensured survival of early Greek literary works. Translations into Ethiopian are the only complete versions that have been found of some manuscripts.

During the early days of Islam, some of MUHAMMAD's first followers were protected by tolerant Ethiopian Christians. However, the Muslim conquest of North Africa, including Alexandria, ended Ethiopia's control of trade on the Red Sea, which had been a major source of its power and influence. Arabs also fought their way south into parts of Ethiopia. The official religion of Ethiopia remained Christianity, however.

Loss of its sea trade forced Ethiopia to look inland to develop its interior resources and to find new trading partners. It moved its capital south from Aksum to Agaw in the middle of the highlands. Later Ethiopian kings viewed Aksum as the national holy city. They continued to trace

* **Persian** referring to the ancient culture of Iran that continued to rival Greek civilization during the early Byzantine period

The Church of St. George is one of several Christian churches at Lalibela, Ethiopia, that are carved from solid rock. Some of these churches are carved directly into the mountainside. Others are freestanding.

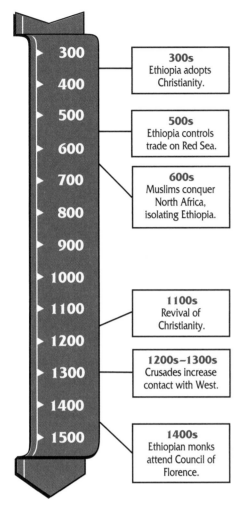

300s
Ethiopia adopts Christianity.

500s
Ethiopia controls trade on Red Sea.

600s
Muslims conquer North Africa, isolating Ethiopia.

1100s
Revival of Christianity.

1200s–1300s
Crusades increase contact with West.

1400s
Ethiopian monks attend Council of Florence.

their ancestry back to its ancient rulers, and they returned to Aksum to be crowned.

The adoption of Islam by some of the people who lived on the Red Sea coast further weakened Ethiopia's ties with the Christian world. Muslim states also developed in southern Ethiopia. However, they became fully integrated into the Christian Ethiopian Empire. Conflicts did occur—there were Christian, Muslim, and Jewish states—but the different religions for the most part tolerated each other, and Christianity remained dominant. Especially in Egypt, Christians in southern Muslim lands also looked to the Ethiopian rulers for support.

There was a major revival of Ethiopian Christianity in the late 1100s during the rule of Ethiopia's Zagwe dynasty. Another reform occurred in the middle 1400s.

Later Contacts with Europe.   European interest in Ethiopia increased as a result of the crusades to Jerusalem. There was a legend about PRESTER JOHN (Priest John), ruler of a legendary kingdom in the East who was supposed to help regain the Holy Land. One of the theories was that Prester John was the king of Ethiopia, and Pope Alexander III wrote a letter to Ethiopia in 1177 seeking an alliance. However, his messenger never returned.

Nonetheless, tales of Prester John persisted and became part of the MINSTREL tradition; the idea of an alliance also did not die. In 1317, a Dominican monk who later became an archbishop in Persia advocated a joint European-Ethiopian crusade against the Muslims in which Ethiopia would blockade the Red Sea trade. According to an Egyptian chronicler of the 1300s, Muslims feared just such a "great alliance against Islam" between Ethiopia and Europe. Ethiopian rulers themselves also discussed crusades of their own to liberate Jerusalem.

In the late Middle Ages, interest in Ethiopia remained high for commercial and religious reasons. King John II of Portugal saw Ethiopia as a route he could use to steal some of the spice trade from Venice, and Henry the Navigator of Portugal undertook his explorations of the west coast of Africa in hopes of finding a sea route to Ethiopia.

Ethiopian and European rulers also sent religious missions to each other. In 1441, during their church reform, monks from Ethiopian monasteries in Jerusalem attended the Council of Florence to discuss Christian unity, and the papacy established a house for Ethiopian pilgrims behind St. Peter's in Rome. These pilgrims increased European interest in the history, culture, language, and customs of the ancient Christian land of Ethiopia. (*See also* **Christianity; Crusades; Islam, Conquests of; Jerusalem.**)

Exchequer

The Exchequer is the principal treasury of England. Its name comes from the checkered tablecloth used in the Middle Ages to keep the royal accounts. Each column of squares on the cloth stood for coins of a certain value, and totals were calculated by moving counters on the cloth.

The Exchequer grew from a central treasury established by WILLIAM I THE CONQUEROR. During the reign of HENRY I, this treasury was enlarged and given responsibility for most royal finances. By the 1300s, the English Exchequer was one of the most efficient financial systems in Europe.

There were two divisions of the Exchequer—the Lower Exchequer and the Upper Exchequer. The Lower Exchequer was responsible for keeping financial records throughout the year, receiving money, making payments, and transporting money for royal use. Money was heavy—it was all in metal coins. The Upper Exchequer's job was auditing—that is, making sure that the king received everything due to him, and that payments made on the king's behalf were proper.

* **audit** official examination of financial accounts and records to check their accuracy

Audits* by the Upper Exchequer were held twice a year. During these audits, SHERIFFS appeared before the Exchequer to report on all official financial transactions in their counties. The sheriffs' records were checked on the checkered cloth, to determine whether they owed more money or had paid too much. The Lower Exchequer received the money from the sheriffs, counted it, tested its metal for quality, and issued receipts, while the Upper Exchequer reviewed payments to and from the royal accounts.

At first, when the king and his household traveled, he was sent money from the Exchequer, which was located in London. But in the reigns of EDWARD I and EDWARD III, many functions of the Exchequer were taken over by royal household treasuries. This was partly for convenience during the king's journeys, but also because English barons tried to control royal spending by placing supporters in the Exchequer. So the kings increasingly bypassed the Exchequer and gave financial control to other divisions of the royal household.

By the late 1300s, kings were no longer free to do this. PARLIAMENT established procedures for collecting taxes, auditing the Exchequer, and controlling any misuse of funds. The Exchequer again became the chief treasury of England. It remained so for the rest of the Middle Ages. (*See also* **Money; Taxation.**)

Excommunication

* **sacrament** religious ceremony of the Christian church, considered especially sacred, such as Communion and baptism

* **heresy** belief that is contrary to church doctrine

* **penance** task set by the church for someone to earn God's forgiveness for a sin

To medieval Christians, church membership was vital. Being able to worship and to receive the sacraments* marked a person as a full member of the community. It was also thought to be the way a person could be saved from eternal damnation. Excommunication meant expulsion from the church. Interdict meant a closing down of the local church. The two were the worst punishments imaginable.

In the early Middle Ages, the two punishments were very similar. Both implied that a heresy* was involved. The purpose of both was to make people mend their ways and rejoin the church and society. The church official who imposed the penalty was the one who forgave the offenders and readmitted them to the church. Forgiven offenders swore to obey the church and to do charity work, go on a pilgrimage, or perform some other penance*.

The term *interdict* meant a punishment that was imposed on a community. In 586, when a bishop was murdered in Rouen, France, all the local churches were closed by interdict; nobody could worship or take Communion. Since an interdict crippled the operation of an entire church or group of churches, only a pope, bishop, or high church official was allowed to impose one.

* **mitigation**   condition that makes a hardship less severe

Interdicts might occur if people protected, listened to, or even associated with those who had been excommunicated. Groups were judged guilty by association. However, some church thinkers, even early on, felt this was unjust. In 869, the bishop of Rheims criticized an interdict in Laon because the dying were denied forgiveness and innocent children were denied baptism. By the 1000s, mitigations* were being observed. Churches under interdict could open for baptisms. Dying people could receive final Mass. This made interdicts less severe than excommunications because they no longer meant damnation.

By the 1100s, interdicts and excommunications had become quite common. They were imposed for lesser crimes: forgery, for example, and lying in court. Church court judges excommunicated people who refused to come to the court or to obey a court decision. Four times a year, churches issued lists of crimes punishable by excommunication. Later still, mitigations began to become privileges. Pilgrims, crusaders, priests, monks, and nobles might get special treatment, or they might be safe from any but papal interdicts.

Though interdicts and excommunications were both greatly feared, excommunication, the individual punishment, was generally considered more serious. In fact, two kinds of excommunication had developed by the later Middle Ages. Minor excommunication was like an interdict against one person; the offender was excluded from the sacraments but not from the church. Only in major excommunication was an offender completely cut off from the church and supposedly from the chance to go to heaven. This punishment was considered so severe that sufficient warnings had to be given before it was imposed.

* **Protestant**   referring to movements against the Roman Church begun during the 1400s and 1500s and the religious traditions and churches that emerged

The most common excommunication procedure was performed in a court. The judge declared, "I excommunicate you," and then the church announced the excommunication so that people would avoid the condemned person. But on special occasions, a formal excommunication service was held in the cathedral. The bishop and twelve priests stood in a circle and cut off "from the body of the church this corrupt and unhealthy member." Excommunications remained in use well after the Middle Ages, and they were used by Protestant* churches as well as the established churches of the Middle Ages.

Exploration

See map in Vikings (vol. 4).

Three major reasons for exploration in the Middle Ages were the spread of religion, conquest, and trade. The faith of Islam was carried east into northern India by Arab traders, and it reached as far west as Spain during the Islamic conquests. After the Germanic migrations of the 400s, the greatest early travelers in Europe were the warlike Vikings. In the later Middle Ages, the quest to find a sea route for trade with Asia prompted Spain and Portugal to finance voyages down the eastern coast of Africa and eventually across the Atlantic Ocean. By 1500, vast new lands in Asia and in the Americas had been found by European explorers and colonizers.

Early Traders and Explorers

In the early Middle Ages, the most active travelers in western Europe were the VIKINGS, who sailed south and west from SCANDINAVIA to raid, trade, and colonize. Meanwhile, European knowledge of the lands to the east was limited. Starting in the 600s, the ancient trade routes from Constantinople to China were mostly traveled by Muslim traders. Jewish and then Italian traders brought Asian goods into Europe from Muslim lands, but Europeans generally knew little about India, China, and other parts of Asia. Interest in the East grew after the CRUSADES and after adventurous travelers returned with tales of the riches of the East.

Scandinavians.   In the early Middle Ages, the Vikings, or men of the *vik* (bay), took to the seas in their longboats as pirates, explorers, traders, conquerors, and colonizers. Other Europeans gave them different names—Northmen, Norsemen, Varangians—but they were all Vikings from Scandinavia.

Beginning in the 700s, Swedish Vikings (the Varangians) sailed east and founded settlements in the BALTIC COUNTRIES. From there, by following rivers and portaging* from one river to another, they penetrated deep into the Slavic territories of Russia, reaching all the way south to the Caspian and Black Seas. They founded several city-states in the area. One was established by RURIK at Novgorod. Another was settled at KIEVAN RUS farther to the south. The Viking rulers of Kievan Rus dominated the other city-states. They also sent their Slavic subjects, called "Russians," on raids against CONSTANTINOPLE in 860 and again in 941. They even traded with the Muslims in the Islamic capital of Baghdad.

Seafaring Vikings from Denmark and Norway conquered the northern isles of Scotland, raided the Scottish and English coasts, and sailed northwest to settle Iceland about 850. Then they sailed farther, to Greenland, where they established a colony that survived for several centuries. On a trip to Greenland, Leif Eiriksson by mistake reached North America (the northern tip of Newfoundland), a land he called Vinland.

Vikings also sailed to Ireland, taking Dublin in 836 and invading the Irish interior. They conquered some of the ANGLO-SAXON kingdoms in

* **portaging** carrying of boats or goods from one body of water to another

St. Brendan, an Irish abbot of the 500s, was a famous navigator and explorer who became a hero of legendary tales. In *The Navigation of St. Brendan,* compiled about 950, Brendan sails off to find the mythical Saints' Promised Land. This illumination shows the crew's encounter with a whale. In truth, there is some evidence that St. Brendan reached the New World before the Vikings. St. Brendan is the patron saint of sailors.

England. They captured land in Normandy. No settlement was safe from Viking raids if it was near the Atlantic coast of Europe or reachable from a river that flowed into the Atlantic. Vikings sacked Seville in Spain. Several times they sailed up the Seine River to loot Paris. By 859, they even reached Morocco and entered the Mediterranean, where they found new cities to raid.

Jews and Italians. From the 800s through the 1000s, Jewish traders traveled extensively, acting as middlemen between the Muslims, the Byzantines, and western Europe. An Arab writer in the 800s wrote of Jewish merchants who went "from West to East and from East to West, by land and by sea" and were able to speak "Arabic, Persian, Romanian*, Frankish, Spanish, and Slavic."

As Italian ports became the point of contact for trade between Europe and Asia, Italians replaced Jews as middlemen between West and East. VENICE, which maintained regular relations with the Byzantine Empire, became Europe's leading commercial port, as the crusades stimulated European contact with the East. Amalfi, PISA, and GENOA also became prosperous ports. Italians took control of the Mediterranean by driving Muslims from Corsica and Sardinia and by capturing the Muslim capital of Tunisia in Africa.

Explorations of Asia. The crusades brought western European settlers, often known as Latins, to the eastern end of the Mediterranean. In the late 1000s, the First Crusade established the Latin Kingdom of Jerusalem. In the early 1200s, the Fourth Crusade led to the creation of a Latin Empire of Constantinople. From these beachheads in the East, explorers and diplomats from western Europe traveled to central and eastern Asia.

In the mid-1200s, western Europeans made contact with the MONGOL EMPIRE. The Latin emperor of Constantinople sent Baldwin of Hainaut as an ambassador to gain Mongol support against the Turks. Pope INNOCENT IV sent the Franciscan Giovanni Pian de Carpine to Mongolia to seek support against Islam. In 1254, the French king LOUIS IX sent William of Rubruck east, again to Mongolia. The report William sent back to Louis is considered a masterpiece of geographical writing.

A year after William of Rubruck left for Mongolia, the father and uncle of Marco POLO, Italian merchants from Venice, had gone to China (Cathay) and returned with large profits. In 1271, they set off again, this time with Marco, who was 17. They traveled overland to Chandu (Xanadu), the summer residence of the great Mongol khan Kublai, emperor of China. Marco worked for the khan and soon became an important Mongol inspector. He did not return to Venice until 1295.

Marco Polo wrote about the wealth and splendor of China and other exotic places in Asia in a book called the *Book of Marvels.* Along with the earlier accounts by William of Rubruck and Giovanni Pian de Carpine, Polo's tales began to awaken interest in traveling. Another book called the *Travels* of Sir John Mandeville, though largely fictional, was, however, the most popular travel book of the time. Translated into many languages and read widely throughout Europe, it did much to increase interest in the wealth of the East. During the next century, a Muslim traveler, IBN BATTUTA, made an even longer journey to India and China. His travels lasted more than 27 years, though they were less well known to Europeans.

* **Romanian** name sometimes used for Greek or Byzantine because the Byzantine Empire was descended from the ancient Roman Empire

See color plate 4, vol. 3.

Later Explorations

The travels of Marco Polo and others increased the desire of western Europeans to trade with the East. Since Muslims controlled the overland trade routes, however, Europeans had to find a way of reaching Asia by sea. Europeans particularly wanted to discover the source of spices, which Italian merchants could buy only from Muslim traders. It is curious that the European kingdom farthest west—Portugal—became the one in the best position to find the sea route to Asia.

Exploring Westward.   Unlike Venice, which faced toward the east, the ports of Genoa and Pisa, on Italy's northwestern coast, were well placed for trading with Muslim Spain. When Seville in Spain became Christian in 1248, the city granted Genoese merchants extensive trading rights. They were given their own district with a warehouse, and the king of CASTILE leased Genoese ships and hired Genoese admirals. He also borrowed money from Genoese merchants, making them his bankers. Profits from this trade helped finance the first voyages to America.

Italian sailors also established commercial relations with PORTUGAL. Genoese ships sailed through the Strait of Gibraltar and north along the Atlantic coast. They docked in Lagos in southern Portugal on their way to the great international market of BRUGES. By the 1300s and 1400s, Italian merchants from Genoa, Florence, Naples, and Venice were all sending regular convoys of ships from the Mediterranean into the Atlantic Ocean.

Looking for a Sea Route to India and China.   In addition to wanting to trade directly with India and China, European Christians hoped they might find new allies there against the Islamic world. Stories were told about a Christian priest called PRESTER JOHN who ruled an empire somewhere on the way to India. The only way to reach it seemed to be by sea.

As early as 1291, two brothers from Genoa sailed south along the west coast of Africa, mapping the coast and looking for a route to the Indian Ocean. However, they were lost at sea. In the early 1300s, Genoese sailors working for the king of Portugal discovered and laid claim to the Canary Islands. Later, navigators sailing northwest from the Canaries to catch the trade winds* that would blow them back to Europe discovered more islands—the Madeiras and the Azores—which they also claimed for Portugal. Discovery of these Atlantic islands led to further Portuguese exploration down the west coast of Africa to Guinea, to capture slaves to work on the new islands.

Guinea became a major trading center for gold as well as slaves. The Portuguese also pushed farther south in hopes of discovering a sea passage to India and China or a way to make contact with Prester John. This passage was finally discovered when Bartholomew Dias sailed from Portugal in 1487. A storm drove him past the southern tip of Africa, and he contacted land again about 200 miles past the cape, on the east coast of Africa.

King John II of Portugal, realizing that the Indian Ocean had been reached, arranged a secret expedition to spy out the new ocean, which until then had been sailed only by Muslim ships. Pero da Covilhão, disguised as a Muslim merchant, traveled through Egypt to the Red Sea and then sailed to Goa, the future capital of Portuguese India. On his way back, he mapped the complete eastern coast of Africa before returning to Portugal, again by way of the Red Sea and Egypt.

Remember: Consult the index at the end of Volume 4 to find more information on many topics.

* **trade wind** wind blowing almost constantly toward the equator

Lost at Sea

King John II of Portugal refused to finance Columbus's proposed western voyage to Japan, but he appointed a Flemish sea captain in 1486 to lead a similar expedition. Ferdinand van Olmen was to search for the island of the Seven Cities. It was believed to be in the Atlantic Ocean about halfway between Europe and Japan.

At the end of the winter of 1487, van Olmen set out with two ships and six months of supplies, but he was never heard from again. When Columbus made his crossing five years later, John was no longer so interested in the island because Dias had discovered another route to India.

This Portuguese quest to arrange direct trade with Asia was finally completed by Vasco da Gama. After sailing south along the coast of Africa and rounding the Cape of Good Hope, he enlisted the help of an expert Muslim navigator to guide him across the Indian Ocean. His arrival in Calicut, India, in 1498 marked the beginning of Portugal's trading supremacy in the East and of Europe's colonization of Asia.

Christopher Columbus. Columbus was the son of a poor weaver from Genoa. Like many other Italian sailors, he went to Spain and Portugal to find work, and he gained experience on several voyages. He traveled to the eastern end of the Mediterranean, to northwestern Europe, to the Gold Coast of Africa (Ghana), and possibly even to Iceland. Around 1484, he approached King John of Portugal with the idea of making a voyage to Cipangu (Japan) by sailing west. (The sea passage around Africa to the Indian Ocean was not discovered until three years later.) John turned Columbus down, so Columbus next approached the rulers of the newly united kingdom of Spain with the same proposal. However, Columbus was at first refused in Spain too.

Columbus's brother tried to enlist support for the voyage in France and England, but he also was unsuccessful. By this time, however, Portugal had gained access to the Indian Ocean, and Columbus finally succeeded in convincing Isabella of Castile, now queen of Spain, to finance his expedition. In three ships—the *Niña, Pinta,* and *Santa Maria*—from the small seaport of Palos, Columbus sailed to the Canary Islands. Then, on September 6, 1492, he set out westward across the ocean.

On October 12 (now celebrated as Columbus Day), a sailor in the *Pinta* spotted San Salvador (Watling's Island) in the Bahamas. Columbus immediately assumed it was one of the islands of Japan. When he learned from the inhabitants about a rich land nearby, he thought of Marco Polo's Cathay (China). Actually the island was Cuba, which he reached on October 27. Columbus also discovered Haiti, which he named Hispaniola (Little Spain). This first voyage of Columbus (he made three more) paved the way for further European exploration and colonization of the New World. (*See also* **Missions and Missionaries, Christian; Trade.**)

Fables

From the time of Aesop, a legendary Greek storyteller from the 600s B.C., fables have been a popular way of teaching behavior. Often presented as animal tales that will appeal to children, fables are short fictional stories that illustrate serious moral points. Many fables are still popular today. One example is the Hare and the Tortoise, in which a hare loses an easy race by being too confident.

Fables were very popular in the Middle Ages. Many collections had been written down by ancient Greek and Roman authors, and some of these works survived and remained influential. The most famous during the early Middle Ages was a series of five books by Phaedrus, written in the year A.D. 50. Phaedrus's work itself was lost between the years 800 and 1500. However, many other Latin and medieval authors modified and borrowed from it, and so it remained popular.

Fables were a popular source of both entertainment and education during the Middle Ages. This is an illustration of the story "The Tortoise and the Two Ducks," taken from the *Fables* of Bidpai, from the 1400s.

Medieval fable collections were often called *Isopets,* after the original Aesop. One of the most influential fables was known as the *Romulus*—supposedly translated from Greek by an author of that name. The *Romulus* collection was available in Latin prose and in several Latin verse versions—notably one attributed to Walter of England in the 1100s. More than 100 manuscripts preserve copies of Walter's Latin verse tales. Translations from Walter's original work also exist in French, Italian, Portuguese, Spanish, German, Hebrew, and other languages.

Another set of ancient fables that came into medieval literature was a collection by a Latin writer named Avianus. His name led to another name for fable collections: *Avionnet.* In addition, a whole set of popular medieval stories about a sly fox called Renard (later Reynard) and a vain cock named Chantecler (later Chantecleer) was developed in France in the 1100s. Called the *Roman de Renart,* this collection of stories has a simple narrative style and moral endings that sound like old proverbs.

Fables were not only used for entertainment and schooling. They were also cited in sermons, and they are included in books of examples that were prepared for preachers in the later Middle Ages. Some churchmen approved of this type of example. Others, including Thomas AQUINAS, argued that fiction had no place in religious truth. A similar argument had been made years before: the ancient Roman author Cicero wrote that the authority of "fabricated things" was not to be trusted.

Fables also influenced literature. An important early poetess, Anglo-Norman writer MARIE DE FRANCE, may have been part of the court of Henry II of England. In addition to her adventure stories and love stories (called lays), she wrote a volume of fables. Fables are also related to the tradition of fabliaux, or comic short story-poems about people who trick one another in all kinds of ways. These works influenced the writings of Italy's Giovanni BOCCACCIO and of England's Geoffrey CHAUCER. In fact, one of Chaucer's *Canterbury Tales,* the Nun's Priest's Tale, is a fable about Chantecleer. In addition, later poets such as the French writer La Fontaine have drawn on the rich tradition of medieval fables.

Fairs

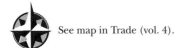

See map in Trade (vol. 4).

Fairs were important to the economic and social life of the Middle Ages, particularly in areas such as western Europe where at first too little TRADE was carried on to support permanent trading centers. Fairs provided safe, organized places for merchants to exchange goods. They stimulated spending, created demand for new products and raw materials, and encouraged merchants to travel and trade more extensively. Fairs brought manufacturing and commerce to places that had lacked contact with other areas, spurring the growth of major CITIES AND TOWNS.

Typical fairs lasted anywhere from one day to several weeks. They took place at fixed times of the year, usually during a holy season or at the beginning of a religious holiday. Located at national frontiers or at boundaries between provinces or counties, fairs also served an important social function. They were a source of amusement and entertainment and allowed people from distant places to meet, socialize, and share news.

Fairs were sometimes called markets. However, markets and fairs were not the same. Markets were local and focused more on the buying and selling of goods to individuals. Fairs, held less frequently, drew people from long distances, particularly merchants who bought and sold foreign goods. Because different currencies were used and the value of money constantly varied, money changers were needed to weigh coins, verify their authenticity, and estimate their value.

Merchants from the same town or region often banded together to ensure their safety and increase their profits. They chose leaders to protect their interests. Disagreements would arise, but local authorities provided courts and judges to settle disputes in a timely manner. To attract foreign merchants, local rulers also provided other services and privileges. They waived or reduced taxes and tolls and offered protection against theft, arrest, or mistreatment. They sometimes provided armed guards, not only within the fairgrounds but also along roads leading to a fair. By guaranteeing order and protection to merchants, the rulers helped fairs grow.

Islamic, Byzantine, and Slavic Fairs.   The Arabs and Byzantines were experienced traders from the start of the Middle Ages. The warlike bedouin* tribesmen before the time of MUHAMMAD had held fairs in Arabia at religious festivals and at other times of peace. However, during most of the Middle Ages, Muslim traders conducted commerce on a regular basis in large cities where shops and markets were open for business most of the time.

Islamic rulers permitted subject peoples to hold fairs, in which Muslims participated as well. In Jerusalem, for example, a Christian fair was held each September at the feast of the Exaltation of the Cross. In 680, the fair was described as "an important gathering of different peoples coming from everywhere to trade."

Muslim pilgrimages also involved considerable trade. Mecca, the religious capital of the Islamic world, served as a huge fair for the many thousands of Muslims who gathered there during the hajj*. Buying and selling continued for a week after the religious ceremonies ended. A visitor to Mecca in the 1100s wrote about goods from North Africa, Ethiopia, Yemen, Iraq, India, and many other places: "At this fair, enough merchandise is sold in one day so that if it were divided among all the countries of the world it would create well-patronized markets."

As in the Islamic world, most commerce in the BYZANTINE EMPIRE took place in the permanent trading centers of CONSTANTINOPLE and other cities. However, international fairs on the frontiers facilitated trade. Places where Greeks and Muslims exchanged prisoners also became fair sites. At these sites, Greek merchants bought raw silk, silk cloth, and perfumes from the East.

Several of the best attended Byzantine fairs remained active until the Turkish invasions. Trebizond on the southern shore of the Black Sea attracted merchants from as far away as GENOA and VENICE in Italy and the Indies in distant East Asia. The Trebizond fairs remained popular through the 1300s. A fair at the port of Thessaloniki on the Aegean Sea attracted large numbers of merchants until the OTTOMANS captured the city in 1430.

Trade routes through the east European lands of the SLAVS connected the Byzantine and Muslim worlds in the south with Scandinavia to the north. The fair sites where Slavic and foreign merchants exchanged goods often grew into fortified towns. At least 25 of the 35 towns in KIEVAN RUS in

* **bedouin** nomadic Arab(s) of the deserts, especially in Arabia

* **hajj** pilgrimage to Mecca that Muslims are required to make once in their lifetime

the year 1000 had begun as trading centers. The two largest—Kiev and NOVGOROD—had quarters for German, Jewish, Armenian, and Scandinavian merchants. The prince of Kiev regularly sent boats full of slaves, fur, and honey down the Dnieper River to Constantinople to exchange them for silk, spices, and wine.

Invasions by Turks and Mongols in the 1200s isolated these Russian trading centers. Novgorod became the only "window open to the West" until Moscow replaced it as the center of the Russian fur trade. Russian traders rarely visited other countries, but foreign merchants traded at local fairs deep in Russian territory.

European Fairs and Markets.   Like the Arabs and the Byzantines, the ancient Romans of the west had cities with permanent facilities for trade. When Rome fell to Germanic invaders in the 400s, however, the old rural fairs or markets of the barbarians were all that was left. What trade took place was over short distances because of the dangers of traveling in western Europe. Gradually, however, the Frankish kings established greater order, and larger fairs began to take place.

Early fairs were largely agricultural and featured the selling of grain, vegetables, wool, leather, and animals. Later, the fairs more and more saw commerce in manufactured and imported products. The oldest European fair—the October fair of St. Denis, just north of Paris, France—is known to have been in existence in the 700s, during the rule of the Frankish MEROVINGIAN dynasty. Organized by the local monastery, it was able to attract many foreign merchants. In the early years, red dyes from Asia were among the goods sold there. The fair was so successful that later another one was organized for the month of June, and merchants began to visit St. Denis twice yearly.

Leaders in other places, too, began to organize cycles of fairs. For example, in the 1100s and 1200s, a series of fairs was conducted at Bruges, Ypres, Lille, Torhout, and Messines in FLANDERS. These were arranged so that between them they covered the entire year. Goods sold included wool, lead, copper, and tin from England; iron from Spain; and quantities of French and Rhine wine.

The famous fairs of CHAMPAGNE were also arranged in a cycle. They served as international centers of European commerce, credit, and currency exchange and as models for other fairs in France and other parts of Europe. International French fairs had long histories in Lyons and Chalon, and important regional fairs were held in Normandy, Brittany, Languedoc, and other parts of France.

The growing cities of Flanders and northern France gradually made their temporary fairs less necessary. The tradition of fairs moved to other, less advanced areas. In the 1300s, Frankfurt became a well-known site for fairs in Germany. At its fairs in the spring and fall, one could find goods from England, Scandinavia, Russia, and Asia. In the 1400s, Leipzig became an important center for the exchange of industrial products from the West and raw materials from the East. After the invention of printing, the Leipzig fairs also became a market for books.

Other western European nations also had notable fairs. Before 1100, Pavia in northern Italy had two great fairs, each two weeks long. The fairs were held near the monastery of St. Martin outside the town. The goods

Remember: *Words in small capital letters have separate entries, and the index at the end of Volume 4 will guide you to more information on many topics.*

traded included tin, copper, iron, silver, weapons, furs, wool, linen, silk cloth, ivory, spices, and slaves. In Spain under Muslim rule, there were apparently no fairs, but after the Christian reconquest, fairs sprang up throughout the peninsula. In London, England, merchants displaying goods at the three-day St. Bartholemew's monastery fair could build their booths in the safety of a walled cemetery. The fair soon outgrew the monastery, however. In Skanör near the southern tip of Sweden, there was a huge fish fair during two weeks in late August. People came from all parts of Europe, and by the end of the 1300s, more than 200,000 barrels of herring were sold there each year.

Family

Families in the Middle Ages differed widely from place to place and from social class to social class—as they do now. Family styles in Byzantine eastern Europe, the Islamic world, and Jewish communities across the medieval world shared certain similarities, whereas the family style in western Europe had separate characteristics among nobles, middle class, and peasants.

The Byzantine World

In the Byzantine Empire of Constantinople, family life was protected by the power of the state and by the Christian church, both of which the emperor headed. Such protection was practical; the economy was in many ways built on the family unit. In the early Middle Ages, Byzantine agriculture relied on independent peasant families, and later on, peasants who rented land from larger landowners. Many other trades—for example, the manufacture of cloth—also depended on family enterprise.

Nature of the Family.   The typical Byzantine family was small, consisting of a father and a mother and their children. This is the type of family most common in the West today, called a nuclear family. It can be contrasted with the extended family, the larger group of relatives that people today generally interact with more rarely: grandparents, uncles and aunts, and cousins.

Extended families also played a part in Byzantine society, especially among aristocratic families, which used marriage to advance their political fortunes. For example, the Byzantine emperor Alexios I KOMNENOS came to power in 1081, first through the help of his immediate family and then through his relations by marriage. Peasants also often worked their land as extended families to increase their productivity. Some extended families lived together, including unmarried cousins or uncles and perhaps the orphans of deceased relatives. But family units most commonly consisted of from four to eight people—the father, the mother, and unmarried children.

The father was the head of the household and manager of the family's finances. The family's name usually was inherited from him, though sometimes the mother's name could be used. The mother was primarily responsible for raising the children. Her role was valued—Byzantine society insisted that the children owed her honor and obedience.

In the early years of the Byzantine Empire, parents, particularly fathers, had great authority over the family and their children. This authority began to weaken in the medieval period, however. Once a child married or achieved financial independence, he or she was no longer under the control of parents.

Laws About the Family.   The state regarded supporting the family unit as a very important task. A law code issued in 741, called the *Ecloga,* is the most important body of laws concerning the Byzantine family. It recognized and protected the nuclear family as the basic economic unit.

Church law was also very specific on the topic of marriage. According to the declaration of an early pope, Leo VI (886–912), marriage was a gift of God given to humankind for the purpose of continuing the species. This was supportive of the state's needs; during many periods infant mortality was high, and the Byzantine Empire suffered from a labor shortage.

Marriages were arranged through an agreement between both sets of parents, though the partners also had to give their mutual consent. The legal age for marriage was set by the *Ecloga* at 15 for a boy and 13 for a girl. However, the age for consenting to a marriage was 7 years and could be even lower in western parts of the empire. Because dedication to a monastic life could not occur until the age of 10, this early age of consent encouraged people to arrange for their children to marry rather than to devote themselves to a celibate* life.

* **celibate** unmarried

Byzantine law was strict with regard to divorce. A woman could divorce her husband only if he failed to consummate the marriage within three years after the marriage celebration, if he tried to kill her, or if he were a leper*. A man could divorce his wife if she committed adultery, tried to kill him, or were a leper. Neither the husband's adultery nor madness was seen as sufficient cause for dissolving a marriage.

* **leper** person who has leprosy

The church also frowned on remarriage. However, because of the importance of having children in the Byzantine Empire, an exception was often made for childless people. They were permitted to marry a second or even a third time, especially if they were young.

The Family and Property.   According to the *Ecloga,* marriage created a unity of persons and goods. The basis of a family's property consisted of the woman's dowry* and the man's marriage gift to his wife. The law protected inheritance of property within a family.

* **dowry** money or property that a woman brings to the man she marries

The dowry could not be sold during the marriage unless poverty was threatening the lives of the children. When a husband died, his wife acquired ownership and control over the family property. The children of the marriage became the first heirs. Finally, if property had to be sold to support the children or because there was no heir, members of the extended family were often the legally preferred buyers. The family holdings were preserved, even if they went to a different branch.

The Islamic World

The family had a very special significance in Islam. As in the Byzantine Christian world, families were encouraged for the purpose of producing children. This was an important Islamic value. Families also cooperated to provide economic support for the traders and wage earners who made Muslim society so successful. But more than Christianity, Islam honored the personal companionship that families provided.

Nature of the Family. In ARABIA before the start of Islam, people centered their lives on the clan or tribe. A clan was more than an extended family. It was a large group of related families whose members supported one another, often warring with neighboring clans. Clans were more important than families for survival and success.

However, under Islam, the concept of a single community of the faithful developed, known as the *umma.* All Muslims were equal under God—men and women alike. This reduced clan rivalries. Islam considered the family the basic unit of society, and marriage relationships flourished.

Though Islam did not encourage celibacy, like Christianity it urged chastity* among the unmarried. One important purpose of marriage was to produce offspring; the birth of children was greeted with great celebration. Polygamy* was even permitted, but it was common only among rulers and among the wealthy.

Marriage was valued for another reason too. The QUR'AN, the Muslim holy book, praised God for creating men and women because, though different, both are capable of love and mercy. In addition to sex and children, marriage enabled them to enjoy *sakina,* a term meaning psychological comfort and gratifying companionship. Good moral conduct was more important in a wife than her physical beauty or wealth, and fathers were advised to choose God-fearing husbands for their daughters. Great rewards were promised in paradise to the husband who was kind to his wife and who faithfully supported her.

Islam established guidelines for married couples to ensure family harmony and stability. The husband was the head of the family and was responsible for supporting it, even if his wife was wealthy. A good wife owed her husband respect and obedience. Women usually stayed home to look after the children, but if their household chores required them to go out, they could. Privileged women tended to stay at home and out of the public eye. When they did venture outside the home, they covered their faces with veils. Peasant women, who had to work, observed modesty by showing nothing of themselves except their faces and hands.

Children were important in Muslim families and were supported by their father until they reached maturity. For a son, this meant coming of age. For a daughter, it meant being married. In return for parental support, children owed obedience and respect. Aging parents with no money of their own became the responsibility of the children.

Brothers and sisters owed each other respect, and a needy sibling was the responsibility of his or her better-off siblings. Other children in the household—for example, the orphans of relatives—might be taken care of but could not be adopted. They retained their old family names. Ties of respect also extended to grandparents, grandchildren, aunts, uncles, and cousins—in fact, to any member of the extended family.

Laws About the Family. Islam permitted the marriage of first cousins, even though it forbade marriage to other close blood relations. The less related a potential wife or husband was, the better. Racially mixed marriages were common and approved.

Family members usually arranged a marriage. The groom's family asked the girl's relatives for her hand. The girl was always asked for her consent; silence was normally taken as a shy agreement. Next a marriage

* **chastity** purity in conduct and intention; abstention from sexual intercourse

* **polygamy** marriage in which either spouse may have more than one mate at the same time

contract was prepared, in which the bride was offered to the groom and a dowry was specified. The groom and bride were thus united by marriage contract as husband and wife. Finally there was a festive wedding celebration involving rich clothing, a procession, and a banquet. The newly married couple might live in either the husband's or the wife's house.

In pre-Islamic days, women were often treated badly and sometimes were completely ignored or abandoned by their husbands. Under Islam, however, a woman had full human and legal rights. She could own property, and the dowry belonged to her. Ordinarily, only men had the right to divorce, but in her marriage contract a woman could specify the right to divorce her husband at will. If she did not do this, she could still apply in court for divorce on the grounds of cruelty or failure by her husband to support her.

The Qur'an recommended that marital disputes should, however, be settled between representatives of the husband and the wife. Only if a husband and wife could not settle their differences could a fair divorce settlement be made.

The Family and Property. The family in Islam was an economic unit as well as a biological and social one. Each family member contributed to the economic well-being of the group by cooking, spinning, food gathering, farming, trading, or working for wages. In the event of a husband's or a wife's death, the surviving spouse as well as his or her parents and children would share in the wealth left behind. If there was no surviving male offspring, the shares of the deceased's estate could be parceled out to grandparents, siblings, nephews, or cousins and other relations.

Western Europe

In contrast to the Byzantine and Islamic worlds, in which the nuclear family played a key role, western European life in the Middle Ages revolved around a much larger group. In fact, the word *family* comes from the Latin word *familia,* which means household. The household was often even larger than an extended family. Its head was usually the father, but the family included parents, distant relatives, loyal friends, and servants. The term *family* also meant one's house, kin, or lineage. In general, the wealthier the family, the larger the household.

Early Western households were crude and not at all private, even for wealthy people. In ANGLO-SAXON England, for example, the hall or main building was the focus of family life. It held long tables and benches where family members, friends, guests, and retainers* ate and entertained. Male guests slept on straw mattresses on the floor of the hall. Women of the family had as their living space separate small buildings outside the hall. There, they slept, talked, and spun into thread the raw wool they had sheared from sheep. The thread would be crafted by these "spinsters" into cloth and eventually made into clothing for the entire household. The women of the household were also responsible for cooking, brewing, and baking. In addition, they made the candles, soaps, dyes, and medicines that would be used by the entire household.

Children received little attention until they were about seven years old since so many of them died. At that age, they were considered ready to be trained. Then they learned largely practical skills. Boys practiced athletic feats, such as running, jumping, throwing the spear and javelin,

---

> **Remember:** Consult the index at the end of Volume 4 to find more information on many topics.

See color plate 2, vol. 1.

* **retainer** person attached or owing service to a household; a servant

and hunting and fishing. Girls learned household skills and by the age of ten were expected to know how to run a household. Few children received any formal education unless they were destined for the church.

feudalism social, economic, and political system of western Europe in the Middle Ages in which vassals gave service to their lord in return for his protection and the use of the land

manor farming estate, usually with a house for the lord and a village for the local farmworkers

Later Medieval Families: Nobles.   Under feudalism*, life in the castles and manor* houses of the later Middle Ages was more civilized than life in the early Germanic halls. Castles started as rough fortresses meant mainly for war, but later, like the smaller unfortified manors, they became suitable for comfortable living. A great hall was still maintained as the center of hospitality, but the castle had many separate chambers called closets for the lord and the lady, the children, guests, and household members.

Many rooms were needed since the household could be huge. In the late 1200s, for example, the household of a minor aristocrat included a steward, a clerk, a chaplain, a marshal, butlers, several kinds of cooks, porters, bakers, brewers, and blacksmiths as well as servants to help in the laundry and kitchen. Each household worker had an assistant, usually a young boy or girl. Most of these officials and their servants lived under the same roof as the lord and the lady and were thus members of the "family."

The responsibility of running the household, managing production, maintaining adequate supplies, and keeping track of expenses and income belonged to the lady of the castle or manor. She was expected to have a knowledge of accounting and to know which rents and feudal fees were owed to the household. Medieval manors were partially self-sufficient. They produced crops and other goods that could either be used on the estate by the household itself or, if a surplus existed, sold at market. Medieval aristocrats moved from one manor or castle to another when the supplies of a residence were exhausted. The lady of the household was responsible for organizing the move of the household's belongings.

Later Medieval Families: Middle Class.   Middle-class families, consisting of a master and a mistress, lived in towns and carried on trades with the help of their children, apprentices, and servants. If they were wealthy, they might have country estates, but they spent most of their time in the city where their businesses were located. Merchant families of the 1300s lived in three-story town houses that were the city equivalent of the manor house. They had a garden in back of the house for growing fruits, vegetables, and herbs. The ground floor of the house contained a salesroom or workshop with a warehouse behind it. On the second floor was the main hall for entertaining, with an adjoining kitchen. The third floor contained the sleeping chambers.

Home life and business were closely related for a medieval merchant. Many merchants taught their trades to their wives and children, who would usually inherit the business. In addition to his wife and children, a merchant often had an apprentice living in his home. This young person—usually about 12 or 13—was brought up by his master as a member of the family. The apprentice lived with the master for 7 to 10 years and learned the master's trade.

A middle-class wife ran the household and helped her husband in his trade. Sometimes she practiced a trade of her own, even if there was no economic reason for her to do so. In England, Dame Elizabeth Stokton manufactured cloth, and Margery KEMPE brewed ale even though she was the daughter of a mayor and the wife of a well-to-do merchant.

The nature of the family during the Middle Ages varied greatly, much as it does today. Marriage was a valued family institution in all cultures and social classes. This marriage scene is from the "Collection of Devotional Treaties," written in France about 1375.

Later Medieval Families: Peasants.   Peasant families in medieval western Europe most closely resembled the modern nuclear family. Since they were too poor to support any servants and their cottages were too small to have other relatives living with them, the household consisted only of the mother, the father, and children. A peasant's house was a rough, one-room dwelling. Walls were made of mud, twigs, or plaster, and roofs were thatched or constructed of wood shingles. The hearth was the centerpiece of the room. This is where the wife cooked the food, and where the family huddled for warmth. Furnishings were sparse, and the family usually slept on straw mattresses, sometimes sharing the same one. There was little privacy.

Women and children tended crops in gardens or worked in the fields gathering grain. They took care of the farm animals. Men made tools and furniture, plowed the fields, and built and repaired their dwellings.

The Lives of Children.   Regardless of class—noble, merchant, or peasant—members of western European medieval families were rarely close to each other emotionally. Parents were unsentimental about their children. They devoted little time to raising them, and the children quickly became part of the adult world. There was no prolonged period of growing up. During the early Middle Ages, children were under the complete control of their fathers until they reached the age of 12. At that age, boys were allowed to bear arms. They became freemen—that is, responsible to the law in their own right.

Later, under the feudal system, the age of majority for boys was raised to 15. Girls came of age at 12 but were not given as much personal or legal freedom as boys. Girls' main role was to marry and raise children. They especially hoped for sons, who would continue the family name and inherit their husband's property.

Aristocratic children probably had the least contact with their parents. Until about age seven, they were raised by nurses. Then they were judged capable of being trained and were usually sent to the homes of other noble families or churchmen to be educated. Young boys learned to perform various services for the nobleman, such as waiting on table, and, later, when they were older, caring for arms and horses. In return for their services, the boys had a chance to observe courtly life and to make good connections. Young girls were trained as ladies-in-waiting. Under the guidance of the lady of the house, they learned to spin, weave, embroider, sew, make clothing, dress wounds, and prepare cosmetics and medicines from herbs. They also learned to sing, dance, play music, and, in some cases, to read and write. The young girl's purpose in the household of a noble family, however, was, first and foremost, to find a suitable husband.

Middle-class children were also frequently sent away from home. If a merchant did not teach his children his own trade, he usually apprenticed them to another one. Some middle-class children attended school before their apprenticeship* began. These schools were often founded by the GUILDS to which the fathers belonged. Both boys and girls could attend elementary schools, where they learned to read and write. But only boys attended grammar schools, where Latin was taught. Once apprenticed to a master, an apprentice looked to him for his training and moral education. Boys could be beaten by their master for bad behavior, though they could protest a master's ill treatment as long as they could prove it. Generally, children were taught to be docile and obedient and to respect authority. The proverb "spare the rod and spoil the child" was popular in the Middle Ages.

Peasant children were the most likely to grow up in their parents' homes. However, their parents had few special skills and little time to give them any education. Occasionally, a village priest might teach a promising lad some Latin or even send him to a local school. But most peasant children grew up illiterate and began working at an early age.

Law and the Family.   Unlike Constantinople and the Muslim world, western Europe had a wide variety of different legal traditions. The customs of the different barbarian tribes exerted a strong influence. So did the laws of the Roman world that the barbarians had conquered. Finally, the Christian church brought another set of ideas about the family to western Europe.

The tribal tradition made the kinship group—the larger extended family, similar to the Arab clan—an important institution of private law. But a child did not become a member of the kinship group unless he or she was acknowledged by his or her father. The early medieval family was governed by the father, who had great power over his children. He could beat them, sell them into slavery, place them in a monastery or convent, or pledge them in marriage. Under the later feudal system, a similar power, though even greater, was in the hands of the feudal lord.

A father's power over a child came to an end when the child reached majority. This was usually 12, and later 15, for boys and 12 (regarded as a marriageable age) for girls. At that point, a young person became independent. The event was important because it established the person as a free, responsible individual who could set up a new household.

* **apprenticed** placed in the care of a merchant or craftsman to learn a profession

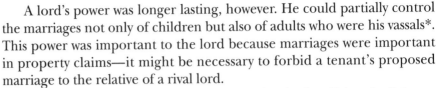

* **vassal** person given land by a lord or monarch in return for loyalty and services

A lord's power was longer lasting, however. He could partially control the marriages not only of children but also of adults who were his vassals*. This power was important to the lord because marriages were important in property claims—it might be necessary to forbid a tenant's proposed marriage to the relative of a rival lord.

Intervention in marriages—like intervention in the affairs of religion—brought the traditional system of law into conflict with the Christian church. Christianity held that marriage was a sacrament blessed by God and should be under the supervision of bishops. So the church sometimes challenged the right of a lord to control marital decisions. It put more emphasis on the personal rather than the property side of marriage. As the church gained influence, this placed more stress on the nuclear family in the West.

Marriage and Property.   Among the Germanic tribes, women were at first under the power of their fathers. After they married, they came under the power of their husbands. Even in this subservient position, a woman did have some rights. She remained a member of her own kinship group and could call upon kindred if her husband mistreated her. Her kin could intervene if her husband injured her or divorced her unjustly. In addition, her personal property descended to her female heirs.

* **fief** under feudalism, property of value (usually land) that a person held under obligations of loyalty to an overlord

Under feudalism, women's rights to inherit property were restricted in favor of male heirs. Feudal lords needed to be able to give fiefs* of land to their vassals to secure their services. Any additional landholdings were usually left to the oldest son. Only if there were no male heirs could a daughter inherit an estate. Even then, her husband would acquire her property and total control over her dowry. Marriages to the only daughters of landowners were thus important property transactions. In addition, if a woman was widowed, she had to receive her overlord's permission to inherit. Neither could she any longer be the legal guardian of her own children. She relinquished this right, too, to her overlord.

Although the legal position of noblewomen worsened under feudalism, their treatment by men ironically improved. The COURTLY LOVE tradition, influenced partly by the Muslim world of Spain, spread into the south of France and then entered the mainstream of CHIVALRY, encouraging men to refine their manners and to respect women. Life in the feudal castle or manor house became more civilized and afforded women more privacy.

Middle-class women could sometimes be more fortunate, gaining legal advantages that even men did not share. For example, a married woman in business could either take full responsibility for her actions or place that responsibility upon her husband. In London in the 1300s, an act of Parliament allowed women freedom to choose as many trades as they wished, whereas men were restricted to one. Business life also allowed medieval women independence. City women were involved in a wide variety of trades and were able to earn a good living. They also had personal liberty and could move about freely.

Jewish Families

The Jewish people in the Middle Ages were scattered. Driven from Palestine by Christians and then by Muslims, they had been forced to settle in many different environments, and they were generally not allowed to own land. This caused them to become traders and scholars rather than farmers. In many aspects, their lives were strongly influenced by the customs of

See
color plate 4,
vol. 1.

the nations in which they lived. While Jewish clothing, books, and other visible elements in their lives followed different styles in the different places they moved to, their family relationships show a striking uniformity regardless of where they settled.

In general, traditional family customs were very male centered. Men could take more than one wife in most places and could keep all the property of a wife after her death. Other Jewish laws also appeared to favor men over women, sons over daughters. Sons were usually the only children to be educated outside the home. Daughters were not heirs unless special legal documents were drawn up for them. Husbands had the right of "correction" or wife beating, though this was disallowed in western Europe. Divorce laws were far more restrictive for women than they were for men. A widow could be required to marry one of the brothers of her late husband, so that her property would stay in the family.

Local laws affected some details of their family customs. In Babylonia, divorce was permissible, and a Jewish bride had to be given away by her father even if she was old enough to be independent. In Toledo, Spain, a surviving husband could inherit only half of his wife's estate, not all of it. These laws reflected the laws of the regions in which people lived. There were, however, great similarities in Jewish family life in all areas, owing to the importance of family life in the Jewish religion, and of religion in the life of the Jewish communities.

Jewish women in the Middle Ages, like women of other religious faiths, often held much higher status than the law suggests. Both in economic life and in religion, they were able on occasion to enter "the world of men," owning capital and learning the Scriptures and the law. (*See also* **Clothing; Feudalism; Nobility and Nobles; Women, Role of.**)

Famine

Food shortages, hunger, and starvation were a recurrent threat during the Middle Ages in both western Europe and the Islamic world. Famine was a major factor influencing population growth during much of the Middle Ages.

In western Europe—which relied primarily on grains, especially wheat, for its food source—bad weather caused wheat crop failures and famine. Too much or too little rainfall was enough to ruin a grain harvest. If the crop failure was extensive or prolonged, hunger, famine, and starvation followed.

In the Islamic world, irregular rainfall and not enough river water for irrigating fields were the main causes of famine, especially along the Nile River in Egypt and along the Tigris and Euphrates Rivers in Iraq and Syria. Other factors that contributed to famine in the Islamic world and in Europe were excessive heat or cold, sudden storms, invasions by foreign armies or bands of raiders, and governments that cared or did little about the problem.

Famine in Western Europe

The heavy reliance of medieval agriculture on grain—especially wheat—made large areas of Europe and England prone to famine. Wheat was widely regarded as the grain that made the healthiest and tastiest bread.

Food in Towns and Cities.   Providing a steady supply of wheat and other foodstuffs to their people was a constant struggle for city governments. Since large towns and cities had to import most of their perishable foods over long distances, townspeople were among the first to feel the impact of crop failures.

The methods that towns and cities used to acquire and distribute food varied. Members of the HANSEATIC LEAGUE in northern Europe stored grain supplies in warehouses in special parts of the city. Cities in the Netherlands sent agents to France, Germany, and the BALTIC COUNTRIES to buy promises of future grain crops. Towns and cities in Italy tried to maintain political control of the surrounding countryside in order to guarantee their food supplies, but large cities such as GENOA, VENICE, and FLORENCE had to rely on distant markets as well.

Because it was landlocked, Florence could not import food by sea the way Genoa and Venice did, and its food-supply problems were among the most difficult in Europe. From 1100 to 1348, the city suffered at least 30 serious food shortages. The famine in 1329 was so severe that one chronicler* reported that at the city's San Michele market "it was necessary to protect the officials by means of guards fitted out with an axe and block to punish rioters on the spot with the loss of their hands and feet."

Venice—perhaps medieval Europe's best-run government—used its impressive naval power to transport grain supplies from distant places. Its extensive sea capability gave Venice control of the coastal areas of the Adriatic Sea, the eastern Mediterranean, and the Black Sea (an outlet for grain from southern Russia). The Venetian city government kept grain prices stable by supplying the city with grain whenever supplies dropped below a certain level. When a wheat shortage occurred in northern Italy in 1268, Venetian ships were able to obtain sufficient supplies in distant Crimea. In the neighboring city of MILAN, another landlocked city, wheat prices shot up 150 percent in two months.

Venice also used grain as a weapon of war. In 1273, the Venetians won their war with Bologna by buying up all the surplus wheat in northern Italy and forcing the starving Bolognese to surrender. In 1380, Venice used a similar tactic to defeat Genoa.

Famine in the Early Middle Ages.   Major famines were rare in the early Middle Ages. Food shortages were mostly limited to local areas and were more the result of poor food distribution than crop failure.

From about 530 to 600, however, famine and plague hit large parts of Europe. GREGORY OF TOURS wrote about a series of famines that struck BURGUNDY between 530 and 570. In Germany, the search for food drove the LOMBARDS south into Italy in the 550s and the 590s. Northern and central France suffered widespread famine in 585. Lombard invasions and severe flooding brought famine to northern Italian towns in the 570s and the 590s. Pope GREGORY I had to double the amount of alms* to the poor and hungry in ROME during these years. The study of the bones of Lombards who lived through these famines showed that they suffered from long-term malnutrition.

Between the late 500s and the year 800, few major famines struck Europe. The 800s, however, marked the beginning of a long period of crop failures, food shortages, hunger, and starvation. Invasions by VIKINGS, Muslims, and Magyars disrupted food production and distribution in Europe.

* **chronicler** person who records events in the order in which they occurred

* **alms** money or gifts given to help the poor and suffering

The Four Horsemen of the Apocalypse are allegorical figures from the New Testament Book of Revelation. They represent conquest, war, famine, and death, some of the hardships that humans will have to endure before the end of the world. The four horsemen, each riding a different color horse, often appear in art and literature. This woodcut was made by German artist Albrecht Dürer in 1496–1498. Famine appears at the center, holding a set of balances to weigh "a measure of wheat for a penny."

* **relic** object cherished for its association with a martyr or saint

* **gallows** wooden structure consisting of a crossbeam on two upright poles, used for hanging criminals

At the same time, it is possible that new plant diseases began to appear. Between 857 and 950, about 20 major famines hit Europe. They were severe enough that the increased local death rates and lowered birthrates in the regions affected led to an overall decline in the growth rate of the population of Europe.

During this time of famine, allegations appeared that starving people ate human flesh to stay alive. One chronicler writing about conditions in ARAGON observed, "Destitution at last reached such a pitch that men began to devour each other and the flesh of a son was preferred to his love." All over Europe, there were reports of human flesh—called "two-legged mutton"—for sale. An Austrian who claimed to have tried it said that the human meat tasted salty, like pork.

Although famines decreased in the late 900s, they returned again in the 1030s, when excessive rainfall caused a series of poor harvests that led to widespread food shortages across Europe. Hungry hordes came to monasteries to beg for food. In 1033, the monastery of Cluny in eastern France distributed carcasses of salt pork to 16,000 people, while the monks of St. Benoît-sur-Loire fed 600 beggars on a single day. Human flesh was said to be for sale in France in 1032 and 1033. One chronicler described in vivid detail the different grades and prices of human flesh that was supposedly being sold in butcher stalls in Burgundy. In the 1040s, when crops failed in northern Europe for three successive years, reports of cannibalism (the eating of human flesh) surfaced again. Starving people were also reported to be eating dirt in order to fill their stomachs.

The famines ended in the mid-1000s as the weather improved, the economy grew stronger, and political stability increased. Not only was the weather generally more favorable for agriculture, but the transportation of food improved with the use of pack mules, sturdier carts, and advances in bridge construction. Between 1046 and the early 1200s, major food shortages declined and famines became less frequent. Those that occurred were limited to local areas. The coming of colder, wetter weather, however, brought a new series of major famines that crippled Europe during the 1300s.

Famine Crisis in the 1300s.   A series of unusually wet growing seasons in the early 1300s caused widespread crop failures and food shortages. The years of especially heavy rain that began in 1315 produced the worst decade of famine in European history, as England, France, the Low Countries, and Germany suffered widespread starvation. The chronicler Guillaume de Nangis reported seeing people "barefooted, and many even, except for women, in a completely nude state, together with their priests coming in procession at the Church of the Holy Martyrs, devoutly carrying bodies of saints and other relics* to be adored."

The worst years for Europe's cities were 1315 to 1317. Ypres lost 10 percent of its people to famine in 1316, while in BRUGES the death rate was about 15 percent. German chronicles reported that soldiers had to stand guard at the gallows* in COLOGNE, Mainz, and Strasbourg to prevent desperately hungry people from cutting down the corpses and eating them. People in England reportedly ate dogs, cats, and "unclean things." The spread of typhoid fever, dysentery, and diphtheria increased the human death rate, while other diseases drastically reduced the number of livestock.

Europe's famine crisis continued in some regions until the BLACK DEATH in 1348 killed a third of the population. With far fewer mouths to feed, the demand for food decreased, and food shortages eased between 1351 and 1500. In addition, more moderate precipitation levels and temperatures helped end the crisis.

Famine in the Islamic World

During the Middle Ages, famines played a major role in the Islamic world as well. Although local food shortages were common, medieval chroniclers tended to record only the major famines. Between 661 and 1500, they reported approximately 186 massive food shortages. Because the episodes of widespread hunger that followed military invasions were not included, however, the actual number of famines was far greater.

Major Famines.   The worst famines in the Islamic world were in Egypt, Syria, and Iraq, but they also occurred in North Africa, Muslim Spain, and other areas. Because agriculture in Egypt depended on the flooding of the Nile River to irrigate cropland, an insufficient or irregular flow of river water led to crop failure and to famine. In Iraq and Syria, crop failure was caused more by inadequate rain or snow. Elsewhere in the Islamic world, drought, windstorms, hail, and excessive heat or cold brought on the crop failures that led to famine and starvation.

Famine, however, occurred not only because of bad weather and drought. Locusts, worms, rats, and other pests had a devastating effect on crops. In addition, invading armies, raids by desert tribes, the movement of grain supplies by merchants and governments, and epidemics* among animals that caused shortages of meat and dairy products also played a significant role. Often, famine resulted in the spread of epidemic diseases among humans that caused even more deaths.

* **epidemic** disease that affects a large number of people or animals

Most Muslims lived from day to day without much in the way of reserve food supplies, and crop failure meant immediate hunger and eventual starvation. The widespread fear of starvation is reflected in the Qur'an*, where famine is referred to as a punishment for nonbelievers.

* **Qur'an** book of the holy scriptures of Islam

Consequences of Famine.   Famine influenced everyday life, as people left their homes and villages to look for food. Many peasants went to cities and towns, where food reserves were greater. In times of famine, bands of hungry people roamed the countryside looking for food or items that could be exchanged for food. Death and dislocation disrupted family relations and normal social life. As hungry people became more desperate, incidents of theft, murder, prostitution, and the sale of children—as well as accusations of cannibalism—increased. Islamic chroniclers reported at least 22 instances of people eating human flesh. Suffering from the effects of starvation, people died in the streets or behind their plows. Work animals also died or were slaughtered for food.

Famines slowed the pace of economic activity. Markets, shops, and mosques closed, and food prices skyrocketed. Peasants and artisans worked less because there was less demand for their work, and income and production dropped. The most vivid description of a famine in the Islamic world comes from Abd al-Latif, a BAGHDAD physician who lived in CAIRO from 1194 to 1204. He described a famine that occurred after two successive years of drought in the Nile valley. Many peasants migrated to the cities or left Egypt entirely after the first year, thus making labor harder to find and more costly. Most villages could not irrigate their fields properly because there were not enough people around to help trap the floodwater on the land.

During the PLAGUE that struck during the sowing season of 1202, peasants died in the fields, and military landowners used their troops to farm the land. In the cities, mosques conducted mass funerals. Processions with bodies clogged the roads to the cemeteries. Many corpses lay unburied in homes or by the sides of roads. People deserted their homes and shops, and many had to burn their furniture to fire their stoves. Religious fervor increased, and public prayers for relief from the famine increased. People prayed to Muslim saints for help, and many turned to MAGIC.

Crime rose as desperation increased. Travelers were murdered, and desperate women sold themselves as prostitutes or slaves. On Roda Island in the Nile River near Cairo, hungry bands are said to have hunted down human beings to eat their flesh. There were reports of parents eating their children, doctors eating their patients, and people selling and buying human flesh. Those believed to have committed such crimes were, if caught, burned alive, but few were ever caught.

Famine had an enormous impact on physical and mental health. Hunger often triggered epidemics of typhoid fever and typhus, and malnutrition decreased fertility. Inadequate food was especially damaging to children because it made them susceptible to tuberculosis, diphtheria, measles, diarrheal infections, and rickets. When governments were unstable or ineffective, the famines lasted longer and were more widespread. For example, if the government levied heavy taxes on agriculture, peasants were driven off the land, and irrigation systems were neglected, thus worsening the effects of the famine.

After 1000, an increase in the number of food shortages and famines throughout the Islamic world contributed greatly to political, economic, and social decline in the Muslim world in the late Middle Ages. (*See also* **Agriculture; Climate, Influence on History; Food and Drink; Medicine.**)

Farabi, al-

ca. 873–950
Islamic philosopher
and music theorist

* **Neoplatonism** philosophical system that combines Plato's ideas with elements of Eastern mysticism and Judaic and Christian concepts

Abu Nasr al-Farabi was born in Transoxiana, in western Asia, around 873. His father took him to BAGHDAD, where he studied philosophy, logic, and music theory. Al-Farabi's main interest was in the relationship between logic and language. His teachers included Yuhanna ibn Haylan, a well-respected logician, and Ibn al-Sarraj, an expert in Arabic grammar. In 942, al-Farabi settled in Damascus, Syria, where he lived in relative seclusion.

Although few facts about his life are known, al-Farabi's influence on Arabic thought has been widely accepted. Most of his written commentaries concerned the writings of ARISTOTLE and, to a lesser degree, PLATO. His own philosophy was a version of Neoplatonism*, which he presented in such works as *Tahsil al-Sa'adah (The Attainment of Happiness)*. In al-Farabi's view, the world flows from God in the form of ideas or "intelligences," from which levels of existence flow until the material world is created. Happiness is attained when an individual's soul is in harmony with creation.

Al-Farabi based his theories of Islamic political institutions and religious sciences on the writings of Plato, especially the *Republic* and *Laws*. He influenced several later Islamic philosophers, including IBN SINA and IBN RUSHD, and the Jewish philosopher MAIMONIDES. Several of al-Farabi's works were translated into Latin and studied by medieval scholars and philosophers of the Italian Renaissance.

Abu Nasr al-Farabi is also considered the foremost music scholar in the history of Islam. In his most important work on music theory, *Kitab al-musiqa al-kabir (Grand Book of Music),* al-Farabi explains Greek music and presents an analysis of aspects of Islamic music. (*See also* **Islam, Political Organization of.**)

Fasting

See *Christianity; Islam, Religion of; Judaism.*

Fatimid Empire

* **Shi'ites** Muslims who believed that Muhammad chose Ali and his descendants as the rulers and spiritual leaders of the Islamic community

* **caliph** religious and political head of an Islamic state

* **Sunnites** Muslim majority who believed that the caliphs should rule the Islamic community

* **imam** Shi'ite Muslim spiritual leader who claims to be descended directly from Muhammad

The Fatimids were a Shi'ite* Islamic dynasty that ruled from 909 to 1171. Under the Fatimids, Egypt became the center of an empire that included North Africa, Sicily, Palestine, Syria, and the Red Sea coast of Africa. The Fatimids traced their origins to the house of the prophet Muhammad, through Ali and Fatima, the prophet's daughter (from whom they derived their name).

The Fatimids believed that the caliphs* of the ABBASID Empire were not the legitimate heirs to the leadership of Islam. They considered it their duty and mission to replace the Abbasid caliphate with rulers of their own. Although the Abbasids and Fatimids represented different sects of the same religion, the conflict between them was intense. They differed in their interpretation of the QUR'AN, Islamic theology, and Islamic law, and in their understanding of the role of the caliph and his manner of selection.

Sunnites and Shi'ites.   The majority of Muslims were Sunnites*, who believed that the laws and practices should be determined by the sunna, the practices of Muhammad. When questions arose that were not clearly answered in the Qur'an, a jurist (or specialist in Islamic law) would give a legal opinion based on the sunna. The sunna was also important in helping scholars interpret the Qur'an. The Sunnite caliph did not play an important role in interpreting the Qur'an or in giving legal opinions; those roles were filled by scholars.

The Shi'ites, however, believed that the true teachings of the Qur'an were hidden and that only the insights of the imam* could reveal them. Thus, the imam played an important role in interpreting the Qur'an and acted as a spiritual leader for Shi'ites. Not surprisingly, there were some disputes among Shi'ites over who should be the imam.

The Abbasids and a large majority of Muslims were Sunnites; the Fatimids were Shi'ites of the Ismaili persuasion. Ismailis believed that the imamate should pass through the line of a descendant of Ali named Ismail.

The Rise of the Fatimids.   The Fatimid movement began in 899 when Ubayd Allah assumed leadership of the Ismaili Shi'ites. He established the first Fatimid capital, Mahdia, on the coast of present-day Tunisia. In 969, the Fatimids, under the leadership of an exceptional military strategist

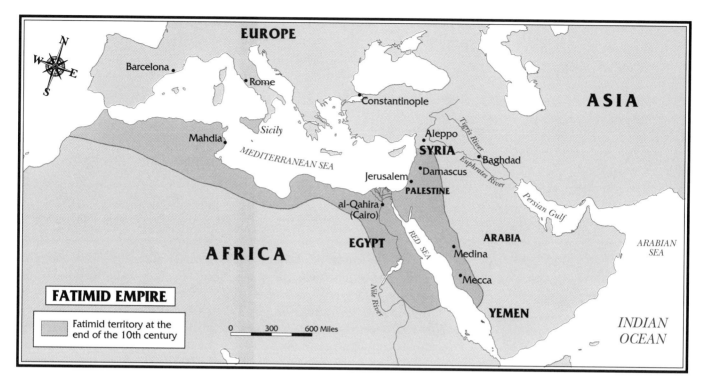

FATIMID EMPIRE

Fatimid territory at the end of the 10th century

0   300   600 Miles

When the Fatimids conquered Egypt, they moved their capital city from Mahdia to al-Qahira (Cairo). Then, as they extended their empire eastward and southward down along the Arabian peninsula, the Fatimids gained control of a profitable trade route to the Persian Gulf. By the early 11th century, Egypt had become the chief commercial center in the Islamic world.

named Jawhar, conquered Egypt. The imam, al-Mu'izz, ruled Egypt from the newly founded city of al-Qahira (Cairo). The imam turned over the administration of the empire to Ya'qub ibn Killis, a Jewish convert to Islam. Egypt prospered, and the imam, supported by a vast network of zealous missionaries and a highly organized bureaucracy, gained power and prestige. For the first time, the Abbasids faced a real challenge to their rule.

Both al-Mu'izz and his son al-Aziz wanted to maintain control over Syria. They gained and lost Damascus several times and were never able to capture Aleppo. One of the greatest successes of the Fatimids in the early years was their reorganization of the administration of Egypt.

During this time, the culture forged by the Fatimids in Egypt flourished. The great libraries and universities they had established became well-known throughout the Islamic world. By extending the empire to Yemen, the Fatimids developed a profitable trade with Asia, creating an alternate route to the Persian Gulf and serious commercial competition for the Sunnite Empire. In general, the economy under the Fatimids prospered.

Decline of the Empire.   The decline of the Fatimids probably began during the erratic reign of al-Hakim in the early 1000s. Driven by religious zeal and personal eccentricity, al-Hakim enacted many harsh measures against the Sunnite Muslims. (He once forbade cobblers from making women's shoes so that women were forced to stay at home.) His destruction of the Church of the Holy Sepulcher in Jerusalem was one action that may have inspired the crusades.

Like the Abbasids, the Fatimid imams faced increasing losses of their power at home. By the mid-11th century, they had to rely heavily on military officials to run their administration. The increase in administrative power under the vizier* Badr al-Jamali ensured that the commercial interests of the empire would be looked after scrupulously. But after his death

* **vizier** Muslim minister of state

in 1094, and with the caliph al-Mustansir's death the same year, the struggle for power that resulted eventually tore apart the empire.

The challenges to Islam in the 1100s—from the Byzantines, Turks, and crusaders—left no room for Muslim dissension, and the Fatimid dynasty withered. By the late 1100s, the position of imam was filled mostly by children of the Fatimid dynasty, further weakening leadership and opening the door to an Abbasid takeover. The last Fatimid ruler died in 1171. Power passed to the Mamluks, who were Sunnites, and Egypt became a Sunnite power. (*See also* **Cairo; Caliphate; Imam; Islam, Political Organization of; Islam, Religion of.**)

Feasts and Festivals

* **penance** task set by the church for someone to earn God's forgiveness for a sin

I n Europe and in the Islamic world, feasts and festivals were a significant part of medieval life. These occasions were religious in nature, but some had origins that predated Christianity and Islam. In neither tradition were the festivals limited to prayer, penance*, and pious observance. Most were joyous public events featuring singing, dancing, feasting, costumes, and entertainment.

Europe

In medieval Europe, feasts and festivals were so frequent that holidays took up more than one-third of the year. The large amount of required leisure posed problems in terms of decreased productivity, reduced profits, and lost pay. Some people criticized the frequency of holidays as unfair to farmers and workers, while others worried that too many feasts and festivals encouraged drinking, gambling, and immoral behavior.

Enforced Leisure. During the Middle Ages, work was prohibited on 126 or more days a year. In addition to 52 workless Sundays, there were more than 40 saints' days and more than 30 local church feasts each year. Moreover, some holidays lasted more than 24 hours. Universities also had holidays. In the 1300s, for example, Montpellier in France celebrated 133 festivals a year, including Sundays.

This significant amount of church-mandated leisure had social and economic consequences since religious holidays interfered with harvesting crops, constructing buildings, and transporting perishable goods. Employers complained that holidays interfered with their productivity and profit, especially when they had to pay their salaried workers a full week's wages for half a week's work. Workers paid by the job complained of lost work opportunities. Others complained that holidays, intended for religious observance, were, in fact, occasions for riotous behavior, sometimes even among clergy, monks, and nuns.

Many medieval holidays associated with the seasons—including Twelfth Night, May Day, and Midsummer Eve—had their roots in pre-Christian fertility rites. Their pagan heritage of songs, dances, games, and food appealed to a wide range of people—people of all ages, social status, wealth, and education. The church knew that rather than condemn the pagan practices, it was better to use them. AUGUSTINE and GREGORY THE GREAT believed that what Christianity could not eliminate, it must adapt to its own purposes.

Eating, singing, dancing, and other forms of entertainment accompanied the many feasts and festivals of the Middle Ages. This illustration from the *History of Alexander the Great,* written in the 1400s, shows the Greek general and conqueror feasting with his nobles.

See color plate 13, vol. 3.

The most elaborate celebrations during the Middle Ages were political—coronations, marriages, births, funerals, and state banquets for distinguished visitors. In 1378, King CHARLES V OF FRANCE celebrated a visit from Emperor Charles IV with a large spectacle in which hundreds of French knights dressed in full armor reenacted the crusaders' capture of JERUSALEM, which had occurred in 1099.

Major Holidays.   The first major holiday of the year was Twelfth Night, which was celebrated on January 5 (the eve of Epiphany), and which concluded the 12 days of Christmas. It was marked by ritual contests between good and evil, such as plays in which the Magi outsmarted King Herod and found the miraculous Christ child in the manger. Country actors, called mummers in England, performed plays about St. George and the Dragon in which St. George overcame an evil knight. A team game called Oranges and Lemons ended with a tug-of-war between sides that represented Winter and Spring in order to see which season was going to triumph. To encourage the rebirth of the land after winter, toasts of spiced ales and wines were offered to the trees. Drinking to the health of fruit trees in country orchards, or symbolically in a hall, was accompanied by loud, vigorous dances.

In February, St. Valentine's Day paid tribute to Love. People decorated the halls with colorful lanterns and played loud, stimulating music. They dressed in long sleeves that could be detached and exchanged with a loved one, and they wore special jewelry, such as a gold knot (symbolizing eternal affection) or a crowned *A* for *amor vincit omnia* (love conquers all). Foods thought to encourage love were served, as well as symbolic treats such as cherry or pomegranate "heart" cakes.

Easter Sunday was the central holiday of a 17-week cycle that began with Septuagesima nine weeks before Easter (including the solemn fast days of Lent) and ended eight weeks after Easter on Trinity Sunday. May Day honored the spirits of trees and woodlands with dances around a Maypole, costumes, hoop rolling, athletic contests, and special foods such as peppermint rice and a lime-glazed "gingerbread man" called Jack-in-the-Green.

Midsummer Eve, St. Swithin's Day, and Lammas Day were summer festivals associated with crops and weather. October ended with Halloween on the eve of All Hallows' (All Saints') Day on November 1. All Souls' Day on November 2 was the day prayers were offered for the souls of the dead in Purgatory. Catherning (St. Catherine's Day) on November 25 honored one of the most famous and learned women saints. Catherine of Alexandria lived in the 300s and, according to legend, was martyred on a spiked wheel of torture before being beheaded. She was the patron saint of lawyers, wheelwrights, rope makers, and carpenters, but women revered her in her capacity as guide and defender of lace makers, spinners, unmarried women, and women students. In fact, Cathernings were especially popular feasts with women, who commemorated St. Catherine with objects that recalled her martyrdom, such as candle circles to jump over or through and Catherine-wheel fireworks.

Christmas Day on December 25 began the Christmas holiday that culminated in Twelfth Night. Each of the 12 holy days was marked by giving and receiving gifts, toasting the health of all present, exchanging kisses under the mistletoe, and eating or drinking special Christmas foods or beverages, such as sweet plum pudding, honeyed gingerbread Yule dolls, and hot elderberry wine.

This steady procession of religious holidays throughout the year provided enough rites, ceremonies, plays, entertainments, singing, dancing, and food to amuse Europeans for much of their daily lives and to provide a balance between work and play.

Islam

The Muslim calendar has two canonical* festivals—the festival of the breaking of the fast and the festival of sacrificing. Although the two festivals are separate and different, they share the same public prayer, called the prayer of the two festivals.

* canonical prescribed by church law

Muslim law books devote a separate chapter to regulations for this prayer. Like the Friday prayer, the prayer of the two festivals must be led by an imam*. However, there are important differences between it and the Friday prayer. The Friday prayer is said shortly after noon, while the prayer of the two festivals occurs between sunrise and noon. Also, instead of the customary first and second call to prayer, the prayer of the two festivals uses a single call (Come to public prayer), which is announced just prior to the prayer. Another difference is that the prayer for the festivals takes place outdoors rather than in a mosque (except in Mecca, where it is held in the Mosque of the Prophet).

* imam Shi'ite Muslim spiritual leader who claims to be descended directly from Muhammad

Festival of the Breaking of the Fast. The first of the two canonical festivals—the festival of the breaking of the fast (id al-fitr)—is celebrated on 1 Shawwal, the first day of the month following Ramadan. Only two duties are required for the festival—attendance at the prayer of the festival and paying the alms* due on the day.

* alms money or gifts given to help the poor and suffering

The alms donation calls for foodstuffs—wheat, dates, raisins, or barley—to be given to the poor and needy, although in actual practice it is often given to family and friends. Every Muslim man is required to give alms, and he must make the donation on behalf of his dependents as well as himself. Popular customs that have evolved around the festival include wearing new clothes, exchanging gifts and visits, and visiting cemeteries.

Worshipers are required to go to the festival on foot, taking one route there and returning by a different route. Some scholars believe that the reason for this practice is that Muslims who are relieved of their sins on the way to the festival should avoid encountering them again by returning a different way.

Festival of Sacrificing.   The other canonical festival—the festival of sacrificing *(id al-adha)*—is associated with the hajj* since it is held on the day that pilgrims to Mecca make their sacrificial offerings at Mina. It is one of the few times Muslims sacrifice. (Another occasion for sacrifice is the offering that occurs seven days after the birth of a child.) The sacrifice on the day of the feast is believed to have started as a commemoration of the near-sacrifice by Abraham of his son (Ishmael in Muslim tradition; Isaac in Judeo-Christian tradition).

* **hajj**   pilgrimage to Mecca that Muslims are required to make once in their lifetime

According to most Muslim legal traditions, the offering of a sacrifice on the day of the festival is not required. However, it is recommended for Muslims who are not traveling and who are wealthy to offer a sheep, a cow, or a camel. The animal must not be blind or lame or have a blemish. The person performing the sacrifice may distribute the meat to anyone he chooses as long as at least a third of the animal is set aside for alms.

Other Observances.   Several other Islamic celebrations connect Muslims around the world with the hajj. The departure and arrival of pilgrim caravans are occasions for celebration. Since the Middle Ages, the ruler of Egypt has sent the cloth covering for the Kaaba* (the most sacred of the Muslim sanctuaries) to Mecca with the pilgrim caravan from Egypt. Often the covering was paraded through the streets of Cairo and al-Fustat before it was sent on to Mecca. After 1200, another practice became common. An empty, decorated litter was carried by the lead camel of the caravan to Mecca. Some people believed it contained a prayer book that was displayed on the return from Mecca.

* **Kaaba**   large stone shrine covered with black cloth. It was a place of worship for pagan Arabs and became the main Islamic place of refuge and protection in Mecca.

The Islamic fast day of Ashura, modeled on the Jewish Day of Atonement, has great significance for Shi'ites* as the anniversary of the death of the martyr al-Husayn at Karbala. It has since become a day of mourning for Shi'ites, who make pilgrimages to Karbala and perform plays that commemorate the deaths of Shi'ite martyrs.

Several nights in the Islamic calendar are of special significance. The night of the ascension marks the night on which Muhammad is said to have ascended to heaven and returned to earth. In some traditions, it is associated with the night journey Muhammad made from Mecca to Jerusalem and back again on the same night. Muslims celebrate the festival with prayers and retellings of the legend.

* **Shi'ites**   Muslims who believed that Muhammad chose Ali and his descendants as the rulers and spiritual leaders of the Islamic community

On another night, the "tree of life"—on which the name of every living person is written—is shaken. The leaves that fall off are believed to contain the names of all the people who are going to die in the coming year. Allah is said to descend to the lowest of the seven heavens so he can summon people to forgive their sins.

The most important Islamic festival is the night of the divine decree. It commemorates the night on which the Qur'an was revealed to Muhammad. Since it is believed that angels descend with their blessings and the gates of heaven are opened, Muslims feel that their prayers are especially effective on that night.

Muhammad's birthday is celebrated with prayers. In FATIMID Egypt, other important birthdays were also observed on that day—those of ALI IBN ABI TALIB, Fatima, the current imam, and al-Husayn. Birthday festivals were celebrated in the Fatimid palace, where the imam sat veiled on one of the balconies and listened to sermons.

Muslims also celebrated Christian festivals with great energy and enthusiasm. In Baghdad, the feasts of patron saints were especially popular. In Cairo, Muslims often joined Christians on the banks of the Nile River to celebrate Palm Sunday, Easter, and Christmas. Egyptians were especially fond of the feast of Epiphany, when Christians paraded through the streets with crosses and burning candles and dove into the Nile (hence the name "festival of diving"). Muslims observed three New Year's Days—Coptic, Persian, and Muslim. The custom on both the Coptic and Persian New Years was for people to sprinkle one another with water. To celebrate the Muslim New Year, the caliph in Cairo staged an elaborate procession with thousands of mounted soldiers, extravagant costumes, and a dazzling display of wealth.

Two other important Muslim festivals—ritual circumcision of boys and the sacrifice on the seventh day after the birth of a child—were family celebrations rather than public holidays. Although Muslim festivals were not as numerous as European ones, they were important to Islamic belief and practice. (*See also* **Calendars; Caliphate; Christianity; Dance; Food and Drink; Games and Pastimes; Islam, Religion of.**)

See map in Carolingians (vol. 1).

See map in Vikings (vol. 4).

*F*eudalism is the word that was used after the Middle Ages were over to describe the arrangement between medieval lords and those who served them. The feudal system evolved from the unstable political situation in western Europe that followed the fall of the Roman Empire. As local lords sought loyal and dependable followers, the system developed.

Feudalism operated on two levels. On the local level, it involved the relationship between a lord of a castle and those who were in his service. On the kingdom level, it defined the political relationship between the king and the powerful lords of his realm.

Lords and Vassals

On the local level, feudalism was a form of government in which a count or a lord of a castle was the military and administrative ruler of his district. Those who pledged their loyalty to him—his vassals—were given land in return for their loyalty and services to the lord, such as fighting in his army or serving in his court. Agreements between lords and their vassals were the foundation of feudalism.

Origins of Feudalism. In the 400s, the Germanic tribes that overran the Roman Empire established kingdoms in western Europe. German rulers divided their kingdoms among their heirs, and the heirs in turn divided their territories into even smaller units. As a result of this breakup of large political areas into many smaller ones, the county became the basic unit of local government. Although the process of fragmentation was reversed in the early Middle Ages under the CAROLINGIANS, later invasions by VIKINGS,

At the highest level, feudalism involved the relationship between a king and his lords. In exchange for land grants, nobles pledged loyalty and military service to the king. Philip of Valois, king of France from 1328 to 1350, is shown here presiding over a meeting with his nobles.

Muslims, and Magyars led to the further division of lands throughout Europe. In many places, counties broke up into even smaller districts called castellanies, which were controlled by the lord of a castle. These castellanies and the agreements between the lord of the castle and his followers became the basic unit of medieval feudalism.

Even in counties where counts kept control, they often turned over most of the rights of local government to the lords of castles, who regarded their rights of government as private possessions. These rights were inherited by their sons or given as marriage gifts to their daughters. Counties and castellanies could even be mortgaged or sold.

Fief. The property or income-producing right that a lord granted was called a fief (*feodum* or *feudum* in Latin, hence the word *feudalism*). The holder of a fief was called a vassal. To serve his lord, a vassal needed arms, armor, a place to live, and support in his old age. Some vassals had small holdings of their own, but these were rarely large enough to meet the vassal's needs. Other vassals were live-in companions to the lord in his castle, but this type of arrangement had its problems. The early castles were not large, and housing and feeding a group of loud and quarrelsome men with large appetites created difficulties. Furthermore, most young knights (as vassals came to be called) did not want to spend their lives living with other men in a castle. They most likely wanted to marry and have their own incomes and places to live. The solution that evolved was to give knights homesteads of their own and sufficient income to support themselves and their families. These early homesteads were small, but in the later Middle Ages vassals were given larger estates. On these estates, the vassal was lord of his domain. Peasants worked the vassal's land for him and paid rent to work small parcels of their own. They also paid to use various facilities on the estate, such as ovens, mills, and winepresses.

A fief was generally inherited by the vassal's heir, but it returned to the lord if the vassal failed to perform his services or betrayed the lord by fighting for someone else. At first, the holder of a fief owed unlimited military service, but that service was later reduced to a certain number of days per year.

The holder of a fief was also obligated to do service in the lord's court. He was expected to pay money when the lord had a special expense, such as a crusade or another long military operation, a payment of ransom, the knighting ceremony of a son, or the marriage of a daughter. These financial services that vassals were expected to provide to their lords were called feudal aids.

Kings and Great Lords

As the vassals gave service to the local lords, these lords in turn gave service to the king. On the kingdom level, however, submission of powerful lords to the king was largely symbolic because the lords tended to be allies rather than subordinates of the king.

Allies of the King. Although, in theory, the great lords were subordinate to the king and owed loyalty to him, in reality, the king had little control over them. Some lords were royal officials who became independent of the king, such as the count of Anjou in France. Others, such as the duke of Normandy, wanted only the king's recognition of the power they already

On a medieval estate, peasants and serfs farmed the land for the lord. In return, they received his protection and a small parcel of land to farm for themselves. Workers also paid to use manor facilities, such as mills and ovens. Workers usually lived in a village near the manor.

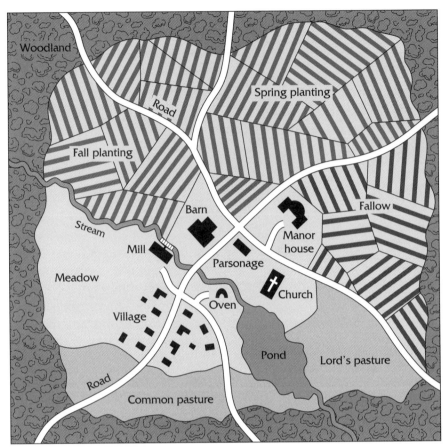

A Medieval Manor

possessed. Great lords—if they chose to—might help the king or attend his court on an important occasion. On their own lands, however, they did what they wanted. Although most great lords eventually pledged their support to the king and became royal vassals, they were not obligated to him in the same way that an ordinary vassal was obligated to the lord of a castle. A feudal tie between lord and king was more of a pact between equals—a duke or a count agreed not to attack the king if the king agreed not to attack him.

Although the great lords rarely attended the king's court or helped him fight his wars, the fact that the great lordships were royal fiefs and the lords were royal vassals helped create the impression of a united kingdom. This pattern of feudalism started in France, then extended into western Germany, into parts of Italy, into Spain, and into England, where it took special shape.

Feudalism in England. In many ways, England represented the most complete form of feudalism. After the Normans conquered England in 1066, all of England was divided into fiefs. Every foot of English land was held either directly by the king's vassals or indirectly by the vassals and tenants of the king's vassals. All royal vassals of the English king owed him military service, court service, and occasionally financial assistance.

The entire structure of English government originated from the royal court, which was served by the king's vassals. The king's court had the authority to give direct orders to any landholder in the kingdom. (But the king could not act arbitrarily or outside the law. Magna Carta, approved in the 1200s, reminded rulers of that fact.)

By the late 1100s, France developed a similar centralized royal government. The Capetians, who went on to become a ruling dynasty in France, began as the counts of Paris and consolidated their power by bringing other counts under their feudal lordship. Germany and Italy, on the other hand, never did develop a centralized royal government, which may explain why they were unable to become unified nations until the 1800s.

Because all land and local governmental rights in England derived from the king, no English earl—even those who were given special privileges because they held exposed border territories—ever became as independent as the duke of BRITTANY or the count of FLANDERS. Ambitious lords might try to increase their power by arranged marriages, legal claims, or even acts of violence, but open warfare and independent action were virtually impossible. Only in Wales (not yet part of England) and Ireland could ambitious barons hope to be semi-independent. Even in these remote regions, however, they were not completely free of royal supervision.

Another factor that limited the possibility of independent action by English lords was the growing reluctance of vassals to perform military service. By roughly the mid-14th century, many knights were not eager to fight for their lord. They continually tried to limit the area in which they were obligated to fight, as well as the number of days they were required to do military service. English vassals had to offer only 40 days of military service, and they insisted that they were not obligated to serve outside England. Lords could no longer expect to receive all the military service their vassals owed them. Vassals willing to serve longer insisted on large payments. Some lords hired knights or men-at-arms who were not their vassals to fight for them, but only lords with large incomes could afford to do so.

English feudalism had set the trend that spread to other parts of Europe. The fragmentation that characterized early medieval feudalism declined with the rise of national monarchies* in England and France. Although a unification of political power was less successful in Germany and Italy, by 1500 much of western Europe was no longer feudal. Although the privileges and titles of the nobility continued, the old feudal terms of *lord, vassal,* and *fief* became almost meaningless. (*See also* **Benefice; Count, County; Inheritance Laws and Practices; Knights, Orders of; Land Use.**)

* **monarchy**   nation ruled by a king or queen

Fishing, Fish Trade

* **saga**   long Germanic narrative poem recounting historical and legendary events

See map in Trade (vol. 4).

Most of what is known about fishing in the Middle Ages comes from archaeological studies of fish remains and fishing gear, from legal and commercial documents, and from household diaries from that time. Interesting and useful information was recorded in court and monastic chronicles, in travel reports, and in medieval poetry, especially Icelandic sagas*.

Marine fisheries have been an important source of food since prehistoric times. The harvest from the sea was much less affected by the seasons, climate, and war than were agriculture, hunting, and raising livestock. The enormous resources from the sea—many times greater than freshwater resources—made up for shortages of other foods.

Until the late Middle Ages, fishermen went only as far from the shore as they could wade or dared to navigate their small boats. In deep water, the main fishing gear was a hook forged of iron or bronze or made of bent wire. During the late Middle Ages, longlines (with multiple hooks) appeared. A line with 120 hooks appeared on an inventory list, dated 1482, from an Icelandic church. On sloping shores, fishermen used traps and nets made of grass, hemp, flax, and wool.

Practically all fish from the sea are edible, but a profitable fishing industry depends on an abundance of fish, providing a surplus that can be traded outside the local area. In northern Europe, cod and herring were the primary catches. In the Mediterranean region, many other varieties were available.

In addition to great supplies of fish, an effective means of transporting them to distant markets is necessary for maintaining a fish trade. At the height of the Middle Ages, a class of fishmongers emerged to link fishermen with distant consumers. English, Flemish, Dutch, and German traders began a long and fierce competition for fish markets. At first, merchants of the HANSEATIC LEAGUE dominated the fish trade of northern and central Europe. In the later Middle Ages, English, Dutch, Germans, and Basques (from Spain) cut into the fish trade of the Hanseatic League.

In northern Europe, during the winter, fish were transported frozen to markets more than 500 miles away. In southern Europe, however, inland towns could obtain fresh marine fish only if located one or two days' journey from the coast. Smoked fish could be preserved for several weeks. The most efficient method of preserving fish was salting. In southern Europe, sea salt was easily produced by evaporation in salinas*, a method used since ancient times. In northern Europe, salt from seawater was obtained by boiling.

Apart from the fish meat, oil was the most important fish product in medieval northern Europe, where it was used as both food and fuel. (Southern Europeans used olive oil.) Another important product was caviar, the unspawned eggs from sturgeon. Caviar is still an exotic and very expensive dish. There was also a market for fermented fish sauces, which were used in cooking.

* **salina**   place where seawater is evaporated, leaving behind huge piles of salt

Flanders and the Low Countries

Throughout the Middle Ages, the area between the North Sea and the Rhine River—occupying modern-day Belgium, Netherlands, and Luxembourg and extending into France and Germany—was known as Flanders and the Low Countries. The county of Flanders (the area between the sea and the Schelde River) played a dominant role in the history of the region. By the year 500, the FRANKS had seized Flanders from the Germanic tribes that occupied the Western Roman Empire. From western Flanders, the Frankish leader CLOVIS launched his conquest of Gaul and founded the MEROVINGIAN kingdom, which later fell to the CAROLINGIANS in the mid-700s.

By the middle of the 800s, Flanders was a military frontier zone, providing defense against the Viking raids that had begun to weaken the Carolingian empire after the death of CHARLEMAGNE in 814. Baldwin I Iron-arm, a military adventurer, ruled Flanders for the Carolingian king Charles the Bald. Baldwin secured his grip on the territory by marrying Judith, the daughter of Charles.

Flanders was a language frontier as well as a military one. In the southern portion of Flanders, people spoke a French dialect known as Walloon. In the north, people spoke a Germanic dialect known as Netherlandish, which is the basis of modern Flemish or Dutch. The linguistic frontier still exists in modern Belgium, marking the division between Dutch- and French-speaking Belgians.

Early History.   The history of Flanders was determined by the fortunes of its neighbors: the Norse, English, French, and Germans. Its strategic location, controlling several major riverways into Europe and its prosperous textile industry, made it a tempting target for monarchs on every side. With the weakening of the power of the Holy Roman Emperor following the death of Otto I the Great in 973 and a similar decline in the power of the Capetian* nobles, the Flemish counts became virtually independent. In this environment, a series of capable rulers improved the economic health and political stability of the region. Baldwin V (1035–1067) arranged for the marriage of his daughter to William I the Conqueror, king of England and duke of Normandy. In this way, he strengthened the bond that existed between England and Flanders, an alliance based on the interdependence of the Flemish textile industry and the English wool industry. Following Baldwin's example, Robert the Frisian (1071–1093) established ties with Denmark through the marriage of his daughter to the Danish king. Robert's son, Robert II (1093–1111) was one of the most celebrated princes to participate in the First Crusade.

The long line of Flemish counts descending from Baldwin Iron-arm ended with the son of Robert II, Baldwin VII (1111–1119), who died without heirs. The countship passed to Charles the Good (1119–1127), another grandson of Robert the Frisian. Charles was an exceptionally able ruler, leading Flanders through some desperate times, including a famine in 1125. Charles's success caused some resentment among the powerful feudal families that had lost power during his administration. In 1127, Charles was murdered. A vivid account of the murder, the punishment of the conspirators, and the civil war over succession was given by the count's clerk, an eyewitness to the events.

French Domination.   Following the murder of Charles, the French king, Louis VI, led an invasion into Flanders in support of William Clito, a Norman descendant of William I. The French king was successful at first, partly because he promised the townspeople local self-government. William eventually lost to Thierry of Alsace (1128–1168), who, with his son Philip (1168–1191), brought Flanders to the height of its political power. Philip supported reforms of the criminal and commercial laws sought by the townspeople. He was further admired for his participation in tournaments and jousts, and for his participation in the crusades. Following Philip's death and the brief reigns of Baldwin VIII and Baldwin IX that ended in 1205, the fortunes of Flanders declined. The region became involved in the struggles between the French and German rulers, and later between the pro-French and anti-French factions of Flanders.

Baldwin IX left only two daughters: Joan (countess, 1205–1244) and Margaret (countess, 1244–1278). Both women came under the protection of the French king PHILIP II AUGUSTUS, who educated them and arranged their marriages to men he thought he could control. Joan's husband,

* **Capetians** princely and royal family that controlled the west Frankish kingdom for several centuries

In the 1200s, France sought to dominate Flemish politics. Strong resistance by the Flemish caused political chaos, economic problems, and local uprisings. This illumination from the *Grandes Chroniques de France,* a medieval history, shows French and Flemish soldiers fighting.

Ferrand of Portugal, attempted to break away from France by forming alliances with King JOHN of England, Otto IV of Germany, and a confederation of Low Country princes. However, Philip Augustus crushed the allied army at Bouvines in 1214. Margaret married William of Dampierre. Their son Guy had an unsuccessful career as Margaret's successor and was eventually imprisoned by PHILIP IV THE FAIR (1285–1314), who took control of Flanders. By 1300, Flanders was occupied and under French rule.

A widespread resistance to the French officials sent to administer the country developed among the Flemish people. On May 18–19, 1302, in Bruges, they rose up and slaughtered all but a few of the French soldiers and officials. On July 11, 1302, an imposing French army met an ill-equipped force of nearly 10,000 Flemish foot soldiers gathered from the towns and countryside. In the famous Battle of the Golden Spurs that ensued, the French were again routed, and 700 golden spurs were collected from the dead and hung in the church at Courtrai to commemorate the victory. The French sent more soldiers and forced Guy's successor, Robert of Béthune (1305–1322) to accept the harsh terms of the Peace of Athis in 1305.

Catastrophic Times. If the 1200s had been difficult times for Flanders, the next century was one of catastrophe. Robert's successor, Louis of Nevers (1322–1346), supported France at the outset of the HUNDRED YEARS WAR. His support outraged Edward III of England, who placed an embargo* on the trade of English wool to Flanders. The embargo resulted in a decline in the textile industry and a threatened breakdown of the

* **embargo** government order prohibiting the movement of merchant ships in or out of certain ports

*** artisans** skilled craftspeople

peace. Bands of artisans* marched through the countryside destroying looms and any wool they could find.

The political chaos and economic hardship enabled Jacques van Artevelde, a merchant from Ghent, to gain control in 1338 and to lead the opposition to Louis. Artevelde supported Edward III, proclaiming him king of France at their meeting in Ghent in 1340. In return, Edward lifted the embargo on wool. Five years later, an angry mob, annoyed because Edward had not honored his commitments, attacked and killed Artevelde. A GUILD of weavers controlled Ghent for a time. Meanwhile, Louis died fighting for the French at Crécy in 1346, leaving his son, Louis of Male (1346–1384), with a troubled country to govern.

See map in Black Death (vol. 1).

Although accused of being pro-French, Louis was shrewder than his father and tried to follow a neutral course between England and France. He was able to negotiate agreements with the towns and the guilds. He also survived the turmoil of the BLACK DEATH (1348–1350) and managed to enlarge his domain through the marriage of his daughter Margaret to the Burgundian duke Philip the Bold, brother of King CHARLES V OF FRANCE. In 1379, a dispute between BRUGES and GHENT over a canal erupted into a general revolt, and Louis sought help from Charles VI, Philip's nephew. Charles sent an army that quickly defeated the Flemish at Roosebeke in 1382. Among the dead was the body of the Flemish leader of the revolt, Philip van Artevelde, son of Jacques.

Recovery.   Though Flanders was only a province of the larger state of BURGUNDY, Philip the Bold and his successors lavished much attention here and revived the region economically. By the time of Philip the Good (1419–1467), Flanders was once again the most prominent county of the area—the center of a rich artistic and cultural movement that had much in common with the movement known as the Renaissance in southern Europe. The paintings of Jan and Hubert van Eyck and Rogier van der Weyden that have immortalized the merchants and towns are proof of the political and economic achievements of Flanders during this period.

Burgundian rule of Flanders and the Low Countries came to an end, however, as the son of Philip the Good, Charles the Rash (1467–1477), adopted an overly ambitious military policy and lost Flanders to the House of Habsburg. (*See also* **Germany; Textiles; Wool.**)

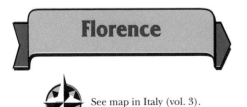

Florence

See map in Italy (vol. 3).

The city of Florence is in the TUSCANY region of Italy, about 145 miles northwest of Rome. Located on the Arno River, the city was established as a Roman colony in the first century B.C. for the purpose of protecting the only practical crossing of the waterway.

During the Middle Ages, Florence (from the Latin *Florentia,* which means town that flourishes) was an important trade center and a prosperous city with a robust textile industry. Its lasting fame, however, comes from its spectacular contributions to art and learning. DANTE, PETRARCH, Donatello, Botticelli, GIOTTO, Michelangelo, Leonardo da Vinci, Galileo, and Machiavelli all lived in Florence, some under the patronage of the MEDICI FAMILY.

The Art of Money

The symbol of both the wealth and the culture of medieval Florence was the florin, the gold coin first struck there in 1252. It was a finely designed coin that was produced to standards of weight so exact that the florin became the standard currency not only in Italy but throughout the world. The first florins were produced continuously and unchanged until 1533.

* **commune**   town in the Middle Ages that established independence from its feudal ruler and formed its own government

* **charter**   written grant from a ruler conferring certain rights and privileges

See map in Black Death (vol. 1).

* **guild**   association of craft and trade workers that set standards and represented the interests of its members

The history of Florence, from the fall of Rome in 410 to the death of Lorenzo de' Medici in 1492, was turbulent. Power changed hands frequently, usually as a result of rivalries within the city that often erupted into street fights. Despite the turmoil, an extraordinary culture arose, one that gave the world some of its greatest scholarship and art.

Early Medieval Period.   Following the sacking of Rome in 410, Goths, Byzantine Greeks, and LOMBARDS ruled Florence for the next 350 years. During this time, Italy suffered economic decline. During the years of Lombard rule (568–774), the city's inhabitants barely subsisted on the agriculture of the countryside.

Following the CAROLINGIAN conquest of the Lombards in 774, FRANKISH officials ruled Tuscany for a time. By the mid-800s, a series of lords called margraves controlled the area. Occasional attempts by church reformers to purge corruption resulted in brief periods of prosperity. Two important developments decisively affected the history of Florence: the rise of the communes* and the struggle between the papacy and the empire, which lasted for centuries.

By 1115, when the ruler of Tuscany, Countess MATILDA, died, the commune system was firmly in place in Florence. The affairs of the city were conducted by consuls, elected by the members of the commune assembled in a *parlamentum*. The membership in the commune was restricted at first to members of the prominent families and trained officials (judges and other administrators). Merchants and laborers were excluded. Slowly, however, more segments of the town were admitted.

By the end of the 1100s, the commune was the dominant political power in Florence. The granting of a charter* in 1187 to Florence by Henry VI (who was crowned Holy Roman Emperor in 1191) was a ceremonial acceptance of an already established fact.

Guelphs and Ghibellines.   Florence of the 1200s was the scene of bitter rivalries that involved virtually all the inhabitants of the city and changed the lives of large segments of the population. The two factions were GUELPHS AND GHIBELLINES, each consisting of a powerful family and its supporters, and each seeking to control the city. The Guelphs supported the supremacy of the papacy; the Ghibellines favored the Holy Roman Emperor and Henry VI's successor, Frederick II. The rivalry often erupted into mob violence, and the Florentine struggle spread throughout Italy.

During the 1200s, the government of Florence consisted of more citizens and fewer aristocrats. The Ordinances of Justice, issued in 1293, further restricted the power of the nobility. Predictably, even the lower classes of Florence became factionalized into two parties, known as the Whites and the Blacks. The latter group gained the support of the pope and the Guelphs. The ascendancy of the Blacks forced the Whites to establish alliances with Ghibellines of other towns and to call on neighboring monarchs for aid. Although one ruler, Henry VII of Luxembourg, attempted to conquer Tuscany for the Ghibellines, his death in 1313 resulted in Guelph control of Florence.

The Black Death.   Florence grew rapidly in the late 1200s and early 1300s, with an estimated population of around 190,000 by 1338. Then, in one calamitous decade, that number was halved by an epidemic in 1340 and the BLACK DEATH of 1348. The guilds* took control of the commune,

The Medici family rose to power in Florence in the early 1400s. Lorenzo de Medici, sometimes called "Lorenzo the Magnificent," was a successful banker, diplomat, and politician who became the unofficial ruler of the city. Because of his patronage of the arts, Florence became an important cultural center.

and guild leaders were remarkably successful in recovering from the effects of the Black Death. There was much to do: bury the dead, restore essential public services, and supervise the massive redistribution of property left by plague victims.

In the 1350s and 1360s, Florence had to defend itself against attacks by neighboring cities, such as MILAN and PISA. In the 1370s, the pope, who had been a benefactor of Florence, became involved in disputes with the city and the commune. The resulting conflict opened the way for the revolt of the *Ciompi,* or clothworkers. A new regime was established, but it lasted only six weeks in the summer of 1378. For that brief time, Florence came very close to full democracy. By 1382, the new commune that replaced the *Ciompi* fell, and Florence was again ruled by the old Guelph families who had ruled the city intermittently for some 150 years.

The Early Renaissance and the Medicis.   In the 50 years from 1382 to 1432, Florence fought with the rulers of Milan and Pisa, sometimes recruiting Venice as an ally. In 1427, Florence extended its rule to the coast, which enabled it to launch a fleet of ships to compete with Genoa and Venice for Mediterranean trade.

The war with Milan was costly, and recovery was slow. When several attempts to extend Florentine rule failed, a banker named Cosimo de' Medici rose to power. Cosimo was a gifted politician and diplomat, able to court powerful allies while quelling civil unrest and challenges to his authority. He managed all this without holding any official position. When Cosimo died in 1464, his sickly but capable son Piero assumed control. Piero died in 1469, and his son Lorenzo, then only 20 years old, became the "first citizen" and unofficial ruler of Florence.

Lorenzo was the most famous member of the illustrious Medici family. Educated in the arts and literature, Lorenzo was an extraordinary diplomat and politician. He forged alliances with rulers, popes, guild leaders, merchants—virtually anyone who could advance his interests and anyone whose interests he could advance, thereby securing each one's loyalty. During Lorenzo's "reign" and under his direction, Florence became the center of art and Renaissance culture. Lorenzo de' Medici's death in 1492 marked the end of the city's supremacy. It occurred on the eve of an event that would mark the end of the medieval period for all of Italy: the conquest by Charles VIII of France. (*See also* **Banking; Commune; Italy.**)

Food and Drink

Food was at the center of the economy during the Middle Ages. Europeans worried constantly about crop failure and the threat of famine and starvation and spent about three-quarters of their income on food and drink.

Food Trades

The food trades—the businesses of buying and selling foodstuffs—were the primary business activities in the markets of all villages, towns, and cities. Grain, salt, fish, and wine were sold locally but were also a major part of all regional and long-distance trade. The securing of food for people at reasonable prices was the main concern of town and city governments. Food trades, therefore, became highly regulated.

Food Trades in the Early Middle Ages. The number of food trades decreased in western Europe following the disruptions caused by the influx of Germanic tribes into the lands of the Roman Empire. The owners of farms and estates grew the food they needed, and food served as a form of money between a lord and his peasants. Peasants paid all or part of their rent with wheat, poultry, or eels, while the lord paid for work with bread or ale. On the estates created by the rise of MONASTICISM, monks not only grew their own food but also produced a surplus that they exchanged at the local market for clothes and other items.

In the early Middle Ages, roads were primitive and transportation was slow. There was no refrigeration to preserve perishable foods. Landowners grew as much of their own food as possible. Lords with two or more estates sometimes moved from estate to estate to consume the food they produced at each place, or they enlisted their peasants to transport the food from the distant estates on a regular basis. Lords who chose not to transport their produce over long distances arranged to have it sold at local markets. Foods that could be preserved for a time—such as wheat, salted fish, and wine—were transported over greater distances more easily.

After 800, agricultural production improved through the use of heavier plows, better tools, more mills, and increased use of the three-field crop rotation system. Greater food surpluses helped stimulate population growth, more commerce, and the growth of CITIES AND TOWNS. By the 1000s, Europe was in the midst of a rapid expansion of trade, with markets, fairs, and urban centers that depended on regular food supplies. The search for adequate supplies of food, especially in years when crop yields were low, resulted in the placement of more land under cultivation. As marshes were drained and forests were cleared, the landscape of western Europe was changed forever.

Rural Food Trades. Beginning in the 1100s, Germans colonized the lands east of the Elbe River and planted grains in the fertile soil of Prussia and POLAND. The introduction of inexpensive grains from eastern Europe led to a decline of grain prices in western Europe. By the late 1200s, eastern-grown grains were transported regularly to German, Scandinavian, English, and Flemish ports by the HANSEATIC LEAGUE, a group composed of several northern European cities. In turn, grain was sent to other parts of Europe. Italian merchants, for example, purchased large quantities of Baltic grain in Sicily and redistributed it throughout the Mediterranean and to Atlantic coastal areas.

The new sources of grain caused many landowners in the West to abandon grain production and to take up specialized forms of agricultural production, such as viticulture (the cultivation of grapes) and livestock farming. Other agricultural enterprises during the Middle Ages included cheese production and the cultivation of olive groves and fruit orchards. The standard of living rose, with people having more income to buy meat, wine, and foodstuffs other than grain.

After 1200, livestock farming expanded with the increased demand for animal products and a rise in profits from the sale of meat, butter, cheese, and wool. As many estate owners and farmers expanded their livestock herds, competition for land sometimes created tensions between livestock owners and grain growers.

Remember: Words in small capital letters have separate entries, and the index at the end of Volume 4 will guide you to more information on many topics.

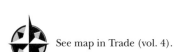 See map in Trade (vol. 4).

By 1300, much of the food grown on large estates was sold in local markets. The owners of large estates, like those of the bishop of Winchester in England, sold about half their grain harvest—an average of 13,000 bushels each year—at the market. However, the availability of grain depended on changing prices, demand, and weather. In the late 1200s and early 1300s, excessive rain caused massive crop failures and widespread FAMINE. Grain cultivation decreased further after the BLACK DEATH in 1348, which killed about a third of the people living in Europe.

Urban Food Trades.   Most medieval towns grew up around places where food was brought to be sold. Many townspeople—between 30 and 70 percent—were involved in food trades.

Urban food traders were divided into four groups. One group, fairly small in number, were gardeners, fishermen, and other workers who brought their food products to market and sold them. A second, much larger group consisted of bakers, butchers, brewers, cooks, and others who purchased raw foodstuffs, processed them, and then sold their products to the public.

A third group of food traders were retailers, such as tavern owners or innkeepers, who sold or served foodstuffs grown or processed by others. This group also included hawkers, people who sold goods on the street by calling out to residents or passersby. Some retailers specialized in the sale of just one type of food, such as wine, bread, cheese, or vegetables. Others sold a wide variety of foods and other items that they bought from peasants, food processors, or middlemen. Retailers of inexpensive foods often barely made a living.

The fourth group of food traders made the highest profits by buying and selling food in bulk. These middlemen mostly traded grain, wine, salt, fish, oils, and spices—as well as certain nonfood items, such as cloth and wool—over longer distances. Their wealth and high status often led them to hold high public office.

Urban Food Policies.   The residents of villages and small towns relied on food from surrounding fields, while those in middle-sized towns depended on regional trade in addition to food grown nearby. The officials of large towns and cities imported much of their foodstuffs, especially grain, from greater distances. A medieval town of 3,000 people needed about 1,000 tons of grain a year. Towns and cities located on navigable rivers and harbors were in a favorable position to provide their inhabitants with a regular supply of food. Supply problems, however, limited the growth and prosperity of some towns and cities.

It became very important for some towns and cities to control the food grown in the surrounding countryside. Town officials outlawed hoarding and purchased grain when necessary. For example, BARCELONA officials sent city-owned ships to FLANDERS, SICILY, and Sardinia to buy huge quantities of grain. City and town governments took even stronger measures in the 1290s and early 1300s, when famines were more frequent and widespread.

The officials of several Italian cities succeeded in establishing political control over nearby rural areas and often used military force to gain and maintain their control in the face of challenges by rival cities. Florence, for example, outlawed the sale of food in a zone three to six miles around the city in order to force producers to sell their food within the city.

Remember: *Words in small capital letters have separate entries, and the index at the end of Volume 4 will guide you to more information on many topics.*

Venice took even more forceful measures. In 1234, its government forced RAVENNA to sign a treaty that required that city to sell surplus grain and salt only in Venice. In addition, Venice used its influence to establish the exclusive right to grain exports from certain regions, such as the lower Po River valley. Venice also succeeded in preventing certain other Italian towns, such as Bologna, from purchasing grain in certain regions. These policies and the sea power to back them up made Venice as well supplied with food as any city in Europe.

Other port cities also established policies that maximized the import of foodstuffs and minimized their export. Officials of some ports required that a specified percentage of every incoming ship's cargo had to contain certain kinds of food, while others imposed heavy duties on food exports or even prohibited them altogether. Many towns and cities set policies favorable to food traders by promising them safe passage to the marketplace and security while they were there, and by guaranteeing speedy and just settlements of business disputes. Many town leaders disregarded the usual restrictions on people doing business who were not citizens or GUILD members to encourage these people to sell produce in their markets.

Town leaders were also concerned about food prices and quality control. They tried to protect the consumer by placing limits on the activities of middlemen. Acceptable retail practices today, such as forestalling and regrating, were frowned on in the Middle Ages. Forestallers bought food from producers before it arrived at the market, or before the market officially opened, and then resold it. Regrators bought the food in the market early in the day, often in bulk, and then resold it later the same day when food was scarcer and prices were higher. To restrict these practices, towns passed laws. For example, in Southampton, England, only actual fishermen were permitted to sell fresh fish, and they themselves were required to bring their whole catch to the market. Town officials were also on the alert for food hawkers, who sometimes sold poor-quality or stolen food.

Towns maintained price and quality controls by taxing the sale of food, with the exception of wheat. These food taxes reduced the profits of middlemen, kept down prices for the consumer, and provided a source of income for towns. Town governments also received revenue from the rents that merchants paid on stalls, shops, and display tables in the marketplace.

Regulation of the food trades was also done by guilds. Individual guilds, such as bakers' or butchers' guilds, not only passed ordinances concerning price and quality but also appointed inspectors and maintained their own courts to enforce guild rules. However, food trade guilds never became as powerful as some other guilds. This was largely because the food trades were considered too vital to the public interest to allow them to fall under the control of any one group.

Many town residents produced as much of their own food as they could. They grew vegetables and herbs in their gardens and kept farm animals, such as chickens and pigs, at home, in poultry sheds and pigsties. As late as 1481, city authorities in Frankfurt were still trying to enforce laws against placing pigsties in front of houses and on public streets.

Kinds of Food

Bread was the most common food in the medieval diet, but grain was also used to make porridge, buns, pies, tarts, and other baked goods, as well as ale and beer. Other foods that supplemented this grain-based diet included meat, fish, dairy products, fruits, and vegetables.

Bread and Grain.   People spent more on bread or on grain used to make bread than on anything else. For example, an unmarried worker in Florence in the 1300s spent at least a third of his wages on bread or wheat, while a family of ten in Genoa bought five and half tons of grain a year. Large noble households, such as that of the earl of Leicester in 13th-century England, used about 300 pounds of grain daily.

To ensure a steady grain supply, town and city governments purchased large amounts and then guarded its transportation routes against thieves and pirates. Some towns had special officials who supervised the sale of grain to the town.

There were basically four groups of grain sellers during the Middle Ages: grain merchants, who bought grain from producers and then sold it to middlemen; local dealers, called cornmongers, who bought grain from producers and sold it directly to consumers; grain regrators, who bought grain in the market and then sold it later in the same market; and grain brokers, who acted as agents between buyers and sellers and received a fee for their services. Some towns and cities imposed harsher penalties on those who made unreasonably high profits from the buying and selling of wheat, rye, barley, and oats than on those who profited from the sale of other food and nonfood products.

While city officials and bakers' guilds did not set the price of grain, they did try to control the price and quality of bread made from that grain. In England, a national bread tax fixed the price of a loaf of bread but allowed its weight to change according to the price of wheat. Officials also regulated the baker's profit by adding a fixed allowance for expenses—fuel, labor, light, yeast, and salt—to the price of the bread and then limiting the baker's profit from the sale. When bakers complained that they were losing money, officials raised the fixed allowance several times. The bread-tax law also gave bread inspectors the authority to fine bakers for selling bread that was poorly fermented*, mixed, or baked. Dishonest bakers were known to put just about anything—including cobwebs or sand—into the dough to increase their profit.

While many bakers made their own bread and sold it in market stalls or shops, most spent the bulk of their time making bread for other people, either by making dough from grain or flour brought to them, or by baking the dough customers brought to them. Thus, many townspeople made their own bread by buying the grain, getting it milled into flour, making their own dough, and then bringing it to the baker for baking. Some brought the grain to the baker to have him make it into dough and bake it. Even in these more limited capacities, however, bakers were able to charge high prices for their services because they owned all the ovens.

In one case, in London in the 1300s, several bakers were charged with fraud. One of the accused, John Brid, cut a trapdoor in the bottom of the box where customers put their dough. A servant hiding underneath opened the trapdoor and sliced off some of the dough "piecemeal and bit

* **ferment** to undergo gradual chemical change in which yeast and bacteria convert sugars into alcohol

by bit, frequently, collecting great quantities from such dough, falsely, wickedly and maliciously." Brid then used the dough he stole from customers to make bread he sold as his own. London authorities punished Brid and the other accused bakers by putting them in the pillory—a wooden frame with holes to lock the head and hands—and hanging dough around their necks.

Meat. Because meat was expensive, it was considered a luxury for most people, except for those who lived in regions where livestock was raised. However, as standards of living rose, meat was eaten more frequently.

The most common and least expensive meat was mutton (from sheep), but pork, beef, lamb, and veal (from calves) were also popular. Many people bought sheep, pigs, or other animals live and then slaughtered them and salted the meat themselves. Others bought their meat fresh from butchers. Cooks and innkeepers sold meat they prepared in the form of roasts, meat pies, and stews.

The high price of meat and its popularity made butchers relatively prosperous. Next to merchants dealing in grain, wine, and spices, butchers made a better living than other food traders and were among the first to form their own guilds. They also profited from the additional sale of meat by-products such as hides, skins, and tallow*.

* **tallow** animal fat used to make candles and soap

The slaughter of animals and disposal of their bones, blood, internal organs, and waste was a continual source of disagreement between butchers and the public. The filth and stench created by the killing of animals in the streets, in the yards of butchers' homes, in slaughterhouses, or in the marketplace itself was intolerable. Large cities, such as London and Paris, banned the slaughter of animals within the city, but the laws were never fully enforced. Many butchers disposed of animal waste by cutting up the remains of the slaughtered animals and throwing them into rivers and streams. Some butchers took animal remains in wheelbarrows to buildings called barrow houses, or outside of town to pits dug especially for waste disposal.

Fish. Fish was a common food in the Middle Ages mostly because the church prohibited eating meat on Fridays and Saturdays, during Lent*, and on certain religious festivals throughout the year. These meatless days, which added up to more than a third of the year, encouraged the catching, selling, and eating of fish.

* **Lent** Christian period of fasting that precedes Easter

Freshwater and saltwater fish were sold salted, dried, pickled, smoked, or fresh. Shellfish such as mussels and oysters were sold fresh by the bushel. Fresh fish was considerably more expensive than preserved fish, which lasted longer. Fresh salmon, pike, trout, carp, and other freshwater fish were valued so highly that feudal lords jealously guarded their rights to rivers, streams, and ponds.

Because fresh fish spoiled so quickly, it was allowed to be sold in the streets. It could not be sold after the second day, however, unless it was properly salted. The sale of fish in the marketplace was subject to regulations similar to those imposed on meat. Sales took place in a special section of the market, and the quality of the fish sold was carefully monitored. Fines were given to fish sellers who continually poured water on their fish to make them look fresher, as well as to those who sold fish outside the designated fish-market area.

Bread was the most common food in the grain-based medieval diet. Meat was generally expensive, and butchers were among the most prosperous of food merchants. In addition to selling meat, butchers prepared and sold animal by-products such as hides and tallow, the animal fat that was used for candles and soap.

See color plate 3, vol. 1.

Town governments took steps to ensure an adequate supply of fish, especially during Lent. The authorities of most seaports required fishermen to carry their catch directly to the market, where they then were allowed to sell their fish to other sellers called fishmongers. Because of the difficulties in preserving freshness and the slowness of transportation, only salted and dried fish could be sold in bulk and shipped long-distance.

Dairy Products. In the late Middle Ages, dairy farming and butter production flourished, especially in Denmark, Norway, and Sweden. Butter, cheese, milk, and eggs were brought to town from the countryside and sold in a special hall or covered section of the market called a "butter cross." The peasants who brought their dairy products to market each week either sold them directly to consumers themselves or to others who would resell them in the market. In larger towns, the sale of dairy products was usually in the hands of middlemen called cheese mongers. These middlemen bought their dairy products from rural producers and estate owners and sold them in town in a shop or market stall. Cheese was made from ewe's milk until the 1300s, when cheese makers switched to cow's milk. At about the same time, butter made from cow's milk replaced lard.

Milk and eggs, which spoiled relatively quickly, were sold mostly retail. Since salted butter and cheese lasted longer, they could be sold wholesale and traded over greater distances. In the late Middle Ages, raising poultry solely for eggs became a specialized business in many parts of Europe.

Fruits and Vegetables. Many people grew most of the fruits and vegetables they ate in their own gardens. Still, those who grew fruits and vegetables had a prosperous trade, especially around the larger towns, where their crops were sold in the marketplace. Many estates and monasteries had their own orchards where apples or olives were grown. During the Middle Ages, the fruit trade was often quite profitable because fruits and nuts had a variety of delicious uses. They were used to make desserts, preserves, cider, oils, and fruit drinks. They were also sold fresh or dried.

Much of the retail trade was in the hands of professional gardeners and rural producers who sold what they grew directly to the consumer in the marketplace. Middlemen occasionally profited by making bulk purchases from the orchards of large estates. There was also a thriving export trade. Traders transported olive oil, dried figs, nuts, dates, and raisins north from the Mediterranean area.

Vegetables were less a part of this trade because most people grew their own. Some townspeople, however, went to the market to purchase vegetables, especially onions and garlic, which stored better than other vegetables and could be shipped long distances. The most commonly eaten vegetables—beans, peas, cabbage, and leeks—were homegrown. If they were traded at all, they were sold close to where they were grown. Because the trade in vegetables was handled mostly by professional gardeners and peasant producers, wealthy merchants and middlemen were rarely involved.

Wine, Ale, and Beer. During the Middle Ages, the wine trade was an international business. In the early 1300s, wine made up 30 percent of English imports and 25 percent of imports in the Low Countries. Wine was in great demand by the nobility, clergy, and wealthy townspeople. The nobility drank more wine than any other class, with aristocratic households spending as much as 40 percent of their budget on wine.

Wine merchants, who were often organized into guilds, transported the wine they bought in large, barrel-shaped vessels called casks. Sometimes they sold it directly to consumers, but more often tavern keepers sold wine to the public. Town governments strictly regulated the retail sale of wine by fixing the price of different grades of wine and by monitoring its quality. Many tavern keepers and wine merchants tried to increase profits by mixing good wine with cheap or spoiled wine, or by adding gum, resin, starch, or sugar to thin wines to give the wines more body and to bring higher prices. Town authorities fined offenders and punished them by making them drink the wine they made or by pouring it over their heads.

Most northern Europeans drank ale rather than wine. In Scandinavia, England, Germany, Holland, and northern France, ale was regarded as a food necessity more than a luxury drink. The ingredients of ale were malted barley, water, and yeast, with herbs and spices added for flavor. In some parts of Europe, ale brewers used oats or mixed grains.

Because ale spoiled after five days, it was brewed frequently, mostly at home by women. Even in towns, commercial brewers were usually women earning extra income for their families. Brewers put stakes or signs up in front of their houses to show that they had ale for sale. A bush or a bunch of ivy on the stake or sign let the local ale-testing officials know that a fresh batch had been brewed and was ready for testing.

Because ale was such a common drink, its price and quality were closely regulated. In England, an assize (or regulation) on ale set the price according to the changing price of the grain from which the malt was made. Village and town governments appointed ale tasters to supervise the quality of the ale. Brewers could be fined for using impure water or bad malt, for selling ale that was old and stale, or for trying to pass off weak ale as a more expensive grade. Town officials also inspected and stamped the measuring containers brewers used. Some brewers used false bottoms or elaborately shaped vessels that held less ale than they were supposed to. Even though brewing laws were hard to enforce, medieval courts prosecuted violators of the ale assize more frequently than any other food traders. Still, most brewers found it easier and less expensive to keep breaking the law and paying the fine than to change their practices.

In the late Middle Ages, beer—an alcoholic drink made from malt, hops, and water—became very popular, especially in Germany and Holland. The hops, which acted as a preservative, gave beer a much longer shelf life than ale, thus allowing brewers to transport their beer over longer distances. Unlike the ale trade, which was primarily a household enterprise, the beer trade became highly commercialized. Beer brewers, mostly male and organized into guilds, stood in contrast to the mostly female ale brewers, who usually were not organized into guilds.

By the end of the Middle Ages, the medieval diet remained largely based on wheat, supplemented by barley and oats in northern Europe and by rice in parts of the south. Grains were made into porridge for breakfast, bread for lunch, and a grain-based gruel* for dinner, with ale and beer made from grain the drink of most people, especially in the north. Although the medieval diet continued to be overwhelmingly grain centered, people supplemented their diet as circumstances allowed with meat, fish, dairy products, vegetables, fruits, and wine. (*See also* **Agriculture; Chaucer, Geoffrey; Famine; Fishing, Fish Trade; Guilds; Trade; Waterworks.**)

* **gruel** thin porridge, or cereal

Forests

* **diocese** church district under a bishop's authority

* **pagan** word used by Christians to mean non-Christian and believing in several gods

Much of Europe was heavily wooded in the early Middle Ages. The exception was some of the lands bordering the Mediterranean Sea, where an unfavorable climate and centuries of intense human activity had depleted ancient forests. Forests were of great value to medieval society. They were a place to hunt and gather food, feed livestock, and obtain timber and fuel. They also served as natural boundaries between villages, counties, kingdoms, and church dioceses*. In addition, they provided a refuge for hermits, outlaws, misfits, and other fugitives from society, including victims of religious persecution. For many medieval people, the forests had an aura of mystery, and some continued the pagan* worship of sacred trees and the belief in forest spirits.

Heavily wooded forests remained a dominant feature of the European landscape until the period from the 900s through the 1100s. During that time, many forests were cleared to make way for farms and towns or to meet the increasing demand for wood. As the forests declined, conflicts often arose among various groups in society over the use of dwindling forest resources.

Restrictions on the Use of Forests.   Before the 600s, there were few restrictions on the use of forests, and anyone could hunt, cut wood, or clear land. For most of the remainder of the Middle Ages, however, forests were set apart from other land by special restrictions on hunting and other uses. The MEROVINGIAN kings of France were among the first to try to control the use of the forests. In the late 600s, they claimed exclusive rights to certain wooded areas in their domain. Their successors, the CAROLINGIANS, also placed restrictions on wooded areas. They set aside royal forests that were subject to special laws. Carolingian law preserved wild animals for the king's hunting and prohibited anyone else from hunting in the restricted areas.

With the decline of the Carolingian Empire and the rise of separate kingdoms in France and Germany, kings continued to control the use of royal forests. At the same time, however, they also gave rights over certain forests to the church or important nobles, who closely guarded their hunting and timber-cutting privileges. By the 1000s in France and the 1200s in Germany, most forests were controlled by local lords rather than by the king.

The idea of the royal forest traveled from France to England as a result of the NORMAN conquest in 1066. WILLIAM I THE CONQUEROR enjoyed hunting, and he issued special laws protecting the "beasts of the forest," which referred specifically to wild boars and several kinds of deer. His BARONS were allowed to hunt these wild animals in specified areas known as chases. In other areas called warrens, they could freely hunt animals except for the so-called beasts of the forest. Gradually, the English royal forest expanded to include more than just wooded areas. In a legal sense, it became a vast game preserve that included non-wooded land, villages, and towns. At its greatest extent, the English royal forest covered more than one-quarter of England.

Administration of Forests.   Special systems of administration were established to manage royal forests. In England, King HENRY II established a strong, centralized administration with various officials. At its head was a chief justice of the forests. Directly under him were wardens, who were responsible for managing particular forests. Under the wardens were foresters, who managed the wild animals of the forest, and verderers, who reported any misuse of timber or misconduct by forest officials. Officials known as regarders made regular inspections of forests to check for breaches of the law. Local courts known as attachment courts prepared cases against those accused of violating the law, and a royal law court, known as the forest eyre, traveled throughout the kingdom to judge the accused.

The violation of forest law in England was a serious matter, and penalties could be very severe. They included mutilation (such as blinding) for killing a deer, and death for a third offense. Such punishments were quite rare, however. Most people found guilty of violating forest law had to pay a fine. Such fines became an important source of revenue for the crown.

In France and Germany, the royal forests were less well organized than in England, and more forestland was controlled by local lords. The king of France appointed *maîtres des forêts* (masters of the forests) to monitor forest income and judge violations of forest law. Other officials were in charge of supervising hunting and the cutting of timber. Nobles or members of the clergy could cut wood in a royal forest as long as they paid a substantial tax on the sale of the wood. French nobles followed similar practices in their own forests. In Germany, a royal forester managed the king's lands, while the nobles placed their forests in the care of a BAILIFF. After the mid-1300s, German nobles became more powerful, and they extended their authority over forests by restricting hunting in entire districts and managing the forest economy under their own laws.

Decline of Medieval Forests.   The growth of towns in the later Middle Ages put a great deal of pressure on forestlands. Large amounts of wood were needed to build houses and other buildings and to provide fuel for cooking, heating, and industry. More land was needed to grow crops to feed urban populations. The result was that many forests were depleted of trees, and forestlands were cleared to make way for agriculture. The problem was most severe in France and Germany. By the 1200s in France, the clearing of forestland resulted in conflicts between nobles and peasant communities over the use of the land, and greater efforts were made to protect the remaining forests. Similar efforts were made in Germany in the 1300s.

England was less affected by such pressures, largely because of its strong, centralized forest administration. Conflicts did arise, however, between the king and barons, who resented the restrictions placed on their own lands. Grievances about the royal forest played a part in the conflict between the barons and King JOHN that resulted in MAGNA CARTA. In 1217, the king issued a Forest Charter, further defining his forest privileges.

By the 1400s, less attention was given to administering and protecting European forests. The BLACK DEATH had killed much of the population in the 1300s, and there was less demand for forest products. Rulers also became preoccupied with other concerns, such as the HUNDRED YEARS WAR, and they neglected the forests. Another factor in the decline of forests was their decreasing economic importance. Kings began to collect taxes from their subjects and relied less on forest revenues. By the end of the Middle Ages, forests had lost much of their importance to society. (*See also* **Hunting and Fowling; Land Use.**)

See map in Black Death (vol. 1).

Fortune

* **allegorical** pertaining to allegory, a literary device in which characters represent ideas, morals, or philosophical or religious principles

During the Middle Ages, Europeans often thought of luck or chance as a goddess, whom they called Fortune. She was the unpredictable and uncontrollable influence on human affairs. She was regarded either as a real goddess or as an allegorical* figure.

Although Christianity did not favor the idea of a goddess of Fortune, neither Scripture nor theology could explain the randomness of human events. Boethius, a Christian educated in the classics, brought the goddess Fortune into the world of the Middle Ages. In the *Consolation of Philosophy,* written while he was a condemned prisoner, Boethius presented the idea that Fortune, although uncontrollable by humans, was less powerful than the Christian God, the Roman god Jove, or Fate. Boethius believed that wealth, fame, and high station in life are neither permanent nor really worth having—an idea that was probably meant to soften the blow, should Fortune decide to take away these attributes.

In this same work, Boethius included the image of the wheel of Fortune. It took on many styles, from delicately drawn miniatures in fine manuscripts to the spectacular rose windows of the cathedrals at Amiens and Basel. Fortune herself was usually drawn larger than human figures to emphasize her greater power. Her victims were depicted as thrown from the wheel by gravity or centrifugal force, and sometimes crushed under the wheel.

Medieval representations of Fortune emphasized her instability and changing nature by showing her with two faces, either side-by-side or back-to-back. She was sometimes shown with one face smiling and the other frowning or with one eye beaming and the other weeping.

Fortune appeared in the works of FROISSART, BOCCACCIO, DANTE, CHAUCER, and other medieval writers and poets. She often appeared in

The allegorical figure of Fortune holds her wheel, while the people on it are randomly thrown off, without regard to age, social class, or any other criteria. This represented the unpredictable and uncontrollable part of human life.

proverbs*, such as the following: "Fortune helps the daring" (a favorite motto in HERALDRY); "Fortune does not stand still, but continually moves"; and "Among men, Fortune is worth more than a plan." (*See also* **Cathedrals and Churches; Glass, Stained.**)

The land known as France today was originally part of the ancient Roman Empire. In the early Middle Ages, Frankish rulers formed an empire made up of territory in what is now France and Germany. This empire split in the 800s, and the western half became the kingdom of France. By the end of the Middle Ages, France was one of the most important nations in Europe.

The Frankish Kingdoms

Gaul. In ancient times, France was known as Gaul. Julius Caesar conquered the area in 51 B.C., and it soon became a prosperous part of the Roman Empire. The Gauls adopted the Latin language and built Roman-style cities. But in the 400s, the Roman Empire began to decline. Germanic tribes from central Europe—including the Franks, the Visigoths, and the Burgundians—invaded Gaul and drove the Roman rulers out.

In the 480s, the Frankish leader Clovis united the tribes living in Gaul into a kingdom under his rule. He made Paris the capital of his kingdom, which stretched from the Pyrenees Mountains in the south to the Rhine River. Several of Clovis's descendants reigned after him. They became known as the MEROVINGIAN dynasty*, and this dynasty held the throne until the early 700s.

The next dynasty to gain control of the empire was the CAROLINGIANS. The greatest leader in this dynasty was Charlemagne, who reigned from 768 to 814. He expanded the empire and established a strong imperial government. Through the palace school and monasteries, he supported advances in culture and learning.

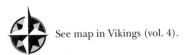

See map in Vikings (vol. 4).

After Charlemagne. When Charlemagne died, a struggle ensued among his heirs for control of the monarchy. The empire was divided into independent regions. VIKINGS raided the weakened empire, ravaging the countryside and even trying to capture Paris. The barons of the western region eventually joined together in 888 to elect a king, named Odo. Odo was the son of Robert the Strong, an important Frankish nobleman.

The new king had only limited power. The royal domain, where he lived, was surrounded by independent counties or principalities, such as BURGUNDY, Normandy, BRITTANY, and AQUITAINE. The king ruled his own domain but could not control the nobles and bishops who held estates and monasteries in the principalities.

When Odo died, more of Charlemagne's relations came forth to claim the throne. The dispute between them ended in 987 with the election of Hugh Capet, another descendant of Robert the Strong. A continuous line of kings drawn from this family, the Capetians, ruled France for much of the Middle Ages.

The Capetian Dynasty

Hugh Capet ruled from 987 to 996. When he came to power, his royal domain was small and consisted of land around three major towns: Paris, Orleans, and Laon. This royal area became known as the Île-de-France—the island, or core, of the king of France. The court of the early Capetians dealt mostly with local affairs in the royal domain and was not much different from those of the great nobles.

Outside the royal domain, the kings faced difficulties in dealing with their subjects. The dukes and barons in the French counties lacked any sense of unity and often fought over their territory, creating even more instability. In addition, many of them did not respect the king's authority. For example, one powerful family held the counties of Vermandois, Troyes, and Blois, surrounding the Île-de-France. They were persistent enemies of the Capetians, who had to seek help from the dukes of Normandy and the counts of Anjou to protect the royal domain.

The monarchy* had much better relations with the church. The king was considered God's representative and was anointed* with holy oil by a priest to mark his special status. The bishops swore loyalty to the king and even sent troops to help him in times of crisis. In return, the king promised to support the Christian faith and to defend the church from enemies.

Hugh Capet asked the bishops to make an important change in the monarchy. In place of the system of electing kings, he wanted to make the throne hereditary. He planned to follow the principle of primogeniture, or inheritance by the eldest son. The bishops agreed and anointed Hugh's eldest son, Robert, with holy oil to ensure his right to succeed his father as king. From this time on, the survival of sons became especially important to the Capetian kings. Some of them married and divorced a succession of wives until a healthy son was born. The system was a success and gave the Capetians an uncontested claim to the throne for more than 300 years.

Growth of Royal Power.   In the 1100s, the Capetians tried to strengthen the king's authority in the royal domain. They felt that, in order to triumph over their rivals, they must first ensure the loyalty of the Île-de-France.

The first ruler of this period, Philip I, reigned from 1060 to 1108. He appointed local officials called *prévôts* as administrators. They carried out royal commands, judged lawsuits, and collected payments owed to the king. Much of the countryside was ruled by castellans, nobles who lived in castles and protected and governed the surrounding area. Philip chose loyal members of the lower nobility as prévôts so that they could help him control the more unruly nobles.

Philip's son, LOUIS VI, ruled from 1108 to 1137. He continued his father's efforts in the royal domain. He focused on winning the loyalty of townspeople. Improvements in trade and manufacturing led to the rapid growth of French towns in the 1100s. Louis agreed to issue charters of privileges to many towns, giving them greater independence.

Louis also changed the nature of the royal court. He made the positions of the household officers—such as the CHAMBERLAIN, chancellor, and SENESCHAL—into more significant jobs. These officials, who accompanied the king on his travels, gradually took on more important responsibilities.

* **monarchy**   nation ruled by a king or queen

* **anoint**   to put holy oil on a person at a religious ceremony or coronation

Remember: Consult the index at the end of Volume 4 to find more information on many topics.

The chancellor, for example, was originally in charge of the king's chapel but was given the power to draw up the royal charters as well.

The household officers came from prominent families, including those of the castellans. When Louis discovered that one group, the Garlande family, was becoming too powerful, he dismissed Stephen of Garlande, who was serving as both chancellor and seneschal*. In Stephen's place, the king took on a young monk named SUGER, who had been his friend since boyhood. Suger also became abbot of a great abbey* at St. Denis.

An excellent diplomat and manager, Abbot Suger became one of Louis's closest advisers. He believed strongly in the importance of strengthening the French monarchy. He developed a theory of government with the king as lord over all the dukes and counts. As Louis subdued the rebellious regions of his domain, many knights and castellans became his vassals*. This was the first step toward fulfilling Suger's vision.

Abbot Suger also advised Louis VII, who followed his father on the throne and reigned from 1137 to 1179. As a young man, Louis VII was an energetic soldier. But difficulties arising during his reign eventually broke his spirit. The Second Crusade, which he launched in the 1140s, ended in failure. When he returned, he found the counties outside the royal domain—such as Flanders, Champagne, and Anjou—increasing in power by acquiring more land and forming alliances with each other. By 1154, Henry II of Anjou held regions exceeding those of the French king.

In addition, Louis's marriage to ELEANOR OF AQUITAINE, heiress to vast territories in France, did not produce a son. Only many years later, after divorcing Eleanor and marrying twice more, did Louis have a son. By then, his health was failing, and his son, PHILIP II, found himself king at the age of 14.

Philip II Augustus.   Philip II, however, went on to make a significant impact as king. He brought about fundamental changes in the government, defeated some of his most powerful rivals, and greatly enlarged the kingdom. He began the governmental changes by replacing the barons on his council with more effective administrators of lesser rank. He also emphasized the role of Paris as the capital of the kingdom. Previously, the court often traveled through the countryside to collect taxes and settle disputes. Now the prévôts and the judges, known as BAILLIS, performed these jobs and came to Paris to report on their progress.

Improved record keeping and the establishment of permanent buildings to store public records in Paris made the government more efficient. Revenues increased enough to fund a regular army. For the first time, the Capetians possessed a well-organized administration and enough military strength to challenge the great barons.

In 1191, Philip claimed some of the territories surrounding the royal domain after the count of Flanders died. His actions created ill will against him in the north. After Philip's conquest of Normandy in 1204, the English joined with northern French and Flemish lords and the German emperor, who opposed Philip.

In 1214, these allies launched a two-pronged attack on the northern and southern sections of the royal domain. Philip's eldest son, Prince Louis, met the southern forces and checked their advance. Philip met the northern armies on the fields of Bouvines in one of the rare full-scale

* **seneschal** person who manages property and financial affairs, such as for a royal court

* **abbey** monastery under the rule of an abbot or abbess

* **vassal** person given land by a lord or monarch in return for loyalty and services

A Royal Coronation

At Philip II's coronation in November 1179, the procession plainly showed the power of the French barons. The count of Flanders bore the 14-year-old king's sword and presided over the banquet. The three sons of the count of Anjou appeared in great splendor, with the eldest carrying the crown. The archbishop of Rheims, a brother of the counts of Champagne, anointed and crowned the king. Young Philip cut a frail figure beside these mighty barons, but he seems to have been undaunted. By his mid-20s, he was ruling with confidence and authority.

* **heretic** person who disagrees with established church doctrine

* **crusader** person who participated in the holy wars against the Muslims during the Middle Ages

* **regent** person appointed to govern a kingdom when the rightful ruler is too young, absent, or disabled

See color plate 6, vol. 3.

battles of the century. By day's end, Philip's troops captured the northern barons, and the German emperor fled the field.

With this victory, Philip secured his hold on much of the Angevins' land. By manipulating marriages and family inheritances, he claimed additional lands so that he was soon in military control of Normandy, Brittany, Maine, Touraine, and Anjou. Along with Artois, Vermandois, and Valois—which had passed to the crown several years earlier—these lands tripled the size of the royal domain.

However, new land was of little lasting value unless it was incorporated into the royal government. Philip assigned prévôts to the new territories to collect revenues. Teams of the king's representatives circulated throughout the counties, performing judicial and administrative duties. All of these officials came to Paris three times a year, keeping the court informed about events in the new districts.

Normandy, the former heartland of the Angevins, became the cherished possession of the French kings. The victory at Bouvines brought peace during the closing years of Philip's reign and eliminated all possible challengers to royal authority in the north of France.

Philip's successes inspired members of the court to glorify him in literature. The historian Rigord of St. Denis gave him the title of "Augustus" because he "augmented" the royal domain. William the Breton, Philip's chaplain and a witness to the victory at Bouvines, completed a life of Philip begun by Rigord, glorifying him as a conqueror and the hero of a powerful nation. Their newly acquired resources and authority made the Capetians undisputed masters of a vast realm in the 1220s.

After the death of Philip II in 1223, his son, Louis VIII, succeeded him and ruled until 1226. Although his reign was short, he achieved a decisive victory against the CATHARS in southern France. The Cathars were Christian heretics* who had established an independent church based on their religious views. They were also known as Albigensians, after their stronghold in the city of Albi. Crusaders* had been trying to silence them for many years. Louis's forces finally overcame the heretics and their supporters in 1226.

Louis IX (St. Louis). When Louis VIII died, his wife, BLANCHE OF CASTILE, became regent* for their young son, LOUIS IX. This caused a revolt among the northern barons, who disliked Blanche because she was from Spain; they still considered her a foreigner. Yet Blanche proved to be a capable ruler and had a dominant influence on the government for the next 25 years.

Like his parents, Louis IX, who ruled from 1226 to 1270, made effective use of his power. He was pious and strong, and his moral and political leadership made France one of the most important countries in the West. His first major task was to hold on to the regions his forefathers had captured.

Occasional rebellions against royal domination still erupted in some of the conquered regions. In addition, there were strong, local customs in provinces with long histories outside the king's realm. Louis used a method first developed by Philip II of allowing the provinces to keep their own government institutions as long as they were loyal to the crown. In Normandy, for example, the Norman courts and systems of financial

* **principality** region that is ruled by a prince

* **crusades** holy wars declared by the pope against non-Christians. Most were against Muslims, but crusades were also declared against heretics and pagans.

* **saint** Christian who is officially recognized as a holy person by the church

accounting remained in place, but officials from the Île-de-France held the most important posts. Some local practices were so effective that the king adopted their best features for the whole country.

In the south of France, particularly in the province of LANGUEDOC, there was more resistance to royal authority. After the Capetians defeated the Albigensians, they installed military governors in the region to prevent any further uprisings. The southerners resented the presence of these harsh officials, who reported any rebellious activity and confiscated the property of members of the opposition.

In addition, the Treaty of Paris (1229) made Alphonse of Poitiers, Louis IX's brother, the heir to Toulouse, the most important principality* in the south. Alphonse soon gained control of the southwestern county of Poitou. Resistance to these royal maneuvers spread, and the growing opposition gained support from allies in England. In 1242, however, Louis IX's forces overcame the rebels in a series of battles. Later, Louis built a new town on the south coast, Aigues-Mortes, a symbol of royal authority. He also forced the leaders of the opposition to contribute men and materials for its construction. The king went on a crusade* in 1248, taking these same leaders with him to prevent any further troubles, and sailing from his new royal port.

When Louis returned from his failed crusade in 1254, he set about improving his government, making genuine attempts to respond to requests from the people. His policies won the loyalty of subjects in both the north and the south. He sent teams of investigators around the country to hear and evaluate complaints against the royal administration. They listened sympathetically and, if necessary, paid citizens for wrongs done to them—such as illegal seizures of property during the Albigensian crusade or ill treatment received at the hands of French authorities. They also removed any officials found guilty of unusually cruel acts.

Louis IX's reforms left no part of his kingdom untouched. He reorganized the Parlement of Paris (the chief French court) and thoroughly examined the Parisian city government to eliminate corruption and wasteful spending. He also improved the relationship between the monarchy and the church. The care and decency he exercised led many to see him as the ideal Christian monarch of his day. After his death, the church declared Louis to be a saint*.

However, there were still lingering problems that threatened royal authority. One was the appanage system, a tradition of endowing young princes of the royal family with large tracts of land. Some of these princes neglected their domains or died without heirs. Fortunately, the crown was able to recover much of the property when ownership came into question, so that, at least during the 1200s, there was no significant loss of land.

Several territories were still in the hands of great barons, and these posed another problem for the Capetians. Here again, luck was on the side of the monarchy. The government purchased some lands, such as the region around Mâcon. Marriages between members of the royal family and those of powerful dukes and counts brought Provence, Champagne, and Burgundy into alliance or directly into the royal domain. In provinces such as Brittany and Flanders, which had supported rebellions, royal forces maintained control through military strength, commanding local leaders to recognize the king's sovereignty.

Art and Architecture

Plate 1

St. George fights the dragon in this 15th-century manuscript illumination from Novgorod, an important cultural center of medieval Russia. St. George was a favorite saint of the Russian people and is often depicted in Russian art. Although St. George was revered by ordinary mortals, it is said that his "deeds are known only to God."

Plate 2

Italian artist Giotto di Bondone worked primarily in fresco, a painting technique in which color is applied to moist plaster and chemically bonds with the plaster as it dries. *Christ Entering Jerusalem,* painted in 1306, is one of a series of frescoes that Giotto created for the Scrovegni family chapel in Padua, Italy.

Plate 3

Karlstein Castle was built near Prague, Bohemia, by Emperor Charles IV and completed about 1365. In the elaborately decorated Chapel of the Holy Cross, shown here, the walls are studded with large semiprecious stones and lined with paintings of saints. The vaulted ceilings are covered with gold.

Plate 4

The Bayeux Tapestry is perhaps the best known of medieval embroideries. It is a pictorial narration of the events surrounding the Norman conquest of England. Much of the tapestry depicts the Battle of Hastings, fought between Norman and Anglo-Saxon troops in 1066. This scene shows Norman knights fallen under the hill of Senlac.

Plate 5

Medieval tapestries generally were produced for noble and wealthy patrons. While their practical purpose was to help insulate drafty dwellings, many were also masterpieces of art and craftsmanship. This detail from a French tapestry shows a lady with a unicorn. Tapestries often pictured stories that were meant to instruct and entertain medieval audiences.

Plate 6

Stained glass windows were the crowning glory of Gothic architecture and are among the most beautiful examples of medieval art. Stained glass scenes in church windows depicted episodes from the lives of Christ, the Virgin Mary, saints, and other religious figures. This stained glass window from Canterbury Cathedral in England, dating from the 1200s, depicts the magi speaking with King Herod.

Plate 7

Mosaic art—a technique that uses small pieces of colored stones and precious metals set in mortar—was practiced primarily by the Byzantines. This mosaic of Christ is from the church of Hagia Sophia in Constantinople. It was made in the 1200s.

Plate 8

Until the invention of the printing press in the 1400s, all medieval books were written by hand and some were beautifully illustrated. This page is from the Book of Kells, one of the most famous illuminated manuscripts of the Middle Ages. This book of the Gospels was kept in the monastery in Kells, Ireland, from the early 800s until the 1600s.

Plate 9

A diptych consists of two hinged panels that could be folded shut for travel. Diptychs were often used as small altarpieces in churches or for private devotion. The Wilton Diptych, shown here, was painted in England in the late 1300s. It shows saints (left) presenting King Richard II to the Virgin Mary and the Christ child (right).

Plate 10

This illumination of a lion and lioness is in a Persian manuscript titled "Advantages Derived from Animals" that was written by Ibn Baktishu in 1295. The book is also known as the Morgan Bestiary. Bestiaries are catalogs of real and mythical creatures that describe the appearance, habits, and symbolic significance of the beasts.

Plate 11

The entrance portal to the shrine of Imam Riza, shown here, is located in the Mosque of Gawhar Shad in Iran. It dates from around 1418. Islamic custom forbids the use of images of people or animals in a religious context. As a result, Islamic art features rich, intricate geometric and floral designs in its religious buildings, manuscripts, and other art forms.

Plate 12

This stave, or wooden, Christian church was built in Borgund, Norway, about 1150. It is believed to be modeled on pagan temples. Both crosses and dragon heads protect the church from the powers of evil. Between 500 and 600 stave churches were built in Norway in the Middle Ages, most of them in the 1100s. Only a few have survived to the present day.

Plate 13

This Armenian miniature from the 1100s or the 1200s shows Christ walking on water. Armenian art resembles aspects of both Byzantine and Eastern art. Many high-quality illuminated manuscripts were produced in Armenia during the Middle Ages.

Plate 14

The Coptic church was founded by early Egyptian Christians. This painting on wood, made in the 600s, is from the church of St. Menas in Abu Mina, Egypt. It shows Christ, holding a jeweled book in one hand and embracing St. Menas with his other arm.

Plate 15

The Gothic statues depicting the Annunciation and Visitation adorn Rheims Cathedral in France. Based on the Gospel of Luke, the two figures on the left show the archangel Gabriel announcing to the Virgin Mary that she will be the mother of Christ. On the right, Mary visits her pregnant cousin, Elizabeth, who, after being barren for many years, will become the mother of John the Baptist.

Philip IV the Fair.   When Philip IV the Fair came to power in 1285, he had an opportunity to build on the successes achieved by his grandfather, Louis IX. He was a skillful ruler, but his forceful ways sometimes made him unpopular. One of his first conflicts involved the territory of Gascony, on the southwest coast of France. Gascony was a possession of the English king, but Philip decided to claim it for France. His campaign, which failed, left another problem in its wake.

Philip knew that he needed to raise money if he intended to go to war with England. Normally, the French king would call on the church to contribute funds in such a crisis. But the pope*, BONIFACE VIII, claimed that the king could not tax the clergy without the pope's permission. Because the papacy* had often called on the French monarchy for help in times of trouble, Philip resented the pope's interference, and a serious conflict erupted between them.

Philip had a great deal of public support in this dispute. In the eyes of the French people, the king was esteemed as the heir of Charlemagne and of the saintly Louis IX. Pope Boniface, on the other hand, was known to be ambitious and eager for more power. An insulting war of words began. The pope made extreme statements about papal authority and the freedom of the church from royal control. Philip summoned a council of nobles, churchmen, and townsmen to defend his position. Finally, in 1302, the French arrested the pope. Although he was rescued, he soon died. After the brief term of office of Benedict XI, Philip supported the election of a French archbishop* as Pope Clement V, who established his papacy at AVIGNON in southern France.

The victory over Pope Boniface encouraged Philip to forge ahead on other religious issues. He expelled the Jews from France in 1306 and seized their property. He then turned his attention to the Knights of the Temple (known as the Templars), a religious order of knights dedicated to protecting sites won by the crusaders in the Holy Land. Over the years, the Templars had grown wealthy and powerful in Europe. Philip accused them of heresy, and, with the reluctant support of Pope Clement, the Templars were formally suppressed in 1312. This was followed by the execution of their leaders and the confiscation of their property.

When Philip's reign ended in 1314, there was growing resistance to the harsh policies of his later years. But most French people of the time had great respect for the monarchy and took pride in the accomplishments of the Capetians. In 1328, the death of Philip's son Charles IV brought this powerful dynasty to an end.

The last hundred years of Capetian rule strengthened the foundations of the French state. The monarchy functioned as the supreme authority in the kingdom. Although there were few checks on the king's use of his power, the high moral standards set by St. Louis and the fear of rebellion led most rulers to act with care. In the legal sphere, the appellate* system, with the Parlement of Paris at its head as the highest court, emphasized the role of the central government and instilled a sense of order.

Paris was still growing, but elsewhere the population leveled off around 1300, first in the countryside and then in the towns. In rural areas, many peasants living as serfs* obtained their freedom by paying large sums to their landlords. The economy suffered setbacks as the result of a depression that began in the late 1200s, with high prices and unstable

* **pope** bishop of Rome and head of the Western Christian Church

* **papacy** office of the pope and his administrators

* **archbishop** head bishop in a region or nation

* **appellate** referring to a judicial system in which a higher court has the power to review the decisions of lower courts

* **serf** rural worker with little or no freedom who was sometimes sold along with the land he worked

money in circulation. The prosperous commercial fairs that had been held in Champagne for many years fell into a decline, and trade in the region suffered.

French culture continued to thrive, primarily in the cities. The University of Paris flourished as a center for theological studies under such scholars as Thomas AQUINAS and BONAVENTURE. Orleans, Toulouse, and Montpellier also had influential schools and universities. At the same time, popular religious movements, based on the ideas spread by the Cathars, criticized the worldliness of the church and promoted the quest for a purer, more spiritual life.

The lively, artistic environment of the day is apparent from architectural triumphs, such as the Sainte Chapelle built under Louis IX, and the literature of courtly love*, such as the ROMAN DE LA ROSE. Works of history, including those of the monks at St. Denis, recorded the traditions and events that were considered meaningful and captured the general mood of confidence in the country's future success.

The Valois Dynasty

When Charles IV, the last Capetian king, died in 1328, he had no sons. His closest male relative was his nephew, EDWARD III OF ENGLAND. The French were wary of encouraging any English claim to their throne. The French barons instead chose Charles's cousin, PHILIP OF VALOIS, who became Philip VI. He was the first of a dynasty of Valois kings who ruled France through the end of the Middle Ages.

Time of Disaster.   In 1348, French optimism received a blow in the form of the BLACK DEATH. This deadly disease swept through the cities and towns, disrupting every aspect of society. As the population fell, there was a shortage of workers and the economy faltered. Further outbreaks of the plague occurred in 1361 and 1374.

While the plague took its toll in the towns, peasant farmers suffered from the effects of war. There were civil wars in Normandy and Brittany in the 1350s and 1360s, as well as invasions by the English. Between these conflicts, unemployed soldiers roamed the countryside, raiding crops for food and burning fields to prevent their enemies from getting supplies. Occasional crop failures due to poor weather conditions contributed to these problems, causing widespread FAMINES. Epidemics, famines, and warfare continued to varying degrees over the next hundred years, so that by 1494 the population of France was only about half that of 1314.

As the economy became unstable, the crown tried to raise money by manipulating the value of the currency and imposing new taxes. These policies were not entirely successful and even caused some revolts.

The Hundred Years War.   The uneasy peace with England soon collapsed, and in 1337 the two countries went to war. The series of struggles that followed, known as the HUNDRED YEARS WAR, lasted until 1453. The second Valois king, John II, who ruled from 1350 to 1364, tried to initiate economic improvements to overcome the effects of the plague and the war. However, John's efforts were cut short in 1356, when Edward, Prince of Wales, captured him at Poitiers. The French had to impose taxes on their people to pay the huge ransom for the king's return.

---

* **courtly love** mannerly, idealized form of love that became popular in the Middle Ages, especially in literature

 See map in Black Death (vol. 1).

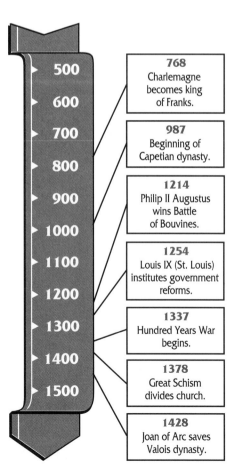

500	
600	**768** Charlemagne becomes king of Franks.
700	
800	**987** Beginning of Capetian dynasty.
900	**1214** Philip II Augustus wins Battle of Bouvines.
1000	
1100	**1254** Louis IX (St. Louis) institutes government reforms.
1200	
1300	**1337** Hundred Years War begins.
1400	**1378** Great Schism divides church.
1500	
	1428 Joan of Arc saves Valois dynasty.

The Hundred Years War was not one long war but a series of conflicts fought between England and France. The dispute concerned English territories in France and England's claim to the French crown. At the Battle of Crécy in 1346, an army of 10,000 English defeated a French army twice its size. The French army's crossbows proved to be no match for the skill and speed of the English longbow archers.

* **theologian**   person who studies religious faith and practice

When King John died, his frail and studious son, CHARLES V, came to the throne. Charles had some successes against the English forces but could not take their main strongholds at Calais and Bordeaux. He also faced a pressing crisis in the church.

The papacy had been based in Avignon for many years until, in 1378, Pope Gregory XI moved it back to Rome. After his death, the new pope, Urban VI, soon turned others away from him with his violent temper. Urban's opponents installed another pope, Clement VII, at Avignon, while Urban continued to reign in Rome. Disregarding the advice of French theologians*, Charles supported Clement's election. The situation, known as the Great SCHISM, caused alarm throughout the Christian world.

Charles's son, Charles VI, was only 11 years old when his father died in 1380. As he grew up, he suffered from insanity, and his uncle, the duke of Burgundy, and his brother, Louis of Orleans, fought over the right to govern in his place. Their dispute erupted into civil war in the early 1400s.

By 1415, the ongoing wars with England flared up as well. This time, the English king, HENRY V, inflicted crushing defeats on the French at Harfleur and Agincourt. The Treaty of Troyes of 1420 declared Henry V the heir to the French throne, in place of the son of Charles VI. This seemed to be the end of the Valois dynasty until, two years later, Henry V died.

CHARLES VII, the disinherited prince, soon had a second chance at the monarchy. In 1428, the English advanced towards Orleans, and a peasant girl, JOAN OF ARC, came to see the prince. She claimed to have heard saintly voices urging her to restore Charles to his throne. With Joan's help, the French defended Orleans, and Charles finally received his crown. Inspired by these events, the French army gradually drove the English out of France, ending decades of war.

Louis XI, Charles's son, ruled from 1461 to 1483. He oversaw France's recovery from the wars and gathered together the pieces of territory that had returned to the crown. He established an effective central administration, stabilized the currency, imposed annual taxes, and maintained a regularly paid army. The kingdom now extended farther than at any time since the days of the Franks, and it began to resemble the modern French state. (*See also* **Capet, Hugh; Champagne, County of; Charlemagne; Commune; Crusades; Flanders and the Low Countries; France, Representative Assemblies; French Language and Literature; Henry II of England; Law; Normans; Toulouse.**)

France, Representative Assemblies

* **clergy** priests, deacons, and other church officials qualified to perform church ceremonies

* **nobility** persons forming the noble class; aristocracy

* **vassal** person given land by a lord or monarch in return for loyalty and services

* **provincial** referring to a province or an area controlled by an empire

Medieval FRANCE had different types of representative assemblies. Some were local assemblies consisting of representatives from various provinces, counties, and towns. There were also national assemblies whose members came from certain social classes, such as the clergy*, the nobility*, merchants, and peasants. During the 1300s, these national meetings were referred to as assemblies of the three estates. The first estate was the clergy, the second estate was the nobility, and the third estate was a diverse group that included merchants, artisans, and peasants. By the end of the 1400s, these national meetings were called the Estates General, a term that is still used today.

France's representative assemblies, like those in other countries, were the forerunners of modern representative government. The assemblies were based on the idea that an individual or group of individuals could legally represent others and make commitments for them. The existence of the assemblies depended on two factors: a tradition in which a ruler consulted subjects on important matters, and the organization of society into recognizable groups from which representatives could be chosen.

Although various assemblies had met in France since the early Middle Ages, an established system of representative assemblies did not develop until the rise of FEUDALISM in the ninth and tenth centuries. Under the feudal system, a lord had the right to require his vassals* to give him aid and counsel. To do this, he had to summon them to meetings. French kings thus held meetings of their leading nobles and clergy. Dukes and other nobles summoned their vassals as well, which gave rise to provincial* and local assemblies.

These early French assemblies usually included only the upper classes of society. In the early 1200s, the growth of towns and the rise of merchant classes led to the need for representation for other groups as well. As a result, towns and various groups appointed representatives with varying degrees of authority to act in their name. These representatives were instructed as to what they should seek at assemblies and what they should grant in return.

Beginning in the late 1200s and early 1300s, French monarchs convened a number of large national assemblies to deal with political, financial, military, and governmental matters. Yet these national assemblies never gained power as great as that of England's PARLIAMENT, which developed during the same period. One reason was the great strength of France's provincial assemblies. France was a much larger country than England, and it contained many different regions with different cultures and languages. The leaders of these regions jealously guarded their rights and only reluctantly ceded power to the king. Moreover, a number of medieval French kings disliked the national assemblies and favored a decentralized system with provincial and local courts and assemblies. These assemblies levied taxes, raised armies, strengthened fortifications, repaired roads, and supported schools. They also appointed representatives to defend the interests of the province or locality before the king and his council. These provincial and local assemblies thus took on much of the responsibilities of government. At these levels, the French people of the Middle Ages attained the greatest degree of self-government. (*See also* **Taxation.**)

Francis of Assisi, St.

ca. 1182–1226
Founder of the
Franciscan Order

St. Francis is one of the most honored medieval saints. In founding the Franciscan Order, he insisted on poverty for himself and his followers, since Christ and the apostles had been poor. St. Francis is shown in this illumination surrounded by scenes from his life.

Francis is probably the most honored saint of the Middle Ages. He was born at Assisi in the central Italian region of Umbria. Even in his own time, he was regarded as living a life that closely resembled the life of Jesus.

Francis was the son of Pietro di Bernardone, a wealthy cloth merchant, and Giovanna, called Lady Pica, whose ancestry was part French. He was baptized Giovanni but was called Francesco, referring either to his mother's ancestry or his father's business trips to France.

In school, Francis learned to read and write, and he acquired a basic knowledge of arithmetic, poetry, and music. He did not go to a university but began to learn his father's trade. Like many young people of his time, Francis developed a taste for French songs and knightly legends.

Friendly and well-liked by his peers, Francis dreamed of chivalric adventure and glory. In his early 20s, he pursued his dreams by joining military expeditions, in which he fought for Assisi against Perugia. He was captured and held for a year. Then, a year after his release, he went off to fight again. On the battlefield at Spoleto, he believed he had a calling, or religious experience, that marked the beginning of his intense conversion.

Dissatisfied with his old life, Francis withdrew from his family and friends and sought instead the company of outcasts, such as beggars and lepers. Cloth became an important item in his conversion. One day Francis took his father's cloth to market; he sold it but then gave away the money he had earned. His father was so angry that he imprisoned Francis. Francis formally renounced his family before the bishop of Assisi, and, in a gesture that shocked everyone present, he stripped himself naked and handed his clothes to his father.

More confident about his life's direction by this time, Francis organized a band of followers. They lived in caves outside the city, begged for food, and preached the Gospel. In 1210, when they numbered 12, they went to Rome, where they eventually gained approval for their way of life from the pope, INNOCENT III.

See color plate 5, vol. 3.

* **sultan** political and military ruler of a Muslim dynasty or state

* **itinerancy** moving from place to place

* **stigmata** marks on the hands, feet, and body resembling the crucifixion wounds of Christ

* **canonize** to officially declare (a dead person) a saint

In 1212, a young woman named Clare, from a noble family of Assisi, asked to join the company of Francis and his followers. His response was to help her organize a religious community for women, the Poor Clares, at the church of San Damiano at the edge of Assisi.

Over the next few years, hundreds of people joined the movement, as the order spread its activities throughout Italy. The first ventures outside Italy took Francis to Egypt in 1219, where he preached the Gospel before the Muslim sultan*. While he was away, some FRANCISCANS at Bologna accepted the gift of a house, creating the first major conflict within the order over the ideals of poverty and itinerancy*.

There was a spontaneity about Francis that attracted people to him. Although ragged in appearance and without training in either theology or oratory, he won the admiration of scholars for his clarity of expression. Stories in which Francis communicated with birds, fish, wolves, and other animals circulated—and still do—about him. His "Canticle of Brother Sun" is one of the earliest ecological hymns of praise honoring all creatures.

At the end of his life, Francis underwent an intense mystical experience and emerged bearing stigmata*. Before his death, only his close companions knew about the wounds. He was canonized* within two years, and a church was constructed to house his remains and to serve as a focus for the rapidly growing Franciscan Order. (*See also* **Canonization; Friars; Hospitals and Poor Relief; Inheritance Laws and Practices; Mysticism; Saints, Lives of; Women's Religious Orders.**)

Franciscans

Francis of Assisi established the Franciscan Order between 1206 and 1210. It differed from other religious orders in that Francis insisted on poverty for himself and for his followers since Christ himself had been poor. Other religious orders were often removed from society or else concentrated their efforts on the influential elite. The Franciscans had an exceptionally broad appeal, serving both rich and poor. The earliest Franciscans lived in caves on the outskirts of Assisi, begged for food, and preached the Gospel. During the 1200s, the order spread to more than 1,400 convents, and its missionaries went to many countries beyond the Christian world. The Franciscans have endured to the present, but not always with the ideals Francis held.

From the early years, there were disagreements. Many members kept to Francis's strict ideals of poverty, but others were more practical. For example, they explained the gift of a house by maintaining that the benefactor still owned the house and that they had only the use of it. The Poor Clares (a religious community for women) had wanted to lead a Franciscan life of wandering in poverty, but not even Francis could allow religious women to live outside a convent.

Shortly before his death in 1226, Francis named Brother Elias as his successor, and the movement expanded into northern Europe and the Near East. However, Elias lived in a luxurious manner, and he was eventually deposed. A faction known as the Spirituals emerged around 1250, adhering strictly to the original ideals of the order. A compromise was reached when BONAVENTURE, a Franciscan friar* who as a child had been

* **friar** member of a religious brotherhood of the later Middle Ages who worked in the community and relied on the charity of others for his livelihood

saved from a near fatal illness by St. Francis, became head of the order. Bonaventure argued that the order had to change with the times as Christianity itself had, and his moderate line brought a temporary peace to the order. The conflict between the strict Spirituals and the more moderate Conventuals reignited after Bonaventure's death and continued for several years. After the severe crackdown on the Spirituals by Pope John XXII, in which some were burned to death, the Spirituals were driven from the order. The doctrine of the absolute poverty of Jesus and his apostles was declared heretical*, and the remaining Franciscans prospered.

* **heretical** characterized by a belief that is contrary to established church doctrine

Spiritualists continued to turn up from time to time and distributed writings about St. Francis, holding up his fidelity to the ideals of poverty. The Spirituals were eventually succeeded by a group of friars calling themselves the Observants. They were faithful to the original ideals of the Franciscan order but were less extreme than the Spirituals. In the early 1500s, Pope Leo X sought to permanently resolve the disunity in the order. In his bull, or edict, of May 1517, he recognized the primacy of the Observants. At about the same time, the Conventuals went their own way as a separate order.

During the years of dissension, people lost interest in the work of the Franciscan friars. Then, with the European discovery of the New World, the order was revitalized, as Franciscan friars went abroad to Christianize the native peoples. (*See also* **Avignon; Dominicans; Friars; Grosseteste, Robert; Heresy and Heresies; Hermits; Hospitals and Poor Relief; Innocent IV, Pope; Leprosy; Women's Religious Orders.**)

Franks

* **coronation** ceremony during which a leader, king, or queen is crowned

The Franks were a group of Germanic tribes that migrated to western Europe along with other barbarian groups as the Roman Empire declined. The Franks were the first of these groups to establish a lasting state. The empire they created was the foundation for what was to become France and Germany. The basic elements of medieval politics—law based on local traditions, the rule of Christian kings, and coronation* ceremonies—were all creations of the Franks.

Beginning in the mid-300s, the Franks had increasingly close contacts with the Romans in northern Gaul (modern France). During that period, the Franks were divided into two main groups—the Salians and the Ripuarians. A Salian king, CLOVIS, eventually united the Franks and eliminated all rival Frankish kings. By the end of his reign, Clovis had extended Frankish rule to include much of what is now France, western Germany, Belgium, and Luxembourg.

The Franks allowed all groups under their control to follow their own traditional laws. This was an important factor in helping the Franks expand their empire. Another important factor was their association with Roman Christianity. The Franks received the toleration and support of the church as they fought other Germanic groups. Their association with the church also started a vital tradition—papal recognition of the secular authority of the king, and the king's acceptance of the spiritual leadership of the church. This relationship was expressed symbolically in the coronation ceremony of kings, which was developed by the Franks.

The power and longevity of the Frankish Empire was such that, even during the later Middle Ages, western Europeans often were referred to as Franks. (*See also* **Charlemagne; Coronation; French Language and Literature; Law.**)

Frau Ava

died ca. 1127
German poet

* **recluse** person who leads a secluded life

Frau Ava was the first known female author in German literature. Little is known about her life except her name, which appears at the end of her last poem. Historians think she was a recluse* who died in 1127 in the abbey of Melk on the Danube River in Austria.

Ava wrote four poems, each of which has a religious theme. Together, they form a cycle dealing with Christian salvation from the Old to the New Testament. Ava's learning is evident from the use of Latin and technical terms in her poems and from her use of theological and religious works as sources. Her style is compact, straightforward, and vivid, with much dialogue. Ava probably wrote for a well-educated audience, perhaps lay brothers in BENEDICTINE monasteries, who would have appreciated her poetic meditations on salvation and eternal life.

Frederick I Barbarossa

ca. 1122–1190
Emperor of the
Holy Roman Empire

* **papacy** office of the pope and his administrators

* **feudal** referring to the social, economic, and political system that flourished in western Europe during the Middle Ages

* **electors** independent German princes who chose the German kings

* **duchy** territory ruled by a duke or a duchess

See color plate 10, vol. 3.

* **antipope** one who claims the pope's title but is not recognized in modern lists as a legitimate pope

Frederick I, called Barbarossa, or Redbeard, is considered the greatest king of medieval Germany. Elected king in 1152, he ruled for almost 40 years. The first half of his reign was marked by conflicts with the papacy* and unsuccessful attempts to form a large central European kingdom. He then changed his policies and established a feudal* system in Germany. By doing so, he became a symbol of German unity.

At the time of Frederick's election as king, the German people were badly disunited. Two powerful families, the Hohenstaufens and the Welfs, were threatening civil war. Frederick was related to both families, and the German electors* hoped he could prevent war. Frederick did restore calm to Germany by granting the duchy* of Bavaria to a Welf cousin and the duchy of Austria to a Hohenstaufen cousin.

With peace restored, Frederick turned his attention to his own goal: the restoration of the HOLY ROMAN EMPIRE to its former glory. He planned to do this by creating a large, single kingdom that would dominate other European kingdoms and the papacy as well. He also hoped to subordinate the German princes by reducing their independent authority and eliminating their titles.

Frederick's first step toward achieving his goal was to make an alliance with Pope ADRIAN IV. For doing so, he was crowned emperor of the Holy Roman Empire in 1155. Shortly after that, however, he broke the alliance. In addition, his efforts to gain control of territory in northern Italy led to a long period of war there. Over the next 20 years, his actions turned northern Italy solidly against him. Meanwhile, his support for an antipope* also put him in conflict with the new pope, Alexander III.

In 1176, a military defeat in Italy ended Frederick's hopes of gaining territory there. A year later, he decided to scrap his plan for a central

Frederick Barbarossa was pardoned by Pope Alexander III for breaking an alliance and trying to gain control of northern Italy. Frederick gave up his dream of restoring the Holy Roman Empire to its former glory and concentrated on establishing peace and unity in his own German territory.

European kingdom and to make peace with the pope. He met Pope Alexander III in Venice and arranged a truce.

Freed from his old dream of a large unified kingdom, Frederick changed the course of his rule. Instead of trying to be an absolute ruler, he once again recognized the authority of the German princes. Frederick established a feudal system in Germany similar to those in France and England. The unity that followed made Frederick a hero among the German people.

In his old age, Frederick organized the Third Crusade to save the Latin Kingdom of Jerusalem from collapse. In 1190, at the age of 68, Frederick drowned while leading his crusaders across a river in Asia Minor (modern-day Turkey). (*See also* **Crusades; Feudalism; Germany; Italy.**)

Frederick II of the Holy Roman Empire

1194–1250
Emperor of the
Holy Roman Empire

I n addition to being a Holy Roman Emperor, Frederick II was the ruler of Germany, the kingdom of Sicily, and the kingdom of Jerusalem. He was also a scholar. His court was an important cultural center, and his contemporaries described him as "the amazement of the world." At the same time, however, his actions often brought him into conflict with the pope.

Frederick became an orphan when he was four years old. His German father, Henry VI, had been emperor of the Holy Roman Empire. His mother, a Norman princess, had been the daughter of King Roger II of Sicily. The deaths of his parents led to the succession of his uncle, Philip of Swabia, in Germany and to a long period of anarchy* in the

* **anarchy** state of lawlessness or political disorder

kingdom of Sicily. Frederick was not old enough or powerful enough to rule for many years.

Frederick was crowned king of Germany in 1215 at AACHEN, CHARLEMAGNE's royal city. At the time, he vowed to go on a crusade*. Although this was an important pledge, he went to war with rivals in Germany instead. In 1220, Frederick was crowned emperor by the pope. Once again, he vowed to go on a crusade, and, once again, he ignored his pledge. This time, he went to Sicily to quell a rebellion of nobles and to suppress a revolt of Muslims* living there. His failure to fulfill his crusade vows and his actions against Sicilian nobles undermined his relations with the church.

In 1227, Frederick finally organized his crusade. Shortly after the crusaders set sail, however, Frederick fell ill and had to return. Pope Gregory IX, who did not trust Frederick, was very angry over the crusade's delay, and he excommunicated* Frederick. Nevertheless, Frederick and his army set out again in 1229. But, instead of fighting for the glory of the church, he signed a ten-year truce with the Muslim leader of Egypt. This agreement so angered the pope that he excommunicated Frederick again.

While in the Holy Land, Frederick had himself crowned king of Jerusalem, based on his marriage to Isabella of Brienne, the heiress to that kingdom. Frederick then returned to defend the kingdom of Sicily against papal forces, which had invaded during his absence. He defeated the papal army and arranged for peace. The pope withdrew the excommunications, and, for a time, matters seemed settled between emperor and pope. Soon, however, Frederick began moving against enemies in northern Italy. The pope, who supported the northern Italians, excommunicated Frederick a third time.

When a new pope was elected in 1243, Frederick was regarded as a threat to the papacy because of his control of southern Italy. The pope, INNOCENT IV, called a council in 1245 to discuss the problem. The council urged excommunication of Frederick. This time the excommunication marked a change in Frederick's fate. His armies suffered major defeats, and some of his closest supporters turned against him. Then, in 1250, he suddenly fell ill and died.

Frederick's greatest and most lasting contribution was perhaps his interest in learning. During his rule, Sicily was an important cultural center, with Christians, Jews, and Muslims living and working there. Frederick commissioned translations of Arab and Greek works, and he even wrote himself. In 1224, he founded the University of Naples, the first state-run university of the Middle Ages. (*See also* **Germany; Italy; Sicily.**)

* **crusades** holy wars declared by the pope against non-Christians. Most were against Muslims, but crusades were also declared against heretics and pagans.

* **Muslim** word commonly used to describe people who follow the teachings of the prophet Muhammad

* **excommunicate** to exclude from the rites of the church

French Language and Literature

Perhaps in no other European country are the relationships among language, literature, and national identity as close as in France. During the Middle Ages, a distinctive French language and a distinctive French literature developed as France unified and became increasingly separate from the other western European states. The language and literature became strongly identified with the French kingdom, and they were held in high regard in western medieval civilization.

French Language

The French language has its roots in the Latin language of ancient Rome. It is called a Romance language (based on the language of Rome). Other Romance languages in Europe include Italian, Spanish, and Portuguese. However, during the early years of the Middle Ages, the French language gradually developed a form that made it distinct from these other Romance languages.

Early Developments.   After Roman soldiers conquered the region they called Gaul (modern-day France) between 120 B.C. and 51 B.C., their Latin language gradually replaced the CELTIC LANGUAGE of the original inhabitants. Although Celtic continued to be spoken in isolated areas, the Vulgar Latin (common speech) of Roman soldiers, settlers, and traders became the main spoken tongue. This Vulgar Latin differed from the classical Latin of the great ancient Roman authors.

Vulgar Latin remained the predominant language of France until the decline of the Roman Empire in the 400s. Then, as the authority of Rome declined, other events affected the language. Local speech differences developed freely, and different dialects* arose. Local variations also developed as a result of invasions by VISIGOTHS, Burgundians, and FRANKS. In the 800s, the language spoken in what is now France was sufficiently different from Latin to be a distinct language. It was also different from the languages of surrounding lands. For example, in 842 the two grandsons of CHARLEMAGNE, Louis the German and Charles the Bald, swore public oaths (known as the Strasbourg Oaths) in the two different vernacular* languages—early forms of German and French—of their armies. In these oaths, each man swore that he would not take military action against the other.

Old French.   The period from the 800s to the 1400s is usually called the period of Old French. The early centuries of this period were characterized by regional differences in the French language. Toward the end of the period, regional dialects disappeared, and a more standardized form of the French language developed.

In the Middle Ages, it was customary to distinguish between the languages of northern and southern France. The language of northern France was called the langue d'oïl, while the language of southern France was called the langue d'oc. These languages were so named because of their characteristic forms of the word for *yes* (*oïl* in northern France and *oc* in southern France). Within each of these two broad categories were many different dialects. Major dialects in southern France included Catalan, Gascon, Limousin, and Provençal. Dialects in northern France included Picard-Walloon, Lorrain, Champenois, Angevin, Burgundian, and Norman.

Gradually, the dialect of the Île-de-France region of northern France (the area in and around Paris) became the most important dialect. This was because Paris was the political center of the French kingdom and the most important intellectual center of the country. The dialect of this region was known as Francien, a form of the langue d'oïl. The French language of today is derived from this dialect.

During the later medieval period, the French language grew in prestige throughout Europe. Although Latin remained the main language

---

* **dialect** form of speech characteristic of a region that differs from the standard language in pronunciation, vocabulary, and grammar

* **vernacular** language or dialect native to a region; everyday, informal speech

See color plate 8, vol. 3.

Medieval Passion Plays

The Passion play, developed in the Middle Ages, has survived to the present. The Passion play developed from religious plays known as the *mystères*. They focused on the death and Resurrection of Jesus Christ. By the late 1300s, the *mystères* were spectacular events, with lavish costumes, numerous actors, complicated machinery that enabled angels to "fly" across the stage, and elaborate sets. The productions lasted for hours or even days.

Today, Passion plays are still performed, mostly in Germany. The most famous one is performed in the German town of Oberammergau. The Oberammergau Passion play has been performed once every ten years since 1634, with only three interruptions because of war.

* **pagan**   word used by Christians to mean non-Christian and believing in several gods

* **lyric poetry**   poetry that has the form and general effect of a song

* **saint**   Christian who is officially recognized as a holy person by the church

for scholarly writing, Old French became the most favored of the European vernaculars. The conquest of England in 1066 by the NORMANS, the conquests of Sicily and southern Italy, and the CRUSADES all helped promote the French language abroad. The language became an important diplomatic language, and one enriched by hundreds of words borrowed from other languages. The invention of printing in the late Middle Ages also contributed to the importance of the language as well as to its spread and standardization. In 1539, the French king Francis I imposed the use of the vernacular in his courts of law. From that date, French became the official language of communication in France. It soon replaced Latin and other French dialects in the country and in all areas of French life.

French Literature

Until the 1100s, most forms of writing in France were in Latin. As the French vernacular language developed, however, French literature also developed. By the end of the Middle Ages, France had a rich and varied literature that was admired throughout western Europe.

The earliest documents in vernacular French, which date from the 800s, were written in the langue d'oïl. The *Séquence de Ste. Eulalie* is the first literary work in the langue d'oïl to have survived. It tells the story of the persecution and martyrdom of a fourth-century Spanish girl at the hands of a pagan* king. The other is the Strasbourg Oaths.

By the end of the 1100s, two important literary vernaculars had developed, one based on langue d'oïl and the other on langue d'oc. Langue d'oïl writing focused on the narrative, while langue d'oc was the language best suited to lyric poetry*.

Early French Narrative.   From the early 1000s to the mid-1100s, the most important forms of French narrative were stories of the lives of the saints* and CHANSONS DE GESTE—epic tales of heroes and their deeds.

Lives of the saints were a literary tradition based on the earliest Christian literature. Those written in France usually dealt with holy men and women of earlier times and of places far from France. Few works from this period survive. One of the most famous is the *Life of St. Alexis,* a story of an early Roman saint.

The chansons de geste were epic poems written and recited by traveling entertainers called jongleurs. These jongleurs performed at noble courts, in towns and villages, and along pilgrimage routes. They generally accompanied themselves on stringed instruments. Most of the chansons de geste reflected the crusading spirit of the late 1000s and the 1100s. Many of the poems dealt with the idea of CHIVALRY and included such themes as courtly gallantry, bravery, and loyalty to a king or a great cause. They celebrated the exploits of kings and knights and told the stories of rebellious nobles who took up arms against an unjust king. Jongleurs frequently varied the texts of the poems, depending on their particular audiences. Of the 90 or so chansons de geste that have survived, the most famous is the *Song of Roland.* Composed about 1100, the *Song of Roland* tells of a French knight named Roland who is killed on his return to France from an invasion of Spain.

Over the centuries, the lives of the saints and the chansons de geste underwent many changes. By the late 1100s, there was a greater interest in the here and now. As a result, saints' lives focused on more contemporary saints, and the chansons de geste included more contemporary themes. These narratives became so popular that both genres* were adopted by other European vernacular languages in Italy, Spain, Germany, and Norway.

French Romances.   The 1100s in France saw the flowering of a new type of vernacular literature—the medieval romance. The medieval romance combined features from vernacular history, classical and medieval Latin literature, and the chanson de geste. The earliest romances were actually translations or adaptations of earlier Latin texts. An important feature of these works was the learnedness of the writers. These writers were well educated, and they liked to display their literary training, their knowledge of Latin, and their ability to utilize various poetic devices. The appeal of a romance was in the tale itself, as well as the imagination of the author and the skill with which the tale was written. The medieval romance was meant to be intellectually stimulating as well as entertaining.

One of the most important elements of medieval romances was their combination of literary learning and courtly themes. Romances became a means of examining poetic technique, courtly love*, and the qualities of knighthood. Brave knights were expected to be handsome and well-spoken, kind to ladies, and loyal to their lords. They also had a sense of mission, which sent them on various adventures or quests to prove their worth.

Many medieval romances focused on Celtic themes and subjects, especially tales about the legendary King Arthur of Britain and his Knights of the Round Table. Also popular were the so-called Grail romances, tales dealing with the quest for the Holy Grail*. Another important group of romances dealt with the story of TRISTAN and his love, Iseult. This tale of two tragic and doomed lovers was one of the most famous in the medieval world.

Most of the romances written before the 1200s were composed in verse*. Beginning in the 1200s, however, verse was gradually replaced by prose*. At the same time, many romances were written in cycles, with separate narratives woven together to form one long, epic work. Romance writers of the 1200s also experimented with more contemporary settings instead of those of the legendary past. Some writers of this period also tried adapting the allegory* to the romance. One of the most famous allegorical romances was the *ROMAN DE LA ROSE,* or *Romance of the Rose,* a two-part work written by Guillaume de Lorris and Jean de Meun between 1225 and 1270. This love story, with its treasure trove of poetic elements and innovations, was one of the most influential poems written in Old French.

Two of the most famous romance writers of the Middle Ages were CHRÉTIEN DE TROYES and MARIE DE FRANCE. Chrétien wrote a series of romances based on the legend of King Arthur that referred extensively to themes from the Tristan legend. Marie wrote a collection of short romances called *Lais,* which also were based on Celtic legend and focused on the themes of chivalry and courtly love. Both Chrétien and Marie had considerable influence on later writers, including the famous German writer WOLFRAM VON ESCHENBACH.

Courtly Love Lyrics.   Courtly love lyrics are another important genre in the literature of medieval France. They developed from the works of Chrétien de Troyes and Marie de France, which were probably read aloud at noble courts. The courtly love lyric, which consisted of both words and

* **genre** style or type, especially in literature or art

* **courtly love** mannerly, idealized form of love that became popular in the Middle Ages, especially in literature

* **Holy Grail** cup that Jesus drank from at the Last Supper

* **verse** poetry; composition in meter and, sometimes, rhyme

* **prose** writing without meter or rhyme, as distinguished from poetry

* **allegory** literary device in which characters represent an idea or a religious or moral principle

One of the most famous allegorical romances of the Middle Ages was the *Roman de la Rose,* written in the 1200s by Guillaume de Lorris and Jean de Meun. This manuscript illumination shows one of the crimes of jealousy.

* **satire** use of ridicule to expose and denounce vice, folly, and other human failings

See color plate 6, vol. 3.

music, was sung by the poet or by a performer playing the poet. It told of the poet's love for a lady and the difficulties he faced in wooing her. The courtly love lyric was highly autobiographical and conventional. Unlike medieval romances, which were prized for their originality and uniqueness, courtly love songs were highly regulated in form and content. It was largely due to courtly love lyrics that the tradition of the TROUBADOURS and trouvères was preserved, and these performers helped ensure that song would remain an essential part of the medieval literary experience.

French Literature in the 1200s. The forms of literature that were developed in France during the 1000s and the 1100s—saints' lives, chansons de geste, romances, and courtly love lyrics—continued to flourish and expand into the 13th century. At the same time, the rise of SCHOLASTICISM led to a greater interest in the real world, rather than the ideal, and in observable experiences. This was reflected in changes in literature. Saints' lives of the period dealt with people of the time such as St. Thomas BECKET, and romances were written with contemporary settings and themes.

While older genres changed and expanded, other genres came into their own during the 1200s. One of the most popular genres of the period was the fabliau, or fable. Fables told of everyday things—the deeds, sins, joys, and sorrows of people from all levels of society. The sacred counterparts of fabliaux were the *miracles,* devotional poems that told of the miracles performed by the Virgin Mary on behalf of sinners. Both fabliaux and miracles focused on recognizable human beings caught in circumstances that were familiar to the audience.

The poetry of the period is characterized by attention to "realistic" detail and by comedy, satire*, and playfulness. Humorous poems, such as those dealing with Renard the Fox and his friends, were immensely popular. Although Renard and his friends were animals, they possessed very human character traits. The characters in the Renard poems were so popular that their figures were carved in stone in churches and cathedrals and painted in illuminated manuscripts. Many of the writers of these poems were anonymous.

As realism and historical truth became more important, prose works took on greater significance. Medieval writers of prose often recorded eyewitness accounts of actual events. One of the most important prose works of the period was the *Grand Chronicles of France,* begun about 1270 and completed after 1350. This work, written by various secular scholars, was a history of France—the story of the kings of France from earliest times, their deeds, and the development of the French kingdom. As a result of this work, history writing became highly prized in France. The *Grand Chronicles* was also significant because it reflected the growing importance of the French national character and a pride in French history. Another prose masterpiece of the period was the *Life of St. Louis* by JEAN DE JOINVILLE. This biography of King LOUIS IX recounts Joinville's long association with the king. It is actually both biography and autobiography, since much of the work focuses on Joinville's experiences.

During the 1200s, plays written in the vernacular also became more fully developed. Many of these plays were adaptations of older genres, such as saints' lives and courtly love lyrics. One of the most interesting playwrights of the period was a court poet and musician named Adam de la Halle. His masterpiece is the *Play of the Arbor,* written in 1276. This verse play is a highly comic drama about life in a town, including the gossip, myths, boisterousness, and earthy characters.

French Literature After 1300. French literature in the 1300s was marked by a turning away from realism and a return to the celebration of chivalry and chivalric themes. Day-to-day experience was largely rejected in favor of the ideals of love, poetic art, virtues and vices, and intellectual values. Music and song were important elements in French literature of the period. Genres such as the ballade*, the virelay*, and the rondeau* were refined and perfected. One of the greatest poets and composers to use these and other poetic forms was Guillaume de MACHAUT. Machaut was a skilled professional completely dedicated to his craft. He was perhaps the first major poet to supervise the publication of his work, regulating the order in which his poems were placed within the book and influencing the choice and rendering of the illustrations. Machaut's masterpiece, which was titled *True Story,* is considered to be the first great poetic autobiography in the French language. Its main themes are the poet's love and his craft. The poetic traditions that Machaut renewed were followed by many other medieval writers, including the great English poet Geoffrey CHAUCER, the French writer Jehan FROISSART, and France's first well-known female writer and ardent feminist CHRISTINE DE PIZAN.

French literature in the 1400s was marked by great diversity and innovation. One of the most important genres of the period was the play. By the 1400s, the theater had come to occupy a central position in French national life. The plays of the period were based on both religious and secular themes. Both types of drama borrowed ideas from earlier popular literature, such as saints' lives and chansons de geste. Secular comic dramas and farces* were especially popular. Prose fiction also underwent a renewal in the 1400s, with the verse and prose romances of the 1300s giving way to a new, more realistic literature. Much of this prose literature was satirical, humorous, and realistic in both language and content. In poetry, the works of the poet François VILLON stand out for their honesty and vibrancy. Villon's masterpiece, *Le grand testament (The Great Testament)* recounts his own misfortunes as a scholar, convict, sinner, poet, and lover. Much of Villon's work is filled with a variety of realistic characters and situations.

By the end of the 1400s, France had a remarkably rich and varied literary heritage. The talent of its medieval writers was tremendous, and their creations were equal to those of the classical Latin authors of the ancient Roman world. (*See also* **Allegory; Arthurian Literature; Ballads; Books, Manuscript; Chronicles; Courtly Love; Fables; Greek Language; Latin Language.**)

---

* **ballade** lyric poem of three stanzas in which the last line of each stanza is repeated as a refrain

* **virelay** lyric poem that consists of stanzas of varying length and number and with long and short lines

* **rondeau** poem of 13 lines in 3 stanzas and in which the opening line serves as a refrain at the end of the second and third stanzas

* **farce** light, humorous play characterized by broad comedy and an improbable situation

---

Friars

Friars were male members of the mendicant* religious orders founded in the 1200s. Such orders were characterized by their commitment to poverty. The word *friar* comes from the Latin word *frater,* meaning brother. The principal orders of friars were the FRANCISCANS, the DOMINICANS, the Carmelites, and the Augustinians.

Members of religious orders founded in earlier centuries were called monks. The differences between monks and friars are significant. An

* **mendicant** begging; depending on charity for a living

individual monk joined a particular monastery, not the monastic order in general. He was bound to that community for the rest of his life. The monk had no personal possessions, but the community did. The monastery was private and independent, with its own holdings, usually of land. Monastic activity took place away from affairs of the world and did not include ministering to the population. Monks focused on prayers and celebrations of the Mass.

A friar joined an order, not a particular community. Neither the friar nor the order could own property. At first, friars lived as wandering hermits, preaching and working or begging in a town by day, sleeping in the woods or caves outside the town at night. Eventually the mendicant orders did acquire houses, or friaries, in cities. This property technically belonged to the pope*, but the friars were free to use it. Rather than withdrawing from the world, as monks did, friars actively moved from one friary to another, ministering to the people in the cities.

* **pope** bishop of Rome and head of the Western Christian Church

Froissart, Jehan

ca. 1337–after 1404
Poet and historian

* **Low Countries** flat coastal lands west of Germany, now occupied by Belgium and the Netherlands

* **patron** person of wealth and influence who supports an artist, writer, or scholar

* **romance** in medieval literature, a narrative (often in verse) telling of the adventures of a knight or a group of knights

Jehan Froissart was one of the leading historians of the late Middle Ages. His observations of life in England and France during the HUNDRED YEARS WAR (1337–1453) are an important record of that time and reflect the views of the aristocratic society of which he was a member.

Froissart was born to a middle-class French family and studied for the priesthood. As a young man, he traveled to England to serve at the court of Queen Philippa, the French wife of EDWARD III. From there, he embarked on trips to Scotland, France, the Low Countries*, and Italy. During these journeys, Jehan made friends with nobles and several wealthy patrons*, including Guy of Châtillon, count of Blois, and Wenceslas, duke of Luxembourg and Brabant. Both men sponsored Froissart's poetry and other writing.

Froissart's work included numerous lyric poems that celebrated COURTLY LOVE and a verse romance* about the adventures of an ideal knight, Méliador. The main achievement of Froissart's life was *The Chronicles of France and England*, a history of almost all of western Europe between the years 1325 and 1400. The work was based on his interviews with participants and eyewitnesses to various events and on his own firsthand observations. As a historian, Froissart made a great effort to record the facts accurately, and he traveled widely to seek out corroborating sources. Even so, his work was not without bias; it sometimes reflected the views and prejudices of his royal patrons. Like them, he believed in the values of CHIVALRY and hoped for the return of these values, and he showed little respect for the growing middle class. Nevertheless, Froissart's work provided a vivid picture of life in western Europe during the 1300s. (*See also* **Chronicles; French Language and Literature; Historical Writing.**)

Fuero

The term *fuero* in medieval Spain generally referred to the legal statute granting privileges to a city or town. The *fuero municipal*, or town charter, was the written expression of the immunities and exemptions from general laws and taxes granted to a place by a king or lord. *Fuero* also referred to the hereditary transfer or use of land.

In some ways, a *fuero* was like a bill of rights for the people of a region. A *fuero* might grant freedom of residence, freedom from unreasonable

* **codify** to arrange according to a system; set down in writing

* **Muslim** word commonly used to describe people who follow the teachings of the prophet Muhammad

search, freedom to will property, or common use of pasturelands, forests, and water. During the early Middle Ages, the law of the VISIGOTHS had been in force in Spain, but in practice unwritten local custom prevailed as the source of law. Such customs were later codified* in the form of *fueros*. The oldest *fueros* appeared in the 900s, and many early ones were written in Latin. Others were drafted in the local language of the people.

Historians of Spanish law classify the *fueros* in "families" of similar content. Regional *fueros* appeared later, and some were the work of professional lawyers. These *fueros* achieved their fullest development in the 1300s and 1400s. In Aragon and Valencia, regional *fueros* were the work of the CORTES, or parliament. Some *fueros* were granted to encourage the colonization and repopulation of land Christians reconquered from the Muslims*.

Roman and church common laws gradually replaced this patchwork of local laws and privileges. In time, the *fueros* were reduced to a few instances of local law embedded within the common law. This change was a complete reversal of the old Spanish legal traditions, whose diversity had reflected the social and political divisions of Christian Spain. (*See also* **Law.**)

Fur Trade

The central and northern areas of Russia were the main sources of fur for the European fur trade. Furs, a sign of power and wealth, were in great demand among the nobility. This detail from a stained glass window in Chartres Cathedral, France, shows furriers at work.

During the Middle Ages, large quantities of Russian furs were exported to Europe, Byzantium, and parts of Asia. Furs, which were a sign of wealth, status, and power, were in great demand, especially among the ruling classes. The fur garments of royalty and nobility used large numbers of animal skins, or pelts. King John of France possessed a coat made of 366 pelts, and when Marie of Savoy was married in 1426, one of the gowns in her trousseau was lined with 618 sable skins.

Russian Fur Trade. While fur-bearing animals were found throughout medieval Europe, those living in the north were more prized because animals living in the colder climate were bigger and had fuller coats. The central and northern parts of Russia, which possessed a great abundance of fur-bearing animals, were the main sources of fur for Europe.

Four main groups of workers were involved in the Russian fur trade. The first group caught, killed, and skinned the animals. This group consisted of peasant farmers in central Russia and of Lapps (from Lapland) and other herders who lived in northern Russia in cold regions where farming was not possible. The second group consisted of the tax collectors, merchants, and raiders who acquired the furs by barter or force. This group brought the furs to eastern European markets, where merchants from all over the world came to buy the famous Russian pelts. A third group then transported the pelts to trading centers scattered across Europe and Asia from LONDON to SAMARKAND. A fourth group consisted of the merchants who bought the furs, had them sewn, and then sold the fur garments in local markets.

Trade with Europe and the South. From the 800s to 1000s, the VIKINGS developed trade routes to the rich fur lands of Russia through the BALTIC COUNTRIES and through northern Norway into Lapland.

By the late 900s, NOVGOROD had become the main center for the export of Russian furs to the west. Its conquest by MUSCOVY in the 1470s

* **Byzantium** ancient city that became Constantinople; also refers to Byzantine Empire

marked the passing of the northern fur trade into Moscow's hands. Russian, Volga Bulgar, and Muslim merchants also exported Russian furs south to Byzantium*, central Asia, and the Middle East. (*See also* **Hanseatic League; Kievan Rus; Trade.**)

Furniture

I
n medieval Europe and the Islamic world, furniture was less common than today. Its design and use reflected the different traditions and social conditions of each society.

European Furniture

In general, the furniture of western Europe in the medieval period was massive and severe. Constructed of various types of wood, it had simple lines, and designs were fairly uniform throughout a geographical region. Because of its expense, furniture was found primarily in wealthy households and churches. The living conditions of medieval peasants were quite primitive, and few peasants owned items that would be considered furniture today.

Household Furniture. Household furnishings in Europe tended to be few and simple during the Middle Ages. The homes of wealthy merchants and the castles and manor houses of the nobility were, by modern standards, sparsely furnished. People wealthy enough to own furniture often had several homes. When they traveled from one home to another, they took with them all their valuable possessions, including their furniture. When invasion or war threatened, wealthy people could move quickly with their few pieces of furniture. The practice of moving furniture from place to place is still reflected in some European languages. In both German and French, for example, the word for furniture means "movables."

The demand for movable furniture inspired special designs and the extensive use of fabrics. Folding chairs, tables with removable tops, chests, and cushions were common. One such portable design was the curule chair, a type of chair with a leather or fabric seat and legs that folded. When not in use, this chair was folded flat. Unfolded, its legs formed an X shape. Since cloth could be folded and carried easily, canopies and draperies were a popular feature of medieval furnishings.

The most basic piece of medieval furniture was the chest. Chests were used for moving and storing all types of goods. Their flat tops could also be used as tables for eating, as benches for sitting, or even as beds for sleeping. Locked chests were often used to store valuables. Chests that contained valuables were sometimes given to churches for safekeeping.

* **tankard** large mug for drinking

Other pieces of furniture used for storage were dressers, buffets, and cupboards. Medieval dressers had an open set of shelves where cups and tankards* were stored. Buffets, which could be open, closed, or partially open, always had at least one large open shelf for storing or displaying glasses, plates, or other items. Although dressers generally were used to store items out of public view, buffets were used to display items. Buffets often occupied a prominent spot in a medieval home, where visitors could appreciate the owner's prosperity. A type of cupboard known as an ambry or armoire contained a set of shelves set behind a door. It was used to store arms, housewares, or food.

Medieval households were, by modern standards, sparsely furnished. Furniture was generally large in size and simple in design. This massive oak armoire, or cupboard, was made in France in the 1100s. Behind the door of the armoire are shelves that could be used to store weapons, food, or household goods.

Medieval tables were used mostly for dining. Since large amounts of food were served at banquets, these tables were long and heavy. They often consisted of a flat top resting on a separate frame. During banquets, important family members and distinguished guests might sit at a "high table" placed on top of a platform and beneath a cloth canopy. Other family members and guests would be seated at side tables. Special side tables known as credenzas or credences were used to hold food about to be served.

Chairs had special significance as symbols of authority in the Middle Ages. Therefore, they were usually reserved for the most important members of a household. Rarely did a castle have more than three chairs—one each for the master, his wife, and an honored guest. A person of great power and authority usually sat in a chair placed on a raised platform beneath an elaborate canopy.

One of the most important pieces of medieval furniture was the bed. Beginning in the 1300s, wills often specified who was to inherit the "best bed." Many medieval castles did have separate bedrooms, but in some castles beds were placed in the large, open halls. Therefore, beds were designed for privacy and protection from cold drafts. From the 1100s, beds had roofs and canopies made of rich fabrics such as velvet, satin, or silk. To ensure privacy and protection, some beds were constructed with three wooden walls and a fourth side of curtains. During the daytime, bed canopies or draperies were pulled back so that the bed could be used as a couch. The sleeping area of a bed had a foundation of straw or wool. Feather beds*, sheets, blankets, and embroidered quilts were layered on the foundation.

* **feather bed** quilt or sack stuffed with feathers and used as a mattress

Gothic Furniture

In the later Middle Ages, European furniture design and decoration was inspired by the architecture of Gothic cathedrals, with their soaring pointed arches and carved decoration. Chests and cupboards were enriched with rows of pointed arches and highly ornate decoration known as tracery. Tables, chairs, and benches had similar types of design and ornamentation. Beds were plain, but elaborate canopies and draperies were hung to resemble the spires and towers of cathedrals. The favored wood used in Gothic furniture was oak.

In view of the massive size and heavy look of medieval furniture, carpenters and owners used colorful fabrics, carved decorations, and bright paints to make their furniture more attractive. Canopies and draperies made of luxurious fabrics covered some pieces of furniture or hung above them. Colorful fabrics were also used to cover the seats and backs of some furniture and to make pillows. Delicate designs and scenes of medieval life, legends, and biblical stories were carved into the wood. Furniture was also painted in vivid shades of red, green, and gold. The great halls in medieval manor houses and castles were not rich in furniture, but the furniture they contained was beautiful and richly decorated.

Church Furniture. Medieval churches and other religious buildings were often better furnished than the homes of the wealthy. In part, this reflected the greater security of churches, which were less vulnerable to attack and to political and economic changes. Unlike castles and manor houses, which were left empty from time to time, churches were used throughout the year. This stability enabled churches to accumulate furniture. It also made possible the use of grander, less portable furniture, since this furniture was not moved from place to place. Because some church furnishings were considered almost as holy as the altar itself, special rules governed the construction, use, and removal of church furniture.

One important element of church furnishing was seating. For many centuries, the only chair found in a church belonged to the bishop. It was called the cathedra. To this day, a church used by a bishop is known as a cathedral, meaning a church with a bishop's chair. The cathedra was usually an armchair with a high back. Made of richly decorated wood, stone, metal, or ivory, it stood on a raised platform beneath a canopy. At first, the cathedra might be found in various places inside the church. Eventually, however, it became a permanent part of the altar area, typically behind the altar or to the left of the altar.

Benches built against the wall or stools provided seating for other clergy members, although benches for the lay worshipers did not appear until about the 1200s. Before that, people stood, sometimes using sticks to support themselves. During confessions, priests would sit on a type of seat called a shriving stool, usually a heavy chair with arms. Closed confessional boxes were not introduced until the 1500s. Anyone required to kneel before the altar used a type of small kneeling bench called a prie-dieu or *genuflexorium.*

The enclosed choir became a common church furnishing after the 1000s. Made of wood or stone, it contained a series of stalls or compartments facing one another. These stalls were usually on a raised platform and had a high back. Within each stall was a type of hinged seat that tipped up. In the upright position, the seat had a shelflike projection called a misericord. Standing choir members could support themselves on the misericords during long church services.

Medieval churches contained various desks and tables. As priests chanted the Mass or read lessons, they stood behind high desks or stands called lecterns, upon which books were placed. These lecterns were of two types—either portable or fixed in one spot. Most churches also had two special reading desks called ambos. One, located to the right of the altar, was used for reading from the Epistles*. The other, located to the left of

* **Epistles** letters from the apostles to the early Christians

* **Gospels** accounts of the life and teachings of Jesus as told in the first four books of the New Testament

* **sanctuary** part of the church around the altar

* **host** bread blessed during a Mass and said to be the body of Christ

* **baptismal font** basin used to hold holy water in the baptism ceremony

* **holy water** water blessed by the priest and used in various church ceremonies

* **Muslim** word commonly used to describe people who follow the teachings of the prophet Muhammad

the altar, was used for reading from the Gospels*. Rising 20 feet or more above the church floor, the ambos often were decorated with stones, jewels, or elaborate carvings. Lessons and sermons could also be given from a raised pulpit. The most important table in church was the *credentia,* a small table on which the sacred bread and wine for the Mass were placed during the service.

Churches used a variety of chests, boxes, and cupboards, some of which were set into the walls. These were used to hold sacred oils, books, altar equipment, and clothing for the clergy. The sacred bread and wine were stored in special locked cupboards set into the wall of the sanctuary*. During the later Middle Ages, the sacred host* often was stored in enormous "sacrament houses" built near the altar. Some of these had gigantic towers and pinnacles that reached toward the ceiling. Special locked boxes were used to receive alms, or donations, for the poor.

Other church furnishings included different types of candlesticks and oil lamps, crosses, carved sculptures, and items used during the Mass. Water buckets and basins, including baptismal fonts*, were very important for holding and carrying holy water*.

One very special item found in churches was the organ. Organs provided church music as early as the 700s. By the 1200s, organs were common in larger churches, and they were found in virtually all churches by the late Middle Ages. At first, they were small and portable, but organs eventually became very large, fixed pieces of furniture requiring constant care and maintenance.

Like the medieval household, the medieval church was adorned with rich and colorful fabrics. Curtains and canopies hung from ceilings, on walls, and over doors. Decorated cushions were placed on chairs, stools, and benches. On festive occasions, the stone floor of the church was covered with straw and colorful carpets were placed on top. Brightly colored banners were used in church processions. The richly decorated furnishings and fabrics of the medieval church provided a glorious spectacle for churchgoers, a reminder of the church's wealth and power. For the poor, it provided a great contrast to their own lives and helped inspire a sense of awe in their religion.

Islamic Furniture

Islamic homes were even more sparsely furnished than those in western Europe. Indeed, European travelers sometimes described Muslim* homes as "empty" or even "uninhabitable." This criticism, however, fails to account for the different history, customs, and traditions that distinguished the Islamic world from the European one.

In part, the difference between European and Islamic furnishings reflected different origins. The medieval European world traced its traditions to the urban culture of ancient Rome. The Islamic world, on the other hand, traced its traditions to Arab nomads who roamed freely throughout their desert lands. Even after the Islamic world developed a great urban culture, its traditions, furnishings, and language continued to reflect nomadic origins.

Life in the medieval Muslim home was lived mostly on ground level. Instead of using chairs, Muslims usually sat on carpets and cushions on the ground. They ate their meals this way at tables that were small, low, and portable. After eating, these tables were removed and the cushions might be taken away as well. Food was served in different types of serving dishes. Some dishes had legs attached; others had removable bases. Instead of using plates or spoons, people took food directly from serving bowls.

Not all medieval Islamic furniture was low. There were stools and chairs with wooden or metal legs, but these were not used for meals. High tables and benches were built for use outside the home. Royal courts sometimes had large thrones modeled after those used in the BYZANTINE EMPIRE. Another type of royal throne was a long reclining couch similar to those used in ancient Rome. These thrones might be used for important public occasions or ceremonies, for private meetings with officials, or for feasts.

In Muslim society, seating levels indicated class distinctions. A person seated on a throne or a high stool was from a very high social class. A person from a lower social class sat at a lower level—on two cushions, on one cushion, or on the carpet itself. People of the lowest social class squatted directly on the ground.

Beds also reflected social rank. A bed with legs was considered the ultimate in luxury. The next best bed was one with a frame. Other beds might consist of a mattress alone, ranging from one of good quality to a simple mattress laid on the ground, a sleeping mat, or just a carpet. The poorest people often slept directly on the bare ground. The use of a bed with a frame for both sleeping and relaxing became fashionable among the upper and middle classes toward the end of the 800s.

Although the Muslims had no cupboards, they had a variety of chests, cases, and boxes for storing items. Muslim homes also had recesses set into the walls and racks on which to hang things.

Throughout the Islamic world, furniture was generally similar in style. The Muslim style persisted for centuries, long past the medieval era. While households and churches in Europe became more elaborately furnished as time went on, Muslims maintained their traditions until the early 20th century. (*See also* **Lighting Devices.**)

Games and Pastimes

One of the most enduring images of the Middle Ages is of armored knights on spirited horses rushing toward each other, lances poised to strike, as a festive crowd roars its approval. This type of contest, known as a joust, was just one of many medieval pastimes. Most games and pastimes in the Middle Ages were more peaceful. People participated in two types of games—action games and "sitting games." These types of games were found both in Europe and in the Islamic world.

Action Games. People in the Middle Ages played a number of games that required physical activity or ability. Some of the more active of these games were similar to modern sports. In fact, many of the action games of the Middle Ages have survived the passage of time and developed into modern versions.

Modern games such as blindman's buff, leapfrog, tug-of-war, and hide-and-seek are derived from medieval games that were popular with both children and adults. In the medieval version of blindman's buff, known as hoodman-blind, the player who was "it" kept a hood on his or her head.

The other players took their hoods off, knotted them, and struck the blindfolded player with the knotted cloth. In the medieval version of leapfrog, called frog-in-the-middle, players tried to touch, pinch, or slap the player who was "it" as he or she crouched on the floor.

People played several types of ball games in the Middle Ages. These were not equivalents of present-day ball games because of the balls that were used. Rubber was unknown in Europe in the Middle Ages, so balls generally were made of leather or fabric stuffed with rags. Therefore, they did not bounce. In the medieval version of stickball, players would throw a fist-sized, rag-stuffed ball into the air and then hit it with a stick. Handball or fives, a forerunner of tennis, was played by batting a ball with bare hands. A game called tennis, played with racquets, was first mentioned in English literature about 1400. Two versions of a bowling game were also popular in the Middle Ages. In one, a single ball was aimed at nine wooden markers. In the other, one ball was thrown at several other balls spread over the ground. Both versions of the game were played outdoors on a grassy lawn. Other ball games included hurling, a forerunner of field hockey, and football, a game with rules similar to the modern game of soccer.

Some medieval action games were more strenuous and competitive. Among these were stone tossing, wrestling, fencing, and archery. These games were real tests of strength and skill. In addition, practice in fencing and archery was good preparation for battle.

Since citizens of most medieval towns and villages served in militias*, it was important for men to know how to handle the weapons of the day. By the 1400s, most European cities had schools of fencing that taught courses and awarded diplomas such as "master of the long sword." Fencing was done with wooden staffs called quarterstaffs, with swords, or with pole arms*. Quarterstaff fencing required great skill because the staff was used both as a weapon of attack and as a means of defense. Both ends of the staff could be used for a blow or a thrust, and a daydreaming fencer could be taken by surprise from an unexpected angle. Sword fencing involved using a metal-edged sword with which to strike, and a buckler, or small shield, to help deflect blows. Striking sword against sword was avoided because of possible damage to the sword's edge.

In archery, medieval sportsmen practiced their skill at shooting arrows from longbows* and crossbows*. Annual shooting contests were held in many towns and cities, during which the most skilled shooters would take aim at man-sized targets or fake animals. The best marksman was declared "king" of the shooters for the year and was exempted from paying taxes during his "reign." The worst shot was awarded a pig as a consolation prize.

The Tournament. The most spectacular sporting event of the Middle Ages was the tournament. During the period of the Roman Empire, imperial armies used tournaments as military exercises to prepare for war. In the Middle Ages, the tournament became a formalized sporting event with specific rules of combat and conduct. It was also limited to knights. Developed first in France in the 1000s, the medieval tournament gradually spread to other parts of Europe.

The medieval tournament was composed of several classes of events. The most popular of these was the joust. In this test of power and skill, two armored knights on horseback would charge at each other along wooden

* **militia** army of citizens who may be called into action in a time of emergency

* **pole arms** shafted weapons with axlike cutting blades

* **longbow** archer's weapon about five to six feet in length for the rapid shooting of arrows

* **crossbow** weapon consisting of a bow fixed crosswise on a wooden stock; the arrow, drawn taut by a spring, is launched by an archer

barriers called lists. The object was to strike the oncoming rider with a blunted lance and unhorse him. If both knights remained in the saddle, an extra point was awarded to the one who had shattered his lance. The broken lance proved that the knight had hit his opponent squarely and with the greatest possible force. Other tournament events included the melee, the baston event, and the foot combat event. The melee involved groups of knights fighting on horseback. In the baston event, pairs or groups of knights on horseback tried to knock the crest off opponents' helmets with blunted swords or wooden clubs. The foot combat event was a fencing exhibition in which knights fought each other with lances or swords, sometimes both. Originally, tournaments were fought with the same equipment used in battle, except that weapons were blunted. Gradually, however, special armor and shields were developed just for tournaments.

Tournaments were festive occasions. They were often accompanied by parades and pageants in which men and women acted out stories from ARTHURIAN LITERATURE. Fake castles might be set up so that gallant knights could "storm" them and "rescue" beautiful damsels using flowers as missiles and weapons. Tournaments with pageants became a popular annual attraction in some wealthy cities. At some county fairs and local festivals, pretend tournaments provided humorous entertainment. Villagers would wear tubs, buckets, or baskets instead of armor and engage in boisterous jousts.

Sitting Games.   The "sitting games" of the Middle Ages consisted of various card games, dice games, and board games. Cards were introduced into Europe from either China or India in the late 1300s. Among the earliest European card games was a "war" game. Card games soon became so popular that a law was passed prohibiting workers from playing them on work days. The earliest known signs used on cards were swords, cups or chalices, coins, and staves. These signs represented the four classes of medieval society: nobles, clergy, merchants, and peasants. The organization of a medieval suit of cards with a king, a knight (which later became a queen), a squire (a jack), and faceless foot soldiers (the numerals) corresponded to the organization

Both secular and church authorities tried to ban dice playing, a popular form of gambling. This French manuscript illumination from the 1400s is titled "Temperance and Intemperance." While the women on the left have chosen prayer and quiet activities, the men on the right have been unable to avoid the temptation of a dice game.

of a medieval army. The modern suit signs—spades, hearts, diamonds, and clubs—were introduced in France in the early 1400s.

Dice became the classic gambling game throughout the Middle Ages. The church, however, was opposed to this type of gambling, and secular and church authorities passed numerous bans on dice games.

Medieval board games included nine-men's morris, "hunt" games such as fox and geese, and backgammon. Each of these games involved moving pieces around a board according to specific rules. Backgammon, which incorporated dice as well as the playing pieces, was one of the most popular medieval board games. The most prestigious board game, however, was chess.

Chess originated in India in the 500s and spread through the Islamic world to western Europe at the time of the CRUSADES. Unlike other games—which were banned at various times because they were thought to be a corrupting influence—chess was generally held in high esteem as a game that improved people's minds. Chess is a "war" game. When the game originated in India, its "men" represented the organization of an Indian army, and their moves were styled after actual military tactics. In Europe, the game was changed according to European practices. For example, certain pieces came to represent prominent figures in medieval society—the bishop, the knight, the castle, and the king and the queen.

Games in the Islamic World.   The teachings of early Islam tended to view games as distractions from the serious business of life and preparations for the hereafter. Nevertheless, children and adults did play games. Most boys and girls, for example, played checkers-type games, games in which pebbles were placed in holes, and games that involved throwing dice or bones. Swinging on swings and seesawing were also common amusements. Action games involved running, jumping, and playing with balls, as well as games that used animals and birds for racing or fighting. Gambling was prohibited in Muslim society, however, since it was denounced in the QUR'AN, the Islamic holy book.

Adult games often involved intellectual thought and sharpness of wit. As in Europe, the most prestigious board game was chess. Backgammon, which originated in the Middle East, was also popular. Skill at chess and backgammon was viewed as the sign of an educated person, and those who were particularly skilled were called "masters." Since they also taught strategy, such games were approved of for military leaders and princes as preparation for actual warfare. Field sports were also encouraged for the same reason: they helped provide physical exercise and development for future warriors. (*See also* **Armor; Knighthood; Warfare; Weapons.**)

Gardens

Gardens have been found in every civilization, from ancient times to the present day. People of every culture have cleared, planted, and tended plots of land for practical or ornamental purposes. One of the most famous gardens is the biblical Garden of Eden, in which Adam and Eve lived before their fall from grace. During the Middle Ages, gardens played an important role in daily life in both Christian Europe and the Islamic world. They were also an important element in much medieval art and literature.

European Gardens.   Although no medieval European gardens have survived to the present day, evidence of their main features and characteristics can be found in literary and other sources. Large or small, secular or religious, medieval European gardens shared similar characteristics. Of foremost importance was their utilitarian purpose. Gardens served a very practical need in medieval society: they provided fruits, vegetables, and medicinal herbs for secular households and religious communities. Many plants that today are considered ornamental—such as lilies, poppies, and irises—were found in medieval gardens not because they were beautiful but because they were useful. Lilies were used to cure snakebite, poppies were used to lessen pain, and irises were used to make starch for washing.

Most medieval gardens shared a similar form and structure. They were carefully constructed, enclosed spaces surrounded by walls, hedges, or fences made of woven branches. There was little or no view of the surrounding countryside. Thus, the focus of gardens was inward. Within a garden enclosure, the land was subdivided by low and high fences and trelliswork, around which various vines and trees were arranged. Sometimes, in manor houses or castles, garden trellis arbors were shaped into houses, tents, or pavilions where lords and ladies could rest, meditate, and enjoy fair weather.

Within the enclosed garden space were raised beds of plants, flowers, and shrubs. These beds often were arranged in geometrical patterns, with straight paths made of sand, gravel, or low-growing herbs running between them. The center of the garden sometimes contained a well or a fountain of elaborately carved stonework. Topiary, the art of forming plants and trees into unusual shapes, appeared in the late 1400s. Royal or princely gardens often contained topiaries of various animals and birds. Seats fashioned from brick or wooden boards and covered with turf were positioned against garden walls or trellises, allowing people to sit and view the garden. Some gardens might also contain a section of meadow grasses mixed with sweet-smelling herbs and flowers. Thus constructed, the medieval European garden was useful not only for the plants it contained but also because it provided a place for enjoyment and quiet meditation.

Medieval monasteries often had several gardens, each with a specific purpose. Sometimes there was a garden in the cloister*, a square space that was open in the center and surrounded by roofed walkways. The central area was crossed by paths that met in the middle. The cloister was reserved for monks or nuns to use for walks, reading, the copying of books, or silent prayer. Another space might be set aside as an herb garden, where small aromatic plants such as fennel, sage, mint, and rosemary were grown. These plants were picked by the monastery's herbalist, who used them to make medicines. A third garden space might be used for growing kitchen vegetables such as onions, celery, parsley, lettuce, and carrots. Fruit and nut-producing trees might be planted in another area. Flowers were rarely grown unless they had medicinal uses.

Like their present-day counterparts, medieval gardeners faced the endless tasks of clearing the garden, planting, and keeping the garden orderly and neat. All this work was done by hand. One of the earliest accounts of gardening was written by the German monk Walafrid Strabo in the mid-800s. His account and the plan in the library of the Swiss monastery of St. Gall are two of the earliest documents describing medieval gardening.

* **cloister**   covered passageway around a courtyard in a monastery or convent

Gardens provided fruits, vegetables, and medicinal herbs for households and religious communities. Some plants also had a symbolic importance. The lily, for example, stood for purity and was often associated with the Virgin Mary; the red rose symbolized the suffering of Christ. This illumination, entitled *Garden of Paradise,* is from Germany in the 1400s.

* **martyr** person who suffers and dies rather than renounce a religious faith

Walafrid describes his problems in clearing and planting his small enclosed garden with just a few tools—a rake, a spade, and a knife. He describes the laborious tasks of clearing the land of roots and other debris, sowing and planting seeds, watering planted areas, and building raised beds. Walafrid also lists some 30 plants that he grew in his garden, and he describes their different properties and virtues.

Many plants and flowers in medieval gardens were not only useful; they also had symbolic and religious importance. The lily, for example, was a symbol of purity and was associated with the Virgin Mary. The red rose was a symbol of blood and a reminder of the suffering of Christ and Christian martyrs*. A group of 13 trees planted together symbolized Christ and his 12 disciples. These symbolic characteristics of medieval European gardens reflect the importance of religion during the period and its connection to everyday life.

Islamic Gardens.   To Medieval Muslims, gardens had great symbolic importance. The Arabic terms for garden, *rauda* and *janna,* imply a heavenly "paradise," a place where the holy enjoy the grace of God. Medieval Muslim gardeners used the patterns of ancient Persian landscape design to create formal, enclosed parks for their royal rulers. A plot of land was divided into four smaller, raised plots, with a pool of water or a fountain in the center. The presence of water was the most important feature of an Islamic garden. Since most of the Islamic world had a hot, dry climate, water was needed to irrigate the garden's plants. Water also had symbolic importance. As water flowed out from the garden's central pool or fountain to enrich the four plots of the garden, it symbolized the waters of the earth flowing to enrich the four quarters of the globe.

Unlike European gardens, Islamic gardens were designed with beauty in mind rather than for their usefulness. Because of their beauty and religious symbolism, Islamic gardens were much loved by Muslims.

Some owners chose to be buried in their garden plots, thus creating a final resting place within a symbolic paradise.

Gardens in Art and Literature. Medieval art is filled with depictions of gardens. Many paintings of the Virgin Mary, for example, show her within an enclosed garden surrounded by flowers whose symbolic meanings (carnations as a symbol of divine love; violets as a symbol of humility) remind viewers of her life or character. Medieval stained glass windows often show Adam as a gardener in the Garden of Eden. The elegant illuminated manuscripts of the 1400s often depict scenes of gardens during the different months of the year. Medieval TAPESTRIES often contain flower-filled backgrounds suggesting a garden.

One of the most beautiful descriptions of a garden from the Middle Ages is found in the *Romance of the Rose,* written in the 1200s. This long prose poem describes grassy lawns covered with yellow, white, and red flowers. Its garden has a magical quality, much like a dream.

In the Islamic world, carpets were woven to reflect the beauty of gardens. In fact, ancient carpets provide an excellent idea of what Islamic gardens may have looked like. These "garden" carpets are usually geometric in style with elaborate borders and a central design. The colors are jewel-like, and flowers abound. Looking down on them gives the impression of looking into a garden. (*See also* **Agriculture; Islamic Art and Architecture; Monasteries;** *Roman de la Rose.*)

Gems and Jewelry

Using the technique of setting colored gemstones into gold, Germanic artisans created beautiful crowns, book covers, and jewelry. The imperial crown of the Holy Roman Empire, shown here, was made in the 900s.

Wealthy medieval people wore necklaces, bracelets, earrings, rings, and pins. Jewelry was made of gold or silver inlaid with precious stones, including sapphires, emeralds, and carved cameos or enamel. Jewelry could be made in symbolic shapes such as the cross, or it could contain representations of holy figures or scenes from everyday life.

During the early medieval period (500s–900s), Byzantine jewelry continued to use forms and techniques inherited from ancient Rome. Many Byzantines used the traditional Roman gold fibula, or clasp, to fasten their silk and gold-embroidered garments. A Byzantine innovation was the pectoral cross worn on a gold chain that hung around the neck. Gold crescent-shaped earrings and pendants also were very popular among the Byzantines and others under their influence. In KIEVAN RUS (present-day Russia), for example, male and female aristocrats wore crescent-shaped pendants suspended from elaborate headdresses.

The crescent shape was also popular in Islamic jewelry of the 1000s to the 1200s. In contrast to Byzantine artisans, Muslims tended to form the crescents of filigree and granulation (clusters of small gold balls). They used the same techniques in designing necklaces and pendants. A characteristic of Islamic jewelry is the repetition of such motifs as birds and geometric shapes—a habit derived from the ancient Near East.

The jewelry of the VISIGOTHS, LOMBARDS, and FRANKS was greatly influenced by the Byzantines. Like the Byzantines, these barbarian tribes arranged colored gemstones against a gold background. They used this technique to create gorgeous covers for books, royal crowns, and other

* **cloisonné** enamelwork in which areas of color are separated by tiny metal bands embedded into the surface

* **guild** association of craft and trade workers that set standards and represented the interests of its members

* **city-state** independent state consisting of a city and the territories around it

* **pomander** small bag or box containing aromatic herbs; used to scent clothing and guard against the plague

items. The Franks also used the fibula, either in gold or cloisonné*, on their clothing—often in pairs, with one on each shoulder. The gold, disk-shaped fibula remained an essential article of dress until the 1200s.

During the period of the CRUSADES, knights returning from the Holy Land brought back exotic gemstones, which inspired the practice of gem cutting, and the West became important in jewelry production. By the late 1200s, PARIS had a gem-cutters' guild*. French trade with the Italian city-states* of VENICE and FLORENCE and the patronage of the royal court spurred new levels of creativity.

In the 1300s, both men and women throughout Europe wore brooches, finger rings, gold chains, and pomanders*. Laws began to be introduced to regulate jewelry wearing according to rank. The chain was the emblem of knightly dignity, and each order of knights had its own badge. By the end of the 1400s, prosperous townspeople had the right to display jewelry, and production increased with cheaper materials (such as silver) to meet demand. (*See also* **Byzantine Art; Clothing; Islamic Art and Architecture; Trade.**)

Genghis Khan

**1155–1227
Conqueror and founder of
the Mongol Empire**

See
color plate 11,
vol. 3.

* **steppe** vast treeless plain of southeastern Europe and Asia

The Mongol born as Temüjin, later known as Genghis Khan (Universal Ruler), overcame early hardships to become the unifier and ruler of the nomadic tribes of Mongolia. At the height of his power, he ruled an empire that stretched from eastern Europe to the Sea of Japan.

Temüjin was the son of Yesügei Baghatur, nephew of the last elected khan of the Mongols. When Temüjin was nine years old, the Tatars poisoned his father. Abandoned by the other Mongol tribes, the family barely survived. To prevent Temüjin from avenging his father's death, the Tayichi'yud tribe captured him. He escaped and found support from To'oril, ruler of the Kereyid tribe and a friend of his father's. In 1196, a gathering of the important Mongol tribes proclaimed Temüjin their overlord, a position also sought by Jamuqa, a boyhood friend and *anda*, or sworn brother.

Five years later, Temüjin defeated Jamuqa with the help of To'oril's army, and the two allies then ruthlessly defeated the Tatars. By 1205, Temüjin had defeated all his enemies, and the following year, at a congress of the Mongol tribes on the Onon River, Temüjin was proclaimed Genghis Khan.

In 1211, the Mongols began the conquest of China in earnest and succeeded when Peking fell in 1215. Next they focused their energies westward to the territories beyond the steppes* of Asia. The Mongols were skilled warriors and military strategists, and they efficiently conquered lands almost as quickly as they could reach them. Because of their fierceness, however, the Mongols were regarded as inhuman by Europeans and other Asians.

Temüjin himself was a man of great physical strength and personal appeal, who had a talent for military tactics and organization. He valued loyalty, granting generals of whose allegiance he was certain a free hand in their campaigns. His last great campaign was the conquest and annihilation of the Khwarezm people of Afghanistan. After he returned to

Genghis Khan ruled an empire that stretched from eastern Europe to the Sea of Japan. Because of their skill and ferocity in battle, Mongol warriors were considered ruthless and were greatly feared. This French manuscript page shows Genghis Khan in a more serene setting, being served at his table. To the Mongol people he had great personal appeal.

Mongolia in 1225, Genghis Khan began plans for a new campaign, this time against the Tanguts. He died in 1227, however, before it was completed. (*See also* **Mongol Empire.**)

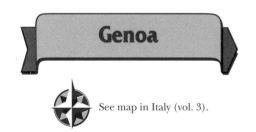

Genoa

See map in Italy (vol. 3).

* **barbarian** referring to people from outside the cultures of Greece and Rome who were viewed as uncivilized

Genoa is a city in northwest Italy. It has a small, natural harbor located at the head of the deepest gulf of the Mediterranean Sea. This feature helped the city develop into an important port. At its peak, in the 1300s, the port of Genoa was part of a vast network of trading links that stretched as far as India and England. For a time, Genoa's greatness rivaled that of VENICE.

A small city had occupied the site of Genoa since pre-Roman times. During the Roman period, it was an important stop along the route between Rome and northern Europe. In about 642, the town was sacked by barbarian* invaders and reduced to a small fishing village.

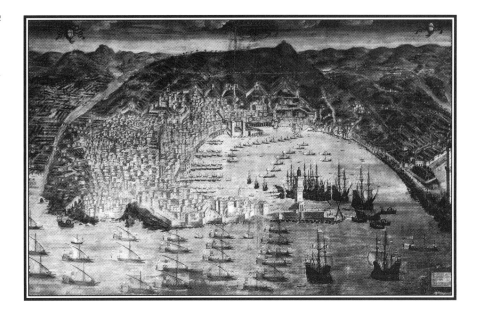

Genoa became an important port during the Middle Ages. At one time, it rivaled Venice in trading power and prestige. By 1481, when this panoramic view of the city was painted, Genoa was struggling with problems brought on by the plague, the Hundred Years War, and ineffective government within the city.

Between 930 and 935, a series of Muslim raids stirred the Genoese to action. Genoa and the nearby coastal city of PISA joined forces to defend themselves against the Muslims and to take the offensive. Their raids on Muslim strongholds in Sardinia and Tunisia brought booty and power to northwest Italy and forced the Muslims back. Genoa gradually became an important trading power. Genoese ships sailed east to Egypt and Syria and west to Provence in France and to Catalonia on the Spanish coast. By 1088, Genoa was larger and more prosperous than ever before.

The CRUSADES provided additional opportunities for greatness. Genoa provided many of the ships and supplies needed to transport crusaders to the Holy Land. While its ships were in the East, the city established numerous trading colonies. These colonies, which usually included a seaport, consisted of just enough territory to provide a stopping place where merchants could trade in security and comfort, without interference from nearby authorities.

The trading system established during the crusades led to Genoa's greatest era. By 1293, the city was one of the busiest ports in the world. Genoa had trading colonies as far east as the Black Sea coast. Overland routes linked it to trading centers in India and even China. To the west, Genoese ships sailed to England, Morocco, and even the Canary Islands. The city itself had become one of the largest in Europe, with a population approaching 100,000.

In the face of such glory, no one was likely to guess that Genoa had reached its peak of power and prosperity. The city's decline was small at first, brought on by political instability and ineffective government. Then Genoa was struck by the plague*, and external problems, such as the HUNDRED YEARS WAR, also took their toll. By 1346, the city's population had fallen to about 50,000, and many buildings stood empty. Still, the city struggled to recover, and it became more deeply involved in banking and exchange. Then, in 1453, the fall of Constantinople resulted in the loss of almost all of Genoa's colonies in the east. With characteristic energy, Genoa turned its face westward, toward Spain, in search of new economic opportunities. One of those Genoese people seeking opportunities in

* **plague** disease that swept across the medieval world several times, including the Black Death in the mid-1300s

Spain was Christopher Columbus. (*See also* **Italy; Lombards, Kingdom of; Ships and Shipbuilding.**)

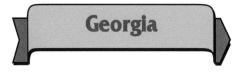

Georgia

* **Tatars** descendants of the Mongols who raided Georgia beginning in the 1200s

Georgia is an ancient country located along the Black Sea coast in the western part of Transcaucasia, a region of the Caucasus mountain range that separates Europe and Asia. The country is divided by mountains into an eastern and a western region. For most of Georgia's history, these two regions were separate countries.

The people of Georgia are divided into many tribes, speaking different languages. Most Georgians are Christians who follow the Greek Orthodox rite, but some are Muslims. Groups of Armenians, Germans, Jews, and Tatars* have also lived in Georgia for centuries. The traditional livelihoods of the Georgian people have included farming, gardening, stock breeding, and various arts and crafts.

For much of its history, Georgia's fate was tied to the conflicts and rivalries of larger powers surrounding it—the Romans, Persians, Byzantines, Arabs, and Turks. Each of these powers sought to control Georgia and make the region a part of its empire. By 532, the BYZANTINE EMPIRE and Persia had divided Georgia between them, with western Georgia controlled by the Byzantines and eastern Georgia controlled by the Persians. Beginning in the 640s, the Arabs pressed into the region, and they soon dominated it. The Arabs relied on a powerful local family, the Bagratids, to represent their interests. By the 900s, Arab power in the region began to decline, and the Bagratids developed several relatively powerful and prosperous kingdoms. Bagratid rule was marked by a revival of industry, commerce, architecture, and literature. During the reign of the Bagratid monarch Bagrat III (978–1014), Georgia became united for the first time.

After the 900s, Georgia was threatened by both the expansion of the Byzantine Empire and the rising power of the SELJUK TURKS. The united Bagratid kingdom of Georgia stood as a buffer between these two groups. The Georgian monarchs managed to maintain peaceful relations with the Byzantines, and they won a series of military victories against the Turks. In 1122, the Georgian capital of Tbilisi was retaken from the Muslims, ending nearly 500 years of Muslim control.

The high point of medieval Georgia occurred under Queen TAMAR, who reigned from 1184 to 1212. After ending a rebellion of Georgian nobles in 1191, she launched victorious campaigns against her Muslim enemies and established a powerful and prosperous kingdom. Soon after she died, however, the Mongols invaded Georgia in 1220 and conquered the country. Under Mongol rule, Georgia fell into near anarchy*, and the country was split into various semi-independent states ruled by local princes. Meanwhile, the power of the Georgian monarchy declined, and the kingdom entered the twilight of its glory.

* **anarchy** state of lawlessness or political disorder

During the 1300s, the Georgian monarchs made a last, desperate attempt to free their kingdom from Mongol rule. In 1327, under King Giorgi VI, the Mongols were driven out of the land, and Georgia was united once again. But in 1386, the Mongols returned under their fierce leader TAMERLANE and reconquered the country. Although briefly reunited in the early 1400s, Georgia soon split once again into tiny kingdoms and principalities. Thereafter, it remained divided until the modern era. (*See also* **Armenia; Mongol Empire.**)

German Language and Literature

The first German writing began in the early medieval period with translations of LATIN works and religious poems written mostly in MONASTERIES. However, later in the Middle Ages, German prose writing emerged, and other kinds of poetry—allegories, lyrics, and romances—became widely popular.

German Language

The Germanic tribes of Europe spoke many different dialects* during the Middle Ages. Those spoken in the north and in the Low Countries* were called Low German. The people who lived on the higher ground of central and southern Germany spoke a dialect called High German, which eventually became modern German.

During the Middle Ages, the High German dialects went through three stages of development—Old, Middle, and New High German. Old High German refers to the German dialects spoken and written from about 700 to 1100. During this period, writing consisted mostly of translations and religious texts composed by monks. The earliest German works were mostly glossaries and translations of Latin originals. The first known German book, *Abrogans* (765–775), was a Latin-German word list.

In the Middle High German period (1100–1350), the number and range of High German texts increased dramatically, as new types of poetry appeared. Religious texts continued to be written, but German poets turned increasingly to subjects from history and legend. Many of the best medieval German poems were written between 1170 and 1250 (called the classical Middle High German period). After 1250, there was an increase of German prose* writing that included histories, city chronicles, law codes, sermons, and the writings of German mysticism*.

During the New High German period (1350–1650), High German dialects blended, and German spelling and pronunciation gradually became more standardized. The New High German that took shape at the end of the Middle Ages became modern German.

German Literature

The three main types of medieval German poetry were allegory, lyric, and romance. Although these types sometimes overlapped, with elements of each appearing in the same poem, they established distinct literary forms that influenced later generations of German writers.

Allegory.   An allegory is a story that uses symbolic characters or settings to express ideas about human life. Allegories appear to be simple stories at first, but careful examination reveals another level or interpretation of the story. Allegories initially were woven into other works, but later they stood on their own as independent texts.

* **dialect** form of speech characteristic of a region that differs from the standard language in pronunciation, vocabulary, and grammar

* **Low Countries** flat coastal lands west of Germany, now occupied by Belgium and the Netherlands

* **prose** writing without meter or rhyme, as distinguished from poetry

* **mysticism** belief that divine truths or direct knowledge of God can be experienced through faith, spiritual insight, and intuition

German religious writers, who learned from Christian theologians* and the Bible, often used animals as symbols for certain traits or moral ideas. For example, the lion represented Christ because of its strength. The first person to include allegory in a German text was the monk Otfrid of Weissenburg. His life of Christ, *Evangelienbuch* (864–867), was the earliest rhymed poem ever written in German.

The early full-length allegories were religious works intended to explain Bible stories and sacred texts. However, even after allegories became independent creations, they continued to appear within larger works. One such example is the poem *Der Streit der vier Töchter Gottes (The Debate of the Four Daughters of God),* which contained a commonly used allegorical dispute. Two of God's daughters, Truth and Justice, insist that humans be condemned for their sins, while his other two daughters, Mercy and Peace, plead that they be forgiven. Christ settles the dispute by offering salvation.

In many medieval religious allegories, the Seven Deadly Sins (Pride, Envy, Wrath, Sloth, Avarice, Gluttony, and Lechery) played a prominent part. Often they lined up in battle formation and fought against corresponding virtues or allegorical personifications such as Repentance, Confession, and Penance.

Some medieval German writers used the game of chess as an allegory to discuss politics and society. The chess pieces represented various groups in society—rulers, judges, knights, governors, and craftsmen. The most popular German chess allegory was the *Schachzabelbuch* by Konrad von Ammenhausen (1337). He filled his work with colorful details and had a particularly sharp eye for the tricks craftsmen used to cheat their customers.

German allegories of love dealt with the nature of love between man and woman. *Die Jagd (The Hunt),* written by a Bavarian nobleman Hadamar von Laber in the mid-1300s, told the story of a hunter (the lover) pursuing his game (the beloved lady). The hunter's hounds represented the lover's virtues, moods, and attitudes.

Lyric. Lyric poetry flourished at courts in Germany between 1050 and 1350. Lyric poems were sung, often to the accompaniment of stringed instruments, such as the harp, lyre, or fiddle. They were usually about COURTLY LOVE.

There was a strong tradition of popular ballads and dance songs in medieval Germany with which court singers entertained their noble audiences. One story from 1020 told of a group of teenagers in Saxony who sang and danced in the churchyard at Christmas. However, their chanting, leaping, and stomping disturbed the local priest. When he ordered them to stop and they refused, he put a curse on them that forced them to keep dancing for an entire year.

See color plate 10, vol. 3.

The first members of one group of lyric poets, called minnesingers, were themselves members of the nobility. This illustrious group included Baron Friedrich von Hausen, councillor to Emperor FREDERICK I BARBAROSSA; Rudolf II of Fenis, count of Neuenburg in Burgundy; and King HENRY VI OF GERMANY.

Great court festivals provided occasions for poetry recitals. In 1184, French and German singers performed at the festival that Frederick I held on the occasion of the knighting of his sons. WALTHER VON DER VOGELWEIDE, a famous poet who worked at the courts of several European kings, traveled to Vienna in 1203 to sing at the two-week wedding feast of Duke Leopold VI.

German lyric poets used themes of CHIVALRY and courtly love borrowed from French TROUBADOURS. The German poets sang about the pains of love they suffered and praised the virtues and perfection of their beloved. The imagery of FEUDALISM often figured in their lyrics. The poet usually portrayed himself as a vassal* and his beloved lady as the one he is sworn to serve. The poems were sometimes set in a spring or winter landscape to express the singer's mood. One popular type of love lyric was the dawn song—a dialogue between two lovers who must separate at the first light of day. Usually set in a garden or in a castle chamber, the dawn song is about the grief the lovers feel when they have to part.

After the beginning of the Third CRUSADE in 1187, crusade songs were sung at the court of Frederick I Barbarossa. These poems were about the anguish the poet feels when he has to leave his lady to go on a crusade and about his conflicting loyalties—serving God or serving his lady.

Lyric poets, who were members of the nobility, sang almost exclusively about love, but traveling professional singers, who supported themselves by singing, sometimes took up other subjects. Others, who depended on the generosity of patrons* for their livelihood, sang in praise of their sponsors.

Romance.   By the late Middle Ages, long narrative romances had gained popularity in Germany. Some German romances told the history of the German people. The most famous such poem was the *Nibelungenlied,* a romance based on legends about an ancient German hero, Siegfried, and members of a family called the Nibelungs.

Most other German romances retold stories from ancient Greece and Rome. The Greek king Alexander the Great and the Trojan War were common subjects of romance. German poets learned about these events from ancient histories or from French romances that used the same subjects. They also used stories from the *Aeneid,* a long epic poem by the Roman poet Virgil.

Stories about King Arthur and his court also had a powerful appeal to romance writers. Arthur was familiar to European readers through the *History of the Kings of Britain,* written by Geoffrey of Monmouth in the 1130s. Geoffrey's descriptions of Arthur's court, based partly on Welsh legend, helped to spread the ideas of chivalry and courtly love. Arthur was seen as a wise, kind, and courteous king, and the rules of courtly behavior practiced by his knights set a standard for an ideal society.

German romances generally followed a pattern. They told the story of a hero, beginning as he left home on a journey or quest. He then had a series of adventures along the way, from which he learned important lessons. Upon completing his quest, the hero returned home to his court and to his beloved lady, who faithfully waited for him. Love and adventure were important themes in medieval romances. Knights held women in high esteem and performed daring feats to show themselves worthy of a woman's love.

Christian virtue was another important theme for German poets. Rather than show characters engaged only in a series of adventures,

* **vassal** person given land by a lord or monarch in return for loyalty and services

* **patron** person of wealth and influence who supports an artist, writer, or scholar

Romantic Revival

In the late 1800s, legends from German medieval romances regained their popularity through the operas of Richard Wagner. His *Parsifal* and *Lohengrin* are based on medieval poems, and the medieval poet Wolfram von Eschenbach is a character in *Tannhäuser.* Wagner's four-part operatic masterpiece, *Ring of the Nibelung,* uses myths from the *Nibelungenlied,* and *Tristan* is based on Gottfried von Strassburg's poem from the early 1200s. Today, these operas are performed throughout the world.

German romances often portrayed their heroes helping people who were in danger.

The three greatest German writers of romance during the Middle Ages were Hartmann von Aue, WOLFRAM VON ESCHENBACH, and Gottfried von Strassburg. Hartmann von Aue's poem, *Iwein,* written about 1102, was based on a French poem called *Yvain* by Chrétien de Troyes. In the poem, Iwein embarked on several adventures designed to win the respect of his wife, Laudine. However, his adventures caused him to lose his reason at one point. He recovered with the help of a woman, whose love he refused (remaining faithful to his wife). When he finally returned home, Iwein had a happy reconciliation with Laudine. In his poem, Hartmann tried to show how the Arthurian code of conduct helped people act in a moral way.

The hero of Wolfram von Eschenbach's romance, *Parzival,* began as one of Arthur's knights, but he then pursued a higher set of values as a

Wolfram von Eschenbach's famous Arthurian poem, *Parzival,* was written in the early 1200s. It is based on the French story *Perceval* by Chrétien de Troyes, but it contains many original elements. Parzival's goal was to be the perfect, chivalrous knight. Ultimately, he finds his honor by dedicating himself to helping the weak and the oppressed. This illumination shows scenes from Parzival's quest.

knight of the Holy Grail. In Christian legend, the Holy Grail was the cup used at the Last Supper. Grail knights strove to achieve moral purity and find the Grail. Wolfram contrasted the Arthurian code, based on the individual quest of each knight for worldly honor, with the religious devotion of the Grail knights who sought the common good. In the poem, Parzival changed from his early blundering efforts to join Arthur's court to his later dedication to help the weak and oppressed.

Gottfried von Strassburg's great poem, *Tristan and Isolde* (ca. 1210), was based on the Celtic legend of Tristan, his uncle King Mark of Cornwall, and the king's bride, Isolde. According to the legend, Tristan and Isolde fall in love after they unknowingly swallow a love potion. Their love brings them both joy and great sorrow. In his exploration of the meaning of love, Gottfried rejected the standard Arthurian rules about relations between men and women. Instead, he stressed the artistic, intellectual, and religious aspects of true love, which he valued more highly. (*See also* **Arthurian Literature; Celtic Languages and Literature; Flanders and the Low Countries; French Language and Literature; Minstrels; Mysticism; Troy, Story of.**)

Germany

* **duchy**   territory ruled by a duke or a duchess

See map in Carolingians (vol. 1).

During the Middle Ages, Germany evolved from a cluster of duchies* and tribal lands into a kingdom with thriving cities dominated by a strong ruling class. The kings of medieval Germany tried to revive the HOLY ROMAN EMPIRE founded by CHARLEMAGNE, often seeking the support of the church for their efforts. Although they succeeded in establishing Christianity throughout their lands, the attempts at reviving the empire failed. Instead, the monarchy became weaker, and local nobles and urban leaders gained power and independence.

The Carolingians, Saxons, and Salians

The Carolingians.   In 843, Louis the German, Charlemagne's son, received the East Frankish kingdom, consisting of the land that eventually became Germany. The kingdom extended between the Rhine and Elbe Rivers as far south as modern Hungary. It was a heavily forested region, inhabited by tribes—such as the Alamanni, Bavarians, Saxons, and Thuringians—who followed their own clan leaders. These tribes had learned about Christianity only a few generations earlier from monks who had visited the region in the 700s. There were still very few towns.

After ruling for more than 30 years, Louis died, and his three sons divided the kingdom. However, two of them, Carloman and Louis the Younger, soon died as well. Their lands passed to the youngest brother, Charles III. In addition to the East Frankish kingdom, Charles became king of Italy and of the West Frankish kingdom.

The East Frankish nobles, unhappy with Charles's rule, rebelled against him. They named Arnulf of Carinthia, Carloman's illegitimate son, as their king. The rebellion showed the powerful influence of the nobles and also contributed to a new sense of identity among the people of the region, who were beginning to be known as Germans.

When King Otto I of Saxony took over the duchy of Franconia, he became more powerful than any of the German dukes. He then conquered the Magyars and the Slavs, opening up the eastern Danube valley to German settlement. In these territories, he increased the authority of the church.

In addition to joining forces against the king, ambitious nobles were carving out their own strongholds. In Saxony, Bavaria, and Franconia, powerful local leaders established themselves as dukes, with control over the property and families in their districts.

The problems of the kingdom soon overwhelmed Arnulf. Both the Vikings from Scandinavia and the Magyars, a nomadic tribe in Hungary,

GERMAN EMPIRE

- German Empire in 962
- Associated States
- Frontier Territories

KINGDOM OF DENMARK

BALTIC SEA

NORTH SEA

Lübeck

Hamburg

Bremen

Brandenburg

Elbe

KINGDOM OF POLAND

FRIESLAND

Utrecht

EASTPHALIA

Magdeburg

River

SAXONY

WESTPHALIA

Antwerp

LOWER LORRAINE

Cologne

Rhine River

HESSE

THURINGIA

BRABANT

FRANCONIA

Frankfurt

Prague

KINGDOM OF BOHEMIA

FLANDERS

Moselle River

Mainz

Trier

Worms

Nuremberg

MORAVIA

Metz

Regensburg

AUSTRIA

UPPER LORRAINE

Strasbourg

Danube River

BAVARIA

Vienna

KINGDOM OF FRANCE

ALSACE

SWABIA

Augsburg

BATTLE AT LECH RIVER (955)

Salzburg

Lech River

CARINTHIA

HUNGARY

Geneva

A l p s

KINGDOM OF BURGUNDY

Legnano

Milan

VERONA

Verona

Venice

Turin

LOMBARDY

Po River

Rhône River

KINGDOM OF ITALY

Genoa

ADRIATIC SEA

N W E S

0   50   100 Miles

PROVENCE

MEDITERRANEAN SEA

Pisa

were raiding the country, resulting in constant warfare between them and the Germans. The reign of Arnulf's son, Louis the Child (900–911), was equally troubled. He was the last of the CAROLINGIANS on the German throne.

The Saxons.   The end of Carolingian rule changed the monarchy significantly. From this point on, a small group of prominent nobles elected each new king. They sometimes chose a near relative of the dead king, but not always. In the first election, held in 911, Duke Conrad of Franconia became king. Seven years later, the nobles elected Henry of Saxony. Henry's election gave Saxony special importance as the king's home region. Several generations of Saxons ruled the kingdom in the 900s and 1000s.

Henry's primary task was to stop the invasions of Germany's borders. To do this, he first negotiated a truce with the Magyars in 926. Several years later, he defeated the Slavs, a tribe living along Germany's eastern border. These victories gave Henry the personal prestige he needed to control the German dukes, who still tended to assert their independence against the king.

Henry's son, OTTO I THE GREAT, became king in 936. He took over the duchy of Franconia, combining it with Saxony to ensure that he was more powerful than any of the German dukes. Otto's approach to the Slavs was different from his father's. He decided to conquer them and convert them to Christianity. He founded a monastery at Magdeburg as a mission center, which was soon so successful that he appointed several bishops in the new lands.

In a battle at the Lech River in 955, Otto resoundingly defeated the Magyars. This victory opened up the eastern part of the Danube River valley to German settlement. Henry and Otto relied on the church to help overcome tribal loyalties and control the nobility. They appointed bishops and abbots familiar with their policies and enlarged the church's estates. Otto gave some bishops entire counties to govern.

The Saxon kings also tried to conquer some of the other territories of Charlemagne's empire, notably Lorraine, Burgundy, and Italy. Henry won control of Lorraine in 925. In 951, Otto had himself crowned king of Italy. Then he married Adelaide, daughter of the king of Burgundy. As more pieces of the former empire fell under Otto's control, his supporters felt he had achieved greater status than the other kings of the time. Many longed to revive the past glory of Charlemagne. Accordingly, Pope John XII crowned Otto emperor of the Holy Roman Empire in 962. This coronation set an example for future German monarchs to follow. Many of them were also separately crowned emperor after becoming king.

Otto's son, Otto II, gained the throne 11 years later and continued his father's quest for power in Italy. He called himself Emperor Augustus of the Romans. He tried to take over southern Italy, but Arab forces annihilated his army at Calabria in 982. The following year, his three-year-old son, OTTO III, became emperor.

Otto III's mother, Theophano, and his grandmother, Adelaide, ruled the empire until the young emperor was able to assume control. Beginning with Otto I, the court had become a place where German culture flourished, and this continued under Otto III. Writers and artists produced great works of scholarship, architecture, sculpture, and painting.

Claiming that the restored empire should eventually include all Christian lands, Otto III tried to bring Poland under his rule through negotiations with the Polish duke, Boleslav. Otto's efforts to win Poland through negotiation were in vain, however, and his successor, Henry II, attacked Poland. Henry's reign (1002–1024) brought the Saxon dynasty to an end.

The Salians.   A new ruling family, known as the Salians, then came to power and held the German throne for more than 100 years. The first Salian king, Conrad II, was followed by his son, HENRY III, then his grandson, Henry IV, and then his great-grandson, Henry V. All were deeply involved in changing the German church.

Henry III appointed four German bishops as popes. With Henry's support, these popes instituted reforms to eliminate corruption and poor management of church affairs. The papacy* gained in influence, and the church in Germany became the strongest in Europe. The power of the papacy, however, became a problem for Henry's son, Henry IV, when he came into conflict with Pope GREGORY VII. Gregory wanted to free the church from the king's control, but the king thought otherwise and maintained his right to appoint bishops. This battle of wills, which was known as the Investiture* Controversy, continued under Henry V. The two sides finally reached a compromise in the Concordat of Worms (1122). The effect of the compromise was to limit the king's power over the church and, in general, weaken the monarchy.

The Hohenstaufens

After the Salians, the Hohenstaufens gained control of the throne and became the most powerful German ruling family of the Middle Ages. The dynasty began with dukes in Swabia and eventually produced six monarchs who reigned in the 1100s and early 1200s: Conrad III, FREDERICK I BARBAROSSA, HENRY VI, Philip of Swabia, FREDERICK II, and Conrad IV.

The reign of Frederick I Barbarossa (1152–1190) was long and eventful. Like many of his predecessors, Frederick wanted freedom from papal control. To achieve that, he claimed that his authority came directly from God and, therefore, did not need the pope's approval. Frederick made his position quite clear when he refused a request to hold the stirrup of the pope's horse and to lead the animal.

Soon after becoming king, Frederick placed a small group of nobles, including his cousin, Henry the Lion, in charge of Germany. He then left for Italy to be crowned emperor. He hoped to conquer the northern Italian cities of Lombardy as well as the kingdom of Sicily. But the Lombard cities formed an alliance (the Lombard League), combining their forces to fight the emperor. They defeated him at Legnano in 1176. Frederick barely escaped from Italy.

Frederick was succeeded by his son, Henry VI, who also had a particular interest in Sicily since his wife, Constance, was related to the Sicilian king. Four years into Henry's reign, his army successfully invaded that kingdom, and he became king of Sicily. For many years, Sicily remained in German hands.

* **papacy** office of the pope and his administrators

* **investiture** act of installing a person in high office, such as a bishop

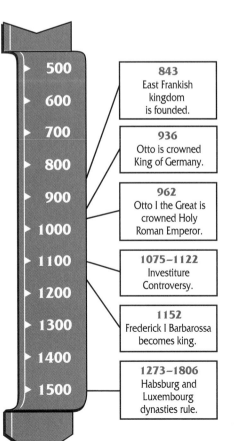

843
East Frankish kingdom is founded.

936
Otto is crowned King of Germany.

962
Otto I the Great is crowned Holy Roman Emperor.

1075–1122
Investiture Controversy.

1152
Frederick I Barbarossa becomes king.

1273–1806
Habsburg and Luxembourg dynasties rule.

A dispute over succession followed Henry's death. Despite serious opposition, a group of nobles elected Henry's brother, Philip of Swabia. Another group supported Otto of Brunswick, the second son of Henry the Lion. A few years later Philip was murdered, and Otto gained the throne as Otto IV.

Otto soon made enemies of both the king of France (Philip II Augustus) and the pope, who arranged for a new election declaring as king Frederick II, the son of Henry VI. Philip Augustus resolved the conflict between Otto and Frederick by defeating Otto in battle at Flanders and sending Frederick the golden eagle from the captured imperial* flag. But the long battle for the throne had weakened royal authority.

* **imperial** pertaining to an empire or emperor

Frederick II placed his son, Henry, in charge of Sicily and Germany. He then left for Italy, hoping to conquer the Lombard cities. From Italy, Frederick joined a campaign, led by the pope, against religious heretics* in Germany. Henry, however, objected to the campaign, and the pope excommunicated* him. Frederick, to his son's displeasure, returned to Germany.

* **heretic** person who disagrees with established church doctrine

* **excommunicate** to exclude from the rites of the church

In an effort to keep his father out of the country, Henry gave his support to the Lombards, a move that greatly angered Frederick. When Frederick reached home, he imprisoned Henry for the rest of his life. Henry's brother, Conrad IV, succeeded Frederick in 1250. Hohenstaufen rule in Germany ended four years later with Conrad's death.

In spite of political turmoil, the Hohenstaufen years were regarded as a time of economic and cultural vitality in Germany. Millions of acres of forest were cleared, and hundreds of new towns were established. Germany's territory expanded eastward, and German merchants controlled much of the trade on the North and Baltic Seas.

Major literary works were created during this period, including poems of chivalry and courtly love: Hartmann von Aue's *Iwein,* Wolfram von Eschenbach's *Parzival,* and Gottfried von Strassburg's *Tristan.* The great epic poem the *Nibelungenlied* appeared in the early 1200s. German architects and artisans of this period built the magnificent cathedrals of Bamberg and Naumberg.

The Habsburgs and Luxembourgs

The departure of the Hohenstaufens from the German throne left the country in disarray. No strong ruler emerged to unite the country or to fend off outside invaders. In a disputed election in 1257, two foreign princes, Richard of Cornwall and Alfonso X of Castile, claimed the German crown. At the same time, the French occupied parts of Germany, and the Swiss, who lived in southern Germany, began to remove themselves from the empire. Legends began to circulate about the return of the powerful emperors. One version claimed that Frederick II was asleep in the Thuringian mountains and would be summoned by God to help his nation.

The instability ended with the election of 1273. By this time, the selection of the king was conducted by an Electoral College, which consisted of three archbishops (from Mainz, Trier, and Cologne), three powerful nobles (from the Rhine, Saxony, and Brandenburg), and the king of Bohemia. The Electoral College chose Rudolf of Habsburg, the first member of the HABSBURG DYNASTY to rule Germany.

Along with the Habsburgs, another powerful family, the Luxembourgs, provided candidates for the monarchy in the 1300s. In 1308, the electors chose Henry VII, the first Luxembourg monarch. Henry, like many other German kings, believed that conquering Italy was the way to restore the Holy Roman Empire. But he, too, was hindered by the northern Italian cities. After his death, a disputed election led to an eight-year civil war. Louis, duke of BAVARIA, who was supported by the Luxembourgs, emerged as King Louis IV the Bavarian.

Pope John XXII, who feared a strong ruler in the empire, vigorously opposed Louis, who wanted to limit the power of the papacy. Louis went to Italy to demand the imperial crown, but he finally succumbed to the pope's opposition. In his place, another Luxembourg king, Charles IV, came to power.

Charles made his court at Prague, one of the leading cultural centers of Europe, and he founded the University of Prague. In 1356, he issued the Golden Bull, an important legal document that defined the procedure for electing the German king and listed the titles and territories of the electors. In issuing the bull, Charles attempted to strengthen royal authority. But, at the same time, the bull gave the electors immense privileges. They became an elite group among German nobles.

In 1438, the Habsburg king Albert II took the throne. From then until the end of the empire in 1806, the Habsburgs reigned. In Austria, they ruled into the early 1900s.

As the Middle Ages came to an end, the Habsburg kings Frederick III and his son MAXIMILIAN I ruled the kingdom. They had costly battles with two of Germany's important neighbors—Hungary and France. First, Frederick lost a war for possession of Hungary and Bohemia. Then, Maximilian married Mary, the heiress of Burgundy, hoping to restore the empire's fortunes elsewhere, but it took him years of bloody campaigns to win acceptance in his wife's land. Moreover, the war brought Germany into direct confrontation with France, which was the most powerful country in Europe at that time.

Rise of the Nobility and the Great Cities. In the 1400s, with the German monarchy at a low point, the nobles and leaders of Germany's major cities acquired unprecedented independence over their own affairs. More than 100 important nobles (princes, dukes, landgraves*, and margraves*) won sovereignty in their regions, giving them complete authority over justice, administration, coining money, and road and river tolls. As a result, the territories of the nobles came to resemble independent states.

There were about 80 major cities in Germany at this time, and they, too, became increasingly powerful. The cities grew in size and population and became prosperous centers of trade and finance. Visitors praised the German cities of Cologne, Nuremberg, Augsburg, Lübeck, and Frankfurt as splendid places. For greater strength, the cities formed alliances, such as the HANSEATIC LEAGUE and the Swabian League, pledging to assist each other. Although the monarchy still existed, by the 1400s much of Germany's political, economic, and cultural leadership came from the city leaders and the nobles in the countryside. (*See also* **Austria; Burgundy; Cities and Towns; Count, County; Duke, Duchy;**

* **landgrave** noble who had jurisdiction over certain lands

* **margrave** noble appointed as military governor of frontier territory

German Language and Literature; Germany, Representative Assemblies; Lombards, Kingdom of.)

Germany, Representative Assemblies

* **imperial** pertaining to an empire or emperor

* **dialect** form of speech characteristic of a region that differs from the standard language in pronunciation, vocabulary, and grammar

In the late Middle Ages, representative assemblies emerged in GERMANY and other parts of western Europe out of an increasing need of rulers to seek support and money (especially for war) from their subjects. Assemblies also gave some influential groups—such as the clergy, nobility, and townspeople—the opportunity to protect and advance their interests.

Imperial Assembly (**Reichstag**). For most of the Middle Ages, the German emperors of the HOLY ROMAN EMPIRE did little more than invite other German princes to their court to confer and settle disputes. They certainly did not consult with representatives of the vast majority of the people who were their subjects. However, toward the end of the medieval period, political assemblies developed as a way for the emperor to seek political and financial support and for powerful social classes to defend their rights.

Although representative assemblies were a way for the emperor and the people to respond to various political and economic issues, there were certain obstacles that prevented representatives from gathering. The enormous size of the German Empire meant that members of any imperial* assembly had to travel great distances for the meeting. In addition, there was no common language. People in the vast empire spoke Italian, Slavic, and French as well as many different German dialects*. Furthermore, in the late Middle Ages, the German emperor was not strong enough to control the powerful German princes, who ruled their own territories and fiercely defended their independence.

In the 1400s, an imperial assembly called the *Reichstag* was created with the support of the German electors, a group of seven bishops and nobles officially designated to choose the kings of Germany. As the monarchy weakened, these electors took over additional responsibilities of government. When war broke out between Germany and the Hussites of BOHEMIA in the early 1400s, the *Reichstag* met regularly to raise money and plan defense. Each group that was asked to contribute financially to pay for the war—the clergy, princes, and townspeople—attended the assemblies.

The *Reichstag* soon began taking on more governmental duties. At the Diet of Worms in 1495, the assembly declared its commitment to defend the peace and established an imperial court. The assembly was divided into three groups called colleges—the electors, princes, and townspeople. The nobles in the first two groups dominated the assemblies.

Other Assemblies. Local assemblies also emerged during the late Middle Ages. The German Empire was made up of several hundred political territories called principalities, counties, duchies, or bishoprics, depending on the title of the local ruler. Assemblies formed in many of these territories and included members from different levels of society—the clergy, knights, townspeople, and even peasants. In some places, such as

Bavaria and Württemberg, strong territorial assemblies developed, while in other places assemblies never developed or met briefly and were quickly disbanded. Many towns and cities formed their own urban assemblies, where municipal leaders met with citizens to discuss matters of mutual concern. (*See also* **Austria; Bavaria; Cologne; Germany; Kingship, Theories of.**)

Gerson, John

1363–1429
Theologian, reformer, and spiritual writer

* **theologian** person who studies religious faith and practice

John Gerson was a French theologian* who played a major role in settling the crisis created in the Roman church by the existence of two rival popes, a conflict that became known as the Great SCHISM.

Gerson's career was spent at the University of Paris, where he became university chancellor in 1395. He actively tried to resolve the Great Schism by recommending that both the pope in AVIGNON and the pope in Rome resign. When the schism continued unresolved, he joined those calling for a church council to settle the problem. Gerson was a leading force at the Council of Constance, which brought the schism to an end with the election of a new pope in 1417.

Gerson also called for church reform and wrote extensively on spiritual matters of interest to monks, laypersons, and children. One of his last writings was a defense of JOAN OF ARC, the young French heroine who led French soldiers in the HUNDRED YEARS WAR and who eventually was burned at the stake for HERESY. Gerson's final years in Lyons were among his most productive. Through his writings, he continued to advocate church reform and spiritual renewal. (*See also* **Christianity; Paris; Universities.**)

Ghazali, al-

1058–1111
Islamic jurist, theologian, and mystic

* **vizier** Muslim minister of state

Abu Hamid Muhammad ibn Muhammad al Tusi al-Ghazali was born in eastern Iran. His early training was in Islamic law and later in Islamic theology. Nizam al-Mulk, the powerful vizier* of the Seljuk sultans, was so impressed with al-Ghazali's scholarship that he appointed him chief professor in the Nizamiya (a college for teaching Islamic law) of Baghdad.

In 1095, al-Ghazali experienced a spiritual crisis that caused him to lose the power of speech for a time and resulted in his abandoning his prestigious academic career to lead the life of an Islamic mystic, or Sufi. Al-Ghazali believed that purely rational aspects of religion had drained Islam of its spiritual content.

During this period of his life, al-Ghazali wrote his most important work, *The Revival of the Sciences of Religion*. In that book, he was able to reconcile traditional Islamic beliefs and practices with MYSTICISM, which previously had contradicted each other. Al-Ghazali also wrote an important book relating the theories of various philosophers. Because he was so thorough in discussing the theories he criticized, his works actually made philosophical ideas better known in the Islamic world. In 1106, al-Ghazali resumed lecturing and continued teaching until his death in 1111. (*See also* **Farabi, al-; Ibn Rushd; Ibn Sina; Islam, Religion of.**)

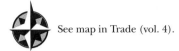

See map in Trade (vol. 4).

* **magistrate** ruling official of a town

* **guild** association of craft and trade workers that set standards and represented the interests of its members

Ghent became one of medieval Europe's great commercial and industrial centers. As early as the tenth century, it was one of the leading towns in the county of Flanders, in present-day Belgium. Ghent reached its peak in the 1200s and was most famous for its wool industry. During the late 1200s, Ghent produced more wool cloth than any other European town.

Ghent is located where the Schelde and Lys Rivers meet and flow into the North Sea. This position made it an ideal trading center. The rivers offered transportation from inland towns and villages to the sea, and the North Sea provided easy access to England and other neighboring countries. At first, this location was not an asset, however. It made the town easy prey for enemy raids. In 853, 879, and 881, the NORMANS raided the town and occupied it, destroying much of the town's commercial quarter. The destruction gradually led to the creation of a new commercial area and the steady growth of the town into a bustling urban center. By 1000, Ghent was famous for its annual fair and its fine wool cloth. The townspeople had also gained property rights and a significant amount of economic independence from the count of Flanders, the feudal ruler of the region.

The period from 1100 to 1300 was Ghent's greatest era. In the 1100s, the town grew rapidly and became self-governing. A body of local magistrates* supervised urban affairs, such as law enforcement, the courts, commerce, taxation, fortifications, and public works. Ghent's industrial and trading strength reached its height in the 1200s. During this period, traders imported raw wool from England. Local crafts workers wove this wool into fine cloth that was sold throughout Europe. Traders from Spain, Italy, southwestern France, and the Baltic Sea region came to the town for its cloth.

Ghent's wool industry produced a wealthy class of cloth makers and merchants that dominated the economic, social, and political life of the town. During the 1200s, the power of this class became hereditary. Ghent's magistrates all came from this class, and it excluded all others from participating in government. At the same time, less-powerful merchants and workers, such as butchers and shoemakers, organized themselves into craft guilds*. Over time, tensions rose between this working class and the wealthy, ruling class. After 1300, there were repeated, unsuccessful attempts by the craft guilds to seize political power in order to improve the economic condition of workers.

In the 1300s, Ghent faced economic problems, as the wool industry began to decline. The outbreak of the HUNDRED YEARS WAR between England and France, in 1337, added to Ghent's troubles. Town merchants traded with both countries, but England was the more important trading partner since it supplied the raw materials for Ghent's wool industry. Yet the feudal lord of Flanders, Count Louis of Nevers, favored the French cause. King EDWARD III OF ENGLAND banned the export of wool to Flanders in an attempt to force the count to support England, but the count refused. In desperation, Ghent and other towns formed a military alliance with England. Despite the alliance, Ghent continued to decline. England had begun making more of its own wool cloth and no longer needed Flanders as an outlet for its raw wool. Italy also was becoming a manufacturing center, producing its own cloth. Unable to find new markets,

Ghent began to shrink in wealth and size, and it lost its commanding importance as a center of commerce and trade. (*See also* **Flanders and the Low Countries; Wool.**)

Giotto di Bondone

ca. 1267–1337
Painter and architect

Giotto di Bondone, perhaps the most influential painter of the 1300s, was born near Florence, Italy. He broke new ground in painting and set the style for future generations of painters. His most important contribution to Western art was his use of narrative composition and expressive gestures to convey powerful human emotions.

Historians know little of Giotto's early life. He studied art in Florence and painted at St. Peter's in Rome, where he met and was influenced by other artists and sculptors working there. In 1330, he entered the service of King Robert of Anjou, the French ruler of the Italian city of Naples, and he most likely learned of the French GOTHIC PAINTING style while at the ANGEVIN court. Four years later, Giotto returned to Florence as the chief architect of the Florence Cathedral. He designed the cathedral's famous bell tower.

Giotto worked primarily in fresco, a method of wall painting in which paint is applied to fresh, moist plaster. In creating a fresco, colors are mixed with water and then applied to the wet surface, where they chemically bond with the plaster. Artists had used this method before Giotto; what makes his contribution so important was his sculptural and naturalistic style. In his paintings, Giotto designed massive, dignified figures who seem to possess an emotional inner life. The Byzantine style adopted by earlier Italian painters depicted the human form in a remote and emotionally limited way. In contrast, Giotto's solid and monumental human figures convey a whole range of expressions, gestures, and poses from a quiet calm to anguished despair.

Giotto's most famous frescoes were painted for the Scrovegni family chapel in Padua, Italy. *The Lamentation,* painted in 1305–1306, is one mural in the series depicting *The Lives of the Virgin Mary and of Christ.*

Giotto's greatest and best-preserved achievement in fresco painting was the series of murals depicting the *Lives of the Virgin Mary and of Christ,* which he painted for the Scrovegni family chapel in Padua, Italy. He painted these frescoes in 1306 when he was in his late 30s or early 40s. Twenty-two separate scenes cover the walls of the chapel with detailed narrative scenes in three-dimensional settings. Giotto carefully calculated every element of these paintings—the architecture, figure placement, gestures, color choices, composition, and use of solid and empty spaces—for maximum effect. In doing so, he strongly conveyed to the viewer the psychological conditions of the people whose story was being depicted.

The *Life of St. Francis* in the Bardi Chapel in Florence is another series of frescoes, generally dated in the 1330s. It shows Giotto's style as it developed toward the end of his career. This work is simpler, concentrating on the essential aspects of the story of St. FRANCIS OF ASSISI. Giotto used muted shades of gray, pink, and brown and placed fewer figures in each scene. The total impact is dramatic and powerful. Giotto's art, in which he portrayed figures as humans instead of ICONS, served as a bridge between the medieval period and the Renaissance. (*See also* **Byzantine Art; Florence.**)

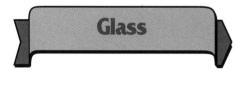

See color plate 6, vol. 1.

Glass

Glassmaking was an important industry throughout the Middle Ages. Glassmakers throughout Europe provided the materials for a cathedral's stained glass windows, for common household containers (bottles, bowls, and goblets), and for the much-desired mirrors and lamps of wealthy nobles and merchants.

Glassmaking in northern Europe can be traced back to Roman times. Sand, fuel, and either soda or potash were needed to make glass. Early glassmaking used soda, a salt compound that had to be imported from the Mediterranean in Roman times. However, northern European glassmakers around the year 1000 began using potash in place of soda. Potash is a compound of potassium found in wood ashes, and it was readily available in the woodlands of northern Europe. This change to the use of potash permitted glassmakers to move their operations to the forested regions of northern Europe. Glassmaking sites existed in the area around the Rhine River as well as in France and the British Isles. One drawback of potash glass, however, was that it deteriorated over a long period of time, and not much potash glass from this era remains today.

Italy, which had been the center of the Roman Empire and where people probably never had forgotten the art of glassmaking, also was a major center of glassmaking. Glassmaking in Venice began in the 900s or earlier, and, by the late 1200s, VENICE was the undisputed leader of glassmaking in Europe. Northern Italian cities, including Florence and Padua, helped spread the manufacture of soda glass outside Italy.

Techniques for making glass were described in the early 1100s by Theophilus, a Benedictine monk, possibly from Cologne, Germany. Theophilus describes the operation of a glass furnace and the glassmaker's technique of elongating and shaping a blob of molten glass into a vessel.

* **gilding** covering with a thin layer of gold

Everyday glassware was usually pale green in color because it was difficult to remove impurities to make clear glass. Some glass was milky white, and glass could be colored deliberately with metal ores. Surface decorations were added by etching, cutting, engraving, enameling, gilding*, and painting.

Sheets of window glass were prepared in a process called "muffing." This process existed during Roman times and continued throughout the Middle Ages into the 1500s. In the "muffing" process, cylinders of molten glass were split with a hot iron and, while still soft, were spread flat with iron tongs and a smooth, flat piece of wood. The flat sheet of glass was allowed to cool before being cut. The cutting was accomplished by using first a red-hot iron and then a "grozing iron," a notched tool that nibbled away at the edges until the desired shape was attained.

Another method for making window glass was the crown technique. In this method, small circular window panels similar to flat glass plates were set into plaster or other frames. Each technique had advantages: "muffing" created a single large rectangular sheet, and the crown technique preserved the brilliancy of the glass.

Sheet glass was important for one of the most sought after items of the Middle Ages: the looking glass, or mirror. The city of NUREMBERG in Germany became a leading producer of mirrors in the Middle Ages. The German mirror had a convex surface (curved outward) and was backed with silvering, or a metallic mixture made of tin or lead compounds. German master craftsmen were hired by Venetians in the 1300s to help establish a mirror-making industry in their glass center in Murano. Mirrors were so popular in medieval Europe that mirror makers, called "mirrorers," had their own guild in the 1300s. (*See also* **Glass, Stained; Technology.**)

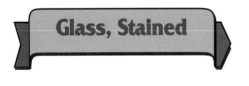

See color plate 6, vol. 2.

The church windows made of colored glass are among the most exquisite examples of medieval art. The term *stained glass* is somewhat misleading, however, since staining was just one method of coloring glass. Medieval artisans used colored glass extensively to create windows for the Gothic cathedrals and other buildings of the later Middle Ages.

The basic techniques for making stained glass date back to the 800s. Metallic oxides were fused to the glass in a melting pot. The colors, obtained from metal ores, were restricted in number and consisted of red, blue, yellow, green, and rose purple. Despite the few colors, the variations of shading resulting from the firing process enabled artisans to create wonderful effects of light and shadow. Highlights on the face, hair, or clothing of a figure were made by applying a light gray wash over the surface and then picking out with the butt of the brush handle the areas to be highlighted before the glass was fired.

To create a stained glass window, artists—often working in teams—prepared a rough sketch, or cartoon, of a design. Then, using a red-hot cutting instrument, workers cut colored glass into small, specially shaped pieces. Once the colored pieces were cut, they were fitted into channeled lead strips, the junctions of which were soldered together with a hot soldering iron. The whole image was then fitted into a framework of iron called an armature. When fully assembled, the window was a kind of "glass painting."

The art of stained glass reached its glorious peak between 1150 and 1250. More than 160 windows of vibrant reds and blues still can be seen in CHARTRES CATHEDRAL in France. People in the Middle Ages believed that light was a metaphor for the way God touches every part of the world. The light entering a cathedral through windows of sacred pictures not only illuminated the interior but enlightened the minds of those inside. Scenes in stained glass told of the lives of Christ, the Virgin Mary, and the saints. These stained glass images were so precious that they were frequently rescued from fire and reset in new buildings. (*See also* **Gothic Architecture.**)

See
color plate 11,
vol. 3.

* **duchy**   territory ruled by a duke or a duchess

The Golden Horde was a branch of the MONGOL EMPIRE that ruled Russia and central Asia in the late Middle Ages. The name refers to the golden tent or dwelling (*orda*) of the khan, or ruler, of the Mongols.

The branch was founded in the 1200s by Batu, who died in 1255. He was the grandson of the great Mongol ruler Genghis Khan. The Golden Horde established its capital at Saray on the lower Volga River. Batu's brother Berke converted to Islam and combined forces with the Islamic Mamluks to create an empire of Turko-Mongolian peoples called Tatars.

After the non-Muslim reign of Möngke Temür ended in 1280, civil conflict between feuding Tatar princes followed. The brief but brilliant reign of Noghay, a grandnephew of Batu, ended in 1299 when he was assassinated by a rival. Özbeg, who ruled from 1313 to 1341, strengthened the khanate (rule of the khan). He reaffirmed the central role of Islam and reestablished control over the Russian princes. By granting the grand duchy* of Moscow to Ivan I Kalita in 1328, Özbeg helped Moscow rise to power.

In the late 1300s, a period of Tatar decline set in despite the presence of the strong ruler TAMERLANE. Lithuania, Moldavia, and Moscow asserted their independence more forcefully against the rule of the Golden Horde. In the mid-1400s, the khanate fragmented further, as local Tatar rulers in Kazan, Crimea, and Astrakhan broke away and established their own states. In 1502, the Golden Horde ceased to exist when the Crimean khan, who was a vassal* of the Ottoman Turks, destroyed Saray. (*See also* **Islam, Religion of; Kievan Rus; Mamluk Dynasty; Muscovy, Rise of; Nevsky, Alexander; Novgorod; Ottomans and Ottoman Empire.**)

* **vassal**   person given land by a lord or monarch in return for loyalty and services

See *Saints, Lives of.*

An underground poetic tradition existed in the Middle Ages that mocked holiness and piety. The authors who created these poems were known as goliards, named after Golias, a drunken priest who appears as a character in many of the works. The goliardic tradition lasted from about 850 to around 1250. Its high point came in the 1100s, as large numbers of university students composed irreverent works in the goliardic style.

The goliard poets wrote in Latin, usually anonymously. Their works praised the pleasures of food, drink, love, and travel, and they parodied religious literature and the ceremonies of the church. Many of the best goliardic works took well-known religious texts and altered them slightly for comic effect. For example, a hymn to the Virgin called "O Good and Delightful Word" became the drinker's song "O Good and Delightful Wine." No subject was too sacred for such treatment, not even the Lord's Prayer and the Mass.

Two of the greatest goliard poets were Hugh of Orleans (ca. 1095– ca. 1160) and a writer known only as the Archpoet, who flourished from 1159 to 1165. The Archpoet's "Confessio Goliae" is the most famous goliard poem. It is noteworthy for its masterful use of words and for its psychological study of why people behave the way they do.

By the early 1200s, church leaders became concerned that the jokes were getting out of hand. They began to urge strict measures against those who sang improper words in church. Also, anyone who claimed to be a goliard risked losing church privileges. As a result, the tradition died out, although its reputation lived on. By CHAUCER's time, "goliard" was a term of insult, but it still suggested verbal skill. (*See also* **Carmina Burana.**)

Gothic Architecture

Gothic architecture is a style of building that developed in northern France around the mid-1100s. From France, the Gothic style spread to Germany, Italy, England, and other parts of Europe. It remained the dominant architectural style north of the Alps for about 400 years. The Gothic style was used in both secular and religious architecture, but its ultimate artistic expression is found in the medieval Gothic cathedral.

The Gothic style reflects a tremendous upsurge in the European economy and a willingness, at least in France, to exploit and experiment with extremes of technology. The style also reflects the cooperation of the clergy (bishops) and secular (nonreligious) powers to create structures that advertised the wealth and culture of the small cities that were beginning to flourish at the time.

Characteristics of Gothic Architecture. Gothic architecture succeeded ROMANESQUE ARCHITECTURE. The ground plan of a Gothic cathedral was a modified version of the early Roman basilica*. The early basilica consisted of a rectangle divided into three aisles: a central aisle, or nave, that ended in a semicircular recess, and aisles on each side. The aisles were divided from the nave by columns carrying semicircular arches. In some churches, intersecting these aisles and perpendicular to them was a rectangular space called a transept. The T-shaped plan became a basic characteristic of Gothic church architecture.

During the Romanesque period, builders used round arches, barrel vaults*, and groin vaults*. To carry the vaults, they built thick exterior walls of stone, punctured by small window openings. The result was a solid, massive-looking building that was dark on the inside. Gothic

* **basilica** in Roman times, a large rectangular building used as a court of law or public meeting place; adapted for early Christian churches, which had an oblong plan with a high central nave, aisles on each side, and an apse (semicircular recess) usually at the east end

* **barrel vault** round arched ceiling made of stone or brick

* **groin vault** arched ceiling consisting of two barrel vaults intersecting at right angles

* **rib vault** arched ceiling formed by intersecting pointed arches

* **flying buttress** stone structure connected to the outer wall of a building by an arch; used to support the vaults

builders modified these elements, creating the distinctive look of Gothic architecture. Instead of rounded arches, Gothic builders used pointed arches. Pointed arches allowed the construction of large rib vaults* over the nave. Pointed arches and ribs also eliminated the need for massive walls and enabled builders to raise the height of vaults and walls and to create more and larger windows. As cathedral walls became taller and less massive, pressure tended to force the walls outward, and builders had to find a way to keep them from collapsing. The solution was the addition of flying buttresses* along the outside walls.

These three features—thin walls, rib vaults, and flying buttresses—were the most distinctive features of Gothic architecture. They enabled builders to construct towering basilicas with arches soaring upward and light filtering through large and beautiful stained glass windows. The Gothic cathedral is sometimes described as a mysterious, spacious cage in which the viewer's eye is carried toward heaven—an awe-inspiring effect that reinforced medieval faith.

The Spread of Gothic Architecture.   The Gothic style of architecture emerged between 1137 and 1144 in the Île-de-France region (the royal domain) around Paris. The first landmark of the Gothic style was the rebuilding of the abbey church of St. Denis. St. Denis was a royal abbey, where the kings of France were buried. The head of the abbey, Abbot SUGER, wanted to make St. Denis the spiritual center of France, so he commissioned builders to create the finest and most beautifully decorated church in the Christian world. The east end of the church was rebuilt. The massive walls of the old Romanesque structure were refashioned and made higher and thinner so that they appeared almost weightless. A rose-shaped stained glass window, the first of its kind, was

The three most distinctive features of Gothic architecture are thin walls, rib vaults, and flying buttresses. This exterior side view of Bourges Cathedral in France, built in the 1200s, shows the flying buttresses characteristically built to help support the cathedral's high interior walls.

Secular Gothic Architecture

During the 1200s, the Gothic style was gradually adopted by wealthy nobles, merchants, towns, and guilds for their homes and meeting halls. Among the greatest examples of this secular Gothic architecture are the great guildhalls of Flanders (modern-day Belgium), town halls in such German cities as Lübeck and Münster, and Italian merchants' palaces in Venice. Use of the lavish Gothic style for these buildings was a symbol of prosperity and pride.

* **facade**   front of a building; also, any side of a building that is given special architectural treatment

* **mosaic**   art form in which small pieces of stone or glass are set in cement; also refers to a picture made in this manner

placed in the west facade*, allowing more light to filter through. The builders of St. Denis also used the pointed arches and rib vaults that marked the Gothic style.

The most famous masterpiece of Gothic architecture is the cathedral of CHARTRES, located about 50 miles from Paris. Rebuilding the cathedral between 1194 and 1220 after a fire destroyed most of an earlier church, the architects of Chartres borrowed and expanded on the ideas established at St. Denis. Its walls soar upward, and its main facade is crowned by two towers. The cathedral's interior is filled with soft shadows and colored light filtering through its stained glass windows. Its exterior portals, or entrances, are covered with fine examples of GOTHIC SCULPTURE.

Other great Gothic cathedrals were built all over northeastern France. Among the finest examples are the cathedral of Notre Dame in Paris and the cathedrals of Amiens and Rheims. The artisans who worked on these magnificent buildings moved from place to place, taking with them the newest architectural ideas and designs. Because of their mobility, Gothic architecture spread quickly to other countries. The expansion of Gothic architecture from France to other parts of Europe resulted in variations of the style. English Gothic cathedrals generally are lower and wider than those of France. They usually have no flying buttresses and have one tower over the crossing of the nave and transept, rather than two at the front. Italian Gothic cathedrals are also broader, and their towers are shortened or are sometimes replaced with domes. The facades are covered with shimmering mosaics* or smaller-scale sculptures. Many Gothic cathedrals in Spain have elaborate ornamentation, often influenced by Islamic styles. By the mid-1200s, the Gothic style had become an international style that dominated European architecture.

The Construction of a Gothic Cathedral.   Vast amounts of time and money were required to build a Gothic cathedral. Money to pay for the buildings came from donations gathered from all classes of society—merchants, clergy, and monarchs alike. Ordinary citizens and clergy united behind the effort, and towns often grew up around a cathedral as it was being built. (Many cathedrals were left unfinished because of excessive expense.) People in different towns competed with one another to see who could erect the most beautiful structure. The construction of a Gothic cathedral took decades or even centuries. Cutting and fitting stone was a laborious and time-consuming task, and raising the cathedral stone by stone using simple hoisting devices and scaffolding was a slow process that required many workers.

A master architect supervised the construction of the cathedral. Most medieval architects were former stonemasons who had trained under other master architects and perfected their skills while working on buildings. The architect's job was to create designs for the building and to prepare plans and drawings before construction began. Details had to be worked out beforehand so that the stones for the cathedral could be cut to their exact size and shape. Full-sized drawings of stones, moldings, and other elements were created to serve as patterns for stonecutters and other workers. After construction began, the architect supervised all aspects of the work to make sure that it was being carried out properly.

The Late Gothic Style.   By the 1400s, the Gothic style was no longer new and dynamic, as it had been in the 1100s and 1200s. The rules of design had become increasingly complex, formal, and regimented. Moreover, local economies were no longer able to support the building of huge cathedrals. At about that same time, architects in Italy began studying the rules of architecture laid down by early Roman architects. As they read the ancient Roman manuscripts and examined the ruins of ancient Roman buildings, they developed another new style, one that imitated the classical architecture of antiquity. The principles of Gothic architecture were put aside, and the classical style was adopted. As a result, the Gothic style slowly disappeared. (*See also* **Construction, Building; Glass, Stained; Gothic Painting; Notre Dame de Paris, Cathedral.**)

Gothic Painting

A style of painting known as Gothic appeared in western Europe around the 1200s, several decades after GOTHIC ARCHITECTURE and GOTHIC SCULPTURE took root there. Gothic painting remained the prevalent style of European painting for the next 200–300 years.

Gothic painting differed in several important ways from the ROMANESQUE ART that preceded it. Gothic painting was more realistic in its representation of figures and used a wider range of colors. It was more complex and varied in its settings and landscapes and more secular* in its attitude toward the stories depicted. Distinct differences in the style, form, and content of Gothic painting developed in different regions of Europe, and the style as a whole went through a great transformation from the 1200s to the 1500s.

Painting during the Gothic period was practiced in four principal forms: frescoes*, painting on wooden panels, manuscript illumination*, and stained glass. Some of these forms were more important in certain parts of Europe than in others. Fresco painting was popular in southern Europe, whereas in northern Europe, particularly in France, stained glass was widely used. Panel painting, popular in Italy in the 1200s, spread to the rest of Europe in the mid-1300s. By the 1400s, it had replaced stained glass as the leading form of painting in northern Europe. Manuscript illumination developed to a high degree in northern Europe but never achieved a similar level in the south.

Gothic Style in France.   In France, Gothic painting was influenced by French Gothic sculpture as well as by Byzantine art and the evolving artistic styles of Italy. Frescoes from the early 1200s contained scenes set in vines and medallions* that also reflected the art of contemporary stained glass.

One of France's most important contributions to Gothic painting is its illuminated manuscripts. The Gothic style in manuscript illumination first emerged in northern Europe in the early 1200s. The manuscript illustrations from this period depict realistic-looking people and clothing.

By the middle of the 1200s, manuscript painting had evolved into a refined, aristocratic style, and its production was centered at the court of LOUIS IX in PARIS. The style was heavily influenced by the art of stained

* **secular** nonreligious; connected with everyday life

* **fresco** method of painting in which color is applied to moist plaster and becomes chemically bonded to the plaster as it dries; also refers to a painting done in this manner

* **manuscript illumination** decoration of manuscript pages with colorful illustrations of figures, scenes, designs, and patterns

* **medallion** circular design often used in wall paintings or windows

* **linear** consisting of lines

* **tracery** ornamental work consisting of delicate interlacings of lines and curves

* **illuminator** artist who painted the illustrations for illuminated manuscripts

* **mosaic** art form in which small pieces of stone or glass are set in cement; also refers to a picture made in this manner

Gothic painting was more realistic than previous styles in its representation of figures and its use of color. While earlier medieval artists were generally anonymous, by the end of the Middle Ages individual artists signed their work and became famous. About 1435, Flemish artist Jan van Eyck painted this *Madonna and Child* in the late Gothic style.

glass. It featured elongated figures that were flattened and linear* in form. The most prominent colors were shades of blue and red—which were popular colors for stained glass in cathedrals—and the scenes were placed within architectural frames.

Largely because of the patronage of Louis IX, manuscript painting became, after stained glass, the second most important art in medieval France. Numerous artists created vast libraries of religious works, BOOKS OF HOURS, and secular books for the king and the nobility. These artists painted miniature figures and scenes in vivid colors and gold. Gothic tracery* provided an elaborate framework for detailed and colorful scenes. Gradually, painters included realistic landscapes in their miniatures, with such features as blue sky or identifiable trees. This technique reached its height in the *Très riches heures,* a richly illustrated manuscript created for the duke of Berry by the Limbourg brothers in the early 1400s. This work, one of the most magnificent medieval manuscripts, illustrates the months of the year with enchantingly detailed scenes of aristocratic and peasant life.

In the 1330s, a remarkable school of painting developed around the papal court at AVIGNON in the southern French region of PROVENCE. The artists of this school created realistic figures in intricate architectural settings and lush garden scenes. Their work, which focused on religious themes, served as an inspiration to manuscript illuminators* at the beginning of the 1400s.

Gothic Style in Italy. Gothic painting developed in and around the city-states of FLORENCE, SIENA, and PISA in the region of TUSCANY. One reason for its development there was the region's long tradition of large wall paintings, either in fresco or mosaic*. This provided an excellent environment for the development of a new style of art.

The Byzantine tradition of panel painting was popular in Italy, and wooden panels were an important medium for the emerging Gothic style. Italian panel paintings in the early 1200s appeared more three-dimensional than earlier ones, and they depicted religious scenes of great emotional intensity. The principal figures in the scenes were still somewhat stiff and conventional, yet the accompanying scenes became richer and livelier.

Major innovations that led to a distinctive Italian Gothic style were made in the late 1200s and 1300s by several painters. Pietro Cavallini's frescoes show people in natural poses with softened expressions, characteristics seen in illuminated manuscripts in France almost 100 years earlier. GIOTTO DI BONDONE created simple, strongly modeled figures set within dramatic landscapes or detailed architectural settings with towers and arches. Ambrogio Lorenzetti painted frescoes of cityscapes and scenes of everyday life. Death became a major theme in Gothic painting in Italy as well as in France during the mid-1300s as the plague ravaged Europe. There was a revival of stark, iconlike images and crowded, rigid compositions.

By the 1400s, northern Italian painters had incorporated various characteristics from the art of northern Europe, especially the elegant, courtly style of painting that was prominent in France. Paintings of the period were filled with aristocrats clothed in brilliantly colored and lavish

Medieval Altarpieces

Altarpieces, often made of wood, were an important feature in the medieval Christian church. Because of their prominent position on the altar, they were beautifully decorated. During the Gothic period, altarpieces became increasingly complex. They were constructed of three panels hinged together (triptych) or more than three panels (polyptych). The scenes painted on an altarpiece depicted religious themes—biblical figures and stories, saints, and martyrs.

* **diptych** a pair of pictures on two panels, usually hinged together

* **altarpiece** painted or carved screen placed on the altar in a church

* **Renaissance** intellectual and artistic movement that began in Italy in the late 1300s and lasted until the 1600s

* **guild** association of craft and trade workers that set standards and represented the interests of its members

costumes. Such paintings were much more secular-looking and ornate than earlier works, and they became typical of the late Gothic period.

Gothic Style in Other Parts of Europe.   Few examples of early English painting survive. What does exist, including frescoes at Winchester Cathedral and Windsor Castle, reveals a delicate, linear style of painting. The most famous English Gothic painting, the Wilton Diptych*, painted between 1380 and 1390, shows a mixture of English, French and other European styles.

The Gothic painting of Bohemia (in the present-day Czech Republic) was influenced by Italian and Byzantine styles. It was characterized by idealized figures in flowing garments. As the Bohemian style evolved, figures became less idealized and more commonplace, with more natural skin tones. They also became more slender and graceful.

In Germany, fine examples of Gothic painting are found on large-scale altarpieces* painted in the late 1300s. These depict complex, lavishly painted biblical scenes filled with drama and emotion. By the beginning of the 1400s, German painting had become highly realistic and detailed. By the end of that century, the work of the German artist Albrecht Dürer reflected both the late Gothic style and the beginnings of the Renaissance*.

From the 1200s to the 1500s, Spain enjoyed a long tradition of panel painting in the Gothic style. During that time, a number of regional styles developed. In the province of Burgos, painting evolved from a rather drab, two-dimensional style to a highly dramatic style that reflected Italian influences. The provinces of Catalonia and Valencia developed a more international Gothic style as a result of having a number of foreign painters working there. On the whole, Spanish artists eagerly adopted the realistic and detailed style of northern European painting.

Secular Painting and the Status of the Artist.   Like Gothic architecture and sculpture, much of Gothic painting focused on religion. Religious topics and themes were major elements of the paintings of the period. Yet, as the Gothic period progressed, art became increasingly nonreligious. One reason was the growth of trade, of cities, and of a wealthy merchant class. People outside the church and outside the aristocracy could now afford to commission artists. The merchant class was increasingly literate, and a growing body of vernacular literature (in the everyday spoken language) encouraged a wide range of themes—religious and nonreligious.

As society changed, so did the status of artists. To practice their craft, painters increasingly were required to join the trade guilds* that were forming at that time. The guilds regulated the craft, and training became highly structured. Painters usually were apprenticed to the workshop of a master, where they had to train for a number of years before going out on their own. This increased professionalism resulted in greater recognition for individual artists, many of whom began to sign their works. This was a marked change from earlier periods, when artists generally were anonymous. By the beginning of the Renaissance, individual artists became famous throughout Europe, and their painting styles became very individualized as well. (*See also* **Books, Manuscript; Glass, Stained; Mosaics.**)

Gothic Sculpture

* **facade**   front of a building; also, any side of a building that is given special architectural treatment

See color plate 15, vol. 2.

* **capital**   uppermost portion of a column

* **buttress**   stone or wood structure that supports a wall or building

* **liturgy**   form of a religious service, particularly the words spoken or sung

* **portal**   large doorway or entrance

During the Middle Ages, sculpture was tied closely to both architecture and religion. Most medieval sculpture was made for the facades* or the interiors of the churches and cathedrals of western Europe, and it reflected religious themes and subject matter. For about 400 years, this church sculpture exhibited the Gothic style that dominated all art forms of the time.

Origins and Characteristics.   The Gothic style in sculpture originated in France around 1150, as the first great Gothic cathedrals were being built. Gothic sculpture developed in tandem with architecture, and sculpted figures were integrated into cathedral design as a way to help people visualize religious themes and stories. The greatest Gothic sculptures in France are found on such cathedrals as CHARTRES, Strasbourg, Amiens, and Rheims.

From France, the Gothic style in sculpture spread across Europe, gradually replacing the Romanesque style that preceded it. Gothic sculpture differed from the Romanesque in several important ways. Gothic sculptures were generally more naturalistic in form than their Romanesque predecessors, and they depicted religious themes and subject matter in a more comprehensive way. Also, in the 1200s, they were organized in rigorously symmetrical and logical ways that reflected the ideas of SCHOLASTICISM.

Among the most important features of Gothic sculpture was the realistic appearance of sculptured figures. Figures were carved in natural poses. The folds and wrinkles of garments fell in natural ways that helped define the positions of bodies. In addition, the faces of people had convincing expressions. Yet, at the same time that sculpture was becoming more realistic, its content became more refined. In the Romanesque period, sculpture often depicted popular stories or legends. In the Gothic period, sculptural programs were often organized around political or moral themes, such as the redemption of the soul and the struggle between good and evil.

Sculpture was used everywhere on Gothic cathedrals. Leaves, flowers, patterns, and figures of people or animals were carved into the stone of capitals*, door frames, buttresses*, and spires. The figures depicted included Christ, the Virgin Mary, apostles, saints, prophets, and Old Testament kings. Since sculpture was an integral part of a cathedral, it was closely related to the liturgy*, and any departure from time-honored traditions was suspect. Thus, Gothic sculptors were well versed in the details of how their religion was traditionally represented. They knew that the Virgin Mary was always shown wearing a veil (a symbol of modesty) and that Christ, the angels, and the apostles were always barefoot, while the saints were shod. By incorporating these details, they made sure that their viewers could recognize the figures represented in their stories, which made their sculpture useful as a teaching aid.

The sculptures on Gothic cathedrals were organized in a logical and orderly fashion. The portals* of most cathedrals contained one of these basic themes: the Life of Christ, the Last Judgment, or the Coronation of the Virgin Mary as Queen of Heaven.

Development and Spread.   From 1140 to 1260, Gothic sculpture changed rapidly, taking a new direction about every generation. These changes led

Claus Sluter was a Netherlandish sculptor whose principal work was done for Philip the Bold, duke of Burgundy, in the later 1300s. At Philip's Carthusian monastery in Dijon, Sluter created several sculptures, including this statue of the *Virgin and Child.* The natural facial expressions and the rich folds of the Virgin's garment are characteristic of the Gothic period in sculpture.

to an increasingly naturalistic and elegant style. In the earliest sculpture of the Gothic period, figures were relatively rigid and only slightly carved out of the surface of the stone. As the technology of carving developed, figures became more sinuous (with supple, winding curves) and three-dimensional. They also portrayed more movement and emotion. Some of the finest examples of this High Gothic style are found at Rheims Cathedral in northern France.

While the Gothic style was developing in France, sculptors from other countries often went there to work on the great cathedrals. These sculptors adopted French ideas and took them back to their own countries, modifying them to suit local traditions and needs. By the early 1200s, the Gothic style of sculpture began to influence German artisans. German sculptors created works of greater emotional intensity than those of France. Their figures displayed less idealized facial types and a different range of expressions—from serenity to torment and intense fear. The remarkably lifelike statues carved for Germany's Naumburg Cathedral are among the finest examples of the German Gothic style.

In Italy, sculptors combined French ideas with inspiration from the classical sculptures of ancient Rome to create a distinctive Italian Gothic style. They worked in marble rather than limestone, which made possible a great deal of fine detail. Italian sculptors often made small-scale statues and lacy carvings to decorate their cathedral facades. They produced intensely passionate figures with highly individual characteristics, sometimes leaning out from their niches as if to speak to the viewer. Fine examples of the Italian Gothic style are found in the cathedral of SIENA.

In England, cathedral sculpture was not as prominent as in other parts of Europe. English sculpture generally was confined to decorative elements and tombs. Sculptures of knights atop tombs in London's WESTMINSTER ABBEY are some of the most dramatic figures in the English sculpture of the period. Many of the tomb statues honor the memory of crusaders who died in the Holy Land.

Eventually, the Gothic style in sculpture broke down. One of the reasons was that church and royal patronage diminished, providing fewer large-scale opportunities for sculptors. Interior sculpture, such as choir screens and votive images*, was in greater demand. Without large cathedral projects to bring sculptors together, these highly skilled craftsmen became isolated and more specialized. These factors contributed to a breakdown of the International Gothic style and to the development of more individual and regional styles. (*See also* **Gothic Architecture; Gothic Painting; Romanesque Art.**)

* **votive images** images offered to holy figures in exchange for protection or blessings

Gower, John

ca. 1330–1408
English poet

John Gower was a well-known medieval English poet. A contemporary and friend of Geoffrey CHAUCER, he was one of the few writers of the time who wrote important works in three different languages—French, Latin, and English.

Little is known of Gower's life except that he was a man of some wealth and perhaps connected to the legal profession. His works deal with human wickedness and the importance of law in helping people choose right over wrong. Gower believed that the only safeguard for society or the individual is obedience to the law of God. His most popular work, *Confessio Amantis (The Lover's Confession),* is a collection of more than 100 tales about the struggle between vice and virtue. The *Confessio* was one of the first books printed in English (1483). Because of his emphasis on vice and virtue, Chaucer called him "moral Gower."

In examining vice and virtue, Gower's poems are full of references to events in his own day, including accounts of the Peasants' Revolt of 1381, the overthrow of King RICHARD II, and even the wool trade. Many of his works include proverbs, illustrations from natural history, and bits of folklore. (*See also* **Peasants' Rebellions and Uprisings; Wool.**)

Grail

See *Arthurian Literature.*

Granada

See map in Aragon (vol. 1).

* **caliphate** office and government of the caliph, religious and political head of the Islamic state

* **Berber** referring to a group of Muslim people from North Africa

* **Sephardic** referring to Jews of Spain and Portugal and their ancestors

* **sheikh** Arab chief

* **vizier** Muslim minister of state

Granada, in southern Spain, was the capital of the Muslim kingdom of that name and was one of the most advanced cities in the Middle Ages. Located at the foot of the Sierra Nevada mountain range, the city lies on three hills, two of them separated by the deep ravine of the Darro River.

Granada's glorious past is linked to the Arabs. After Muslims conquered Granada in the early 700s, the region was governed by the UM-MAYAD caliphate* in DAMASCUS, Syria. Granada became known as the "Damascus of the West." After 1031, it broke away from the Eastern caliphate and fell prey to warring factions from Morocco, finally falling to the Almohads, a North African dynasty, in 1156. Under the Almohads, Granada became the fifth largest city in Spain, with a population of Arab, Spanish, and Berber* Muslims, Spanish Christians, and Sephardic* Jews. The height of its prosperity and culture came later, under the Nasrid dynasty, which began when the prince of Jaén, Muhammad ibn al-Ahmar, took control of the city in 1248.

The prince was the first of an unbroken line of 21 Nasrid sovereigns. Against all odds, they managed to preserve the independence of their small state for some 250 years. During most of this period, they were the sole surviving Muslim power in Spain. The Nasrid rulers formed alliances first with Christian CASTILE and later with the Marinid sultans of Morocco. From 1273 on, the Marinid alliance gave Granada some relief from Christian pressure to the north, and Marinid armies twice defeated the Castilians. Eventually, the princes of Granada commanded a corps of Moroccan troops under Marinid sheikhs*. In return, the Moroccan dynasty took over part of the Nasrid domain. Granada thus enjoyed a unique position of being allied with both Christian Spain and the Muslim regions to the south. Its alliances and its geographic position as a protected stronghold explain its long survival.

The Nasrid rulers established a traditional Muslim civilization. Arabic was the only language used in the city, and Islamic art, literature, and science flourished under their rule. The historian Ibn Khaldun, the geographer Ibn Battuta, and the vizier* and literary figure Ibn al-Khatib were frequent guests at the court of Granada.

Nasrid culture reached its height in Granada during the second reign of Muhammad V, from 1362 to 1391. Much of the ALHAMBRA, the famous palace and fortress, was built at that time. Silks and other textiles of unsurpassed quality were widely exported from Granada. Agriculture and irrigation flourished as never before. The population of the city at that time has been estimated at 400,000. The Arabic saying "Paradise is that part of the heavens which is above Granada" expresses the feeling for that magnificent city.

Some part of Granada's splendor survives, especially the incomparable Alhambra. The city still has an estate from the 1200s set in beautiful gardens and a palace from the 1300s for the Nasrid queens. Other examples of Nasrid architecture include nine bridges over the Darro

In 1492, Granada fell to the Christian forces of Aragon and Castile, ending over 700 years of Muslim rule. After their defeat, many Muslim prisoners were forcibly baptized in the Christian faith. This sculpture, from the Royal Chapel at Granada, shows King Ferdinand of Aragon overseeing such a baptism.

River, a rebuilt covered market known as Alcaiceria, Arab baths, and the Bibarrambla Plaza, which had been the scene of tournaments and bull-fighting.

The later history of the Nasrid dynasty and of the city comes mostly from hostile Christian sources. They recount how the kingdom fell to bitter feuding between the leading noble families. The Muslim rulers added to these troubles by engaging in bitter disputes over who would rule next. As a result of this decline, Muslim Granada was unable to withstand the war waged against it in 1481 by the united kingdom of Aragon and Castile. After a six-month siege, Granada surrendered on January 2, 1492. Granada's ruler, Abu Abd Allah Muhammad XI (called Boabdil by Spanish and other European writers) went into exile in Morocco. (*See also* **Islamic Art and Architecture; Spain, Muslim Kingdoms of.**)

Greek Language

Although Byzantine society consisted of many different peoples and languages, Greek was the language of the dominant culture in the BYZANTINE EMPIRE, especially before the Arab conquest in the mid-600s. The knowledge of Greek provided opportunities for holding leading positions in the church and in state government.

Throughout the Byzantine period, the Greek language was marked by a division between popular Greek and a type of classical Greek used in writing and formal speech. As Christianity spread, so did literary Greek, or Greek used by scholars, especially among the powerful church leaders of the 300s and 400s. Knowledge of literary Greek, however, was never limited to the clergy, as was knowledge of Latin in western Europe. Many ordinary people, such as merchants, understood literary Greek even though they did not use it in everyday life.

The fall of the Byzantine Empire to the crusaders in 1204 briefly interrupted the educational tradition that supported the literary language. But the tradition was revived, first in Nicaea and then in the restored Byzantine Empire after 1261. Western Europeans were hated and regarded as barbarians because they lacked the knowledge of Greek.

At about the same time, a new middle class was beginning to emerge in the cities. The reading public cared little for imitations of the classical literature of ancient Greece, and around 1300 poetry was being written in the vernacular*. The new writing was largely for entertainment and consisted of light subject matter. The written use of the vernacular never became a major literary tradition, and a Greek literary figure of the stature of the Italian poet DANTE (who wrote in the everyday language of medieval Italy) never emerged. (*See also* **Byzantine Literature; Classical Tradition in the Middle Ages; Crusades; Italian Language and Literature.**)

* **vernacular** language or dialect native to a region; everyday, informal speech

Gregorian Chant

Gregorian chant is the music the Western Church used in its services in the early Middle Ages. Also known as plainsong or plainchant, Gregorian chant uses only one melodic line (in contrast to music that uses two or more lines, or is polyphonic).

Historians do not know where the music originated or how it spread to so many parts of Europe before 900. Its name is based on the legend that GREGORY I THE GREAT, who was pope from 590 to 604, received the music directly from the Holy Spirit and gave it to the church.

During the early Middle Ages, Gregorian chant was used in all five major Roman liturgies*—Ambrosian, Celtic, Gallican, Mozarabic, and Roman. Only two of the liturgies survived the end of the Middle Ages and exist today. The Gregorian chant of the Ambrosian liturgy is limited largely to the diocese* of Milan, while the Gregorian chant of the Roman liturgy is the music that is heard today throughout the Roman Catholic Church.

The MASS and the DIVINE OFFICE are the two orders of liturgy that employ Gregorian chants. The chants used in the Mass—the Eucharistic sacrament that reenacts the Last Supper—include the Introit, Alleluia, Offertory, Kyrie Eleison, Gloria in Excelsis, Credo, Sanctus, and Agnus Dei. While some parts of the Mass stay the same every day, other parts and the music that goes with them change every day. While the number of different melodies may never be known, the *Index of Gregorian Chant* of Bryden and Hughes lists more than 11,000 tunes and texts. In the late Middle Ages, Gregorian chants gave way to the polyphonic music that found wide acceptance in the church after 1100. (*See also* **Music.**)

* **liturgies** prescribed rites and ceremonies of public worship

* **diocese** church district under a bishop's authority

Gregory of Tours, St.

ca. 538–ca. 594
Bishop, saint, and writer

* **Gallic** referring to Gaul or France

* **martyr** person who suffers and dies rather than renounce a religious faith

Gregory, the bishop of Tours, wrote about the Frankish church of his time and about the lives of saints. His works are a rich source of information about Gallic* life, education, and culture at the beginning of the Middle Ages.

Gregory was born Georgius Florentius in Avernus in Gaul (France). His family could trace its roots back on his father's side to a Christian martyr* named Vectius Epagatus who died in 177. When Gregory was called to succeed his uncle as bishop of Tours in 573, he began using the name Gregorius in honor of one of his relatives who had been a bishop earlier in the century.

Tours was the site of the remains of St. Martin, bishop of Tours in the 300s, a well-known miracle worker both during and after his life. Encouraged by his mother, Gregory wrote about the life and miracles of St. Martin and about the lives of other Gallic saints. Gregory also wrote a major historical work about the Franks and Frankish Christianity in the 500s. The generally accepted title of this work is *The History of the Franks*. Some scholars, however, prefer the title *The Ecclesiastical Histories* since the main focus of this work is the growth of Christianity among the Franks of Gregory's day.

Gregory's history and saints' lives were very influential in his lifetime and later. His saints' lives served as models for later medieval writers. Gregory's history is a most important source of information about Frankish society, politics, church life, and the LATIN LANGUAGE during the early Middle Ages. (*See also* **Franks; Historical Writing; Merovingians.**)

Gregory I the Great, Pope

ca. 540–604
Pope, reformer, scholar, and author

* **prefect** Roman name for a high-ranking official

* **deacon** church officer ranking below a priest

See color plate 12, vol. 3.

* **doctor** in terms of the church, a teacher whose works have achieved great authority

Gregory was a monk, saint, and scholar who served as pope from 590 until his death in 604. His outstanding leadership increased the prestige and power of the PAPACY and earned him the title of "the Great."

Born in ROME to a prominent family, Gregory was educated in the LATIN classics and probably the law. He served for a year as a prefect* in city government before he decided to become a monk. He founded six monasteries on family property in SICILY and one in Rome where he lived. After Gregory became a deacon*, Pope Pelagius II sent him as a papal ambassador to CONSTANTINOPLE. He lived there for seven years with other Latin monks before returning to Rome.

In 590, Gregory reluctantly left the quiet life of the monastery when he was chosen to be the new pope. Strong leadership was needed after famine, plague, floods, and invading LOMBARDS had destroyed much of ITALY. Gregory worked tirelessly to feed the hungry and help the poor. He strengthened church life by promoting MONASTICISM and educating his clergy. He also made peace with the Lombards and sent monks to distant England to convert the ANGLO-SAXONS.

Gregory's many writings include 854 surviving letters, commentaries on the BIBLE, a collection of sermons, and *Morals on Job*, a long mystical work he wrote for monks. His *Pastoral Care*, written for priests and bishops, and *Dialogues*, stories about Italian saints, were especially influential in the Middle Ages. Gregory was later designated as one of the four doctors* of the early Western Church. (*See also* **Christianity.**)

Gregory VII, Pope

ca. 1020–1085
Pope and reformer

* **depose** to remove from high office

* **excommunicate** to exclude from the rites of the church

Gregory VII was one of the most important and influential popes in the Middle Ages. His belief in the supreme authority of the PAPACY led to a dramatic confrontation with a German emperor.

Hildebrand (his name before he became pope) was born in the region of Tuscany in Italy. He went to Rome, where he became a monk and served a series of popes, beginning with Gregory VI, a church reformer. He followed Gregory into exile in Germany but returned to Rome when another reformer, Leo IX, became pope. After Leo, Hildebrand served four more reform popes before he himself became pope in 1073 and took the name of Gregory VII.

Gregory went well beyond the reform policies of his predecessors. He insisted that the pope was not only the supreme head of the church but also was responsible for all of society and was owed obedience by all mortals, including kings and emperors. Gregory outlined his ideas about the supreme authority of the papacy in the work *Dictatus papae* (1075).

Gregory's position put him on a collision course with the German emperor Henry IV. When Gregory wrote Henry to criticize him for supporting a rival candidate for the archbishopric of MILAN, Henry convened a council of German bishops that declared Gregory deposed*. Gregory excommunicated* Henry and called on the German princes to choose a new emperor. In 1077, Henry crossed the Alps in winter to ask for Gregory's forgiveness at CANOSSA. Although their reconciliation was short-lived, the emperor had submitted and Gregory had won a symbolic victory. This paved the way for the emergence of the powerful papal government of the 1100s and 1200s. (*See also* **Holy Roman Empire.**)

Grosseteste, Robert

1168–1253
Scholar, science writer, translator, and bishop

* **treatise** long, detailed essay

* **theology** study of the nature of God and of religious truth

Robert Grosseteste was perhaps the greatest English scholar and churchman of the 1200s. He was an original thinker who wrote scientific treatises* that contributed much to the advancement of science in Europe.

Grosseteste was born to a humble family in Suffolk and as a young man served as a clerk in the households of the bishops of Lincoln and Hereford. After he received his degree in theology*, he taught at Oxford University and is believed to have been the first chancellor of the university. He had a considerable influence on FRANCISCAN thought both in England and on the Continent. In 1235, Grosseteste was elected bishop of Lincoln, where he spent the rest of his life.

Grosseteste is best known for his scholarly works, especially his writings on scientific matters. He wrote influential commentaries on ARISTOTLE and treatises on such subjects as tides, rainbows, and mathematical reasoning. Grosseteste did much to promote the thought of Aristotle in western Europe and laid the foundations for the philosophical movement called SCHOLASTICISM.

While in Lincoln as bishop, Grosseteste translated many important Greek works into Latin, including Aristotle's *Nicomachean Ethics*. However, he spent most of his energy as bishop running his see (or district) and reforming church practices. Although his zeal for reform often brought him into conflict with his superiors, Grosseteste was widely respected as a true scholar and a conscientious churchman. (*See also* **Science; Universities.**)

Guelphs and Ghibellines

* **heretic** person who disagrees with established church doctrine

* **secular** nonreligious; connected with everyday life

* **commune** powerful self-governing town or city

The Guelphs and Ghibellines were opposing sides in a long struggle for power that pervaded the political life of Italy for more than 200 years. The Guelphs supported the church and the authority of the pope. The Ghibellines supported the HOLY ROMAN EMPIRE and the authority of the emperor.

The Guelph-Ghibelline conflict began with the reign of Holy Roman Emperor FREDERICK I BARBAROSSA and his attempts to restore imperial authority in northern Italy by force. His actions divided Italians; some supported the church and others supported the empire. The Guelphs accused the Ghibellines of being enemies of the church and denounced them as heretics*. The Ghibellines, meanwhile, argued that the emperor would save Italy by healing political divisions caused by the church's interference in secular* affairs. The Italian communes* were divided in their allegiances to the two parties. Great lords and cities on both sides formed alliances, and the conflict became internal warfare on almost a national scale.

The Guelph-Ghibelline conflict reached its greatest intensity in the mid-1200s, as Ghibelline forces supporting Emperor FREDERICK II fought openly with Guelph supporters of Pope INNOCENT IV. By the 1300s, the conflict had lost most of its association with the empire and the church. Instead, it had become primarily a struggle for political advantage between rival Italian families, factions, cities, and provinces. (*See also* **Commune; Italy.**)

Guilds

Guilds were associations of business owners that promoted the interests of their members. They are closely linked with the growth of cities and the expansion of trade in the Middle Ages. Guilds were established to meet the needs of merchants and craftsworkers in towns. They brought wealth and stability that enabled the towns to prosper, and they provided wide-ranging social, educational, religious, and political services.

There were two types of guilds—merchant and craft guilds—they had similar aims. Members of merchant guilds were involved in many types of commerce, such as local and long-distance trade and wholesale and retail sales. The craft guilds specialized in particular trades. For example, guilds covered butchers, bakers, and smiths.

Rise of Guilds.   Guilds had existed in ancient times. Roman trade guilds were mostly social and religious societies that met for festive occasions and religious observances. In times of hardship, Roman emperors took control of certain guilds, such as food suppliers, whose services were essential during times of famine. These guilds disbanded as the Roman Empire and its great cities fell in the 400s.

However, in the Byzantine world, the Roman guild tradition continued into the Middle Ages, particularly in the eastern parts of the empire. The Byzantine government controlled the guilds, demanding taxes and services from them. In Antioch, guild members had to clean the drains and repair fallen columns in the streets. In Alexandria, they had to dredge the Nile River.

Guilds developed in Islamic Iraq and Syria in the 800s. Followers of the Sufi Muslim religious movement helped to organize the guilds. As a result, the guilds included moral and ethical instruction along with craft skills in the training they provided. These guilds helped to spread Islamic civilization to newly conquered lands.

In Europe, guilds reappeared in the Middle Ages and flourished between the 1000s and the 1200s. Trade expanded during this period, and cities prospered. Growing urban populations supplied skilled workers and created a market for large quantities of food and other goods. Business was booming, but both merchants and master craftsmen soon saw a need for regulations to govern the marketplace and for ways to help each other in difficult times.

To regulate competition, guilds adopted rules about work hours and the number of apprentices* a master could employ. They also set standards to maintain the quality of their products. Certain cities were known for their fine cloth, and, to protect a city's reputation, workshops were required to meet a standard of excellence. Guild members took an oath to follow the rules and paid a fine if they failed to do so. The rules varied according to the trade and were adjusted as necessary. For example, in times of warfare the smiths were allowed to work longer hours or to take on more apprentices. A group of officials ran the guild, and a special court enforced the regulations and investigated complaints of unfair competition or poor workmanship.

The guild also served as a charitable organization, arranging burials for deceased members and raising money for widows and orphans. Islamic guilds kept a common fund from which members could borrow in times of need. Many guilds had halls where they held banquets and other social events. The hall served as a social club for members.

The guild met the religious needs of its members. A local church often provided a chapel where guild members worshiped together. Most guilds adopted a patron saint and observed the saint's day with celebrations or acts of charity.

Merchant Guilds. Merchant guilds appeared in medieval Europe earlier than craft guilds. The merchant guilds tended to have wealthier members than the craft guilds and were often more powerful, especially in northern Europe. They were particularly important in port towns. In some towns, such as Venice and Genoa, merchants actually governed the town, and so guilds were not needed to promote and protect trade in those cities.

In the 1100s and 1200s, German merchant guilds formed leagues, or associations, with guilds in other cities to encourage trade with Scandinavia and Russia. These local leagues then combined to form the HANSEATIC LEAGUE, in which merchant guilds from many cities along the North and Baltic Seas cooperated in relative harmony.

* **apprentice** person bound by legal agreement to work for another for a specific period of time in return for instruction in a trade or art

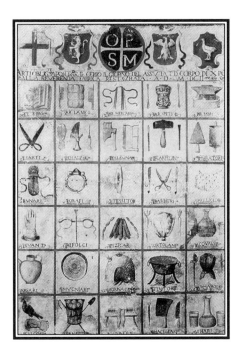

Merchant and craft guilds brought stability to the medieval urban economy. They established and controlled the working conditions of most trades and also provided many social services. Each guild created its own identifying trademark or emblem.

---

* **caliph** religious and political head of an Islamic state

* **journeymen** day laborers

Craft Guilds.   Craft guilds became important in Europe in the 1100s and brought together masters of workshops in a particular trade. In manufacturing towns, such as Florence and Milan, craft guilds became extremely powerful.

The apprentice system was the single most important feature of medieval craft guilds. In this system, young boys (about age ten to early teens) lived with a master craftsman for a fixed period of time. The boys worked without payment and, in return, received food, clothing, shelter, and training in the master's craft. The parents of the boy signed a contract with the master by which they agreed to pay a large fine if the apprentice ran away. The apprentice had to obey the master. Although some masters were cruel and used the boys unfairly, others were kindly and took a genuine interest in a boy's career.

Islamic apprentices made one further commitment. In addition to selecting a master, they chose two other apprentices to whom they pledged lifetime devotion. In this way, the Muslim guilds encouraged strong social ties.

At the end of his term, the apprentice became a journeyman who was free to work for wages for any master. Eventually, he became a master himself, with full membership in the guild. In the Byzantine guilds, a craftsman had to display both competence in the craft and moral character in order to become a master.

Decline of Guilds.   As they became more powerful, the guilds sometimes met with opposition. The Spanish monarchs encouraged the guilds as a means of increasing trade, and several Islamic caliphs* valued the guilds as political allies against the military elite. But elsewhere kings saw in the guilds a threat to royal authority and blamed them whenever price increases and food shortages occurred. In 1219, Frederick II banned guilds from his vast empire in Italy and Germany. In England and France, guilds won legal recognition only after a long and difficult struggle.

Other factors also affected the growth of guilds. By about 1300, many industries were no longer expanding. Competition increased, and guilds limited the number of journeymen* allowed to become masters. Then in 1348, the BLACK DEATH struck Europe. About a third of the total population died. An even greater proportion of the population in the cities died, where the disease spread quickly. Both merchant and craft guilds suffered tremendous losses both in membership and in the demand for their products. In addition, banks collapsed, weakening the economy.

Two new developments further diminished the need for guilds. Craft industries developed in the countryside, where labor was cheaper. These workers did not belong to guilds, which were generally located in cities. Improvements in technology made guilds unnecessary. Specialized trades, such as clock making, depended so much on both secrecy and inventiveness that their members never formed guilds.

Guilds also began to compete for control of city governments. Usually the less wealthy craft guilds rebelled against the leaders of the wealthier craft guilds and the merchant guilds. In Florence, for example, where the wool guild and the merchant guild held political and commercial control, an uprising occurred in 1378. A similar English Peasants' Revolt of 1381 occurred, with apprentices, journeymen, and the urban poor of London joining peasants in rioting against the business leaders who controlled the city.

In Italy, France, and Spain, the merchant guilds eventually lost control of the cities, as strong rulers came to power. Under the mighty Ottoman Empire in the 1300s and 1400s, Islamic guilds also lost their political influence, although they continued to manage their business affairs and maintain their rituals and traditions. Only in Germany, where the monarchy was weak, did guilds remain in control of city governments into the 1400s.

While guilds dominated the medieval marketplace, they presented new ideas of cooperation at many levels of business and society. They preserved standards and levels of skill in important crafts. They also maintained order and established principles of fairness and equality among their members. The guilds' social services lent support to individuals and their families at a time when survival was often difficult.

The economic expansion of the Middle Ages benefited from the mutual efforts of the guilds. Merchant guilds shared business risks and assisted each other in crises. Craft guilds provided a steady supply of trained craftsmen. Regulating prices and competition sometimes protected growing businesses from failure. Cities flourished on the wealth and leadership that the guilds provided during times of rapid urban growth. (*See also* **Byzantine Empire; Cities and Towns; Commune; Trade.**)

Gutenberg, Johannes

ca. 1400–1468
Printer

Johannes Gutenberg is usually said to have been the inventor of the printing press in the West. He is believed to have been the first European to print with movable type cast in molds. His printing process spread across Europe in the late 1400s and influenced mass communication for the next 400 years.

Gutenberg was born in Mainz, Germany, in the early 1400s. His full name was Johannes Gensfleisch zur Laden zu Gutenberg. He called himself Gutenberg after the house in which his family lived. In 1428, he left Mainz and settled in Strasbourg. There he became involved in a number of lawsuits involving his inheritance, a marriage promise, and debts. Documents regarding these lawsuits are an important source of information about his life and work.

The lawsuits reveal that Gutenberg possessed outstanding technical skills and worked in partnership with others. He knew how to cut semiprecious stones for decoration. He was skilled with metals as well, crafting "pilgrim badges," or badges made from soft metal that were cast in molds and bought by religious pilgrims as proof of their journeys. The court documents also show that Gutenberg knew how to raise capital for his business ventures. A court document dated 1439 notes the purchase of lead and other metals, a press, printing types called forms, and a four-piece instrument that could be taken apart (probably a mold for casting type). The document suggests that many printing elements were already in place. However, the process was not sufficiently developed to produce a Bible until 16 years later. That Bible—called the 42-line Bible because of the number of lines on a page—was the first major book ever printed.

Johannes Gutenberg possessed outstanding technical skills. He developed a technique to mass-produce small metal objects by casting them in shallow molds, which may have led to the development of movable type and the printing press. Shown here is Gutenberg's printing press, on which he produced his famous Bible, the first book in western Europe to be made with movable type.

After the death of one of his partners ended the Strasbourg business relationship, Gutenberg returned to Mainz. There he entered into a partnership with Johann Fust, who financed the printing of the Bible, which was completed in 1455. At about the same time, Gutenberg was also printing smaller works, such as papal documents, poetry, and a propaganda pamphlet in verse warning of the danger of an invasion by the Turks after the fall of Constantinople in 1453.

Gutenberg had developed the ingenious method of combining separate letters that were reusable because they were cast in metal. He also designed the most complicated part of the invention—the adjustable mold for casting the hand-set type. The ability to mass-produce books was also helped by the introduction of paper manufacture in Europe in the 1300s.

Gutenberg's partnership with Fust dissolved after the printing of the Bible. A court divided their assets, and the two men went their separate ways. Fust found a new partner and formed a successful printing business. Gutenberg used his assets—profits from the sale of the Bible, his equipment, and his typeface—to produce more books.

The books that Gutenberg produced that have survived show a high degree of perfection. Today, the Gutenberg Bible is valued not only as the first book printed in the West but also as one of the most beautiful books ever printed. Twenty perfect copies are in existence (31 imperfect copies have also survived). (*See also* **Printing, Origins of; Technology.**)

Gypsies

* **nomadic** wandering from place to place to find food and pasture

* **tinker** person who travels about mending pots, pans, and other household articles

The Gypsies are a nomadic* people who appeared in Europe in the late Middle Ages. The Gypsy language provides clues regarding the origins of this wandering people. Their language, which contains many Greek and some borrowed Slavic words, is derived from Sanskrit, the classical language of India. The Gypsies call themselves Romanies, which may be from the Sanskrit word for "man." They are known to have passed through the Middle East (where some are still found) and to have settled later in lands that were, or had been part of, the BYZANTINE EMPIRE.

In much of Europe, especially the eastern regions, they are called *Tsiganes* (or *Tsihanes*), a term that may come from the name of a religious sect of Asia Minor with whom they had contact. The English word *Gypsy* comes from the word *Egypt*. Gypsy leaders claimed that they were Egyptian nobles, driven out of their country by the Muslims.

It is not certain why the Gypsies became wanderers nor how they survived for so many centuries in many diverse places. The earliest records of their supposed ancestors describe them as entertainers and metalworkers. Both occupations would have required extensive travel. Fortune-telling, for which the Gypsies are probably best known, is regarded as a form of entertainment, and ancient traditions regard workers in iron and steel as having semi-magical powers. Wherever the Gypsies went, there was always work for tinkers*, an audience for singers and dancers, and people who wanted their fortunes told. However, they have also been persecuted throughout history—often accused of sorcery, fraud, or theft. In the 20th century, they were among the victims of the Nazi Holocaust.

By 1300, the Gypsies were in Greece and soon after in the Balkans, where they are still found in large numbers. They reached central Europe (Hungary and Bohemia) early in the 1300s, and there is an account of their first appearance in Paris in 1427. They reached England and Spain (where they were highly regarded as singers and dancers) somewhat later. Wherever they went, they told tales of persecution and were welcomed as pilgrims at first, but they soon acquired a bad reputation. By the end of the 1400s, Germany and Spain passed strict laws against them. In England, Henry VIII threatened to expel them if they did not give up their nomadic life and settle on the land. Although harassed and regarded as social outcasts, they clung to their ways and were neither destroyed nor turned into small farmers. They remained a separate and distinct minority in most European countries.

The nomadic Gypsies appeared in Europe in the late Middle Ages. They were mainly entertainers and metalworkers, and these two professions kept them on the move. Although welcomed at first, Gypsies acquired a bad reputation and were later harassed and regarded as social outcasts. This engraving of Gypsies was made in France in the 1400s.

Habsburg Dynasty

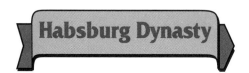

* **dynasty** succession of rulers from the same family or group

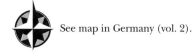

See map in Germany (vol. 2).

The Habsburg dynasty* ruled Austria from 1282 to the end of the Austro-Hungarian Empire in 1918. The Habsburgs were also known as the House of Austria. The name *Austria* was eventually extended to all Habsburg possessions, including parts of the present-day Czech Republic, Slovakia, Hungary, Poland, and Ukraine. Through a series of advantageous marriages, the Habsburgs became rulers of a world empire in the 1500s. Thereafter, the dynasty was divided into separate but closely linked Austrian and Spanish branches. Except for five years in the 1700s, the Habsburg rulers held the title of Holy Roman Emperors or Emperors-elect between 1438 and 1866.

Although the dynasty claimed Roman ancestry, the Habsburgs can be traced to the dukes of Alsace, a region in eastern France. In any case, the Habsburgs were already a powerful noble family in the second half of the 900s. Around 1090, Otto was the first to employ the name *Habsburg*, from the German *Habichtsburg* (meaning hawk's castle), for the family as well as for the castle that had been built about 1020 in what is now Switzerland. Rudolf I of Habsburg, king of Germany from 1273 to 1291, claimed and occupied Austria and Styria, a mountainous region in central and southeastern Austria. He bequeathed those duchies* to his sons in 1282, marking the beginning of Habsburg rule in Austria.

Rudolf and his son Albrecht continued expanding their domains into southwestern Germany. Then Albrecht was murdered, the Swiss defeated his son Leopold in 1315, and Louis IV the Bavarian defeated the Habsburgs in 1322. The dynasty was unable to regain the crown until 1438. The reign of Frederick III, from 1440 to 1493, marked the low point in the fortunes of the family, with the loss of Vienna to the Hungarians. Frederick's perseverance, however, and his strong belief in the mission of his family, laid the foundation for the dynasty's future greatness. In 1496, Philip I the Handsome married Juana, who inherited Spain from her parents, Ferdinand and Isabella. Their son, Charles V, was the founder of the Spanish line. The Habsburg dynasty ended in 1918 with the defeat of Austria-Hungary in World War I and the overthrow of the monarchy. (*See also* **Austria; Holy Roman Empire; Hungary; Maximilian I, Emperor; Switzerland.**)

* **duchy** territory ruled by a duke or a duchess

Hadewijch of Antwerp

ca. 1230–ca. 1260
Mystical poet and feminist

* **mystical** referring to the belief that divine truths or direct knowledge of God can be experienced through meditation and contemplation as much as through logical thought

* **vernacular** language or dialect native to a region; everyday, informal speech

* **lay** not linked to the church by clerical office or monks' and nuns' vows

* **chivalric** pertaining to the customs of medieval knighthood

Hadewijch of Antwerp was one of the most gifted mystical* poets of the 1200s. Her religious prose and poetry in the Old Flemish vernacular* combine power, clarity, and a subtle rebellion against the religious conventions of her day.

Hadewijch was born into a noble family in or near Antwerp, a city in Brabant. She belonged to a lay* Christian order known as the BEGUINES. In her often sad and gloomy works, Hadewijch uses images of a barren, threatening nature to depict the loneliness of the soul. Her major prose work is a collection of visions called the *Visioenen*. Hadewijch also wrote 45 poems. These can be described as religious love songs after the nonreligious love songs of the TROUBADOURS of Provence. In her poetry, Hadewijch depicts the individual seeking union with God, similar to a lone knight roaming the wilderness in search of his true love. The task is a solitary one, and only those with the strongest faith can progress. Her view of the soul's union with God is close to that of the teacher and mystic Meister ECKHART. Unlike most other women mystics of the Middle Ages, Hadewijch believed that mystical union is possible through emotions *and* the intellect.

Hadewijch's favorite technical devices in her poetry are contrast ("I have from love darkness by day") and paradox ("To him all happiness is pain"). She skillfully combines these devices with images of nature, descriptions of bodily sensations, and concepts of chivalric* behavior. No other female poet of the Middle Ages comes close to matching her intellectual discipline and poetic gifts. (*See also* **Courtly Love; Mysticism.**)

See *Sunna.*

**ca. 1320–1390
Persian poet**

Hafiz is the pen name of Shams al–Din Muhammad. Known sometimes as Hafizi Shirazi after his native city of Shiraz (in modern Iran), he was one of the greatest poets of medieval Persia. The *Diwan,* a collection of Hafiz's poems, is one of the masterpieces of medieval poetry.

Hafiz was born around 1320. Little is known about his life except that he spent it entirely in or around Shiraz and that he was educated in Islamic religion and Persian literature. His pen name Hafiz is, in fact, a title given to devout Muslims who have memorized the entire QUR'AN (Koran). Like most poets of the time, Hafiz was supported by royal patrons. Unlike other poets supported by patrons, however, Hafiz devoted little space in his poems to praising his patrons. Instead, he concentrated on the style and emotional content of his poetry.

Hafiz is considered the greatest master of the ghazal, a type of lyric poem that is 10 to 30 lines in length. The themes of his ghazals celebrate the joys and pains of love and the beauties of nature. Their tone ranges from serious to lighthearted. They combine the elements that were most prized in that poetic form—rich imagery, emotional intensity, and subtle allusion*. Hafiz's poems often shift in focus from one topic to another, only to be vaguely connected later in the work. This allows him to bring together a wide range of emotions within a single poem. (*See also* **Arabic Language and Literature.**)

* **allusion** implied or indirect reference, especially in literature

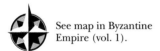
See map in Byzantine Empire (vol. 1).

The church of Hagia Sophia (Greek for Holy Wisdom) in CONSTANTINOPLE was the greatest achievement of Byzantine architecture, and it remains the most famous monument in the modern city of Istanbul. It is also one of the largest buildings that has survived from medieval times.

The construction of Hagia Sophia began in early 532 during the reign of the emperor JUSTINIAN I. It was built on the site of an older cathedral that was destroyed during a revolt that same year. The architects, Anthemios of Tralles and Isidoros of Miletos, employed thousands of workers to complete the structure in a short time. Justinian dedicated the church on December 27, 537, just five years and ten months after construction began.

The design of Hagia Sophia was very original and daring, perhaps too much so, since the building has required various structural improvements over the centuries to keep it standing. The massive central dome, the second largest (after the Pantheon in Rome) to survive from antiquity, forms an enormous canopy over the interior. This dome, the light passing through the many windows under the dome and in the richly colored marble walls, and the gold mosaics that cover the vaults create an impression of weightlessness, which seemed miraculous to medieval viewers.

Construction of Constantinople's Hagia Sophia began in 532 during the reign of the emperor Justinian I. It symbolized the importance of Orthodox Christianity in the Byzantine Empire. After the Turkish conquest in 1453, the church was turned into a mosque, and four minarets were added.

In the Byzantine era, Hagia Sophia served as the seat of the Eastern Orthodox Church. From 1204 to 1261, it was a Roman Catholic cathedral. Following the fall of the city to the Ottoman Turks in 1453, Hagia Sophia became a Muslim mosque. In 1935, it became a museum. (*See also* **Byzantine Architecture; Christianity.**)

Handbooks (Fachschrifttum)

Many medieval books were neither religious texts nor works of literature. They were practical handbooks that contained useful information. The German word *Fachschrifttum*, which means technical or practical writing, is often used as the name for these kinds of books.

New discoveries and technological advances in the late Middle Ages created a demand for up-to-date books on many subjects. The chief topics of medieval handbooks were the seven liberal arts and the seven mechanical arts—a system of organizing knowledge that began in ancient Greece. According to the Greeks, the liberal arts were those considered worthy of a freeman, while the mechanical arts were for slaves.

The liberal arts were grammar, rhetoric (composition), logic, mathematics, music, geometry, and astronomy. Because only educated people read about these subjects in the Middle Ages, books on these topics were in Latin. The mechanical arts were handicrafts, weaponry, navigation, hunting, medicine, court arts (jousting, fencing, dancing, and court entertainments), and the forbidden arts of magic and thievery.

Latin was less appropriate for the mechanical arts as most craftsmen who practiced these trades used the vernacular, the local language spoken in each region. It was naturally much more convenient for them to have handbooks in the language they could read and write, especially since new information discovered in the late Middle Ages was rapidly transforming many fields. For example, by the late 1400s, advances in firearms made all classic military texts obsolete. There was a great need for current handbooks, such as the German military handbook *Feuerwerksbuch* (written about 1420), which could explain the new techniques of warfare.

The CRUSADES and PILGRIMAGES to Rome, Canterbury, and other holy places created a demand for travel books. Greater interest in navigation led to an increase in the number of harbor guides and sailing manuals. Townspeople were eager for books that helped them to copy the customs and manners of the aristocracy. Books on cooking, housekeeping, and gardening were also in demand. Gottfried of Franconia's *Pelzbuch,* a book on horticulture* from the 1200s, was a best-seller that remained popular for centuries.

* **horticulture**   art or science of growing fruits, vegetables, flowers, and plants

Although medieval handbooks often mixed charms and superstitions with sound advice, they helped educate large numbers of medieval readers eager for information on a wide range of subjects. (*See also* **Armor; Encyclopedias and Dictionaries; Medicine; Navigation; Science; Technology.**)

Hanseatic League

The Hanseatic League was an association of north German merchants that controlled much of the trade in northern Europe during the late Middle Ages. This German manuscript illumination from the Hamburg City Charter of 1497 shows the busy seaport of Hamburg, a member-city of the Hanseatic League.

The Hanseatic League was an association of north German merchants formed in the 1160s to secure and protect trade privileges in foreign markets. The league, which lasted 500 years, successfully controlled much of the trade in northern Europe during the late Middle Ages.

The league's first foreign port was on the island of Gotland, located between Germany and Russia in the Baltic Sea. In 1161, the duke of Saxony obtained rights for a group of German merchants to trade safely on Gotland without tolls, or taxes. The Gotlanders were granted the same rights in his territories.

In the 1200s, Germans expanded farther along the Baltic coast. A crusade in the BALTIC COUNTRIES of Latvia and Estonia opened that area to German trade and settlement, and the Teutonic Knights, a German chivalric order, conquered Prussia. These lands yielded an abundance of goods, such as grain, amber, timber, wax, and furs. Merchant members of the young league sought customers for these goods in nearby FLANDERS and ENGLAND.

In the 1250s, the countess of Flanders gave the Hanseatic League trading rights in Flemish cities. The privileges given league members included legal protection, reduced customs fees, and a weighing house for them to use. Merchants from COLOGNE had been trading in England for years. After they joined the league in 1281, the privileges they enjoyed in England were granted to the rest of the league.

League merchants next turned their attention to SCANDINAVIA. After they discovered plentiful supplies of fish and copper there, their trade routes added stops in Denmark, Norway, and Sweden. They traded Baltic grain in Norway for cod; they exchanged the cod in England for wool; they sold the wool in Flanders, where it was made into cloth; and then they brought the Flemish cloth back to Baltic towns, where they sold it for a handsome profit.

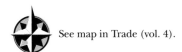

See map in Trade (vol. 4).

The Hanseatic League succeeded for several reasons. Its merchants used advanced business practices, and their ships were better suited for cargo than Scandinavian ones. Also, they had little political interference to deal with because of the weakness of the German emperor, while they tended to be powerful figures in their own communities. Most importantly, the organization of the league was loose enough to allow members independence but strong enough to foster cooperation.

Merchants from LÜBECK assumed leadership because they were among the earliest members and Lübeck was located at the center of a major east-west trading route. In foreign ports, the league established its own market-places, known as *Kontore* (countinghouses). The major ones were in LONDON, BRUGES, NOVGOROD (Russia), and Bergen (Norway).

In the mid-1300s, trade fell off after the BLACK DEATH struck northern Europe and trouble developed over the safety of ships sailing to Bruges. When league members met to discuss these problems, they changed the organization, so that now, instead of merchants themselves being members, their towns were members.

After the league reached its peak about 1370, a long period of decline set in. In the 1400s, competition increased from merchants outside the league. But the league lingered on until 1669, when it held its last assembly. Changing circumstances in Europe, including war and the rise of strong national monarchies, helped bring an end to the league. (*See also* **Fishing, Fish Trade; Fur Trade; Textiles; Trade; Wool.**)

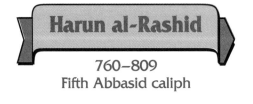

Harun al-Rashid

760–809
Fifth Abbasid caliph

* **caliph** religious and political head of an Islamic state

* **Barmakids** family of Iranian origin that served in the administration of the early Abbasid caliphs

Harun al-Rashid was the fifth caliph* of the ABBASID dynasty. Although he ruled at a time when the Islamic Empire was at its largest and richest, his reign marked a turning point in the history of the Abbasids, as their dynasty began to decline.

The son of al-Mahdi, the third caliph, and al-Khayzuran, a former Yemenite slave girl, Harun was born in Rayy, Iran. He was raised as a prince in the court of Baghdad and was the second heir apparent to the caliphate after his older brother Musa al-Hadi. Harun led two military expeditions against the Byzantines, in 779 and in 781, which reached the shores of the Bosporos opposite Constantinople. In honor of these victories, he was given the title *al-Rashid,* meaning one who follows the righteous path.

Following the death of their father in 785, Musa assumed the caliphate. But he died mysteriously a year later amid rumors that he had been assassinated by Harun's mother and his teacher. Once in power, Harun placed his sons and their supporters, the Barmakids*, in positions of power. The Barmakids administered the empire effectively despite occasional unrest in outlying areas. Industries such as textiles, metals, and paper flourished, and great wealth flowed into Baghdad. Harun's court became the model for the pleasure palace that is depicted in the *Thousand and One Nights.*

Harun then made two decisions that hastened the decline of the empire. In 803, he replaced the Barmakid administrators with a less capable group. Even more serious, however, was Harun's scheme to divide his kingdom among his three sons. His intent may have been to prevent strife among his sons, but his scheme had the opposite effect, as the empire was thrown into a civil war. In the meantime, the western provinces used this turmoil to become virtually independent of the Baghdad caliphate. After Harun's death in 809, the Abbasid Empire entered a long period of decline, though it was to rule for another 250 years. (*See also* **Caliphate; Ma'mun, al-; Thousand and One Nights.**)

Hastings, Battle of

The Battle of Hastings was the most famous battle in English history. The first and most decisive victory in the conquest of England by the NORMANS, it marked the end of Anglo-Saxon rule. The battle itself was a fierce clash between Anglo-Saxon foot soldiers and Norman knights on horses.

The stage for the battle was set in January 1066 when King Edward the Confessor died, leaving no heirs. Among those who claimed the throne were Earl Harold of Wessex and Duke William of Normandy (in France). On his deathbed, Edward had named Harold his successor, and Harold was crowned shortly thereafter. William claimed the throne based on his relationship to Edward (cousins by marriage). William had the support of the pope and claimed that Harold had sworn earlier to support his claim to the English throne.

When William heard that Harold had taken the throne, he prepared for an invasion of England. For several months, he strengthened his forces and built ships to transport them across the English Channel. Meanwhile, Harold built defenses along the coast and waited. In September, Harold's attention was diverted to the north when the Vikings invaded near York. While Harold was fighting the Vikings, William crossed the Channel on September 28 and landed, unopposed, on the English coast. From there, he marched the Norman forces to Hastings, which they began to fortify.

After defeating the Vikings, Harold marched his war-weary army 250 miles to Hastings, arriving there on October 13. The Anglo-Saxons and Normans met in battle the next day. Although Harold's troops were tired from fighting the Vikings and from their long march, they fought hard. The Anglo-Saxon army consisted of nearly 7,000 peasants armed with shields, swords, and battle-axes. The Norman army was about the same size, but it was composed of archers and armored men on horses. They were also fresh and ready for battle.

The Battle of Hastings was the first and foremost victory in the Norman conquest of England. It is considered one of the battles that changed the course of history. Weary from recent fighting with Viking invaders, the Anglo-Saxon army was unable to overcome the forces of the Norman army. This scene from the Bayeux Tapestry shows the death of King Harold during the battle.

As the battle raged, the Anglo-Saxon troops held their ground at first. Their shields stopped the Norman charges, and their battle-axes took a heavy toll on the Norman horses. Between charges, however, the Norman archers fired their arrows and killed increasing numbers of Anglo-Saxons. Harold had placed his men too close together, making it easy for the archers to hit them. Eventually, the Anglo-Saxons weakened. By late afternoon, Harold and his brothers were dead. By evening, the remaining Anglo-Saxon troops fled. The Normans had won, and William soon was crowned king of England. (*See also* **Anglo-Saxons; Edward the Confessor, St.; England; William I of England, the Conqueror.**)

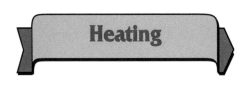

Hätzlerin, Klara

ca. 1430–ca. 1476
German scribe

* **scribe** person who hand-copies manuscripts to preserve them

* **public notary** public officer authorized to certify deeds and contracts and to take depositions

* **necromancy** practice of witchcraft or sorcery

Klara Hätzlerin was one of the best-known German scribes* of the 1400s. In her day, she was the only woman copying German manuscripts who was known by name. Unlike the majority of medieval scribes, Hätzlerin signed her name to the manuscripts she copied, eight of which still exist.

Born and raised in Augsburg, Hätzlerin most likely learned her profession from her father and her brother, who were public notaries* and legal advisers. The manuscripts she copied range widely in subject matter. They include historical texts, such as a description of the coronation of Holy Roman Emperor Frederick III, legal codes, lives of the saints, and texts on the art of hunting and necromancy*. Her most famous manuscript, *Liederbuch der Klara Hätzlerin (Songbook of Klara Hätzlerin),* dates from 1470/1471. The title of the work is somewhat misleading since Hätzlerin did not own or author the work but only copied it. Historians speculate that she might also have helped collect and arrange the texts within it. The *Liederbuch* consists of two sections, one containing 77 love poems and the other 128 songs without melodies. It is an important document because it reflects the literary life and interests of late-medieval German townspeople. (*See also* **Books, Manuscript.**)

Heating

See color plate 2, vol. 1.

Perhaps no technology of the Middle Ages changed people's lives more than the heating systems that evolved during that time. The spread of chimneys even to peasant huts brought social and economic changes across the land, not the least of which was making life more comfortable. Heating technology went through three stages: from ancient technologies to the central hearth to chimney systems.

Ancient Technologies. Medieval Europe inherited heating systems that the Romans had developed for their mild Mediterranean climate. The Romans had used furnaces and piping to provide buildings with central-heating systems. The pipes ran through walls and floors, heating the building rather than the air in the rooms. The system worked well in temperate climates, but not in the chilly north, where cold drafts chased away the warm air that had taken hours to accumulate in the walls of the building.

The Romans also used small warming pans, called braziers, filled with hot coals. These, too, were used throughout the Middle Ages. Braziers heated the air directly, but they did not solve the problem of drafts. They also emitted toxic fumes and needed plenty of ventilation—but ventilation brings in cold air. People had to balance the danger of too little fresh air against the discomfort of too little heat.

The Central Hearth.   Another ancient heating system was the central hearth. This technology brought the primitive campfire indoors. A large trench in the center of a room stored the fuel and fed the fire. An opening in the roof of the structure provided an outlet for the smoke. The fire, however, gave off so many sparks that the room had to be very wide and the walls had to be very high so that they would not catch fire. Another danger was the large fire itself, as people, especially children, sometimes tumbled into the fire pit.

The central hearth was inefficient because it sent most of the heat up to the top of the high room. The system forced people to live together in a large common hall. Privacy was impossible and comfort was rare. Working indoors under such conditions was difficult. Yet, despite these difficulties, the central hearth created a social atmosphere that many people enjoyed. Although chimneys eventually replaced many central hearths, they did not eliminate the central hearth completely. Structures with central hearths existed throughout the Middle Ages.

Chimney Systems.   The medieval solution to the problem of living in cold, drafty Europe was the chimney system. It combined a fireplace, a flue*, and a smokestack into a heating unit, and it was one of the great inventions of the Middle Ages. The fireplace allowed the direct heating of air in a room. The flue moved heat through the building, and the stack let

* **flue** tube or other enclosed passage for conveying smoke or hot air outside a structure or from one part of the structure to another

This 13th-century illumination shows a medieval fireplace. The fireplace reduced the danger of open flames; the flue moved the warm air throughout the building; and the stack provided an exit for the smoke.

smoke escape without bringing cold drafts inside. The system brought many changes to the social life of a household.

Fireplaces were an improvement on the central hearth. They were built into the wall, thus reducing the danger of open flames in the room. A flue linked the fireplace to a smokestack, or chimney. As buildings became larger and more elaborate, flues became more complex. Sometimes flues from different fireplaces came together and led to a central chimney stack.

The chimney stack extended above the roof of the building. The stack allowed the smoke from the fire to escape and, at the same time, prevented drafts from entering. Grills were sometimes placed on the stack to keep small animals and birds from coming inside the house. Sometimes various kinds of covers were used on chimneys to keep out the rain.

Although the system seems simple, it took centuries to develop. The basic system was suggested in a plan for a monastery (St. Gall) in about 820. The plan shows central hearths linked by flues to chimney stacks. By the 1100s, chimney systems had become commonplace, and by 1200, chimney stacks were clearly visible on many rooftops.

Chimney systems led to architectural and social changes. As the danger of sparks declined, ceilings were lowered and rooms were made smaller. Doors were added to rooms and buildings became compartmentalized. Instead of great halls, or multipurpose rooms, people now had private rooms, and the lord of the manor, his family, and his guests ate apart from the servants. Chimney systems and smaller rooms made indoor work much easier. Monks could copy manuscripts through the worst of winter, and university classes did not have to stop because of foul weather.

The need for fuel had environmental implications, however. By the late 1200s, forests around cities were disappearing, as they were cleared for firewood. New sources of fuel were sought and found: brush, peat, charcoal, and coal. London's air pollution from coal smoke was so great that the first clean-air laws were passed in that city in the 1200s.

Hebrew Literature

* **Talmud** large body of collected writings on Jewish law and tradition
* **liturgical** pertaining to formal religious rites and services

See color plate 4, vol. 1.

For much of the Middle Ages, Hebrew literature had a strong connection to religion. The most important influences on Hebrew literature during the early Middle Ages were the BIBLE and the Talmud*.

During the early Middle Ages, Jewish literary activity was confined to the creation of liturgical* prayers, or piyyutum, for use in religious services. The basic form of prayers was well established before the Middle Ages, but prayer leaders were encouraged to compose their own introductions to these prayers. Jewish liturgy in the Middle Ages consisted of two parts: a fixed prose portion that was the same throughout the Jewish world, and an optional poetic portion that varied from community to community and from occasion to occasion. Gradually, local collections of liturgical poetry were compiled.

Many of the religious poets of the early Middle Ages were anonymous. The first poet known by name was Yose ben Yose, who lived in

* **mysticism** belief that divine truths or direct knowledge of God can be experienced through faith, spiritual insight, and intuition

The Sarajevo Haggadah

The Sarajevo Haggadah is perhaps the best known Hebrew illustrated manuscript still in existence. Created in northern Spain between 1350 and 1400, it was thought to have belonged to a Jewish family expelled from Spain in 1492. As it changed hands, the manuscript made its way to Italy, Austria, and then Sarajevo (in the former Yugoslavia). Hidden during World War II, it was later returned to the Sarajevo Museum. However, during the recent war in Bosnia, the manuscript, valued at more than $700 million, was feared lost. Found to be resting safely in a bank vault, it was retrieved and used in the Passover ceremony in 1995 in Sarajevo.

* **treatise** long, detailed essay

* **vernacular** language or dialect native to a region; everyday, informal speech

Palestine before the 600s. Two other early religious poets were Yannai and Kallir. Early Hebrew poetry was relatively simple. Gradually, however, poetry became more complex and secretive, as it was influenced by Jewish mysticism*. Much of this poetry was very obscure, and it became necessary to have a detailed knowledge of the Bible in order to understand it. As a result, only the most educated people could understand religious poetry. Nevertheless, it remained popular throughout the period.

In the ninth century, another discipline of Hebrew writing became important. This discipline was the midrash, or an explanation of the underlying significance of the Bible. This writing was based on material from the Haggadah, or earlier biblical teachings from narratives, prayers, and proverbs. The work of Saadiah Gaon (882–942) became a model for future writers. Gaon, who translated the Bible into Arabic, wrote interpretations of the Bible. He considered the Bible's meaning in both a literal sense (using the usual meanings of words) and from the standpoint of the study of language and philosophy.

By the middle of the tenth century, the center of Jewish learning had shifted to Muslim Spain. At that time, Spanish Jews were fully integrated into Islamic society, and many were steeped in both Arabic and Hebrew culture. The period from the mid-900s to the late 1100s is referred to as the golden age of Hebrew literature because it produced a number of great Jewish writers. Poets of this time included Samuel ibn Naghralla, Solomon ibn Gabirol, Moses ibn Ezra, and Judah Halevi. Halevi's work, which included religious and nonreligious poetry, displayed a mastery of theme and technique. Halevi also wrote *Sefer ha-Kuzari (The Book of Argument and Proof in Defense of the Despised Faith)*, which was an account, in dialogue form, of the reason for the conversion to Judaism by a group of Turks in the eighth century.

This productive period in Spain came to an end in the mid-1100s, when a puritanical Islamic dynasty, the Almohads, rose to power and began persecuting the Jews. The center of Hebrew literature then shifted to northern Spain. Abraham ben Meïr ibn Ezra (1089–1164), who fled Spain in 1140, wrote works on the Bible as well as on Hebrew grammar, mathematics, and philosophy. During this period, one of the most outstanding figures in Jewish history, Moses MAIMONIDES (1135–1204), lived. Maimonides wrote *Moreh Nevukhim (Guide for the Perplexed)*, an important work among scholars who sought to bring together the philosophical concepts of creation and humanity as related by ARISTOTLE and by the Bible.

Another school of biblical interpretation emerged in northern France at about the same time. The most illustrious representative of this school was Rabbi Solomon ben Isaac, known as RASHI (1040–1105). He wrote his treatises* on religion in French, his vernacular* language. In fact, Hebrew was not the spoken language of many Jewish authors in the Middle Ages. Some wrote in Arabic or Greek and others in the Jewish vernaculars of Yiddish (Judeo-German) or Ladino (Judeo-Spanish).

A tradition of using mysticism to explain hidden meanings in the Scripture had been present since the second century. This tradition became a fully developed doctrine in the twelfth century called the CABALA. One of the most famous works of the cabala movement is entitled the *Sefer ha-Zohar (Book of Splendor)*, which was compiled by Moses de Leon. From southern France, this movement later spread to Spain, Italy, and the Byzantine Empire.

Hebrew literature continued to flourish in northern Spain until persecutions in the late 1300s and the expulsion of the Jews from Spain in 1492. This period produced several important writers, including Todros ben Judah Halevi, who wrote highly personal love poetry, and Joseph ibn Zabara, who composed works of rhymed prose that incorporated poems, proverbs, and information of all kinds. Another writer of the period, Judah al-Harizi, imitated classic Arabic styles and dealt with a wide variety of themes. Hebrew literature of this period also included translations of classics originally written in Arabic, Greek, or Latin, such as Aesop's *Fables.*

The emigration of Jews from Muslim Spain after the mid-1100s resulted in the dissemination of Spanish-Jewish culture to other parts of Europe, particularly Italy and France. In the 1100s and 1200s, Jewish poets in Italy and southern France created secular* works that displayed Arabic style. In the late 1300s, a new school of Hebrew poetry emerged, one that used features of Italian poetic forms. The greatest Jewish poet in Italy was perhaps Immanuel of Rome (died ca. 1332). Immanuel wrote many poems in the conventional Arabic style, but he also pioneered the use of the Italian sonnet* form in Hebrew poetry. The blend of both Arabic and Italian influences in Hebrew poetry formed a unique style that continued for the next 400 years. (*See also* **Arabic Language and Literature; Italian Language and Literature; Jewish Art; Jewish Communities; Jews, Expulsion of; Judaism; Spanish Language and Literature.**)

* **secular**   nonreligious; connected with everyday life

* **sonnet**   fixed verse form of 14 lines; also, a poem in this pattern

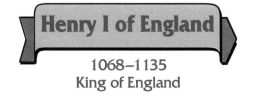

1068–1135
King of England

Henry I, the third son of WILLIAM I THE CONQUEROR, was a shrewd ruler who became king under suspicious circumstances. He was, however, one of the most able medieval English kings. His greatest achievements included the reunification of England and Normandy, the development of a highly effective government, and the establishment of an uneasy peace between the English crown and the church.

When William I died in 1087, his oldest son, Robert Curthose, inherited Normandy. The second son, William II Rufus, became king of England. As the youngest son, Henry inherited money but neither land nor power. Henry's fortunes changed, however, in August 1100. While Henry was hunting with William Rufus, a member of the hunting party, Walter Tirel, shot an arrow and killed the king. Henry rode at once to the city of Winchester to take hold of the royal treasury. Three days later, he was crowned king. Walter Tirel was not penalized for his poor marksmanship, but he instead was given a handsome reward.

At the time of the accident, Henry's brother Robert was returning to Normandy from the CRUSADES. He, too, claimed the crown, and he invaded England in 1101. After negotiations, the two brothers reached a peaceful agreement. Henry remained king of England, but he gave up any claims to Normandy. Henry did not keep his side of the bargain, however. In 1105, he invaded Normandy. He defeated Robert in battle in September 1106, and he imprisoned Robert in Cardiff Castle in England.

Robert remained a prisoner there until his death in 1134. England and Normandy were once again united under one ruler.

Henry I had a difficult relationship with the church. His brother William Rufus had angered the clergy by seizing church property and by forcing Anselm, the archbishop of Canterbury, to flee into exile. When Henry became king, he tried to make peace with the church by promising to end his brother's abuses and by recalling Anselm to England. The pope, meanwhile, was urging reforms to make the church independent of local kings. The pope banned kings from investing* bishops and banned clergy from paying homage* to kings. Anselm supported these reforms, but Henry opposed them. When Henry invested some bishops, Anselm refused to have them consecrated*. The relationship between Henry and the church deteriorated. Finally, Henry and Anselm reached an agreement in 1106. Henry would not invest bishops, but clergy would pay homage to him.

The final crisis of Henry's reign began when his only son, William, drowned while crossing the English Channel. William's death left Henry without a male heir. Since his wife was dead, Henry quickly remarried, but the marriage produced no children. In 1128, Henry's daughter Matilda married Geoffrey Plantagenet and eventually had two sons, Henry and Geoffrey. The birth of these grandsons seemed to solve the problem of succession. In 1135, Henry I died suddenly after eating too many eels. His grandson Henry was only two years old. Matilda should have become queen until her son was old enough to rule. However, one of Henry's nephews, Stephen de Blois, claimed the throne. A long civil war followed, ending in 1154 when the young Henry became King HENRY II. (*See also* **Anselm of Canterbury; Normans.**)

* **invest** to give a churchman the symbols of his spiritual authority. After the Investiture Controversy, only another churchman was permitted to exercise this power.

* **homage** formal public declaration of loyalty to the king or overlord

* **consecrate** to declare someone or something sacred in a church ceremony

---

Henry II of England

1133–1189
King of England

* **patronage** the support of an artist, writer, or scholar by a person of wealth and influence

* **duchy** territory ruled by a duke or a duchess

Henry II was the greatest king of medieval England. His legal and institutional reforms transformed English society and set the stage for the development of the modern nation. A skilled diplomat, Henry ruled over a large empire. His inability to deal with his own family caused many problems. However, Henry was one of the first literate rulers of Europe, and his patronage* of literature and his interest in law and administration made his royal court one of the most accomplished of the time.

Born on March 5, 1133, in France, Henry was heir to the throne of England and Normandy through his mother Matilda, the daughter of King Henry I. After the death of Henry I in 1135, the throne was seized by Matilda's cousin Stephen. This began a long civil war that ended nearly 20 years later after Henry invaded England in 1153 and Stephen agreed to the Treaty of Winchester. Under the terms of the treaty, the crown would become Henry's at Stephen's death. Stephen died the next year, and Henry became king of England.

Through his father Geoffrey, Henry had inherited Anjou and Maine, two provinces in western France. He expanded his control to include the neighboring provinces of Poitou and Touraine. His marriage to Eleanor of Aquitaine in 1152 gave him control of that large duchy* in southwestern France as well. At the height of his reign, Henry controlled a vast territory that stretched from Scotland to Spain, making him the most powerful monarch in Europe. This large empire is sometimes called the Angevin Empire, named after the province of Anjou that was the home of Henry's father.

Because he was born and raised in France, Henry was essentially a French ruler. He seldom visited England, spending a total of only 13 years there during his 34-year reign. Despite his long absences from England, Henry accomplished a great deal there. He reformed English law, creating a system of courts and juries that promised quick and impartial justice. The English tradition of common law* and jury verdicts owes much to Henry's rule. In addition, he created an orderly and efficient system of administration by intelligent and experienced officials.

One of Henry's rare setbacks involved a dispute with Thomas Becket, archbishop of Canterbury, over the relationship between church and state. Becket was a strong defender of church rights, and he opposed Henry's efforts to gain more control over the church and restrict the power of church courts. In 1164, Becket went into exile in France in protest. When he returned to England in 1170, he denounced the supporters of the king, a move that enraged Henry. On December 29, 1170, four of Henry's knights murdered Becket in Canterbury Cathedral. The murder shocked all of Europe and led to an outcry that forced Henry to abandon much of his claim over church law.

Henry also had difficulties with his sons, who were suspicious and jealous of his power and of one another. Henry's rival, King Philip II Augustus of France, took advantage of this situation and incited Henry's sons to rebel against their father. In 1188, Henry's son Richard did so after Henry refused to give him possession of several French provinces. Another son, John, supported Richard's actions. Defeated and depressed by his sons' treason, Henry died on July 6, 1189. His sad end, however, does not detract from his brilliant and enduring accomplishments. (*See also* **Angevins; Aquitaine; Becket, Thomas, St.; Eleanor of Aquitaine; Philip II Augustus.**)

* **common law** unwritten law based on custom and court decisions

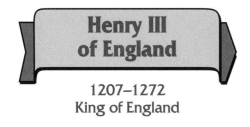

Henry III of England

1207–1272
King of England

* **regent** person appointed to govern a kingdom when the rightful ruler is too young, absent, or disabled

The story of Henry III demonstrates what can occur when a weak king reigns for a long time. Under Henry's long and incompetent reign, England went through a difficult period that culminated in a civil war.

Henry was only nine years old when his father, King JOHN, died in 1216. Ten days later, Henry was crowned king, but the country was ruled by a regent*, WILLIAM MARSHAL, the earl of Pembroke. When Pembroke died in 1219, Hubert de Burgh replaced him. De Burgh's regency lasted until 1232, when Henry dismissed the regent and took command of the country.

Henry lacked political experience and military ability. He chose foreign advisers who were incompetent and disloyal and who had little interest in England's problems. The failed policies of the royal court enabled England's powerful barons to become increasingly restless and discontent.

* **papacy** office of the pope and his administrators

They were finally driven to rebellion by Henry's demand for increased taxes to pay the military debts of the papacy*.

In 1258, Henry met with the barons. The barons agreed to new taxes in return for a series of political reforms. These reforms included the formation of a council that would represent the barons and advise the king. The reforms were agreed to in Parliament and might have succeeded if Henry had not renounced them in 1261. Three years later, civil war erupted. The war ended in 1266 with Henry's oldest son, Edward, defeating the barons, who were led by SIMON DE MONTFORT THE YOUNGER. (*See also* **Edward I of England.**)

Henry V of England

1387–1422
King of England

* **heir apparent** person expected to inherit a throne when the living monarch dies

Although Henry V reigned for only nine years, in that short time he became one of medieval England's most popular kings. An able diplomat, military commander, and administrator, he ruled at a time of relative peace and prosperity at home that was in sharp contrast to the periods before and after him. Henry is also remembered as the first English king who could read and write the English language with ease.

When Henry's father, Henry IV (Henry Bolingbroke), overthrew King RICHARD II in 1399, young Henry was named Prince of Wales, the heir apparent* to the English throne. Though still only a boy, Henry spent the years from 1400 to 1408 helping quell rebellions in Wales. During this period, he learned much about military tactics.

Henry V became one of medieval England's most popular rulers. As a soldier, Henry was known for his ability to inspire his men in battle. Although greatly outnumbered, English forces defeated the French at the Battle of Agincourt in 1415.

Henry became king on March 20, 1413. In his first two years, he devoted much of his energy to subduing religious and political revolts, including two plots to kill him. Soon after, Henry turned his attention to France, renewing old territorial claims. By presenting a series of extreme demands, to which no agreement was possible, Henry had the pretense of legal justification for invasion. In August 1415, he led a large fleet to Normandy and quickly captured the port of Harfleur. He then began a destructive march through northern France to the port of Calais. On October 25, in the village of Agincourt, the English army met the French forces. The English were badly outnumbered, but Henry's years of fighting in Wales had served him well. His clever choice of terrain, the placement of his archers, and his ability to inspire his men led to a stunning victory. After three hours of fighting, 6,000 French fighters lay dead, while the English had only a few casualties.

Other successes followed in 1417 and 1419, and the English pushed deeper into France. Final victory came with the Treaty of Troyes on May 21, 1420. Under the terms of the treaty, the French king, Charles VI, made Henry his heir and agreed to the marriage of Henry and his daughter Catherine. Charles was old, and it seemed certain that Henry would become king of France. Yet, Henry died of an illness in the summer of 1422, only two months before Charles himself died.

In addition to his military campaigns, Henry was very interested in church affairs. He supported efforts to end the Great SCHISM, founded two royal monasteries, and encouraged reforms among the English BENEDICTINES. (*See also* **Hundred Years War.**)

Henry VI of England

1421–1471
King of England

Although Henry VI was king for almost his entire life, he was never an able ruler. During his reign, England lost the HUNDRED YEARS WAR and retreated from France. English politics fell into chaos, and struggles for power among the king's relatives and heirs led to the WARS OF THE ROSES.

Henry was only nine months old when his father, HENRY V, died in 1422 and he became king. His grandfather, Charles VI of France, died two months later, and, according to the Treaty of Troyes, Henry became king of France as well. An infant king, however, could not maintain control of both France and England. The French, under the leadership of CHARLES VII, began a campaign to drive out the English. By the time Henry was 14, France was a lost cause. By 1453, the French had driven the English from most of their land, except the port of Calais.

In England, Henry faced challenges to his crown. In the 1450s, Richard, duke of York, claimed that he was the rightful heir to the throne. The rivalry between Henry and York finally erupted into a civil struggle known as the Wars of the Roses. During the struggle, York was killed in battle. The following year (1461), York's son claimed the throne as Edward IV. Henry fled to Scotland, but he was captured in England in 1465. He was restored to the throne in 1470 as a result of the rivalry between Edward and the earl of Warwick. In 1471, Edward won a military victory at Tewkesbury, and Henry's son and heir was killed in the struggle. Henry

Henry VI became king of England and France at a very young age. His reign, which spanned most of his life, was marred by constant challenges to his crown.

himself was probably murdered in the Tower of London. His only positive contributions to England were the founding of Eton College and King's College, Cambridge. (*See also* **Aquitaine; Joan of Arc.**)

Henry III of Germany

1017–1056
King and emperor

Henry III was one of the most effective rulers of Germany in the Middle Ages. He brought Bohemia and Hungary under his control and reformed the German church. He belonged to the Salians, a family that ruled Germany for more than 100 years. He became duke of Bavaria and Swabia. Then, for 11 years, he ruled as king jointly with his father, Conrad II, who was Holy Roman Emperor. Thus the way was eased for Henry's eventual control.

In the 1040s, Henry forced the duke of Bohemia and the king of Hungary to accept German rule. He also took over the duchy of Lorraine, defending it against the former duke and the French king.

Henry and his wife, Agnes, were deeply religious and felt that the church had fallen into decline and needed reforming. He founded a church near his home in the town of Goslar as a training school for bishops. He appointed bishops and abbots who supported his desire to eliminate corrupt church practices, such as selling church positions for money.

During the papal election of 1046, a dispute erupted among three rival candidates. Henry dismissed all three and selected a German bishop, who became Pope Clement II. Henry later appointed three more German bishops as pope, all of whom helped in the reform movement.

Toward the end of his reign, Henry encountered growing opposition. Nobles in Saxony, Lorraine, Normandy, and Hungary objected to his power. Critics of his reforms said he was interfering in church matters. His strengthening of the church and the papacy would later cause problems for his son Henry IV, who came into serious conflict with Pope Gregory VII. (*See also* **Germany.**)

Henry VI of Germany

1165–1197
King and emperor

Henry VI reigned during an era when German monarchs were trying to expand their empire. He conquered Sicily, a kingdom long sought by Germany. He tried, but failed, to make the monarchy hereditary, and groups of electors continued to choose German kings. He was a poet and wrote verses that were set to music.

Henry was a member of the Hohenstaufens, a powerful family that ruled Germany in the 1100s and the 1200s. He succeeded his father, the emperor Frederick I Barbarossa. At the age of 19, Henry was knighted and married Constance, the heiress to the Sicilian crown.

One dramatic episode of Henry's reign involved his cousin and political opponent, Henry the Lion, duke of Bavaria and the powerful region of Saxony. After a dispute with Frederick I (Henry VI's father), Henry the Lion was outlawed and his territories were taken. Then in 1192, Henry the Lion's English brother-in-law, Richard the Lionhearted, was captured by the then duke of Bavaria and was turned over as a prisoner to Henry VI. Henry VI negotiated Richard's release in return for an

Henry VI succeeded his father, Frederick I Barbarossa, as king of Germany. This illumination from a history of the Welfs (an important medieval German family) shows King Frederick with his sons. The future King Henry VI is on the left.

enormous ransom and annual payments from England. By doing so, the young King Henry VI gained prestige, and Henry VI and Henry the Lion were reconciled.

Henry VI's reign ended abruptly when he died of malaria as he was preparing to go on the Fourth Crusade. He left an infant son and problems of succession that ultimately led to the end of the Hohenstaufen dynasty. (*See also* **German Language and Literature; Germany.**)

Henry de Mondeville

ca. 1260–ca. 1325
Surgeon and lecturer

* **pathology** study of the nature of diseases

Henry de Mondeville was a Norman surgeon and lecturer whose books combined the surgical and anatomical knowledge of Italy and France during the late Middle Ages. His works provided a complete picture of the extent of surgical practice and the day-to-day concerns of a medieval surgeon.

Henry studied surgery at Paris and Montpellier in France and was also familiar with Italian methods. In 1301, he served as an army surgeon for the French king, PHILIP IV THE FAIR, and later with the king's brother, Charles of Valois, and the king's son, Louis X. Although being surgeon to royalty carried prestige, Henry often complained that it brought him little money. He lectured on anatomy at Montpellier in 1304 and at Paris in 1306. He continued to write, practice, and teach until his death, probably from tuberculosis.

His most important works include an illustrated collection of his Montpellier lectures, titled *Anathomia,* and a major text called the *Chirurgia.* This latter work was an ambitious project, which would consist of five sections: anatomy, treatment of wounds, surgical pathology*, treatment of fractures and dislocations, and drugs. Henry was never able to complete it. He explained that the pressure of patients and students left him only enough time to write a line a day. He completed only two sections (anatomy and wounds) and parts of two others (fractures and drugs). The section on surgical pathology was planned but not written. The second section, which includes no less than 17 methods for stopping a hemorrhage, recounts his difficulties in bringing new Italian surgical techniques into French practice.

Unlike 20th-century surgeons, who enjoy great prestige, medieval surgeons were often despised. Most universities did not teach surgery, and people relied on barbers for their surgical procedures. Henry, as a university-trained practitioner, was eager to increase public respect for surgeons and self-respect among surgeons themselves. He insisted on the unity of medicine and surgery. He attacked the contempt that many physicians (healers) expressed for surgeons. Henry believed that surgeons were, in fact, more important than physicians. He explained that the work of a surgeon was visible to all—when a surgeon made a mistake, everyone saw the result. The physician must use his brain, Henry maintained, but the surgeon must use both brain and eyes. Indeed, the surgeon should have five eyes to see all that must be seen during a surgical procedure.

Henry's emphasis on observation made him less dependent on authority and tradition. His innovative thinking led to the creation of new surgical tools. He even used a magnet to remove pieces of iron lodged in a body. He opposed the deliberate creation of pus in wounds by probes or irritants, which was thought to aid the healing process. Henry preferred, instead, the gentle cleaning and rapid closure of a wound after surgery.

Henry's use of drawings to accompany his lectures shows his enterprise. His illustrations were not particularly accurate, however, and they had little influence on the tradition of medieval anatomical drawing. (*See also* **Barber-Surgeons; Medicine.**)

Heraldry

Heraldry refers to the art of designing and describing marks of identification that were used on shields, helmets, and banners in medieval warfare. The basic heraldic symbol—an emblem called a coat of arms—survived beyond the Middle Ages as a sign of a particular family and its status.

Origins.   In the excitement and urgency of battle, the danger of being harmed or even killed by a member of one's own side has always been present. For this reason, since ancient times, soldiers have worn various markings to show who they are. Both the ancient Greeks and the German invaders of Rome wore decorative markings on their shields and helmets. These markings made it easier for soldiers in the heat of battle to tell friend from foe.

A part of the attraction of military life has been the chance for personal glory, and early battles provided the opportunities for combatants to show their individual skill and heroism. Brightly colored markings made it easier to recognize individual warriors when they performed their heroic feats. Unlike modern military uniforms that tend to be dark camouflage without ready markings of personal rank, ancient and medieval markings were designed specifically to catch the eye.

* **insignia** signs of rank

The great difference between ancient and medieval insignia* was the linkage of design to family lines in medieval coats of arms. Insignia were passed from generation to generation. The symbols were legally protected, and it was unlawful for a person to use insignia to which his family was not entitled.

* **chain mail** flexible armor made of small metal rings linked together

Use.   During the Middle Ages, knights wearing chain mail* needed shields for protection from sword blows. They also wore visors that hid their faces, making it impossible to distinguish friend from foe even at close range. The most obvious way to display a mark of identification was to paint an emblem on the largest available surface, the shield, or to mount a crest* on the top of a knight's helmet.

* **crest** decoration at the top of a coat of arms

Commanders of large fighting units carried banners, which were also decorated with various insignia. French knights put their own coats of arms on their banners. The English used a common sign, the Cross of St. George, on theirs. The banners enabled the combatants to see which side occupied a particular portion of the field.

* **squire** aide to a knight

Only knights had coats of arms. Ordinary soldiers, squires*, and others on the battlefield had no insignia of their own and were not allowed to wear the insignia of their lords. Instead they wore badges as a sign of loyalty to a particular family or person. The badges displayed a symbol chosen by a knight or a noble family. The badges were not subject to the same rules or controls applied to coats of arms. Among the most famous medieval badges were the roses of England. The badge of the house of York had on it a white rose, and the badge of the house of Lancaster had a red one. When these two families went to war over the English crown, the struggle became known as the WARS OF THE ROSES.

Officials, called heralds, were charged with keeping records of the many different coats of arms. From the beginning, heralds used a special language to accurately describe the composition of a shield. The slightest error could be disastrous, for a coat of arms identified its wearer. The special terms used by the herald also added to the color and excitement, as a champion's blazon* was called out at a tournament. At first, heralds and other interested parties compiled lists of arms from those who participated in tournaments or were on the army rosters. Later, more comprehensive and general rolls were kept.

Design.   The design of a coat of arms followed certain rules and used two basic colors—one dark "color" (red, blue, black, green, or purple) and one light "metal" (yellow for gold and white for silver). The purpose of using a dark and light color was to create strong, contrasting patterns that could be seen from as far away as an arrow could fly. The color rules were so strictly observed that a knight with the wrong combination of colors could be banned from tournaments. The only exception to the rule was made for the coat of arms of the kingdom of Jerusalem, which combines gold and silver. This was allowed in recognition of the exalted status of the king of Jerusalem among other ordinary kings.

* **blazon** description of a coat of arms

Medieval coats of arms began as fairly simple designs and became more elaborate as the Middle Ages progressed. The *shield* is the most important part of the coat of arms because it gives the identifying sign of the bearer. The *crest,* which sits on top of the *helmet,* often repeats an object from the shield. The *mantling* represents the protective garment worn by the knight. A *scroll* with the knight's *motto* might appear at the bottom. In the Middle Ages, *supporters,* or guardians of the arms, were added. Supporters were usually real or mythical animals, such as deer, lions, or dragons.

Elements of a Coat of Arms

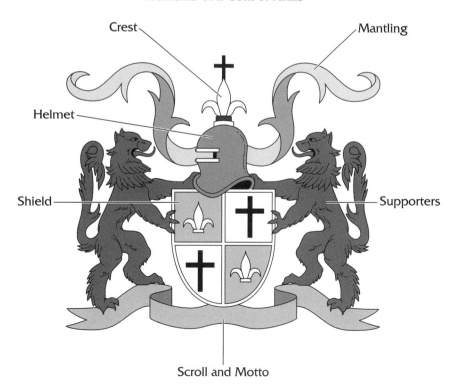

Crest

Mantling

Helmet

Shield

Supporters

Scroll and Motto

The background color was called the field. The main figure was called the charge. Medieval coats of arms tended to be fairly simple—for example, a red field with a yellow charge. Eventually the designs became more elaborate. Special insignia indicated younger members of a family, and sometimes coats of arms were combined when two great families married.

Survival. In the mid-1300s, plate armor replaced chain mail. Since plate armor provided adequate protection for the wearer, shields were no longer needed. The introduction of gunpowder changed the conduct of war still further, yet coats of arms endured. By this time, they had become desirable symbols of family and noble birth. The heralds became experts on genealogy, and their information was critical in issues of inheritances, marriage, property, and other family matters. In England, the king's approval was necessary to legalize a coat of arms. In 1484, Richard III created the Heralds' College of Arms to decide who had the right to have a coat of arms. The College of Arms also chose the elements that were to appear on an emblem. Two years later, the first book in English to describe heraldic insignia, the *Boke of St. Albans,* appeared. Although the Middle Ages were ending, the medieval tradition of family coats of arms continued to be used in tournaments and other ceremonies.

Most nations have abolished heraldry and the privileges associated with the system. However, people in some countries still use heraldic symbols to show their ancestry. Although anyone may create and use a coat of arms, few that are used today are authentic. (*See also* **Armor; Warfare.**)

Herbs and Herbals

* **treatise** long, detailed essay

In the Middle Ages, herbs were highly valued plants that were used not only as flavorings and fragrances but also as health and beauty aids. Books about herbs, called herbals, were popular throughout Europe and the Byzantine and Arab worlds.

Herbs. During the Middle Ages, interest in the medical and nutritional value of herbs was widespread, as evidenced by the large number of herbals and cookbooks, health manuals, and medical treatises*. Herbs were also widely used as beauty aids for both men and women. Herbs such as sage, saffron, myrtle, hellebore, caraway, belladonna, laurel, hyssop, mandrake, and Madonna lily leaves were considered good for skin, hair, and even temperament.

In the Islamic world, interest in herbs was also strong. In the QUR'AN, the plants in Paradise are presented as signs of Allah's power and majesty. The most comprehensive Arab work on the names of herbs was that of al-Dinawari (died ca. 895). Strong Islamic interest in plants is also seen in the descriptions of herbs that are common in Arab, Persian, and Turkish literature.

Herbals. Western European herbals, written mostly in LATIN, were divided into sections on individual plants believed to have medicinal properties. The typical herbal gave descriptions of the plant and its habitat,

The use of herbs for medicinal, nutritional, and cosmetic purposes was widespread during the Middle Ages. This treatise on snakebites comes from a medical manuscript of the 900s. It shows an herbalist making a snakebite potion.

Wedding Present

At her wedding in Constantinople in 512, the Byzantine princess Juliana Anicia received a book about herbs that contained nearly 500 very beautiful, hand-painted illustrations. Leading Byzantine artists had been commissioned to illustrate the various plants described in the herbal. Each illustration had an accompanying text by an early Greek writer, such as Dioscorides. The magnificently illustrated herbal must have been one of Juliana's most prized wedding gifts.

the various names by which it was known, the ways it was gathered, information about the ailments it treated, and instructions on how to prepare it for use as a remedy. Although all European herbals were primarily concerned with plants, some herbals also included discussions about mineral and animal products. The illustrations ranged from crude sketches to highly detailed drawings.

Most herbals were written in prose, but some were in poetry. Many listed the plants in alphabetical order according to their common Latin name. Some herbals had indexes that listed the plants under specific ailments, which made the medical information easier to find. Herbals were used and studied more in monasteries than in universities. Although herbals were compiled throughout the medieval period, their popularity declined toward the end of the Middle Ages. The invention of PRINTING, however, stimulated renewed interest in herbals.

In the Byzantine and Arab worlds, there was also widespread interest in herbals that provided specific information about medicinal plants. The strong Byzantine herbal tradition had its roots in ancient Greece, where the earliest known herbal was the *Enquiry into Plants* by Theophrastus of Eresus (ca. 300 B.C.). Byzantine herbals, which compiled excerpts from Dioscorides of Anazarbus (ca. A.D. 65) and other Greek authors, were prized for their beautiful illustrations.

Once the Arabs discovered the abundance of medical information in Greek and Byzantine texts, Hunayn ibn Ishaq and others translated the works of Dioscorides and other Greek herbal writers into Arabic.

The Arabs then expanded the scope of their herbal knowledge by learning about new herbs through the study of Asian and African plants. (*See also* **Agriculture; Cosmetics and Beauty Aids; Food and Drink; Medicine; Science.**)

Heresy and Heresies

* **theologian** person who studies religious faith and practice

* **canon** a religious law

* **apostles** early followers of Jesus who traveled and spread his teachings

* **secular** nonreligious; connected with everyday life

* **laypersons** nobles or common people who were not official clergy in the church and had not taken vows as monks or nuns. Some monasteries accepted lay brothers and sisters to help them with their work.

Heresy, which comes from *hairesis* (the Greek word for choice), was defined by medieval Christianity as a stubborn adherence to a freely chosen opinion contrary to church teaching. In the eyes of the church, Christians who insisted on holding such opinions after their errors had been pointed out to them were heretics who needed to be excommunicated, or banned from the church and punished. Medieval theologians* compared heresy to a disease that afflicted the church—a deadly disease that needed to be rooted out so that the church could be healthy.

The idea of unacceptable religious opinions existed in Islamic and Jewish traditions as well. However, during the Middle Ages, Muslims were generally more tolerant of religious differences than Christians.

Heresy in the Christian Tradition. Early Christians insisted that belief should be uniform and that only the church had the authority to interpret religious matters. In the late 300s, the Nicene Creed was adopted and the definitive canon* of the BIBLE was established. These actions allowed the church to define more clearly the divinely ordained truth that was handed down from Christ to his apostles*, and then through them and their disciples to the bishops of the church.

The major medieval analysis of heresy was that of Thomas AQUINAS. In his great work, *Summa theologiae*, he defined heresy as "a kind of unbelief attaching to those who profess faith in Christ yet corrupt his dogmas (principles)." Aquinas regarded heresy as the worst form of infidelity, or unfaithfulness—worse than paganism or JUDAISM. He believed that, unlike Jews, Muslims, or other infidels who were outside the Christian faith, heretics were to be punished for accepting the faith and then corrupting it. Aquinas declared that if an accused heretic refused to change his or her opinion after the error was pointed out, the person should be excommunicated and turned over "to a secular* court to be removed from this world by death."

Western European Heresies. In the Christian West, there were two kinds of heresies—learned and popular. A learned heresy was a disagreement with church doctrine by an educated individual. The case of Berengar of Tours (born in 1000) is an example. The church had introduced the idea of transubstantiation, which is the belief that the substance of the bread and wine used during the MASS changes into the substance of the body and blood of Christ. Although the idea was not yet official church doctrine, Berengar was condemned as a heretic for his refusal to accept it. He died in 1088, unconvinced that he was a heretic.

A popular heresy, on the other hand, was a disagreement with church doctrine by a group of laypersons*. Popular heresies attracted many

All Is Forgiven

The Humiliati were a community of Christians in Lombardy, in northern Italy. Their strict religious lives consisted of prayer, voluntary poverty, manual labor, and preaching their message to others. The church Council of Verona, suspicious of their activities, condemned them, in 1184, for "disobedience." They remained outcasts for nearly 20 years, but the church accepted the Humiliati back in 1201.

followers, especially among illiterate peasants and townspeople. The earliest known case of punishment for heresy occurred in 1022, when a group of Frenchmen were condemned and burned at the stake in Orleans for rejecting the Bible. They called the Bible "the fabrications which men have written on the skins of animals."

The 1100s saw a surge of popular heresies in Europe. The heresy of the CATHARS, or Albigensians, was widespread in northern France, FLANDERS, and northern Italy. Cathars believed that there were two gods, one who created good and one who created evil, including the body. They believed that Christ did not have a body, and they refused to eat meat of any kind. In the early 1200s, the church launched a military crusade against the Cathars (called the Albigensian crusade), which was followed by a campaign of persecution by the Inquisition. By 1300, the church had succeeded in destroying almost all the Cathars.

Two university-trained reforming priests who condemned church corruption attracted large popular followings. John WYCLIF (ca. 1330–1384), a teacher at Oxford University in England, maintained that the Bible should be the only source of church doctrine. He was condemned by the Council of Constance in 1415. Jan HUS (ca. 1369–1415) was a Czech reformer who was condemned and burned at the stake in 1415 for attacking the authority of the pope. The followers of both men (LOLLARDS and Hussites) continued their campaigns after their deaths.

Heresies in the Byzantine World.   Beginning in the 400s, various groups separated from the Byzantine Church over disagreements about who Jesus Christ was—God or man. After the Council of Ephesus (431) condemned Nestorius, archbishop of Constantinople, large numbers of Nestorians left the church. Persecution by the church drove many of them into Persia, where they established an active and prosperous church. Nestorians maintained that Christ had two distinct natures—human and divine.

When the Council of Chalcedon (451) seemed to favor the Nestorian point of view, those who supported the idea that Christ had only one physis (from the Greek word for nature)—called Monophysites—left the Byzantine Church. Large numbers of non-Greek-speaking Christians in Syria, Armenia, Egypt, Ethiopia, and other parts of the Byzantine world adopted the Monophysite point of view.

Later Byzantine dissidents* included iconoclasts, who tried to prohibit all religious images (icons), and groups such as the Messalians, Paulicians, and Bogomils who believed that the world consisted of opposite principles (God and matter, good and evil, light and darkness).

Heresy in Islam.   Medieval Islam was more flexible and tolerant of different religious ideas than the Christian church was. Islam had no pope or councils of bishops to prescribe religious belief, nor did it have anything comparable to the Inquisition to root out and punish heretics. The idea of heresy existed in Islam, but it had more to do with problems of religious succession and arguments about the qualifications of one candidate over another.

Differing interpretations about two important events in early Islamic history were the source of most religious disagreements. One event was the murder of the third caliph*, Uthman, by Muslims dissatisfied with the way

* **dissident**   person who disagrees with established opinion

* **caliph**   religious and political head of an Islamic state

* **Shi'ites** Muslims who believed that Muhammad chose Ali and his descendants as the rulers and spiritual leaders of the Islamic community

* **Sunnites** Muslim majority who believed that the caliphs should rule the Islamic community

he was running the empire. The other event was the series of civil wars fought during the CALIPHATE of Ali ibn Abi Talib, who ruled from 656 to 661. Differing attitudes about Ali caused the greatest division in Islamic history—between the Shi'ites* and the Sunnites*. (*See also* **Aristotle in the Middle Ages; Armenia; Augustine in the Middle Ages, St.; Christianity; Icons; Islam, Religion of.**)

Hermandades

The hermandades, or brotherhoods, of Spain took many forms. They could be city councils, groups of noblemen or clergymen, or members of a trade or profession—as long as they were united by an oath of mutual support. Merchants and artisans formed brotherhoods with the power to supervise the quality and determine the prices of their products. Two other types of hermandades were unions of monasteries for religious and defensive purposes, and cities with common commercial interests. Still another kind of hermandad arose when the middle class of a town united against an aggressive lord.

The most important hermandades were political leagues that acted independently of the CORTES, or parliaments. These brotherhoods may have been influenced by the Leagues of Peace that were active in southern France and Catalonia before the hermandad appeared in Castile in the 1100s. The purpose of these earlier organizations was to deal with outlaws and with the abuses of big landholders.

* **bureaucracy** large departmental organization such as a government

Political hermandades in Castile and León campaigned against the policies of ALFONSO X EL SABIO (the Learned) and recognized his son as king. They also sought to counter aristocratic excesses and the abuses of the royal bureaucracy*. The hermandades were active during the reigns of underage kings in an attempt to correct mistakes that the young kings could not deal with. At various times, the brotherhoods lost power, decreased in importance, or disappeared altogether after outliving their usefulness—only to be brought back to life again for a time. (*See also* **Guilds.**)

Hermits

* **contemplation** focused meditation on spiritual things, to develop inner calm and peace of mind

Hermits were people who withdrew from society to live a life of contemplation* and prayer. Christian hermits were inspired by the example of Jesus, who spent 40 days in the desert praying and fasting to prepare for his preaching mission. By the 300s, growing numbers of Christians had renounced marriage and all but a few of their possessions and withdrew to the desert, wilderness, or mountains.

According to the theologian Athanasius of Alexandria, the first true Christian hermit was St. Anthony of Egypt (ca. 250–355). Before Anthony, Christians who chose to live a life of contemplation and prayer did so in or near their own villages. Anthony was the first to live in the desert completely separated from society. He is sometimes called the "father of Christian monasticism."

As increasing numbers of Christians followed his example, the movement spread in northern Egypt, Palestine, and Syria. Some of the Syrian hermits went to the extreme of wearing heavy iron chains, feeding on grass, or living on the tops of columns. With the spread of MONASTICISM in western Europe, the eremitic* tradition gave way to the tradition of monks living together in monasteries and performing charitable works for others. In the 1000s, the eremitic tradition was revived when CISTERCIANS and other monastic orders renewed the emphasis on poverty and a strict separation from society. The eremitic tradition declined in the late Middle Ages and virtually disappeared after 1500. (*See also* **Julian of Norwich; Peter the Hermit.**)

* **eremitic** referring to a hermit

Hildegard of Bingen, St.

1098–1179
Nun, scientist, and writer

* **cloister** part of monastery or convent reserved for the monks and nuns

* **prioress** head of a convent; rank below abbess

Hildegard was famous as a religious personality and as a scientist. Although she lived a quiet convent life, she was one of the great figures of her age—one who exchanged letters with kings and church leaders.

Hildegard was born in 1098 to a noble family of the Rhine valley. She was educated by Benedictine nuns in Disiboden and remained in their cloister* after she was grown. In 1136, she was elected prioress* of the convent, but 11 years later, she and 18 other nuns left Disiboden to enter a newly founded convent at Bingen. She stayed there until her death.

As a child, Hildegard had special psychic gifts—she had experienced visions and auditory messages. She kept these to herself for fear of being considered abnormal. When Hildegard was 43, she consulted with her confessor, Godfrey, who, in turn, spoke to the archbishop. The archbishop encouraged Hildegard to put her visions in writing. She did so in a work called *Scivias,* which brought her immediate fame.

Hildegard was also famous in her lifetime as a healer and physician. She conducted scientific studies and wrote two medical books, *Physica* and *Causae and Curae.* The books contain information about the nature of diseases and their causes and cures that was used by physicians as late as the 1400s. These works are of interest today because in them Hildegard listed drugs and herbs by the German names, even though she wrote her books in Latin.

By the end of her life, Hildegard had become an important political figure through her correspondence with monarchs and religious figures, including Frederick I Barbarossa and Bernard of Clairvaux. (*See also* **Bernard of Clairvaux; Frederick I Barbarossa; Mysticism.**)

Historical Writing

* **chronicles** record of events in the order in which they occurred

* **annals** written account of events year by year

Medieval historical writing included many kinds—histories, chronicles*, annals*, biographies, and biblical commentaries. Much of it was inspired by writings from earlier centuries, including the BIBLE and the works of Roman historians.

Western European Historical Writing. Medieval historians relied on the work of Roman historians, such as Sallust. The Roman poet Virgil, whose *Aeneid* was read as history, was also frequently quoted. However, medieval European history was for the most part the work of Christian writers, many of them monks, who wrote in LATIN. Their main inspirations were the Bible and St. AUGUSTINE.

Medieval writers assumed that the future was inscribed in the past—that is, that all history was foreordained by God. The notion of the six ages of the world and of humans was a popular metaphor in medieval writing. This doctrine stated that the six days of Creation, as recorded in the Bible, corresponded to the six ages of the world, and that these stages also corresponded to the six ages of humans—from infancy to death.

An influential religious historian was St. Jerome, who died in 420. He edited an earlier work, Eusebius's *Chronicle.* The *Chronicle* had synchronized Judeo-Christian and pagan dates up to 325. Jerome extended the history to 378 and translated it from Greek into Latin. This work was held in high esteem in the Middle Ages.

In England, a monk called the Venerable BEDE, who died in 735, wrote the *Ecclesiastical History of the English People,* an important account of early English history. Two notable histories of German peoples were the *History of the Franks* by Gregory of Tours, who died in 593/594, and the *History of the Goths, Suevi, and Vandals* by Isidore of Seville, who died in 636. Annals were also kept throughout western Europe, and stories of the lives of saints were enormously popular.

Historical writing flourished in the 12th century and involved some of the best writers of the time. Works included commentaries on classical rhetoric, annals, and world chronicles written in Latin. Biographies of royalty became popular, such as the *Life of Louis VI* by Suger of St. Denis, as well as autobiographies, such as *The Story of My Calamities* by Peter Abelard. John of Salisbury, an Englishman in exile in France, wrote the foremost work on international politics, the *Papal History.*

Two important developments occurred in late medieval historical writing. One was the increasing use of the vernacular* (especially French), rather than Latin. The monks of the royal abbey of St. Denis wrote a massive series of vernacular histories from the mid-1200s to the late 1400s called the *Great Chronicles of France.* The most revealing biography of a medieval ruler, the *Life of Louis IX* by JEAN DE JOINVILLE (who died in 1317), was also written in French. The other important development was the appearance of vernacular histories about cities or regions, especially those in Italy and Germany—such as the respected town chronicle, *History of Florence.*

* **vernacular** language or dialect native to a region; everyday, informal speech

Byzantine Historical Writing. Byzantine historical works were generally of two kinds—chronicles and narrative history. Chronicles, which were written in strict chronological order, differed from histories, which were arranged by themes and written in the style of the ancient Greek historians.

In the early Middle Ages, Byzantine historians wrote both church and secular (political and military) history. Among the more impressive works from the later period were the *History* of Leo the Deacon, based mostly on Leo's experience at court in the 900s; *Chronographia,* a remarkable history of the Byzantine imperial court from 976 to 1077 by Michael Psellos; the *Alexiad,* Anna Komnena's eyewitness account of the reign of her father, Alexios I Komnenos; and Nikephoros Gregoras's massive 37-volume *Roman History,* written in the 1300s. The consistently high level of

Present at the Fall

The great city of Constantinople lasted well over 1,000 years. Built in the 300s by the emperor Constantine I the Great and named for him, the city fell to the Turks in 1453. George Sphrantzes, minister of the last Byzantine emperor, was the only historian to actually witness the fall of the great city. In his history of the Byzantine Empire, Sphrantzes recorded one of the most momentous events in the history of the world.

Byzantine historical writing made it one of the great achievements of Byzantine civilization.

Jewish Historical Writing.   Although few Jewish histories as such were written during the Middle Ages, an intense interest in the past was evident in Jewish medieval literature. Major religious works discussed the Talmud* and its teachers and interpreters in order to establish an accurate history of Jewish religious authority. In addition, numerous commentaries on the Bible and retellings of biblical stories appeared.

Probably the most popular medieval retelling of biblical history was the book of *Yosippon,* a work written in Hebrew probably in the 900s. It retells the history of the ancient Israelites. However, it then goes on to describe kings, heroes, and villains from the postbiblical period when the Jews lived under Persian, Greek, and Roman rule.

Armenian Historical Writing.   Historical writing in Christian ARMENIA was initially inspired by the Bible, the works of the Greek Christian historian Eusebius, the lives of saints, and other Christian writings translated into Armenian in the early 400s.

The first original Armenian historical work was Koriwn's *Life of Mastoc.* Since Mastoc was the creator of the Armenian alphabet and Koriwn was his student, the work contains valuable information about how the alphabet was formed. The most ambitious early work was the *History* of Movses Xorenaci, a comprehensive chronicle of the Armenian people beginning with the Creation of the world. Movses's *History* glorified the accomplishments of Armenia's kings and princes to the 400s. Historical writing in Armenia flourished for another 1,000 years.

Islamic Historical Writing.   From the fourth to the tenth century, Islamic historical writing was dominated by religious scholars. They looked at the past and judged it according to its preservation of original Muslim standards of behavior. Muslim religious scholars tended to focus on a few events that address certain religious issues rather than to produce a continuous historical narrative. The first of the great histories of this kind was *Sirat rasul Allah (Life of God's Apostle)* by Ibn Ishaq, who died in 768.

Another type of Islamic historical writing was created at the courts of the caliphs*. The histories produced there represented the caliph as Allah's representative on earth and looked to his actions for timeless rules of political wisdom. These historians focused on the entire reign of a caliph rather than on a few selected events. Two examples of this school of writing are the *Tajarib al-umam (Experiences of the Nations)* in Arabic by Miskawayh, who died in 1030, and the *Tarikh-i Masudi (History of Sultan Masud)* in Persian by Abu'l-Fadl Bayhaqi, who died in 1077.

Some Muslim histories began with the Creation of the world, but most dealt with the Islamic period. Others dealt with dynastic or local pasts. Islamic historical writing also included biographical dictionaries, such as the *Kitab al-Tabaqat al-kabir (Great Book of Generations)* by Ibn Sad, who died in 845. It contained entries on 4,250 people from Islamic history, 600 of them women.

One historian, IBN KHALDUN, who died in 1406, left a lasting imprint on historical writing. He was the first historian to argue that history was a

* **Talmud** large body of collected writings on Jewish law and tradition

* **caliph** religious and political head of an Islamic state

true science based on philosophical principles. He stated that a knowledge of history was not the same as a study of facts alone: history should involve the study of the principles of human society. Ibn Khaldun's ideas had a considerable impact on later historians. (*See also* **Byzantine Literature; Caliphate; Christianity; English Language and Literature; Greek Language; Hebrew Literature; Islam, Religion of; Jewish Communities; Latin Language; Qur'an.**)

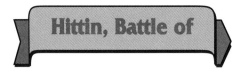

* **principality** region that is ruled by a prince

The Battle of Hittin, fought on July 4, 1187, was one of the most decisive battles in the history of the CRUSADES. It resulted in the defeat and almost total annihilation of the crusader army by the Muslim leader SALADIN. It ultimately led to the Muslim liberation of JERUSALEM a few months later.

By the winter of 1186, Saladin had united various Muslim principalities* in Syria and northern Mesopotamia and controlled all the territory surrounding the kingdom of Jerusalem. His forces were ready to confront the Christians and recapture Jerusalem from them. Open hostilities began in early 1187 when the Christians seized a Muslim caravan that was traveling through the region. By June, Saladin had assembled his armies and was ready to attack. Guy of Lusignan, the king of Jerusalem, responded by assembling his crusader forces. On July 2, the crusaders began to advance toward Saladin's army, despite the danger of confronting the Muslims on desolate, waterless land in the heat of summer.

Soon after starting out, the crusaders found themselves exhausted, thirsty, and surrounded by Saladin's well-rested and well-armed troops. Near the foot of a hill called Qurun Hittin (the Horns of Hittin), the opposing armies clashed. Saladin took advantage of the hot weather by setting fire to dry bushes and grass, covering the crusaders' position in smoke. The crusader army was almost totally wiped out, and most of those who survived were taken prisoner. Only a handful escaped. With their military forces depleted, the crusaders were unable to prevent Saladin and his Muslim forces from capturing Jerusalem three months later on October 2. (*See also* **Jihad.**)

The concept of the Holy Roman Empire, which lasted until 1806, changed over the centuries. On Christmas Day in 800, Charlemagne was crowned "Emperor of the Romans" by Pope LEO III. Charlemagne was the first medieval European ruler to claim legitimate succession from the Romans.

The Holy Roman Empire grew out of the German state that was the eastern part of Charlemagne's empire. In 962, Pope John XII crowned the German king Otto I "Emperor of the Romans" in the tradition of Charlemagne. His son, Otto II, intent on strengthening his hold on Italy, adopted the title "Emperor Augustus of the Romans" in 982.

The emperor Conrad II used the term "Roman Empire" for the first time in 1034, referring to the unification of Germany, Italy, and Burgundy under a single ruler. In 1157, the supporters of the German

By using the term *holy* to describe the empire, Frederick I Barbarossa and his descendants wanted to show the divine origin of their power and their independence from the pope. By the later Middle Ages, however, the strength of territories such as Bavaria and Saxony and of city-states such as Hamburg and Lübeck was more responsible for the survival of the Holy Roman Empire than was the strength of its emperors.

HOLY ROMAN EMPIRE

Holy Roman Empire in 1250

0   100   200 Miles

emperor FREDERICK I BARBAROSSA adopted the term "Holy Empire" to emphasize the divine origin of Frederick's authority. The full title "Holy Roman Empire" first appeared in 1254 and endured until Francis II renounced the title in 1806. (*See also* **Coronation; Germany; Papacy, Origins and Development.**)

Holy Year

* **plenary indulgence** cancellation of punishment for all previously committed sins

Holy Years began in the late Middle Ages as special years of pilgrimage to Rome to earn plenary indulgences*. Originally, Jerusalem was the only place where such pardons were obtained, but when Acre (in Syria) fell to the Muslims in 1291, the trip to Jerusalem became too dangerous. Other locations replaced Jerusalem.

Pope BONIFACE VIII proclaimed the first Holy Year (called a jubilee year) at Rome in 1300. Pilgrims who traveled to Rome and visited its major churches, including St. Peter's, received the much sought after plenary indulgence. At a time when the pope was involved in a struggle with the French king, PHILIP IV THE FAIR, participation in the Holy Year observance demonstrated the obedience of Christians to the pope in Rome. Observance of the Holy Year also boosted Rome's economy. Pilgrims flooded the city seeking the first plenary indulgences ever offered in Europe.

The second Holy Year, which Pope CLEMENT VI proclaimed for 1350, was better organized and even more successful than the first. Later popes reduced the intervals between Holy Years—to 33 years in 1389 and then to 25 years in 1468 (still the interval between Holy Years today). The success of the Roman Holy Year prompted other European pilgrimage centers to proclaim their own Holy Years, though these lacked papal approval. Santiago de Compostela in Spain, which continues to proclaim its own Holy Years, remains an active pilgrimage center to this day. (*See also* **Papacy, Origins and Development; Pilgrimage.**)

Hospitals and Poor Relief

See color plate 2, vol. 3.

O ne of the greatest achievements of medieval civilization was its hospital care. The roots of this care for both Christians and Muslims were in ancient Greece and Rome. Greek hospitals, clinics, and temples dedicated to medical treatment continued in the Roman period under the names *hospitalis* and *hospitalia.*

Christianity built on this Greco-Roman foundation. As buildings near the temple of Asklepios—the god of healing—in Athens served as hospitals for the ancient Greeks, so hospitals in the Christian world were built near churches and monasteries. After the conquests of Islam brought Byzantine lands under Muslim rule, Christian hospitals served as models for extensive hospital construction by Muslims during the Middle Ages.

Byzantine Hospitals. From the beginning of the BYZANTINE EMPIRE, emperors, members of the imperial family, bishops, and wealthy individuals were active in the construction of hospitals in such cities as Constantinople, Alexandria, Antioch, and Jerusalem.

In 335, CONSTANTINE I THE GREAT issued a decree calling for the building of hospitals in Constantinople, Rome, Ephesus, and other cities, and later emperors issued similar decrees. Basil the Great, bishop of Caesarea in Cappadocia, and John Chrysostom, archbishop of Constantinople, built hospitals too.

Medical care also was provided in homes for the elderly and shelters set up to receive strangers, pilgrims, and poor travelers. In fact, in the Byzantine world, the terms *hostel** and *hospital* soon came to mean the same thing. Eyewitness accounts of the fall of Constantinople, in 1453, reported the destruction of many hospitals and clinics.

* **hostel** lodging place or inn

Individuals, churches, monasteries, and certain organizations provided relief to the poor. Emperors, empresses, bishops, priests, monks, and people of all ranks actively helped the poor. On special days—such as coronations, anniversaries, and returns from military victories—the emperor distributed money and corn to the poor. He also distributed bread

Religious orders and church groups were among those who played an important part in the growth of hospitals, nursing care, and relief for the poor. In western Europe, many hospitals were built outside of monasteries and were administered by monks and nuns.

* **diocese** church district under a bishop's authority

* **hospice** house, often kept by monks, where travelers could stop and rest

and clothes to the victims of natural disasters. Female members of the imperial court were especially involved in aiding widows, orphans, and others in need.

Byzantines were expected to follow the example of God's love *(philanthropia)* by providing charity to the poor. The church had the primary responsibility for such aid. Every diocese* and local congregation collected food and clothes and distributed them to the poor on Sundays. People made more generous contributions on Christmas, Easter, Pentecost, and the celebration of the Assumption of the Virgin. Private donations and funds from the government helped the church—usually the bishops—administer its relief programs. Some bishops compiled lists of poor people designated to receive regular help. In the early 600s, the church in Alexandria had a list of about 3,000 poor people who received some aid. In some monasteries, monks stood at the gate to help the poor, and the doors of the monastery's hospice* were always open to poor travelers.

Constantinople and many Byzantine provinces and towns had facilities called *ptocheia* and homes for the elderly. *Ptocheia* were special houses set aside to shelter poor people who were unable to work because of illness, physical injury, or other reasons beyond their control. Beginning with Constantine the Great, many emperors and empresses contributed to the creation and maintenance of these institutions. In addition, the Byzantine government assigned officials to find work for the unemployed, able-bodied poor. Healthy beggars who refused to work were expelled from the capital.

Islamic Hospitals.   Caring for the sick and poor was important in medieval Islamic society as well. The Muslim concern for those in need had its roots in the Judeo-Christian tradition of charity that preceded it. The

QUR'AN urged Muslims to help widows, orphans, travelers, and those in need. The giving of alms (charity) is one of the five pillars of Islam. (The other four are faith, prayer, fasting, and pilgrimage.)

Voluntary donations by individuals rather than government assistance was the basis of Islamic social welfare. Donations were in the form of endowments for mosques, schools, orphanages, hospitals, hospices, Sufi monasteries, the poor of MECCA and Medina, and even drinking fountains and bridges. Such endowments provided the poor and disabled with food, lodging, clothing, schooling, and medical care.

Jews and Christians in the Islamic Empire provided aid and social services to the members of their own communities. Jews actively helped the poor, especially with payment of the poll tax that Muslims had imposed on minorities inside the empire. Christians provided for sick and needy members of their community and set up special "houses for strangers" in the Byzantine Empire. The charitable work of Jews and Christians inspired Muslims to establish their own charitable organizations and hospitals.

* **caliph** religious and political head of an Islamic state

The earliest known example of Islamic charity was the care that the UMAYYAD caliph* al-Walid provided for lepers and blind people in Damascus in 707. The first major Islamic hospital was modeled on the Christian Nestorian hospital and medical school at Gundesapur in Khuzistan, where some of the Nestorians fled after being persecuted in the Byzantine Empire for HERESY. The early ABBASID caliphs in Baghdad summoned doctors from Gundesapur to build the first of the many great hospitals Muslims built in Baghdad, Damascus, Marrakesh, Egypt, and other places. In the late Middle Ages, SELJUK and OTTOMAN Turks continued the Muslim tradition of hospital construction.

In Islamic hospitals, medical care was free and generally available to all. The hospitals had both inpatient and outpatient services, separate wards for male and female patients, and sections devoted exclusively to surgery, eye diseases, the setting of broken bones, mental illness, and internal problems, such as fever and diarrhea. The Islamic hospital also had a pharmacy, a mosque, a library, lecture halls, kitchens, baths, and storerooms.

Although hospital service and poor relief declined in the late Middle Ages in both the Islamic and Christian worlds, medieval civilization set high standards and goals for those who followed.

Western European Hospitals.   In Europe, the development of hospitals and other public charities blossomed in the early 1100s. Before that time, hospitals had been relatively few in number, but by 1150 they were a common feature in most towns and many villages.

The dramatic change from at-home treatment to hospital care may have been connected with rapid population growth, the church reforms of Pope GREGORY VII, and the spread of UNIVERSITIES that increased the number of trained doctors. Certainly the sudden spread of leprosy* across Europe was the single most important factor, since about half the new hospitals were built to treat lepers (people with leprosy).

* **leprosy** chronic, infectious disease that affects the skin and nerves. It can lead to numbness, paralysis, and deformity.

Before 1100, there were only 21 hospitals in all of England, but by 1154 the number had risen to 113. England eventually had more hospital beds—about one bed for every 800 persons—than many parts of the

Medieval Hospital

The Pantokrator hospital in Constantinople, built in 1136 by Byzantine empress Irene, was attached to the monastery and church of the same name. It had 61 beds, as well as a home for the elderly, an outpatient service, a hostel, and a staff of 35 physicians as well as other staff. Two female physicians were in charge of the gynecological (women's medicine) ward. The hospital's diet was mostly vegetarian, and wine was offered in small quantities.

* **Low Countries** flat coastal lands west of Germany, now occupied by Belgium and the Netherlands

world today. In the 1300s, the number of English hospitals peaked at 700. Other European countries showed similar increases in hospital construction.

Many hospitals were built outside of MONASTERIES, which already had a tradition of helping people in distress. Other hospitals were supported by bishops and local nobles. Various religious orders and church groups also were important in the hospital and nursing-care movement. The most famous of these was the Order of the Hospital of St. John of Jerusalem, or Knights Hospitalers, a military-style order that helped crusaders and Christians in the Holy Land. This order operated a huge hospital in JERUSALEM that could treat 2,000 patients, and it operated many community houses elsewhere.

Several nursing groups evolved into regular religious communities, such as the Antonines (founded around 1100) and the Order of the Holy Spirit (founded about 1145). Groups of women called BEGUINES (founded about 1170) did important nursing work in the Low Countries*.

Institutions such as hospitals, monasteries, parishes, and even universities also helped the poor. For many centuries, the church had issued proclamations calling for poor relief. Many of these decrees were first compiled in 1140 in a book of laws called the *Decretum*. These laws stated that the poor deserved respect and were entitled to support from society, including free legal counsel and free education at cathedral schools. In response, the church funded local parishes to provide this relief. In many ways, the poor of the 12th and 13th centuries were better aided than in most other centuries. However, by the later Middle Ages, a number of factors—including the movement of people to cities, the Black Death, and the Hundred Years War—filled the roads with homeless families. As a result, local parishes and institutions became increasingly unable to meet the needs of the poor. In many cases, governments gradually assumed responsibility for the poor and for hospitals and public health. (*See also* **Christianity; Islam, Religion of; Knights, Orders of; Medicine.**)

Hrabanus Maurus

ca. 780–856
Teacher, writer, abbot, and archbishop

* **clergy** priests, deacons, and other church officials qualified to perform church ceremonies

Hrabanus was one of the leading scholars and teachers of the CAROLINGIAN era. His work as a teacher at the palace school in AACHEN and his scholarly writings earned him the title *Praeceptor Germaniae* (Teacher of Germany).

Hrabanus was born in Mainz, Germany, where he also spent the last part of his life as archbishop. Hrabanus studied under ALCUIN OF YORK, adviser to Charlemagne and head of the palace school. He wrote a major 22-volume work called *De rerum naturis (Concerning Natural Things)* and many commentaries on the BIBLE. He also wrote the influential *De institutione clericorum (Concerning the Education of the Clergy*), based on the works of AUGUSTINE, BEDE, CASSIODORUS, GREGORY I THE GREAT, and other Christian writers. In an age when it took months or even years to obtain a copy of a rare text, Hrabanus's work of writing single encyclopedic texts that drew material from many important works and made them available to interested readers filled a real need in educating the next generation of the clergy.

* **abbot** male leader of a monastery or abbey. The female equivalent is an abbess.

For much of his career, Hrabanus was abbot* of the important monastery at Fulda. His religious enthusiasm, however, led to a confrontation with one of his monks that damaged Hrabanus's otherwise admirable career. The monk, Gottschalk of Orbais, had been entrusted to the care of the monastery at an early age and displayed great talent as a poet. When Gottschalk declared he was unsure he wanted to be a monk, Hrabanus grew impatient with him and forced the young man to become a monk against his will. Later, as punishment for his religious views, Hrabanus had Gottschalk imprisoned for life in the monastery at Hautvillers. (*See also* **Encyclopedias and Dictionaries; Latin Language.**)

Hrotswitha von Gandersheim

ca. 935–ca. 1001
Poet and dramatist

* **duchy** territory ruled by a duke or a duchess
* **rhetoric** art of speaking or writing effectively

* **martyr** person who suffers and dies rather than renounce a religious faith

* **pagan** word used by Christians to mean non-Christian and believing in several gods

Hrotswitha von Gandersheim was the earliest and most learned female poet of the early medieval period. She was also the first dramatist since the decline of the classical theater of ancient Greece and Rome.

Born of a noble German family, Hrotswitha entered the Benedictine monastery of Gandersheim in the duchy* of Saxony in 955. Gandersheim was a center of learning, and Hrotswitha benefitted from its lively intellectual climate. She read works of the Roman poets Virgil and Ovid, as well as works of early Christian writers. She received thorough training in the trivium (grammar, rhetoric*, and logic) and in the quadrivium (arithmetic, geometry, astronomy, and music). Above all, Hrotswitha was steeped in the lives of the saints.

Hrotswitha's literary works include eight sacred poems, six dramas, and two historical poems. Her sacred poems, which recount the lives of the saints and the deaths of Christian martyrs*, are outstanding examples of the most popular style of the period. The dramas are Hrotswitha's most important and original literary works. She was the first Christian writer to rediscover ancient classical drama and to use it to create a new literary form—plays in rhymed prose. Hrotswitha used the worldly comedies of Roman dramatist Terence as a model and substituted for his sinful dialogue between pagan* lovers the retellings of the sufferings, loves, and redemption of virtuous Christian youths. The subjects of her plays provide an example of how to achieve a perfect Christian life. Hrotswitha's two historical poems deal with the events of the reign of the first German emperor, OTTO I THE GREAT, and the history of Gandersheim from its founding to 919. (*See also* **Saints, Lives of.**)

Hundred Years War

* **siege** long and persistent effort to force a surrender by surrounding a fortress with armed troops, cutting it off from aid

The Hundred Years War is the name given to the series of wars the kings of England and France fought between 1337 and 1453. The wars consisted of sieges*, raids, sea battles, a few land battles, and long periods of truce. The periodic outbreaks of the Hundred Years War were part of the long and sometimes bitter rivalry between England and France that lasted from the 11th century to the 19th century.

Phases. The Hundred Years War consisted of three major phases. The first (1337–1360) was marked by English victories in France and alliances

Periodic outbreaks of fighting during the Hundred Years War occupied French and English troops from the mid-1300s to the mid-1400s. This illumination from Jehan Froissart's *Chronicles* shows soldiers looting the house of a wealthy Paris merchant. By the time the fighting stopped in 1453, French forces had driven England from all areas of France except the city of Calais.

* **feudal** referring to the social, economic, and political system that flourished in western Europe during the Middle Ages

Teenage Heroine

Joan of Arc lived during the Hundred Years War at a time when the fortunes of France were at their lowest. After she convinced others that she was destined to deliver France, she led a French force that defeated the English and lifted the siege of Orleans. Her leadership and example inspired further French victories.

After Joan was captured, a church court tried her for heresy in the English-held city of Rouen. The court found her guilty and had her burned at the stake on May 30, 1431. She was 19.

with important French feudal* lords. The naval battle of Sluis in 1340 and the subsequent sea battles paved the way for the successful English siege of Calais in 1346–1347. The victory of EDWARD THE BLACK PRINCE at Poitiers in 1356 solidified the vast territorial gains made by the English in northern France during the first part of the war.

The second phase of the war (1360–1413) consisted mainly of English inactivity, but French raids kept England on the defensive. The third and final phase (1413–1453) began with dramatic English gains but ended with England's nearly complete withdrawal from France.

The brilliant victory of King HENRY V OF ENGLAND at Agincourt in 1415, his conquest of Normandy, his marriage to the French princess Catherine of Valois, and his alliance with BURGUNDY in 1420 placed England in a commanding position. However, the lifting of the English siege of Orleans by French fighters under the inspirational leadership of JOAN OF ARC and the coronation of CHARLES VII OF FRANCE turned the tide of the war. By the early 1450s, French forces succeeded in driving the English from most of France. When the disheartened English saw no hope of regaining their French possessions, they gave up and returned home in 1453, leaving only a small garrison to defend the city of Calais.

Characteristics. A surprisingly small amount of time, men, and money was taken up in actual combat. The combined major battles of the war probably lasted a little more than two weeks. Individual battles usually lasted only a day, often less, and most battles involved fewer than 3,000 troops on each side.

Sieges were much more common. They were long, tedious affairs that often dragged on for years. Henry V's mastery of the art of siege warfare was key to his success against the French in the early 1400s.

Medieval fortification consisted of towns encircled by high stone walls and corner lookout towers. Attack featured blockades to starve out the defenders, digging tunnels under the walls, and rolling great wooden towers close to the enemy's walls. From these towers, attackers used slings and catapults* to hurl rocks, flaming arrows, and filth into the town. After 1400, the siege cannon became so effective that it led to the end of the castle and the fortified town.

The sea battles of the Hundred Years War usually involved 20 to 50 ships that resembled floating castles with their slings, catapults, archers, and armed men ready for hand-to-hand combat. The French sometimes succeeded in disrupting supply lines by attacking English convoys crossing the English Channel, but generally English naval forces held the upper hand.

Effects.   During the Hundred Years War, the culture of chivalry* and KNIGHTHOOD thrived, especially in the court of the dukes of Burgundy. Biographies, such as the one about Edward the Black Prince by Sir John Chandos, emphasized heroic virtues and chivalric ideals. The war also inspired poems, patriotic songs, tournaments, and scholarly and historical writings about war, pacifism, royal power, and individual liberties. However, the occasional raids that continued in France during periods of formal truce devastated that country economically. (*See also* **Brittany, Duchy of; Crusades; Heraldry; Normans; Warfare; Weapons.**)

* **catapult** medieval military device for hurling missiles, such as stones

* **chivalry** rules and customs of medieval knighthood

Hungary

The medieval kingdom of Hungary was centered on the plains of the Danube and Tisza Rivers in central-eastern Europe. It included the mountainous regions of modern Slovakia, Ukraine, and Romania. The land was fertile, rich in minerals, and strategically located between the Byzantine Empire and western Europe. Essentially independent and unified throughout the Middle Ages, the kingdom of Hungary survived until the 1500s, when it was defeated and occupied by the Ottoman Turks.

Magyar Origins.   Until the mid-300s, a large part of what is now Hungary was part of the Roman Empire. From then until around 800, it was occupied by the HUNS and other barbarian tribes from the east. In the late 800s, the Magyars, a nomadic* people from beyond the Ural Mountains, conquered the region. Their leader, Árpád, established the first ruling dynasty of Hungary. The Magyar conquest was a crucial event. It marked the start of the Hungarian monarchy and laid the foundation for the political and religious transformation of eastern Europe.

For about 50 years, the Magyars raided neighboring areas and became the terror of Europe. These raids were a factor in the development of the Italian city-states* and in the growth of western Europe's feudal* system. Defeated by the Germans in 933 and again in 955, the Magyars ended their raids and began to transform Hungary into a Christian monarchy. From the mid-900s, Hungarian princes relied increasingly on feudal relationships and the labor of SERFS, or slaves. Meanwhile, both the

* **nomadic** wandering from place to place to find food and pasture

* **city-state** independent state consisting of a city and the territories around it
* **feudal** referring to the social, economic, and political system that flourished in western Europe during the Middle Ages

Beginning in the 1400s, Hungary faced an ever-growing threat from the Ottoman Turks. In 1526, Turkish forces under the command of Süleyman I defeated the Hungarians. Süleyman and his advisers are pictured here during the campaign against Hungary.

See color plate 10, vol. 3.

* **nobility** persons forming the noble class; aristocracy

* **parliament** meeting or assembly of elected or appointed representatives

* **habeas corpus** right of anyone arrested to know the crime with which he or she is charged or to be released

Western and the Eastern Churches attracted the Magyars and helped make Hungary a Christian kingdom. In the year 1000, STEPHEN I was crowned the first Christian monarch of Hungary. Stephen organized a royal administration and established the Roman Church as the official religion of the country.

The Christian Kingdom.   The Magyars built a strong monarchy that was more centralized and powerful than most of those in western Europe. Its strength, along with a rapid population growth, helped Hungary develop rapidly and catch up to the rest of Europe. By 1200, the country had been transformed from a backward society to one that was a full partner in medieval European culture and economics. The foundations established by Stephen I proved to be very stable and helped the kingdom survive through the years of internal conflict and foreign intervention that followed.

The period from Stephen's death in 1038 until the 1100s was marked by repeated civil wars, usually caused by struggles over who would inherit the throne. Yet the country experienced enough stability during the reigns of Kings Ladislas I (1077–1095) and Coloman (1095–1116) to expand its borders. Both monarchs issued laws protecting private property, enforcing Christianity, and safeguarding trade. The reign of Coloman's son, Stephen II (1116–1131), was disastrous. He spent much of his efforts on unsuccessful foreign campaigns. This enabled Hungarian nobles to increase their own power and provided them with a reason to challenge his rule.

For several decades in the mid-1100s, Hungary found itself in the middle of a great struggle between the Holy Roman Emperor, FREDERICK I BARBAROSSA, and the Byzantine emperor, Manuel I Komnenos. Both rulers became involved in Hungary's internal politics and contributed to a period of great instability. Despite such instability and internal strife, the settlement of Hungary and the changes in its society continued. During the reign of Géza II (1141–1162), large groups of settlers came to Hungary from France, Germany, and other parts of western Europe. These settlers received special privileges to ensure their loyalty to the crown. At the same time, Arab traders and travelers in Hungary contributed to a flourishing economy. Under Béla III who reigned from 1172 to 1196, Hungary came into close contact with western Europe, particularly France. Béla's reign increased the power and prestige of the nobility*, and his administrative reforms helped create a rich and well-organized monarchy.

The monarchy declined sharply during the reign of Béla's son Andrew II (1205–1235). Andrew's ill-conceived campaigns against Galicia (a region in present-day Poland and Ukraine) drained the treasury and turned many of the nobles against the king. In 1222, the nobles rose up against Andrew and forced him to issue the Golden Bull. This document limited the king's power and established the beginnings of a parliament*. Among the provisions of the Golden Bull were a guarantee of the right of habeas corpus*, a limitation on military obligations, exemption from taxes, and the right of nobles to resist any infringement of their rights. The Golden Bull is considered the cornerstone of Hungary's constitution—much like MAGNA CARTA in England.

See map in Ottomans and Ottoman Empire (vol. 3).

* **principality** region that is ruled by a prince

Origin of Hungary

The name *Hungary* might have been derived from *Huns*, the early settlers of the region. But a more likely explanation is that the seven original Magyar tribes and the three Khazar tribes that were their allies were known collectively as the On–Ogur, or Ten Arrows, and the Slavic pronunciation of *On–Ogur* is very nearly *Hungary*. Today, more than 90 percent of Hungarians consider the Magyars their ancestors.

The Mongol and Ottoman Invasions. In the spring of 1241, an invasion of the Mongols nearly destroyed Hungary. The Mongol forces stormed into the country, devastating the land, destroying thousands of villages, and killing or enslaving more than half the population. Only the death of the Great Khan, the Mongols' supreme leader in Asia, later that year stopped the Mongol advance. The Mongols retreated and never again threatened the region.

The reconstruction of Hungary after the Mongol invasion led to a rebirth of the country. New castles were built and fortified, and special freedoms were given to many towns. During this period, the power of the nobles greatly increased. Mighty families established small principalities* and began to challenge the power of the monarchy. To balance the rising power of the nobility, the Hungarian monarchs called for representative assemblies so that all groups could air their concerns. The local independence of nobles and their participation in government through representatives remained an important feature of Hungarian politics well beyond the Middle Ages.

During the 1300s, the monarchy regained much of the power it had lost to the nobles. The rulers of this period revived the economy and promoted a version of FEUDALISM in which nobles provided defense in exchange for guarantees of the basic liberties granted by the Golden Bull. Advances in agriculture, population growth, and increased international trade encouraged urban growth, and Hungary reached its greatest territorial extent.

Throughout the 1400s and 1500s, Hungary faced a new threat—the Ottoman Turks. The kingdom built up its defenses, and Hungarian forces waged several successful campaigns against the enemy. In the end, however, the Turks were victorious. At the Battle of Mohács on August 29, 1526, Turkish forces under the command of Sultan Süleyman I the Magnificent defeated the Hungarians. This battle is generally regarded as the end of medieval Hungary. In the years that followed, Hungary was divided into three parts, two ruled by the Ottomans and one by the Austrians. This partition lasted for more than 150 years. (*See also* **Genghis Khan; Holy Roman Empire; Komnenos Family; Mongol Empire; Ottomans and Ottoman Empire; Sigismund, Emperor.**)

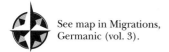

Huns

See map in Migrations, Germanic (vol. 3).

The Huns were a group of tribes from Asia who terrorized Europe for almost a century, beginning in the late 300s. Their migration westward across Asia prior to the Middle Ages pushed the Germanic tribes ahead of them into the Roman Empire. Then the Huns themselves crossed into the empire and, under the leadership of Attila, plundered Gaul and northern Italy.

The Huns migrated from the northern frontier of China across western Siberia and Khazakhstan toward Mesopotamia and Europe. Along the way, various Turkic, Iranian, and Magyar peoples attached themselves to the tribal confederation. After they crossed the Volga and Don Rivers, the Huns defeated the OSTROGOTHS in 375 and then launched major raids deep into Roman territory.

Since the Huns were a loose collection of tribes, they lacked strong central leadership. For example, in the early 400s, some Huns fought against the Romans while others fought with them against German tribes. After a power struggle among the tribal leaders of the Huns, two brothers—Attila and Bleda—emerged as the leaders in the late 430s. In 445, after Attila murdered his brother, the Huns were united. Under his rule, the Huns raided the Roman Empire until the Romans defeated them in Gaul in 451. The following year, Attila invaded northern Italy and threatened ROME before a personal appeal by Pope Leo I convinced him to withdraw his warriors. Following the death of Attila in 453, many of his subjects rebelled, and the Huns broke up into different tribal groupings. (*See also* **Migrations, Germanic.**)

Hunting and Fowling

* **nobility** persons forming the noble class; aristocracy

* **castration** removal of testicles

* **cudgel** short, thick stick or club used as a weapon

* **falconry** sport of hunting with trained falcons

* **hawking** sport of hunting with trained hawks

In medieval Europe, hunting and fowling (hunting for birds) were important activities, particularly among the nobility*. At times, wild game was an important source of nourishment. Yet, hunting for the purpose of obtaining food generally was considered of secondary importance to the hunt, or chase, itself and the festivities associated with it. The hunt provided medieval nobles with an opportunity to display their skill with weapons, and it served as a training for war. The hunt also served as a social activity and a means of recreation.

All social classes in medieval Europe hunted. However, with the rise of FEUDALISM, the nobility began claiming the exclusive right to this activity, especially big game hunting, and nobles made great efforts to restrict the privilege. In the kingdom of the FRANKS, for example, the MEROVINGIAN and CAROLINGIAN monarchs controlled vast hunting reserves and restricted access to them. Offenders were disciplined and often fined. In England under the NORMANS, a large administration was created to oversee the royal forests and to enforce forest laws against hunting. Those who broke the laws were subject to extremely harsh penalties that included blinding, castration*, and even death. The forest laws of the Normans became a source of conflict between the king and the English barons, who saw the laws as an abuse of royal power.

Medieval hunters used a variety of weapons, including bows and arrows, spears, swords, knives, and cudgels* for clubbing small game. Although hunting was largely a male pursuit, women often joined the chase, especially the social activities and festivities surrounding it. Of the women who actually hunted, few hunted for large animals. Many noblewomen, however, became proficient in falconry* and hawking*, and the image of a lady with a hawk on her fist was a well-known theme in medieval art.

While hunting generally was restricted to the nobility, peasants and ordinary people hunted as well, although usually in secret or perhaps openly in remote villages. The lower classes did not hunt for sport; they hunted for food and furs, either for their own use or for sale in markets. The opportunity to hunt depended largely on the authorities in a particular locale. Even in areas where the lower classes were allowed to hunt, hunting usually was strictly controlled. Peasants more often trapped and snared their prey than hunted it. Big game animals could be snared by using screens or nets, self-releasing spears, pitfalls, or nooses attached to a bent tree or branch to ensnare and hang the animals by their paws. Small game could be taken with snares or by stretching nets or pouches over the entrances to their burrows. Even small birds could be snared by using long-hinged sticks that snapped shut with a string to catch the birds' feet.

Because of its importance in medieval life, hunting was a popular theme in medieval literature and art. References to hunting were quite common especially in the courtly romances written for the nobility. Since skill in hunting was considered an essential quality of the ideal knight, the heroes in medieval romances often were shown hunting. Many romances began or ended with a hunt, and hunting often introduced key episodes in the story. In the late 1100s, authors frequently used hunting as a metaphor* for love—courtship became a chase in which the lover (hunter) pursues the beloved (prey). Hunting also was the subject of a number of manuals published in the late 1200s. These manuals provided such information as descriptions of wild animals, instructions for hunting, and descriptions of various kinds of hunting implements. One 13th-century work, *On Hunting with Birds* by Holy Roman Emperor FREDERICK II, stood out as a masterpiece on the subject of falconry. In medieval art, idealized scenes of nobles engaged in hunting were depicted in stained glass windows, in murals, on tapestries, and in illuminated manuscripts.

In the Islamic world, hunting grew out of a tradition quite different from that of western Europe. For the nomadic* Arabs of pre-Islamic times, hunting was an important source of meat. Armed with bows and arrows and aided by dogs, these Arabs hunted a variety of large and small animals. With the introduction of Islam, complicated rules developed about the ritual killing of animals, and these rules affected the nature of the hunt.

After the Islamic conquests, hunting increasingly was engaged in as a sport. Islam encouraged sport hunting as a means of training for the JIHAD, or holy war. Through hunting, Muslims gained fitness and courage, good horsemanship, and skill with various weapons. The development of the sport owed much to the Persians and the Turks, who were superb horsemen and archers. From the late 600s, the UMAYYADS and ABBASIDS practiced large-scale hunting, often spending vast sums on spectacular hunts, the purchase and training of birds of prey, and the creation of fine game reserves.

The Muslims were especially fond of falconry and hawking, and they trained different types of hawks and falcons to hunt. Sometimes these birds of prey were used in cooperation with dogs. They might, for example, be trained to attack large prey in order to slow it down and make it an easier target for dogs. Keen-scented dogs would be used to flush birds from hiding so that the falcons or hawks could attack them in the air.

Some Muslims earned a living through hunting, but it was primarily a sport for kings and the rich. Only they could afford to train and keep the finest birds and beasts of prey. One of the most prized beasts of prey was the cheetah. Used by Muslim rulers and dignitaries from the late 600s, the cheetah was introduced to the courts of western Europe in the 1300s. (*See also* **Bestiary; Books, Manuscript; Forests; Tapestries.**)

* **metaphor** literary device in which an idea is suggested using words or phrases that literally mean something else

* **nomadic** wandering from place to place to find food and pasture

Medieval hunters used a variety of weapons to kill their game. They also used dogs, which were especially effective with larger animals, such as deer. This hunting scene is from the *Très riches heures* of Jean, duke of Berry.

Hus, Jan

ca. 1373–1415
Religious reformer and
Czech national leader

* **theology** study of the nature of God and of religious truth

Jan Hus was a religious reformer who was condemned as a heretic and burned at the stake. His religious ideas, which criticized various church practices, made him a forerunner of the Protestant Reformation. His support of anti-German policies in his homeland of Bohemia (part of the modern-day Czech Republic) made him a national leader and a hero to the Czech people.

Hus was born around 1373 to a peasant family in the Bohemian village of Husinec. He studied theology* at the University of Prague, received ordination as a priest around 1400, and was appointed preacher of the university's Bethlehem Chapel in 1402. He became head of the university in 1409.

Hus promoted two causes during his lifetime: greater Czech presence in the University of Prague (which was dominated by Germans); and the reform of church practices as called for in the writings of the English theologian John WYCLIF. In 1348, King Charles IV of Bohemia founded the University of Prague. Although it was initially dominated by Germans, steady pressure from Czech students and faculty led to greater Czech control. Hus played an important role in this campaign. As a popular and

Jan Hus was a Czech religious reformer who supported the ideas of English theologian John Wyclif. After his condemnation at the Council of Constance in 1414, he was burned at the stake for heresy.

influential citizen of Prague, he also helped persuade King Wenceslas IV of Bohemia to replace a German majority in the town government with a Czech one.

The Czech academics at the University of Prague, including Hus, were deeply involved in the movement for reform of the Catholic Church. Hus had preached eloquently against such church abuses as immoral behavior of the clergy. He also opposed the sale of INDULGENCES, or substitutions that could be bought to avoid performing a penance—a task set by the church in order to earn God's forgiveness for a sin. His protests against the burning of Wyclif's works by the archbishop of Prague in 1410 and his support of certain of Wyclif's ideas created a serious rift between him and the church that eventually extended to the king. In 1412, Hus was forced to leave Prague. During his exile, he wrote his most important work, *De ecclesia (On the Church)*, in which he used many of Wyclif's ideas to argue for the reform of the church and a return to a purer and simpler religious order.

In 1414, Hus was summoned to the Council of Constance to defend his religious ideas. After weeks of fruitless debate (the council was already convinced of his guilt), Hus was condemned as a heretic and was sentenced to death. On July 6, 1415, he was taken outside the city and burned at the stake. His death provoked a revolt by his followers, the Hussites, and years of war between them and the church and between Czechs and Germans. (*See also* **Bohemia-Moravia; Heresy and Heresies; Prague.**)

Husayn ibn Ali, al-

626–680
Grandson of Muhammad and imam of Shi'ites

* **Shi'ites** Muslims who believed that Muhammad chose Ali and his descendants as the rulers and spiritual leaders of the Islamic community

* **caliph** religious and political head of an Islamic state

* **Sunnites** Muslim majority who believed that the caliphs should rule the Islamic community

The son of MUHAMMAD's daughter Fatima and of the Prophet's cousin ALI IBN ABI TALIB, al-Husayn is recognized by the Shi'ite* Muslim sect as the third IMAM, or spiritual and political leader. His martyrdom at the Battle of Karbala on October 10, 680, contributed to the development of the Shi'ite movement.

Born in Medina in 626, al-Husayn was generally uninvolved in Muslim politics, despite a legitimate claim to leadership. Following the death of the caliph* MU'AWIYA in 680, al-Husayn reluctantly agreed to support a Shi'ite revolt against Mu'awiya's son and heir, YAZID I IBN MU'AWIYA. The revolt focused on the city of Al-Kufa, a Shi'ite stronghold in Iraq. Hoping to prevent a challenge to his authority, Yazid sent forces to prevent al-Husayn and his followers from reaching the city. The caliph's forces surrounded the group at a place called Karbala. After attempts to negotiate a settlement failed, the entire group (except for al-Husayn's young son Ali ibn al-Husayn) was massacred.

Al-Husayn's rebellion and death had profound political and religious implications. The murder of the Prophet's grandson shocked many Muslims, both Sunnite* and Shi'ite, and tarnished the reputation of the Umayyad dynasty. The rebellion provided an emotional focus for the Shi'ite movement, and commemoration of al-Husayn's martyrdom became an important part of Shi'ite ritual. (*See also* **Caliphate; Umayyads.**)

Ibn Battuta

1304–1368/77
Muslim world traveler and writer

Ibn Battuta was the greatest of the medieval world travelers. His journeys lasted longer and covered more miles than those of the great European traveler Marco Polo. His traveler's tales, dictated to a writer during his lifetime, provide vivid and detailed accounts of large areas of the medieval world during the 1300s.

Shams al-Din Muhammad ibn Abd Allah Ibn Battuta was born at Tangier in Morocco, North Africa, to a scholarly family. At age 21, he set out on a pilgrimage to the Muslim holy cities of MECCA and Medina. During this trip, he developed a passion for travel and exploration, and he did not return to Morocco for 24 years. Ibn Battuta traveled to southern Russia and through India, reached China, and made two separate trips deep into Africa. He also visited Mecca five times.

During 1325, his first year of travel, Ibn Battuta crossed North Africa to Egypt, where he visited three cities on the Nile: Alexandria, Cairo, and Luxor. He continued through what is now Israel and Lebanon to Syria. He reached Mecca and Medina the following year and spent the next three years in BAGHDAD and other centers in the Muslim Empire.

From Arabia, he journeyed down the coast of East Africa as far as what is now Tanzania. Then he returned to Mecca and started his longest trip—through Asia Minor, the Balkans, southern Russia, and central Asia to Afghanistan and India. He stayed in India almost ten years, working as an official in Delhi for some time. He then made his way through southern India and southeast Asia to China.

Ibn Battuta returned through the East Indies to the Persian Gulf. From there, he made his last pilgrimage to Mecca and Medina. Then, in 1349, he returned to Morocco—but not before visiting the ALHAMBRA in Muslim Spain. His travels still were not complete, however. In 1352, he made a journey across the vast Sahara desert in Africa to the ancient kingdom of Mali.

Finally, Ibn Battuta settled in North Africa. A Moroccan sultan commissioned a scholar to write down the great traveler's experiences in a work called the *Rihla*. In the *Rihla*, Ibn Battuta reports his impressions and reflections, describing everything from political events to types of cuisine. When Ibn Battuta told people at home about the different customs of the places he had visited, many of them thought he had made up these stories.

Ibn Hanbal

780–855
Major Islamic theologian

* **theology** study of the nature of God and of religious truth

* **Qur'an** book of the holy scriptures of Islam

* **eternal** having no beginning and no end; everlasting

Ahmad ibn Muhammad Ibn Hanbal was one of the most important scholars of religious law and theology* in the history of Islam. He was born and died in Baghdad. A small family inheritance enabled him to pursue his studies, which were concentrated on the hadith—stories about Islamic traditions and the prophet Muhammad's sayings and practices. Like other learned men of his time, Ibn Hanbal traveled throughout the Islamic world in order to study the hadith with important scholars.

Ibn Hanbal argued that the Qur'an* and the hadith were the only legitimate sources of Islamic law; he opposed the use of philosophical thinking in interpreting the law. He was involved in a major controversy regarding whether the Qur'an is the eternal*, uncreated word of God or whether it was created by God. The former position was the belief of orthodox Sunnite Islam; the latter was the view of the Mu'tazilite philosopher-theologians who had the support of the ABBASID caliph al-MA'MUN. The caliph instituted a minor inquisition in 833, during which Ibn Hanbal maintained the Sunnite position despite torture and imprisonment. He was released after two years and refrained from public lectures until 848, when a new caliph, al-Mutawakkil, declared the Mu'tazilite position a heresy*. Near the end of his life, Ibn Hanbal was invited to tutor the new caliph's son. But he excused himself because of age and failing health, and he lived the rest of his life quietly outside palace circles. (*See also* **Islam, Religion of; Qur'an.**)

* **heresy** belief that is contrary to church doctrine

Ibn Khaldun
1332–1406
Historian

* **scribe** person who hand-copies manuscripts to preserve them

Ibn Khaldun combined the practical ambitions of political life with the learning of a scribe* and a historian. While traveling throughout the Islamic world of the Mediterranean, he studied the rise and decline of civilizations and developed a theory of history. He then moved to Egypt because, according to his theory, Egypt offered the best prospects for a stable career.

Wali al-Din Abd al-Rahman ibn Muhammad Ibn Khaldun was born to a scholarly Islamic family in Tunis, North Africa. He was trained as a scribe, but because of his quarrelsome nature and taste for intrigue, he had a difficult time staying with one master. Between 1352 and 1375, he worked at various courts in North Africa and Spain. In 1375, he lost his job and retired for a period of study and contemplation.

Between 1376 and 1379, Ibn Khaldun wrote a *History of the Berbers* and the *Muqaddima,* an introduction to his history of Islam. He developed a theory of the rise and fall of civilizations that is still admired for its originality and insight. He traced the strength of a civilization to what he called *asabiya,* meaning loyalty to the group's values and interests. Civilizations flourish for a time but must eventually decline and collapse, to be replaced by new cultures. In some cases, Ibn Khaldun said, the fall of a civilization is not completely ruinous. Cities, skills, ideas, and religions survive the fall.

Ibn Khaldun believed that civilizations in the eastern Islamic world, especially Egypt, were more stable and long-lasting than those of the West. In 1382, he moved to Egypt to resume his public career. For the rest of his life, he held a series of posts as historian, scholar, teacher, judge, and administrator, always looking for the proper balance between the quiet, scholarly life and the excitement of politics. (*See also* **Berbers; Historical Writing.**)

Ibn Khurdadhbih
ca. 820–ca. 912
Geographer

Ibn Khurdadhbih, called the "father of Islamic geography," was a court official for the Abbasids. His account of the roads and kingdoms of his day became the model for Islamic geographers. Officially, Ibn Khurdadhbih was director of the post office in BAGHDAD, a capital city of the eastern Islamic world. He oversaw the sending of mail from one point to another—a job that was close to intelligence work today. Sending messages was not easy, and routes were not always well-known. Ibn Khurdadhbih's special knowledge of how to travel from one place to another made him a pioneer geographer.

Ibn Khurdadhbih wrote several works that have not survived, including books on food and drink and two books on manners. Some quotations from an account of Persian genealogy and from a history have survived, but his most complete and important work is the *Book of Routes and Kingdoms,* the earliest surviving work by an Islamic geographer. It describes the borders, peoples, and countries of the world as Ibn Khurdadhbih knew it, especially the Islamic world. The area where he lived and worked (now called Iraq) became the center of his geography, and he described it and the six great kingdoms that surrounded it. The *Book of Routes and Kingdoms* included colorful tales of curiosities, customs, and traditions of other places. However, it was mainly a work of administrative geography, containing information important for delivering the mail. (*See also* **Postal Services.**)

Ibn Rushd

1126–1198
Philosopher, physician,
and astronomer

Ibn Rushd was a well-known learned man of Muslim Spain. Known as Averroës in the West, Ibn Rushd possessed a keen analytical mind. His written commentaries on the teachings of the Greek philosopher Aristotle influenced numerous medieval and Renaissance thinkers. His influence extended to Jewish thought as well.

Born in the Spanish city of CÓRDOBA to an intellectual and cultured family, Ibn Rushd studied Islamic law and theology. In 1163, a fellow philosopher recommended Ibn Rushd to the Muslim ruler of Spain to write commentaries on Aristotle's work. In 1182, he became chief physician at the royal court and remained there until falling out of favor sometime after 1195. Ibn Rushd was exiled and his books burned. He was reinstated, however, and he then remained in his post until his death in 1198.

Ibn Rushd was a well-known philosopher who lived in Muslim Spain during the 1100s. Known in the West as Averroës, he is most famous for his Arabic commentaries on the teachings of the Greek philosopher Aristotle.

The writings of Ibn Rushd include important books on Islamic law and medicine. He tried to harmonize philosophy and religion by arguing that Islamic law commands the study of philosophy because it leads to the proof of the existence of God. Ibn Rushd's influence continued long after his death. Thomas AQUINAS respected his teachings but attacked Ibn Rushd's argument that philosophic truth comes from reason and not from faith. (*See also* **Aristotle in the Middle Ages; Ibn Sina; Islam, Religion of; Scholasticism.**)

Ibn Sina

980–1037
Physician, scholar, and poet

* **metaphysics** branch of philosophy concerned with the fundamental nature of reality

* **pharmacology** science of drugs, their properties, uses, and effects

The works of Ibn Sina (known in the West as Avicenna) cover many branches of knowledge, including philosophy, medicine, grammar, sociology, and politics. His *al-Qanun fi'l-tibb (The Canon of Medicine)*, a famous treatise on medicine, is still used today in parts of the world.

Ibn Sina was a great Islamic scholar and thinker who was known in the West as Avicenna. Born in the Persian city of Bukhara, Ibn Sina at an early age developed an amazing mastery of the QUR'AN and Islamic religious studies. By the age of 16, he was already a well-known physician. After he successfully treated the Samanid prince, he was allowed to use the royal library, where he continued his studies in various subjects.

By the time he was 21, Ibn Sina was in demand as a physician and scholar by rulers near and far. After Mahmud of Ghazna captured Bukhara, Ibn Sina left his native city and traveled from one Persian city to another, working either as a court physician or a government official. When he did not find the peaceful scholarly life he wanted, he accepted the invitation of a Buyid prince, Shams al-Dawla, to go to Hamadan in western Persia. There he served the prince as his court physician and vizier (minister of state).

After the death of Shams al-Dawla in 1022, Ibn Sina left Hamadan for Isfahan, where he remained for 14 years—the longest uninterrupted period in his adult life. Besides serving as court physician, he also taught in a local school and wrote most of his works—276 in all. Ranging from a massive encyclopedia to short essays of only a few pages, his works cover nearly every branch of knowledge from philosophy and medicine to grammar, sociology, and politics.

His monumental *Kitab al-shifa (The Book of Healing)* is divided into four sections—logic, natural philosophy, mathematics, and metaphysics*. It was the largest encyclopedia of knowledge composed by one person in the Middle Ages. Ibn Sina also wrote a shorter version of this monumental work called *Kitab al-najat (The Book of Deliverance)*. His last major philosophical work and his most personal statement about his views was *Kitab al-isharat wa'l-tanbihat (The Book of Directives and Remarks)*. His other important philosophical works included *The Book of Guidance, Fountains of Wisdom, The Book of Origin and End,* and the visionary *Treatise of the Bird.*

Ibn Sina also wrote several medical texts. The most important and influential is *al-Qanun fi'l-tibb (The Canon of Medicine)*. It is possibly the most famous work in the history of medicine. Its five volumes cover the principles and practice of medicine, diseases of the organs, diseases not confined to a specific organ, and drugs. After being translated into Latin, the work served as the bible of medicine in the West almost up to the modern period, and it continues to be used in India and the Islamic world. Among Ibn Sina's 40 other medical works is *al-Urjuza fi'l-tibb (Poem on Medicine)*, which medical students used to memorize the principles of medicine and pharmacology*.

Ibn Sina also wrote a number of short essays on mystical and religious subjects, including commentaries on the Qur'an. In addition, he was an accomplished poet in both Arabic and Persian. Many of his poems about philosophical and medical subjects have survived to this day.

In 1037, while accompanying the ruler of Isfahan, Ala al-Dawla, on a military campaign, Ibn Sina fell ill. He died of a stomach spasm in Hamadan shortly afterwards. His mausoleum*, rebuilt in the 1950s, is one of the major sites of historical interest in IRAN today. (*See also* **Arabic Language and Literature; Medicine.**)

* **mausoleum** memorial building to house a tomb

Ibn Taymiya

1263–1328
Scholar and teacher

One of the most influential thinkers of the medieval Islamic world was al-Shaykh Taqi al-Din Ahmad ibn Taymiya. Authorities were distressed both by his ideas and by his pronouncements, which aroused public controversy and disorder.

Ibn Taymiya grew up as a refugee from Mongol invaders. The MAMLUK rulers at first provided shelter to him and his family, and he spent most of his life in DAMASCUS and Cairo. There he studied and became an expert in the religious tradition of IBN HANBAL. During the crisis years from 1299 to 1303, when the Mongols threatened the very survival of the Mamluks, he was a leader of the political resistance and was ardent in denouncing the faith of the Mongols.

Ibn Taymiya first came to the attention of the Mamluk authorities in 1293, when he protested a sentence against a Christian who was charged with having insulted the prophet MUHAMMAD. In 1313, Ibn Taymiya returned to Damascus to resume teaching. His opinions on Islamic law, particularly divorce, again earned him the displeasure of government officials. Defying an order to remain silent on this issue, he was imprisoned for five months. In 1326, he attacked the popular practice of visiting the tombs of saints. When he continued to circulate his views from prison, he was denied pen and paper. He died in prison a few months later. His funeral turned into a great public demonstration of mourning, and his tomb became a pilgrimage* site. His writings are still considered important in some areas of the Muslim world, particularly in Saudi Arabia. (*See also* **Caliphate; Mongol Empire; Sunna.**)

* **pilgrimage** journey to a shrine or sacred place

Iceland

See *Scandinavia.*

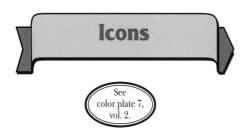

Icons

See color plate 7, vol. 2.

Icons are images of holy figures or events painted on wooden panels or walls. Especially prominent in Orthodox Christianity, they are regarded by Eastern Christians as sacred objects of devotion before which the faithful pray, light candles, and offer incense. Icons are displayed in churches, monasteries, and homes. In Eastern Orthodox churches, icons often are displayed on an iconostasis, a large screen on which many icons are mounted in a particular order. Erected between the

* **sanctuary** part of the church around the altar

* **nave** main part of a church or cathedral between the side aisles

* **Hellenistic** period after Alexander the Great (356–323 B.C.) during which Greek ideas spread throughout the Mediterranean world

* **apostles** early followers of Jesus who traveled and spread his teachings

sanctuary* and the nave*, the iconostasis separates the worshipers from the ceremonies occurring at the altar and serves as the visible focus of worship for the congregation.

Portrait icons probably evolved from funeral portraits of the Hellenistic* era and from the emperors' portraits that were honored throughout the Roman Empire. By the early Middle Ages, icons had taken on a Christian significance, and they usually portrayed Jesus Christ, the Virgin Mary, the apostles*, the prophets, and the saints. A standard format for icons developed during the medieval period. This was characterized by half- or full-length figures presented frontally or in a three-quarter view against a flat background. Three-dimensional effects were played down in order to emphasize the spiritual nature of those represented rather than their human characteristics. Eventually, the rules of icon painting were codified and collected in special manuals, which icon painters were expected to follow closely.

Early Christians generally believed in the Old Testament laws against "graven images." Yet a religious art developed, which often portrayed

Icons, images of holy figures, became an important part of Eastern Orthodox Christianity and a predominant form of Byzantine art. This icon of *Christ the Savior, Source of Life* was painted by John Metropolitos in the late 1300s.

biblical events and people. Such artistic likenesses were common by the 400s. Images of Christ became especially popular. At the same time, however, some Christians remained opposed to the use of religious images and considered them a form of idolatry*. They argued that worship without images was purer and more spiritual. This argument erupted in the 700s, when the Byzantine Church was faced with a controversy known as iconoclasm.

The iconoclastic controversy began in 726, when the Byzantine emperor Leo III publicly condemned religious images. Leo ordered the destruction of all icons and began to persecute those who defended them. Leo's successor, Constantine V, continued these policies. Those who criticized the use of icons, called iconoclasts, based their arguments on the Second Commandment, which forbids the making of idols. They also argued that both God and his son, Jesus Christ, are undefinable and, therefore, impossible to represent as an image. Those who defended the use of icons argued that the Second Commandment was intended for Jews rather than Christians. They agreed with the iconoclasts that God is undefinable, but they argued that Christ was a real man who could be represented. Indeed, they believed that Christ should be represented so that all might know his human form. Those who defended icons also made a distinction between honoring an icon as an object worthy of respect and worshiping an icon, which would be a form of idolatry.

In 787, the Byzantine empress Irene convened the Second Council of Nicaea, which defended icons and justified them as objects worthy of respect. The controversy erupted again, however, in 814 under Emperor Leo V and continued until 842, when the iconoclastic view was finally defeated. Thereafter, icons became a significant feature of the Eastern Orthodox faith and an important component of BYZANTINE ART. (*See also* **Byzantine Empire; Christianity.**)

* **idolatry** worship of physical objects, such as an image, as a god

---

Illuminated Manuscripts

See *Books, Manuscript.*

Imam

I n the simplest sense, an imam is a man who leads Muslim worshipers in prayer. More broadly, an imam is the supreme political and religious leader of the Muslim community. The term *imam* means the same as the term *caliph*, except that *caliph* usually refers to nonreligious authority and *imam* refers to religious authority. *Imam* has different meanings for the Sunnite* and Shi'ite* Muslim sects.

Sunnites believe that the imam should be elected by the Muslim community or selected by a predecessor (a person who has previously occupied the position). There can be only one imam at a time, and he must be descended from the Quraysh, the Arab tribe to which MUHAMMAD belonged. Sunnites believe the imam must embody honesty and integrity and have knowledge of the shari'a, the religious law of Islam. The main task of the imam is to protect Islamic traditions and law and to defend the faith.

* **Sunnites** Muslim majority who believed that the caliphs should rule the Islamic community

* **Shi'ites** Muslims who believed that Muhammad chose Ali and his descendants as the rulers and spiritual leaders of the Islamic community

According to the Shi'ites, the imam is a spiritual as well as a religious and political leader. They believe that he is divinely guided by God and free from sin, and that he has, like Muhammad, perfect knowledge of all things. For Shi'ites, the imam must be a direct descendant of Muhammad. They reject the Sunnite idea that the imam can be elected, and they insist that he is designated by God through the Prophet or through another imam. (*See also* **Caliphate; Islam, Political Organization of; Islam, Religion of.**)